THE COLLECTED
POEMS
AND SELECTED
PROSE

Harry Ransom Humanities Research Center Imprint Series
Published from the collections of the HRHRC

Stuart Gilbert. *Reflections on James Joyce: Stuart Gilbert's Paris Journal.*
Ed. Thomas F. Staley and Randolph Lewis. 1993

Ezra Pound. *The Letters of Ezra Pound to Alice Corbin Henderson.*
Ed. Ira B. Nadel. 1993

Nikolay Punin, *Nikolay Punin: Diaries, 1904–1953.* Ed. Sidney Monas
and Jennifer Greene Krupala. Trans. Jennifer Greene Krupala. 1999

Aldous Huxley, *Now More Than Ever.*
Ed. David Bradshaw and James Sexton. 2000

STANLEY BURNSHAW

THE COLLECTED
POEMS
AND SELECTED
PROSE

FOREWORD BY THOMAS F. STALEY

UNIVERSITY OF TEXAS PRESS, AUSTIN

Grateful acknowledgment is made to George Braziller Inc. for
permission to reprint poems from *In the Terrified Radiance*
and Chapters 6 and 5, respectively, from *The Seamless Web* and
Robert Frost Himself; to Susan Copen Oken for permission to reproduce
the photograph on page 179; and to Arthur Rosenblatt for permission to
reproduce his drawing on p. 274.

First edition, 2002

Requests for permission to reproduce material from this work should be
sent to Permissions, University of Texas Press, Box 7819, Austin, TX
78713-7819.

∞ The paper used in this book meets the minimum requirements of
ANSI/NISO Z39.48-1992 (R1997) (Permanence of Paper).

Library of Congress Cataloging-in-Publication Data
Burnshaw, Stanley, 1906–
[Selections. 2002]
The collected poems and selected prose / Stanley Burnshaw. — 1st ed.
p.   cm. — (Harry Ransom Humanities Research Center imprint series)
Includes index.
ISBN 0-292-70909-9 (alk. paper)
I. Title.   II. Series.

PS3503.U65 A6   2002
811'.52 — dc21
2001052226

FOR SUSAN COPEN OKEN

CONTENTS

IN THE TERRIFIED RADIANCE (1972)

MIRAGES:
Travel Notes in the Promised Land (1977)

LATER POEMS (1977–)

FOREWORD

Stanley Burnshaw has had a long and distinguished career in the literary life of the last century. I know of no other figure whose contribution to American letters has been so versatile and various. Printer, publisher, essayist, editor, critic, translator, playwright, biographer, and, most of all, poet, Burnshaw is a "man of letters" in the richest meaning of the term.

Burnshaw's career as a publisher began in 1937 when he co-founded the Cordon Company. Two years later he created The Dryden Press, which would become famous for its brilliant typography and editing. He continued personally to run the Press until it merged with Henry Holt in 1958; he then became Vice President and Editorial Director. Throughout these years, Burnshaw published a number of landmark books, among them the first comprehensive anthology of African-American literature, *The Negro Caravan* (1941), Stith Thompson's *The Folktale* (1946), *Grandma Moses: American Primitive* (1946), Edwin Sutherland's *White Collar Crime* (1949), Christina Stead's *The Man Who Loved Children* (1965), and Lionel Trilling's *The Experience of Literature* (1967).

From 1934 to mid-1936 Burnshaw worked at the *New Masses* as co-editor and as literary and theater critic. His review of Wallace Stevens' *Ideas of Order* inspired a lengthy Stevens poem, "Mr. Burnshaw and the Statue," in *The New American Caravan,* to which Burnshaw "replied" twenty-five years later in the *Sewanee Review.* For years he was in touch with Robert Frost, with whom he had early formed a close and lasting friendship, capped with his editing of Frost's final volume in 1962. In 1983 the London literary journal *Agenda* published "A Special Stanley Burnshaw Issue," which included a portrait by Christina Stead. And there is more I might add about the intervening years — his teaching, his lecturing on literature, his proposal that NYU create a Graduate Institute of Book Publishing (1958–1962). His engagement in the world of letters was all consuming.

Burnshaw's core career has been as a poet, publishing poems and reviews in 1924 at the age of eighteen. At nineteen he wrote perhaps America's first environmental poem, "End of the Flower-World," having been shocked by the depredations of industrialism which he witnessed firsthand as a copywriter with the Blaw-Knox Steel Company in Blawnox, Pennsylvania. In 1936 his first book of verse, *The Iron Land,* appeared, a narrative of a steel mill interspersed with clusters of personal lyrics. Other volumes of poetry followed, among them the play *The Bridge* (1945), *Early and Late Testament* (1952), *Caged in an Animal's Mind* (1963), and in 1972 *In the Terrified Radiance,* new and selected poems, of which Allen Tate said, "I hope it will place Mr. Burnshaw at the top, where for many years he has deserved to be."

As a critic, Burnshaw began with reviews of books by Frost and Cummings in *The Forum* (1924, 1925). Eight years later *André Spire and His Poetry* appeared, the fruit of a chance encounter with the poet at the Sorbonne: a critical study with forty translations and a pioneering essay on *vers libre* first published in *Poetry.* Three other works (which are still in print) followed: the classic *The Poem Itself* (1960), *The Modern Hebrew Poem Itself* (1965), and *The Seamless Web* (1970), winner of an award (1971) for creative writing from the National Institute of Arts and Letters.

The present volume, as Professor Morris Dickstein observes, has been long overdue: the author's definitive collection of all the poems that he wishes to preserve followed by an inclusive selection of his prose. It offers the dual-biography *My Friend, My Father* in its entirety, together with essays no longer in print and the core chapters of *The Seamless Web* and of *Robert Frost Himself.* "No one else," wrote Alfred Kazin in 1990, "has done so much to show us just what poetry is. No one else writes with such keenness and freshness about poets in their lives and their words." And few have written so widely and so well.

Thomas F. Staley
September 24, 2001

EARLY AND LATE
TESTAMENT

(1952)

For Robert Frost

The poetries of speech
Are acts of thinking love
— *Poetry: The Art,* p. 31

EARLY AND LATE TESTAMENT

Time of Brightness

Before it happens, before the sudden destruction
By your own hands or another's, let it be told.
It is better to know than to mourn what never was.
There is too much brightness here.   Look at the leaves.
Green light burns your eyeballs; the lids close down
To open darkness.   There at least you can see.

Figures are swimming up from nothingness.   Reach for them!
What if they twist and slither away the instant
You strive for a catch, like the withering purple shapes
Staring up under sea waves: something is there
To be sought and known.   You knew the dark before
The explosion into light; you read the outlines
Once.   Are those eyes now lost?

It was not always
This bright on earth.   You could image shape, you could tell
A cloud from a stone when you cared to look.   What was it
Prodded your sleep into waking, shaped on your tongue
Words to be said to earth, your discovered home,
Syllables of serenity such as a man
Sure in belief could say to a more-than-loved

> *For you must always be a moving song*
> *And we must always follow for your sound*

Nothing under the words? — It is not too late
To strain for remembered sight . . . or are the eyes
Grown alien to lost colors past estrangement?

3

There still is darkness in your veins, alive
With early voices: Hear, if you cannot see!

There was a wail of quiet.   Then I heard
A rat's white, hollow strumming on the floor.
The tent-flaps rumbled in a husky word
Born of a wind's last roar —
While up above the shore
Wet webby grayness skidded down a tree
And wrapped the water's limbs in curdling cold.
Then like a cry crackling the slow sea
A sling of sunflame whipped the gray to gold —

Children voices we have used for gracing
The walls of our hollow houses, slender songs
Drifting across the waters of darkness, covering
The heavier sounds of a later, desperate wish:
Save them for a season of calm, for a time
You can dare to revel again when a rush of leaves
Falls in a shower of music to the ground.
Turn from them now: listen for what lies under them:
There is still time, the sounds may still be alive,
You may hear them yet or think you hear — but if only
The sudden beat of blankness floods your ear, come back,
Come out of the dark and into the loud light.
Reason-mind is not wholly weak; it can tell
High from low and the gross distinct; it must tell:
There is nothing else to know with, now that the reach
Of eye and ear is cut.

You will move slowly:
This mind has no muscle of flight; it plods the ground
Traversed before.   Trust it to trace the imprint
Of the signatures before and reconstruct
Your early and later testaments.   It is safer
To crawl and think with this earthbound light, searching
Through tedious streets than to dream at an ocean's edge
For a possible heavenly answer traced in air
By a wind that drags a cold wave's moonwhite hair.

Bread

This that I give you now,
This bread that your mouth receives,
Never knows that its essence
Slept in the hanging leaves

Of a waving wheatfield thriving
With the sun's light, soil, and the rain,
A season ago, before knives
And wheels took life from the grain

That leaf might be flour — and the flour
Bread for the breathers' need . . .
Nor cared that some night one breather
Might watch how each remnant seed

Invades the blood, to become
Your tissue of flesh, and molests
Your body's secrets, swift-changing
To arms and the mounds of your breasts,

To thigh, hand, hair, to voices,
Your heart and your woman's mind . . .
For whatever the bread, do not grieve now
That soon a flash of the wind

May hurry away what remains
Of this quiet valiance of grass:
It entered your body, it fed you
So that you too can pass

From valiance to quiet, from thriving
To silenced flesh, and to ground:
Such is our meager cycle
That turns but a single round

For the deathless flesh of the earth,
For the signless husks of men dead,
For the folded oceans and mountains,
For birds, and fields, and for bread.

The Iron Lands

In the hour before dawn a strange people
Goes forth, whose mournful sounds you cannot hear.

Strangers riding this road morning or evening
See two massive hills and a river between
Then suddenly the houses, streets, and people . . .
"Another dull milltown," and go their way.
But some come here each day
Morning till evening; were it not for their hands,
This town might be what strangers think it is
Until, sighting the houses, streets, and people,
They say "Another dull milltown" and pity.
Millhands scorn such words:
Care-full that here their mouths are fed, their hearts
Have learned to fear-and-love-and-hate this ground
Where every day they come to pour their strength
In the black sheds that cover up the town.

Six years ago I came here.   My eyes saw
First two hills and a river and then a plain
Of graveled rooftrees smoking in the sun —
Twenty miles from a vaster maze where hands,
Deep in treasures torn from the ground, have piled up
A reeling golden city glowing in gloom.
Tying the towns: this brooding Allegheny:
Voiceless river of grime and death — but flame

More blinding than imaged Athena when a May morning
Churns the waves into breasts of foaming gold.

Across the river I saw the double, scarred
Pennsylvania hillsides baring the kisses
Of a hundred plunging rivulets, and their cargo
Of rain, leafage, and soil,
Dragging the colored hills to the leveler wave . . .
Then southward, beyond the rim of the town:
Acres of countryside shaking with sunlight
Where any hunter could trail a chipmunk or rabbit,
Plunder a blackberry field, or climb a deep maple
Clustered with sleeping birds —
But I had traveled here for something starker
Than staring.   I marched toward a thick building,
First of the gates of stone:
Over the doorway glared a legend known
As godhead in a world
Of hammer, piston, granite, tower, and fire.

This was six years ago.
I passed the doors and stayed.   Since that first hour
I have seen many men, have mixed with thoughts
I had not dreamed were men's . . . And every day
Morning till evening we are here; our arms
And days move to a steady song of wheels.

Do I Know Their Names?

Do I know their names? Are they too many?   Count them
As faceless tribes, each wearing a symbol
For the act of hands timed to a song of wheels.
One wears a letter for words, another a curve
Of traceries burned in blue, one shows a flame
Of iron melted to rivers, one wears jagged
Lightning lines for invisible essence moaning
Through copper cables, one wears an anvil-and-blade.

Count them as symbols rapt and deaf in rooms
Beating with silence.   Some of them have forgot
The noises of outer air; they forget to remember
Morning till evening every day till evening.
Then they remember, and some of them look for their faces,
Peer through the shattering image, search for the self
Under the symbol suddenly shaking with sounds —
With hissing angle, bellowing flame, with groaning
Lightning, howling anvil, screeching blade —

For a Workers' Road-Song

Strange that this ripple of birds we hear
Has always sung in the May of the year
Over the road where thousands pass
In the warm ripe wind that lifts from grass,

But stranger that we should have a thought
For a bird or the smell that a branch has brought,
Who give our strength at a wheel that yields
Each day new weapons to ruin fields.

All Day the Chill . . .

All day the chill.   Near and far
Motion congeals to a glassy stare:
Faces and houses cold accursed
Clenched in the stone of time, until
The town is a freezing mind whose will
Is cracking with pain and waiting to burst —
While the dynamos whir in the sheds of steel.
The powerhouse of steel distributes pain.
And you outside this world, why do you dream there

Helpless in adoration, plating the structure
With a suppliant's crust of images till it become
A gorgeous-hideous *thing* that must build or crash?

Are you afraid to look at the face beneath
The image-plate?   It has no eyes or ears —
Sleek unviolent mass whose metal coils
Drool black oil and grease and breath and blood
And send through the copper cables whatever essence
You and I ordain. — Look at its face!
Look at your own face
Congealed to a stare clenched in this stone of time.

Will You Remake These Worlds?

The air is weighted down by floods of smoke
Folding over the dark November river.
Silence outside — hollow silence of streets
Emptied of people.   Railroad whistles, thuds,
Clanging of steel bars in the yards, and the thin
Screams of a far boat-whistle cut the stillness.
Inside the buildings: silence,
Where men from these and other empty streets
Cling to their paper, pencil, compass, angle.

I pass by offices, walk to a third building:
Each storey one vast room
Checkered with desks and tables where designers,
Typists, clerks, tracers, hold to their stations
Clicking out work, like soldiers menaced
By a need for conquering — and yet I know
Most men and women fastened to these rooms
Long each instant for evening,
Wait for its freeing arms from the weights of day.

Watching the faces, steadily I awake
To countless other millions

In countless other walls like these: young men
And women beseeching someone to end the daylight,
Bring on the darkness, blot out the sun —

Will you remake these worlds in your time of strength?
The soil holds food and water, the broad earth
Measureless force waiting for use in the golden
Worlds plotted by dreamers:
Would you become answering gods to your prayers?
Break the clench of air with a singing sound?
Fling your sun out of the iron ground?

THIRD TESTAMENT

A Coil of Glass (I)

Somewhere there is a coil of glass within
Whose range the fire of stars
Thousands of light-years gone gives back the gleam
Once shed from earth —
Lost light of crumpled hours.

He who finds this glass
Reclaims at will whatever sleeps in time.
Nothing that was need ever fade so long
As air floods the redoubts of space and worlds
Roll on their pivots:
All the dead years sleep
On the faces of quiet stars.

Whoever owns this glass may one day turn
The lenses toward the face
Of the farthest star and bring at last a sight
For which men grieved through lightless
Centuries: first moment

A seed of dust unloosed the multiple flowers
Bound in its atom strength, and locked the shapes
In one vast whole of interbalanced need,
And broke forever the vile or sacred sound
Of earth before men quarreled with the ground.

Anchorage in Time (I)

On pavements wet with the misty wind of spring
We walk while our bodies burn
For places where hands of trees draw sleep from a brook
And the air is damp with fern . . .

If waters image cloud, a man can see
A heaven underneath, but if he change
To look up at the sky, let him remember
His anchorage to earth.   Whoever stares
May see suddenly over blue pools of sky
Moving foam of cloud: at once his mind
Fevers for truth, for his anchorage in time,
Balancing earth and heaven in his eyes . . .
Then wakes from staring and puts back the sea
And sun in place, yet never again certain
Which eyes to trust, saying in voiceless words:

What is a man, who strides against the light:
A coat of flesh drawn on the bracing bones?
And the furled earth beneath his feet: a skin
Of sand muffling the burning ribs of stone?
Or is his blood an impulse of all breath:
Flesh fused with bone in one vast atomy
With sand and stone — with earth, whose ground and fire
Speaks for all breath?   Which eyes to trust, which eyes? . . .

Let those who search look to their anchorage
In time, before they balance earth and heaven.

This War Is Love

You, whoever you are:
Dare you believe men died to make a world
Where children breed on bitterness and despair?

Reverence mercy by thriving day,
Worship tenderness when the soft bloom
Of night lowers, but know that these
Are gods of doom
Leading you slowly, helpless away
To a faithless tomb.

In the dim hours of slow emergent
Hope heed the wild voice of the brave
Striving against their masters, shouting
"No words can save —
Struggle is all of blood's commandment:
This war is love."

A Coil of Glass (II)

A book might be the lens of pure hard tears,
The coil of glass that sights whatever sleeps
In time — gone light of earth holding the crumpled hours.
Focus the glass at will: look at the man —
Adam, Arthur, Christ.   Look at the woman —
Lilith, Iseult, Helen.   Light up the brain
Of the priests and kings, the file
Of heroes set on the seeded steps of time.
Then watch these idols crash on the floor of your mind.

Mythless your heart breaks
On the edges of days revived.   Nothing can heal

The wound until you learn the lens, until you know
Builders of myth were men whose hungering minds,
Cutting through shells of sense, needed to image
The fact they hoped to see.

Focus the glass at will: it may show how men
First rose up, lost in the jungle's day
And found themselves in the dim fraternities of blood-and-mind,
Only to lose themselves again in a darker
Fiercer jungle, where wind
Is scissored by screams from a lightless ground,
Where feet trample on bleeding skulls —

Our world — our father's world. . . .   Our night is broken
In a coil of glass.
Look through the pure hard tears.
What do you see?
Whose hands are pushing up through the darkness?   Whose eyes
Carry a flame of signs that tell how the earth's
Long fierce darkness shall be plumed with suns?

Hero Statues

And have you read the record stones,
The marks in clay, the printed grass,
The profile of succussive time?
Come tell me what it shows!
"There are too many traces yet not enough,
Too many signs yet a monotone
Always throbbing across the clay, the grass, the tabled stone,
Beating across the deserted pavements,
Under the houses, under the piers of the bridges . . ."

Though bosomed by the same ground
And driven by the same sun,
A wolf no more assigns
His safety to a man,

Than man, whose lifted hope,
Dazzled by heaven and hell,
Can trust his fate to heroes
To do with as they will.

Now in an hour of frenzy
To find a vaster worth
Than death-through-fear the fathers
Decreed for man on earth

They smash the hero statues,
Accuse the idiot lust,
Spit in the tombs of glory
That canonize distrust,

Summon the world to cancel
Truce with murderer-dust.

Dialogue of the Heartbeat

I

The sun came up at five o'clock,
At six o'clock the sun went down;
None of us saw it, no one alive
Here or in any town.
Clenched in the stone of our will, we forgot to look,
We forgot to remember.   We always forget to remember.

It is warm and safe in our private room.   We can hear
Syllables of our mouths; we watch and reach for
Words of our lips: invisible flowers floating
In our glitter air, shaking us with their spells.

Is it not good, this air in the stone house
Of our will?   It is richer than any outer air,
Than perfume of raindrenched grass on October mornings,
The steady helpless breathing of wind against trees:
It is brighter than any brightness of outer air.

II

Clouds on a winter night
Can blot out all the stars
And cover up the moon,
Backed by the bitter force
Of wildly gathering air:

So, when invisible wind
Drives to the level crust
Of ground, no living bastion
Hopes to hold back the thrust

But shudders under the weight
Of plunging tons of sky
That shake the iron hills
Like soft black miles of sea,

That stun rock-rooted trees
Powerless under the might,
And draw from their birdless boughs
Weak cries against the night

Such as a man might utter
In helplessness to defy
With the summoned battalions of thought
The brute will of the sky.

The Bridge

We build a bridge from here and now to tomorrow.
Can you hear the words its gesture speaks
As it towers over us, tall, huge,
Cutting the sky with its spire,
Clutching the ground with its feet?
Is its path from our shores racing
Across the water, charging
To span the sea in a leap?

Does it say we must seize tomorrow,
Tear it out of the air, compel the future
To come to us here and now?
Does it say we must stand and make eyes ready
To know the new as its far light swims
Slowly up from the darkness: wait, hope, listen?

Or would it say: Hungering hands
Can tear at mists, but passion is not enough:
Tomorrow eludes the blind wild will, yet silence
Waiting passive in hope can never grow
Creation out of the air?   Has it said to you: Quicken
Your blood with enormous thought: tomorrow listens?

Our bridgehead leans toward the far horizon
To mix with a far light flooding.   Look, the arms
Reach out to greet the future: outstretched arms
On whose young strength we hang our road
Till tomorrow raise a bridgehead:
Tomorrow also stand with outstretched arms
That the two bridgeheads may meet, the old and the new
Join hands to close the ocean.

You see no light, you say?
Nothing beyond?   No bridge?
No outstretched arms? — We see it
Whether or not they range the air: half of whatever we see
Glows in cells not signalled by our eyes.
If men lived only by the things they knew
The skin of their hands could touch, they soon would die
Of starved need.   The shapes of sensate truth

Bristle with harshness.   Eyeballs would cut on the edges
Of naked fact and bleed.   The thoughtful vision
Projected by our driving hope creates
A world where truth is possible: without it
The mind would break or die.

Heartbeat Obbligato

Though sung with fierce belief
And lit with crystal day,
The songs the young men sang
Our hearts have cast away.

Flesh they had fever-chilled
Creeping through time has shed
The tissues of young manhood:
Our blood has changed its red.

So must our tongue contemn them,
Our brain resist belief
Ever it bloomed to music poured
From those childish shells of grief.

We in our iron day,
Duped by caress, alone
Trust the clean, fierce burden
The fist can wring from stone.

Yet from such hollow cadence
Our will would hazard change,
And our heart, fed on a ruthless song,
Thirst for a farther range —

For the grace notes of a fugue
Where the budless mind can pore
On a plagal cadence of hope
That might justify its war:

Pale mind that beats to a music
Scored for its coward age:
A tomtom of the heartbeat
In a key of frozen rage.

End of the Flower-World

Fear no longer for the lone gray birds
That fall beneath the world's last autumn sky,
Mourn no more the death of grass and tree.

These will be as they have always been:
Substance of springtime; and when flower-world ends,
They will go back to earth, and wait, and be still,

Safe with the dust of birds long dead, with boughs
Turned ashes long ago, that still are straining
To leave their tombs and find the hills again,

Flourish again, mindless of the people —
The strange ones now on a leafless earth
Who seem to have no care for things in blossom.

Fear no more for trees, but mourn instead
The children of these strange, sad men: their hearts
Will hear no music but the song of death.

Looking for Papa

I

The clear white waters of the moon
Double in hills the earth-shadow more
Than the metallic flaming sun
Or the most frozen star.

You who need an altar-god,
Turn from the stars, turn from the sun;
Though suckled by the mother sun,
Fly to a moon.

There you can learn the mystery
Whereof the best of gods are made —
Beautiful coldness, and over all
A strange shade.

II

All the sad young men are looking for papa,
The sad young men who think they were bad young men,
And their fathers and their grandfathers who were young
Once and are old: all the old young men,
And the women too, and the children: every one —
They are all looking for papa . . . burdened papa,
Helplessly procreant papa who never was born
Or found.
          Shall we join the hunt?   Is it a game?
A wonderfully solemn game, and very sad.

Let's look for him then.   In the sky, in the sea, in the ground,
Any where at all, above us, below us, so long
As we look outside.   Be sure to look outside
Ourselves. . . .   Poor wandering papa,
Bright and invincible and always outside, always outside;
We must never allow him entry; we must never let him come in.

Among Trees of Light

Always men on earth have sought the wondrous
Mist-shadows for sacredness; all else lay
Too far from heaven:

In the night's darkness, we said, are symbols stranger
Than ever day with all its magic and dazzle
Could hide away.

Older now with empty hands, emerged from darkness,
We move among trees of light, striving to learn
The flaming mind

That beats in every glitter of day; we gather
Figures of light none of the dark's adept
Could find, fond

In the shadow-mists.   Searching till leaves lay bare
Their sleeping suns, we dare accept as much
As fire unlocked

Can show, however the embers freeze or scorch us,
Fearful that eyes alone, or thought, or love
Alone, can capture

Nothing beyond the reaches of singleness:
Not light but the mirrored glow of a burning wish.

Coasts of Darkness

A tribe of hearts will endure
A chartless night unknown.
Drawn toward the coasts of darkness,
No man who starts alone
Bondless returns unbroken,
Though first his heart rejoice,
Freed from human speeches

That had always muffled the silence —
Now he will know its voice

Rousing his sleeping wraths,
Ringing gongs of his hate:
They close in around and above him
Blindingly while they wait
For the torment in his blood
To strangle his bondless heart
Till it plead to mercies that scorn him —
Then can his frenzies start:

Moon, from your dizzy ledge,
O scream through his crazy night!
Spill through weird shaking trees
Live stones of bleeding light!
Swift through his eyeballs level
Beams that may pierce his skull:
Nail down his feet, moon, possess him
Till he is glutted full.

And then if his blood still fevers
To brave alone the wild ground,
Flood through his mouth till his body,
Freezing and burst by your flaming,
Screams for your love and is drowned.

In Strength of Singleness

Green maples, men have told,
For want of summer showers
Will burn each leaf to gold,
Striving against the hours
Of thirst with fevered flowers.

Wherefore who walk abroad
In black October night

May think that boughs lash out
Across the gazers' sight
Delirious golden light

To summon every force
Defiant of their pain,
In strength of singleness
As much as need for rain,
As all denied will strain

To make the heart despise
A love withheld too long,
Hide it in heady lies
Or drown it under cries
Of proud pathetic song.

Blood

Cats move like water,
Dogs like wind . . .
Only when bodies
Have shut out mind

Can they learn the calm
Motion of dream.

Would we could know
The way men moved
When thought was only
A great dark love

And blood lay calm
In a depthless dream.

It Was Never This Quiet . . .

It was never this quiet here — always the wind
Raging through branches splattering hail, bellowing
Above and under crags, always rocks
Plunging into crevasses, breaking and killing
Birds and creatures of land, always the screams
Of flesh clawing at flesh.   The sudden silence
Batters the eardrums.   Will we learn to sleep?
The calmness is too strange.   We were bred for fierceness
By furies of hate; now we must utterly trust
A love beyond the eyes of fear.

Go to your glass, if you will: there is brightness there.
What can it show that you have not always known
In the dark of your body?   Nothing until you look
Under the eyes of your fear, and then beyond,
Where sight becomes acknowledgment.   Nothing
Is born without a shedding of singleness:
Arms that embrace are an outward reach for safety,
No more no less than an infant's grasp for love;
No more no less than any creature's of sky
Or sea or land surging from starved estrangement
Toward unities of kind, in great dark love.

The sustenance of sympathies that drive
The blood dissolves the red
Of tooth and claw; yet must the logic scaled
To provables believe that only war
Is love and struggle blood's command — till thought
Probes at the surfaces, pursues the images
Into the darkness, into the range of fear,
Into the silence . . . where the stillnesses
No longer batter the eardrums.   And the calm
Has shed its strangeness.   We can wake and sleep.

> *To know the voice of grass*
> *Slitting the brown earth shell,*
> *Sound of the chrysalis birds*
> *Breaking the husks of air,*

Why run to search the sweep
Of edges where they fell,
Once you have found your words
Descanted with the sound

Of slow unburdened power
That overwhelms this hour:
Time's strange compacted flower
Of birth converged with death

In wild unravelling spring —
"O many-bodied breath
No sooner lost in shape
Than in your singing found. . . ."

When Was It Lost?

When was it lost?   Can you say who covered it up?
Who saw it before it disappeared into darkness?
When did we start to forget?   A million years
Ago, two million — more than the breaking rays
Show through the clocks of stone? — And then the sudden
Noises of tongue and lip, while the body motioned
A sign: the sound and signal once set wild
And never tamed until enfleshed in words
And speech and symbol — infinites of mind
To open immensities, salvage the dear
In images, range through blockades of time
Forever: sudden speaker of words holding
The force of his masteries.   Can the mind contain
Earth in a symbol and still be one with earth?
If speech is thought and thought is sight, can sight
Find unities as much as separateness?
So long as the self is safe, the worlds within
And without are at one in dream — but the speaker wakes,
Fearful of sleep, with mastery force in the hands
Of others awake.

Will they use it in peace?   Can he trust
His safety ever again in sleep, and always
The menace, the possible blow?   Throw down the dream:
You cannot sleep again.   Doomed to waking,
Your worlds within and without at war, look harshly
Above and around: safety is all: protect
Fearing body with eyes of brain, till sight
No longer sees above and around but an image
Warping through the veil of itself, and gathered
For the sake of one against all others and else
Outside.   Enemy earth: enemy man:
Enemy tribe: enemy nation: furies
Shrieking all day across the blackened skies,
Under the splintering cities. . . .

Listen, listen!
Walk outside and listen!   What do you hear?
Wordless sounds.   No sounds.   But not less true
For wordlessness.   Will you ever know my thought
When you stand outside, until you become a part
Of myself?   There is no enemy.   Listen without
And within.   Hear them again together: the self
Was at one before in safety, awake and asleep
Before the coming of fear.   There is time to learn
The wordlessness of wills in your body's dark.

Woodpecker

Woodpecker hovering out of the dawn,
Weaving through arches of sleeping leaves,
Why do you pass the living boughs
To strike at my cabin's eaves?

To find a sweet like the sweet you draw
From the poplars, take your drills of fire
Out of these sapless hemlock halves
Shaped to a man's desire.

And since with nail and beam we have made
A mystic leafless tree you must go
For food to the files of green-leaved boughs
Where the live rootsaps flow:

Know that whatever nourishment moves
In our tree we save for a time bereaved
When age must feed itself on truth
The will of youth believed.

Voices in Dearness . . .

I build my house to keep out vermin, damp,
Decay, and time.   Poems embalm belief
With words; paintings lay out the growing brightness
In shrouds of color; sculptures mummify
Flesh softness into rock.   Can a daisy think?
Whatever is learned at last, we alone can summon
Fire, can touch a match to the logs and quicken
A cold black house with locked-up light of the sun.

Once in a dream I searched a globe, holding
Candles to see whatever might wait within.
Trustful, I pried at the sphere, tore it,
Looked inside.   It was empty dark:
Hollow earth of nothingness in the core.

Waking, I walked to the window; looked at the sky
Of morning overhead and the growing brightness
Below.   My land was alive:
Miracle breathings of flesh and leaf joining
Voices in dearness everywhere.

There is no wasted land until we cover it
With dryness of the heart in weariness,
Deny our anchorage to a land bedded
On a basalt continent that turns on seas

Distilled from waters blown from a time and place
We can never reach or touch, propelled by light
Of a sun beyond beholding: circled flesh
Contained within a sphere, straining to tear
Through the shell, range the beyond, and flee the hollow
Nothingness of the core.

Open your eyes
To the words, the rock, the color; take what they hold
Of fever-summoned calmness — more than enough
To quicken and sustain the truce you need.
Accept them: they are all you have, though flawed
By desperate griefs and strident symmetries,
Maimed by concussive will — as all that lives
Sustains through whole con-fusion.   Nothing pure
Can cope with time, unbrazed to the impure —
Look for no perfect art except in death.

Song Aspires to Silence

Song aspires to silence.
Men of defiant words
Look to the breaking moment
When blood will shed the fever,

Freed of the ceaseless striving
To fasten mountains and seas
And tame the resistless wills
Of hell and heaven defiant.

Song aspires to silence:
The fear that drones above
The rapt fury of song
Seeks its calm in driving

The blood to bury in words
The ever-unnameable love
That plunders the mind and storms the bewildered heart.

Anchorage in Time (II)

The vast stone trunk of mountain lifts above
The ground no more nor less than its rocky knees
Have sunk in tight brown earth, while everywhere
Water is steadily grinding down the hills;
Water will pour the powder into the sea
Until the day the suns no longer boil
The air or scorch the grass,
Blowing from the pale disc of yellow stone
Not flame enough to melt the frozen wave
Blinding the rock and sea —
Hot earth become ice-star.

Yet must the mind woven of blood believe
An imaged vision scaled to an anchorage
In time, and watch eternities emerge
Out of the baseless dust: eternal spring
Conferred on land where cubicles of flesh
And thought must name themselves safe from the ardor
That walls apart all striving unities;
Admit no future fiercer than this river
Raging over cascades of ice the winter
Sun will soon take down.

The mind believes as much
As blood believes, nor grieves for surer purpose
In the immense star-endless curl of space
Than sea's or hill's or frail ephemeras'
Of air, but takes the earth and sun for truth
Eternal in a treasured now, and love
Its anchorage in time.

Two Men Fell in the Irish Sea

Two men fell in the Irish Sea
And when they had drowned they began to think.
The first said *Water is eyes, all eyes.*
And he shook off his flesh to become pure sight
Till his body changed into waves of light.

But the other, blinded, began to drink
The sea with his ears: *It is sound, pure sound:*
Listen, listen, and we'll be free
Of our eyes at last.

                Though he wasn't heard,
He awaited the first man's answering word;
And when there came no friendly sound,
The veins of his mind swelled into rage
Till the voice of his will, too sharp to bear,
Craved release into plangent air . . .

Two men fell in the Irish Sea
And when they awoke above, they could claim
To each other the truths they had found below.
It is light, said one — and *light is death,*
He thought.   Thought the other: *And so is sound —*
But he said *There is nothing below for eyes:*
We must listen to water.

                With brazen breath
They could argue, parry, fume, and blame,
Safe on land where they could not think,
Drowned in more than hearing or sight
And twisted by dream.   The two who fell
In the sea would fight the appeals of air
Blowing against their minds until
They could learn to balance in one calm thought
The winds of waking, the waters of sleep.

POETRY: THE ART

In the Form of an Apostrophe to Whitman

I used to read your book and hear your words
Explode in me and blast new passageways
Deep in my brain, until its crowding rooms
Held more light than my head could balance.   Now
That the tunnels all are cut, I pace the rooms
Looking for you, though certain I shall find
No more of you than you yourself could gather
Out of the pieces of self.   The years have burned
The sharpness from the edges: I can fit
The pieces, but the mortar must be mixed
Out of our blending wills.   Others have tried
And failed.   I too shall fail if I forget
How thought can range beyond the last frontiers
That common sense has civilized with names.

Others who looked for you have made you say
Words you might have said if they were you:
Have lost you in their passion for a phrase.
The private man's infinitude defies
The singleness they look for when they strive
To sort your various colors to a scheme
Of thought-and-action.   Desperate for pattern,
They make the key *Calamus* and they twist
Your other selves around the centerpiece,
Losing you in that love.

                    And others forge
A key of social thought that cracks apart
When words and actions contradict: *Walt Whitman,*
You said you love the common man!   Where were you
When Parsons' friends were hanged?   Were you asleep
Or writing more fine words about mechanics

And farmers? — How much cosier for you
To prate about democracy than live it —
You, its self-appointed poet!

Others,
Seeking you in your plangent celebrations
Of science and the holiness of flesh
And earth, end with a fierce *You too, Walt Whitman,*
You flinched, you stumbled, hankering for a "soul" . . .
The substances of sense too harsh, too bitter
A truth for you to live by!   Underneath
Your protest boils the soft romantic sickness
Of all the Shelleys, Heines — bright lost leaders
We hoped were men.   You were afraid of the dark:
You who had thundered "Science is true religion"
Sang the groveler's wooing song to Death
And God and Spirit! . . .   Hide, at least, the image
Revealed: the gaudy chaos of a man
Reviling his own faith!

But who can dare
To arbitrate the depths of you that anger
Against your tranquil self?   I am not certain:
I have seen the signposts of contradiction
Planted by men impotent to discern
The harmony beneath the subtle wholeness,
And in their self-defense erect confusion
On quiet entities.   A poet's words
Are signatures of self — the many selves
Subsumed in one profounder sense that knows
An all-according truth: a single eye
Uncovering the countless constellations
Of heart and mind.   Wherefore the syllables
Reach outward from the self in an embrace
Of multitudes.   The poetries of speech
Are acts of thinking love; and I must find
The thought that grows the center of your passion.

And so I say to those who precontemn
The message of *Calamus* as the flowers
Of twisted love what Plato showed of truths

Uttered by poets.   And I say to those
Who spit upon your social thought *"Respondez!"*
The human race is restive, on the watch
For some new era — some divine war —
Whose triumph will entrench a brave good-will
Among the common people everywhere —
The trodden multitudes for whom you clamored
A new and tender reverence.

But for those
Who sneer because you looked for lights beyond
The planes of sense, there is no final answer
If they deny the mind its birthright freedom
To range all worlds of thought and sense and vision.
Everything that can be believ'd is an image of truth —
The images refined to great and small
Will cluster into orbits of belief
And hold together as the planets hold
By kinship and denial, in one vaster
All encompassing circle.   Let the sneerers
Proclaim your chief intent or keep their silence
Until its name is found.

It is not found,
The answer to your central search — "the problem,
The only one" — *adjust the individual*
Into the mass.   For we have just begun
To fit the world to men, men to the world;
And we shall stumble till the single heart
Discovers all its selves and learns therefrom
How singleness and multitude can live
In valiant marriage.   With your hungry hope
You pierced the shells of feeling, trumpeted
Into your country's ears, and flooded strength
Into the wavering hearts of men lonely
For courage to fulfill their need: to thrust
Their single faith against the massed-up wills
Of many.   "Sing your self!" you told them.   Listening,
They pledged the valors of the inward man.
And others turned from you with dull, deaf ears,
Afraid to listen, waiting to be taught
The trial-and-error way of rats in a maze . . .

A poem "is," some men believe.   I say
A poem "is" when it has spread its root
Inside a listener's thought and grows a tree there
Strong enough to burst a room in the brain,
And bring its branch to blossom.   Then the host
Forgets the verse and ponders on the mind
That made this seed of growth . . . as I forget
Your poem: as I strive to learn your mind,
Thinking that when I come to understand,
I may begin to touch serenities
You saw beneath the springs of pain that nourished
Your world that was beginning — dim, green world
Trembling with death-and-birth: divinest war.

ODES AND LYRICS

To a Young Girl Sleeping

Into this room of sleep let fall
    The moon's dimmest bars —
Glitter might rouse her still hands lying
    Paler than water-stars;

And let the nightwind calmly flow,
    Lay but the frailest words
On her whose face is a shadow softer
    Than evening birds'.

Innocence

Je suis jaloux, Psyché, de toute la nature.
          — CORNEILLE

In desperate dream of sleep a man
May accuse innocence.   Fearing the will
Of ardors everywhere, he can charge
Rays of the sun with kissing your face,
Accuse the wind of fondling your hair,
Rage that the air you breathe rushes
Tremblingly to touch your lips
And the silks draping your bosom and arms
Cling like hands to the moons of your breast . . .

Wading in desperate dream asleep
Or awake a man may make of heedless
Chimes a glow of beckoning truth,

Grieve to watch their burden shred
Past his reach into gatherless air:

Is sight thereafter pain-compelled
To look for the lost in a blazing world?
Drawn by trust to the trace in his eyes,
Must he believe it will one day grow
A force to quicken the corpse of dream?

Wave

No man can live on truth
Found from the rays of light,
But he must mix with truth a dream
Of truth outranging sight.

Nor can he live believing
Part of the earth his own:
Nothing of earth can be possessed.
All you have sought and known —

Tower, face, and mountain,
Wisdom, word, and tree —
Ride the corroding wave that drops
All in a hollow sea.

Even the hidden ground
Where your dead loved one lies —
The wave will split apart the vault,
Care-less of sacrifice,

And crack the brazen shroud,
Seize the pale skin and bones
And gnaw them into dust
And feed them to the stones.

Event in a Field

When the small lips of rain
Ceaselessly press at the flesh of ground,
When the gold rods of sun
Plunge in heat through the creviced grains:
However its arms resist, —
Though it bristle a skin of bitter clay
And draw in its bones from the rods of fire —
If growth once fibered its strength, land
Must give up its will to the will of air
And haven a womb for flowers.

More than a hope: this waste of clay
Unlocked from its eyeless stare, now reveling
Under a rollicking foam of daisies,
Buttercup, Indian paintbrush, green . . .
Lakes of moaning color flaming
Leaves raveling wind.

More than vision: a sign —
The possible hung clear
Above the copeless chasm of land and sky,
Burning through mists of a mind
When will wavers, fearing the rescue of tears.

The Fear

A Sonnet to the Earth

Because your flame was torn from burning skies
And spun in space to find a course or fail,
We cannot look at you with children's eyes
For we are children of the same travail;
Nor can we let our calm become too strong
Or build contentments in the path we found,

For you must always be a moving song
And we must always follow for your sound.

Though yielded to your song's enchantment, none
In our tribe of flesh can give his heart's release
To certainties — thus do we mock or wrong
Your will, torn by our fear of stark caprice
That questions why we follow in your song
Arcs that may break us both against the sun.

Midnight: Deserted Pavements

La chair est triste, hélas, et j'ai lu tous les livres . . .
— MALLARMÉ

Nightwind beating against the deserted pavements
Carry the town to my window.   I sit alone
With invisible cries from countless city rooms
Stifled, this midnight moment, to one far groan.

Upward: the blue-snow heavens bare time's body
Lunging in wild star-patterns across the sky,
The temptress dance of time whose music would flood
My waking, could it smother the steady cry

Of foundering human voices, near and far,
Tonight and ages done — the triumphal drum-
Phantom no mind can pierce whose desperate bleating
Confounds the starsong now, the hope to come —

The flesh is sad . . . and all the books are read.
Eyes blur at the darkness, straining to see
The face of earth a hundred deserts beyond,
The time of earth a thousand ages to be.

Random Pieces of a Man

(Address to the Reader)

Disown the face deciphered from the book:
No one but you could draw it from the mazes
Of selves wandering undisguised beneath
A line, a twist of sound.   Because the phrases

Suppress as much as they avow, denying
More than a sound's signal, what you see
Might be proclaimed of any man who speaks
Only what can be spoken faithfully

Without danger, pacing his heart's edges,
Safe from its fire core.   He has no names
To hold such heat; everything held in words
Is lava cooled: you read the ash of flames

And only such as he placed upon the page
For you to see, chosen from all his pure
And grave designs.   Where did you hope to trace
His inexpressibles of love and fear

And grief, the laughter seized and lost, the pain
Denied its song?   Though some of him is here,
The missing stares unguessable — while you,
Guarding the profile, lovingly secure

The random pieces of his time tumbled
Luckily on a page. — Oh, hold him close!
Uncertain alien, once: to you no longer
Strange.   Alas, a pattern: calm, morose,

Fretful, and other adjectives that stamp
A new cliché. — Now that you see him bare,
Will you still prize him?   His addiction (verse)
Scarcely captivates.   How could it compare

With any colorful frenzy? — Come confess:
He lacks élan . . . — If all I say is true,

Why do you scorn my words, unless the face
Deciphered from the book is chiefly you?

Waiting in Winter

They were tired, tired, and outside
The wind was cracking boughs and breaking leaves
With stones of freezing water.   Once they heard
A whistle leap and groan against the night
Like a dying bird.

Though winter-sickened, yet they tried to watch
In wonder through the window at the snow,
Content no more to feel their teardrops flow
Upon their faces as a kiss of rain,
While in their bodies gnawed the old, limp pain
Of those who live too long on love.

They were so chill, they slipt their scraggly hands
Around each other's arms. — Sleep always stills,
They thought; maybe its shroud would close the day
Of two gray walkers, wordless, old, and bled
Of trust and unbelief,
Waiting in winter, withered by a sun
That overbloomed their hearts and now was dead.

Outcast of the Waters

No man has seen the wind, though he has heard
Always since he was young a faceless flow
Of moaning from the blue enormous bird;
But only the wind's touch could make him know,

As only the green's prevalence could prove
The tides of birth that slake the loving ground
To sight too slow to see a tendril move
And ears that never range the growing sound:

Young outcast of the waters, still unsure —
Fathered on land but mothered in a sea
Whose terrible bright naked shadows lure
In lovely lust that will not let him free:

How can he hope to gather from her wave
More than a dye dissolved in light, to find
The substance of the shape, unless he brave
Her wraith of bodies burning in his mind?

Restful Ground

I have known solitudes, but none has been
Such as I seek this hour: a place so still
That the darkened grasses wake to no sound at all
Nor flutter shadowy fingers in a wind.

I have known quiet in places without dark trees,
But after this clanging of hours I seek a silence
Where the only motion is the quiet breathing
Of dark boughs gazing on the restful ground.

Days

Strange to be torn away from your embrace
        In the cold dawn,
To be taken far from your face, your silence,
        To be drawn

Past streets, fields, rivers, toward a place
    Miles, miles away
Where senseless words and images clog the mind
    Till the end of day,

When, turning back to you, I wonder, moving
    Through twilight haze,
If we must live only in meeting and parting
    The rest of our days.

Willowy Wind

Now let us two lie down in willowy wind
And raise eyes upward upon pale cloud
And watch birds flutter soft-weaving wings;

See pale cloud-drift float and idle by
To melt in the windy waters of the sky . . .
Gaze only above us, nor wonder why.

Then turning eyes inward, remembering cloud,
Hope that our bodies be taken into the stream
Of wind, and wish our blood a willowy dream.

THE HOLLOW RIVER

(December 19, 1938–January 11, 1940)

Speak these lines that no one will understand
Except the friends who know; and they must turn
From listening.   Memory-mind survives
By sure decay; a thinking grief that fattens
Kills the host.   Speak of the child who lived,
Strove for breath, fainted and laughed, cried
And sang, and died and lived a thousand hours
Through one misfated year, until the morning,
Babbling her song, she suddenly ceased breathing,
Sank in her mother's arms.   I write these lines
Against my hand, contemptuous of the pen,
Fighting the heavy gush of words until
The brutal deed of verse is done.

— Walking once in a thicket, I slipped on a pebble
And headlong fell on bedded vines, and suddenly
Saw a river growing out of darknesses
Choked with briared trees and bushes, arched
With thistles and wild roses.   Overhead
I saw no sky, but everywhere were drops
Of light: blue petals of the sky, white petals
Of cloud foam, red-gold petals of the sun.
I heard the light there make a heavenly sound;
The rainbow water tasted of heaven dew . . .

The pure disdain of art can compensate
For sense with quick imaginings.   Dear art,
Certain in expectation of the calm
You salvage from the wreckage of your love:
Deny your mummied sweetness owes its substance
To the soft corpse of fact you cover over.
— But look! weeds are pushing up from that flesh . . .

O cold, sad counterfeit of song, of a world
That dangles nowhere, lacking anchorage
In time and space — dear helplessness
Of verse to elegize this heart whose sounds
Were tiny waterfalls that brightened air —
Fragment songs of my sunbird . . .

Whoever loved the earth as a beloved,
He or she was a comrade.   I could ask
Wanderers why they searched the world for a friend
When they could find each other as they watched
The same tree bend, the same green rainwind blow.
Now that the sickness hangs on me, I see
In every sunset furying chemistries
That build the color glories, till I see
My own mirage: a box of ashes holding
The transmutation of my sunbird's song.

— Walking once in a thicket, I tripped on a rock-fault
And fell head-first against the matted screens
Of vine stalk.   When I wiped my eyes I could see
The grave of a river: parched, hard, and nothing
Growing out of its skin.   I lavished water
Into the bed, I diverted the spring rains
And channeled heavy autumn floods.   I saw
The gray skin dry the water, then I heard
A wind coughing out of a hollow river . . .

— They question me.   They pry into corners,
Looking for scraps with pieces of thought.
There were no words.

I build a house on the grave of a hollow river.
I brush my arms against the trembling walls.
I look out through the panes.
The light that filters through shakes with fear.

I put the house in order:
Drain the pipes clean, let the liquid out;
Close down windows, lower springless blinds;

Whatever air, let stay there; shut up the house:
Make it a grave for the winds; lock the door
Of its hearth; throw the key in the well whose depths
Are dry with the homing waters of thousand, thousand
Hollow rivers of men.

November 1940

SECOND-HAND POEMS

ANONYMOUS ALBA

En un vergier soiz folha d'albespi

Sheltered beneath white hawthorn boughs,
A woman held her loved one close
In her arms, till the watchman cried abroad:
God! It is dawn! How soon it's come!

"How wildly have I wished that the night
Would never end, and that my love
Could stay, and the watchman never cry
God! It is dawn! How soon it's come!

"My love-and-friend, but one more kiss,
Here in our field where the small birds sing;
We shall defy their jealous throats —
God! It is dawn! How soon it's come!

"Still one more close embrace, my love,
Here in our field where the small birds sing,
Till the watchman blow his reedy strain —
God! It is dawn! How soon it's come!

"From the wind beyond where my love has gone,
Thoughtful, contented, I have drunk
A long deep draught of his breath — O God,
God! It is dawn! How soon it's come!"

(ENVOI)

Flowing with grace and charm is she;
Her loveliness draws many eyes,
Whose full heart throbs with a true love —
God! It is dawn! How soon it's come!

CHARLES D'ORLÉANS

Le temps a laissié . . .

The weather's cast away its cloak
Of wind and rain and chilling haze;
It wears instead embroideries
Of crystal sunlit rays.

There's not a beast or bird but sings
Or cries out in his own sweet strain:
The weather's cast away its cloak
Of wind and cold and rain.

The whole wide earth is clothed anew:
River, fountain, and brook now wear
Drops of silver, strands of gold:
The weather's cast away its cloak
Of wind and rain and cold.

ANDRÉ SPIRE

Nudités

> *Hair is a nakedness.*
> — THE TALMUD

You said to me:

I want to become your comrade,
I want to visit you without fear of troubling you;
We shall spend long evenings in talk together,
Thinking together of our murdered brothers;
Together we'll travel the world to find
A country where they can lay their heads.
But don't let me see your eyeballs glitter

Or the burning veins of your forehead bulge!
I am your equal, not a prey.
Look: — my clothes are chaste, almost poor,
And you can't even see the curve of my throat.

I answered:
Woman, you are naked.
Your downy neck is a goblet of well-water;
Your locks are wanton as a flock of mountain goats;
Your soft round chignon quivers like a breast . . .
Woman, cut off your hair!

Woman, you are naked.
Your hands unfurl upon our open book;
Your hands, the subtle tips of your body,
Ringless fingers that will touch mine any moment . . .
Woman, cut off your hands!

You are naked.
Your voice flows up from your bosom,
Your song, your breath, the very heat of your flesh —
It is spreading round my body to enter my flesh —
Woman, tear out your voice!

ANDRÉ SPIRE

Ce n'est pas toi . . .

It wasn't you I was waiting for
Since the beginning, always.
It wasn't you I saw in my dreams —
Boyhood dreams, young man's dreams.
It wasn't you I searched for
In the pretty bodies I loved,
Nor was it you I watched descending
The hills in a blaze of light.

— We were going our separate ways,
Our paths suddenly crossed
And we held out our hands to each other.

The days have fled,
My beloved . . .

ANDRÉ SPIRE

Nativité

> *Knowest thou the time when the
> wild goats of the rock bring forth?
> Or canst thou mark when the hinds
> do calve? They bring forth their
> young and they are delivered of their
> sorrows.*
>
> — JOB

The cat lies on her back,
Tender eyed, open mouthed,
Pale curved tongue rose-tipped . . .

The cat gasps in the night . . .
A star in the midst of branches
Gleams cold, like the rings
Of a glow-worm moving through leaves.

Now tiny heads and paws swarm
On the cat's belly softly warm.

No wind.   A leaf falls.

ANDRÉ SPIRE

Un parfum éternel . . .

Smoke from heaps of turnip top
Rises, bends, and lowers
Toward the milky mists now floating
Among the furrowed clods.

Behind their steaming horses
Gigantic peasant forms,
Ploughing the muddy earth,
Labor as on a sea.

Suddenly: twigs glisten.
The leaves change into mirrors:
Heaven lives!   I possess a shadow.
The silence breaks in tatters.

My boots are light as air —
Blue rains down everywhere.

From the sea of clover blossoms
An eternal perfume rises:
My dog dives in this sea,
Then he looks at me, stretches his legs,
And his jaws chew at the wind.

He stops and I go forward
And a pheasant flies off in a cry.

Baisers

Wind, you who have often caressed my face,
What kisses do you bring me today?
What temples and bodies have you fingered in passing?
Where did you gather these strange perfumes
Of love or of death?

What lightbeam drawing up water has forced your breath?
To dry what tears and waves and roads?
What pollens are you bearing? — for which of the eager flowers?

Wind, you who have often caressed my face,
What will you take from me this blue-gray evening:
Toward whose brow will you carry my grief and dream?

Friselis

Ripple: smile of the water,
Shatter and stir the mirrored sky
Till the house, head-down in the river,
Mints the ore of the sun.

Ripple: awakening wheat
Slumbering near a water's edge,
Fuse with the hot-trembling air;
Rise up, chant of the harvest!

And mingle with other waves
Falling and rising everywhere
— Thunder, warmth, and love and light —
Through which the gods utter and lead
Without commands or signs:

Ripple of interworlds,
Of our earth and of our sky —
Ripple, vibration, caress:
Kiss of the gods.

ANDRÉ SPIRE

Volupté

Voluptuousness of watching evening
Cover over with velvet eyes
The wars of the cape with the sea.

Voluptuousness of watching night;
Discovering in its blinking lights
The eyes of a laughing child.

Voluptuousness of thinking, speaking;
Sometimes saying less than you might;
Of always keeping secret more
Than one corner in your heart.

Voluptuousness of movements, sounds,
Of dreams; of loving some,
Of hating others; and always yearning
For the end of cruelties.

And chiefly, of feeling in the midst of cares,
A hand — each day less subtle —
Tighten your lungs, make your limbs heavy,
Harden your heart,
And gradually remake your being into a thing.

CAGED IN AN
ANIMAL'S MIND

(1963)

For Leda

All thought is clay
And withered song
— CLAY, p. 85

THOUGHTS ABOUT A GARDEN

Historical Song of Then and Now

Earth early and huge,
No eye dared hope to travel
The palette of its rage

Till, late, they learned to wind
Shackles into its veins,
Shrank it to fit a cage.

So trust contracts to fear.
The tribes give up their feuds.
All wars are now one war.

And will you indict this breed
That strained against a code
Where safe-and-fed was good?

Fled from the mothering wood,
It found in its hand the thought
To light up endless day,

Revel with sleepless eye,
Make of itself a god,
And the veins a level sun —

Now it stumbles, dwarf in the maze
That the thinking hand had spun.
Blind in its blaze of stone,

Whom can this breed indict
That its sun is a blast of darkness,
That light is always night?

Summer

Summer is here — gone is a carol's search —
And light is everywhere: his breadth and height
Dazes the world.   What if this vastness scorch
My lids of flesh?   Its hour will come for flight.

The hour is near — what would a carol bring?

A wind of birds crushes against the night,
Its seeing stones are falling —

                              Cling, O cling,
Voice of my dark, even with blinded sight!
What if this summer cinder to eyeless white
The lavas of color glorying on your wing:

My earth must die in black.

                              Till then, sing, sing,
Voices — my darkness striving to be light!

Ravel and Bind

Whatever: it bears a glow
Above; a seed below,
Thinking might never know
In like-unlike confined:

Lest it erupt and flow,
What can we make with mind
But sorts according to kind
From the worlds of ravel and bind.

Caged in an Animal's Mind

Caged in an animal's mind;
No wish to be more or else
Than I am: a smile and a grief
Of breath that thinks with its blood,

Yet straining despite: unsure
In my stir of festering will
Testing each day the skin
Of this wall for a possible scar

Where the questioning goad of the gale
Forever trying my bones
Might suddenly gather and flail
And burst through the wall. — Would rage

Be enough to hold me erect,
Dazed in the unknown light,
And drive me on with no more
Than my strength of naked will

To range the inhuman storm,
Follow wherever it lead
And answer — whether I hear
A Voice or only the voices

Of my own self-answering scream
In a void of punishing calm?

Ancient of Nights

The broken wisdoms of the ancient lore
Float on the breath of night.   There is no road
Anywhere smitten with dark that you can tread
Safe from the swarm of glances that ensnare,

The instant day decays.   Try to enclose
A body of their fire! — a fleck of air
Blows in your hollow hand.   No sooner seize
A beadstring of those rays! — the staying stare

Mocks at your desperation; while they press
Steadily on your arms, against your hands,
Press in a time-dissolving wave that binds
Comfort and terror into a lost caress,

So glances enter though the clay defies:
The temple of the body's skin has eyes.

Symbol Curse

Tree and river = leaf and water?   Perhaps.
But after an instant's staring: matter and mold,
Then matter-mold shrunk to their sublimate,
Tree and river being too vast to hold.

I crush their sensuous presence so as to save
The fatal essence whispering into thought:
Symbol to me . . .   And what am I now to them?
But what I am to myself? — an aye, a given,
Standing for nothing more: the mere beholder,
To nothing — creature, life, or death — beholden?

Then die from me, symbol, die! that I may fly back
To you, water-and-leaf, river-and-tree,
Cured of the killing thought. . . .   I have you whole,
O pure presence swelling my ears and eyes!

The Valley Between

Man with brow in the air,
Man with the spine erect,
Forepaws hung at the sides,
Drop your head to the grass:

What can you hear down there?
Nothing, nothing, nothing!
Listen, listen, listen,

Man with head in the air:
Raise it higher and higher
To the plain of alarming birds:
What can you hear up there?

Nothing, nothing, nothing!
Listen, listen, listen,
And hear whatever they are,

The voices calling you, calling
From the grass, from the plain of birds,
And up from the valley between
Where you batter a path alone

With your new-won stifle and knees.
Head unsure of the emblems,
Unlinked to below or above,

Hearing no sound but its own,
Reels on the friendless shoulder;
Eyeballs riving with fear
Leap left, leap right, for the course,

While the shanks below push forward,
Right leg, left leg, forward,
Forward, endlessly forward,

Onward, endlessly onward . . .
Keep spine erect from falling!

Face from questioning backward!
So ever ahead and onward,

Onward, helplessly onward,
Onward, helplessly onward —

Thoughts about a Garden

Open windows and crack the cloud:
Strike!   It is never and always time —
Always never — the poles of a nothing

Between but a nonsense song, a nonsense
Cry of waiting.   Every moment
You suck in breath your life hangs

On a thread of air.   So breathe, speak,
That the thread hold, lest it snap and drop you
Gasping through seas of space.   Is your trust

Young enough to believe that flight
But one more storm and one more wave
To cast you up?   The sailor of Egypt

Sank from his shipwrecked boat in a gale's
Black to the island, slept with his heart
His lone companion, and so in peace

Beneath the night of a tree, ever
Embracing shade.   But your heart wavers
In any darkness on any shore:

Only your thought is sure — and thought
Hangs on a thread of air.   Then rush
Into the garden: crack a breach

In the wall of cloud that hides the always-
And never-answering ground of bloom.
Its truth hangs on your thread of thought:

Enter burdened with all you believe!

Petitioner Dogs

Much of the night we sleep
And we doze much of the day
And when awake we watch,
Eat, murder, or play.

Pathetic? Quite. We're dogs.
How could we hope to thrive
Blocked from the human secret?
Lend it! — we too shall live

Like you who dreams and knows
And dreads. It is not too late
To muzzle our brains with grief
And thus rectify fate.

How long must we stay content
To drag our animal breath
From sleep to waking to sleep
In a practice life-and-death?

You will guide, O friend? Then begin:
While we vainly sniff at the air,
Let us vainly paw at the ground
Till we slobber in your despair.

Father-Stones

When all your gods have been carted away and the father-stones
Lie cracked into shapeless meal

And the iron mother-faces
Fester in red under dissolving waters —

Now when your leveled pantheon
Cannot enjoin even a wind, where will you turn,

Where will you look for the yes, the no, the possible,
Probable gate of light?

— Hack your way through arbors of discontent.

Night of the Canyon Sun

Lying above the rim
Of this hollowed world: my sight
Held in the never-believing
Night of this dark, suddenly
Floods with love for the sun.

But you, black sun, why you
Alone of the guardian terrors?
Beneficent sun, cold warmer,
Whose flood transfused to leaf
Propels the broods on earth?

Shall mouth resist with praise —
Mouth of your tissue — striving,
Fed on yourself, green sun,
Maker-sustainer? I carry
Within the horns of my skin

The same pure arcs that listen
On the infinite's beach of fire,

The same forever wisdoms
Churning, out of whose gasps
The living and dying spheres

Unroll.   Then hail, my unquenchable
Day! white sun and only
Turner of sea-bed, mountain,
And helplessly flowing waters,
Whose law's caprice compels

Breathings of ice to burst
My axe of stone and knowledge.
O mountain- and vision-breaker,
How long will the heart stay blind
To your bitterly building might?

The moon is a frozen thought
But yours is the symbol fused
With the tendrils of its sign
So vastly strewn that desire,
Scanning the lights of dark,

Passed you by in the search
Of fire.   Eye of your flaming
Graces not mine alone
But drives me outward onward
To gather a calm that men

May grow when their bodies learn
To meet the guardian terrors
With unexalting prayer.
Wherefore, against all shadows,
In the hard plain light I cry:

"Consume-sustain your sun
That feeds and consumes our flesh!
Gorge on the bones for worship
And flee your dark!   Oh smother
The god in the sun with his passion

Not to adore: to know!"
An echo beats through the dark

From the wailing rites of fear
To maim the words of light:
"Never to know but adore."

— Speech falls back from the air,
From the canyon, into my ears.
Who will be heard: the shadows?
My sun of the desert night?
Till words are made to utter

Reverberations of light,
No man will speak to a man
Of what can only be found
In loneliness as he moves
Unaware in search of his heart.

A Recurring Vision

Down, down, gone down,
Gone down and under the sea,
Past harbor, streets, and piers — the sun
Has drowned.

       So up with the lights,
Up, up in the streets!   Let cars
Dazzle at curbs, spit light, make a flare
For whatever man or woman gropes
In the alleys home.

       You must drive out black:
Remember, its fingers would reach for your throat
At the death of day.   Black is cold
In a city of night or a cave.

       Then light the stones
In all the storeys!   Turn up the bells
Of fire, tier on piling tier,

Till the panes burst and ring in the comfort
Of light — which is heat.   Turn on sound —
Its rays are warmth.   Pour it on floors
Till they shake the walls. — Look!   You live
Though the sun drowns in the sea. — Scorn!
You can tally survival, measure your miles
Of wire, tons of your stone, steel,
The heights and depths of quantified heat
That keeps your throbbing through nights of ice —

But sometimes
In the late morning I see your same stones wearing
Wreaths.   All through the day I see black webs
Hang from the towers, they sway from ledges, they are caught
In the hair of the ginkgo trees.   I watch them float on roofs
And swirl down toward pavements.   They crowd walls, everywhere
Watching with an unknown unknowable stare
That eats at eyes that stare back till those eyes
To save themselves fling up
From the level below to the level above, to the sky, to a colorless foam
Above.   Whatever they find there
Soothes and holds them motionless.
Is it blankness of day? blankness of night?
A fiercer double disdain?

Midnight Wind to the Tossed

I glared at the wind, the wind glared back.   The window
Walls us apart.   Where have you gone? — No answer.
Better that way.   A truce is made, the issue
Thrown to a farther night.   At last: good-night!
But fire comes creeping into the sky, the room,
Eyelids.   Oh, what are walls?   "Scatter their stones!"
Why?   "For the reachless roses.   Wake up!"   Roses?
        "And listen:

A free man needs no house: only a fool
Lusts in rooms for calm: only the old

And young can always sleep: only the tossed
Wrestle with shadows, striving to close fingers
On shapes of loving. Wake! To be purely free,
Speak to your hands until they drop from your arms.
Cherishing is to touch, covet, and seize."

THE AXE OF EDEN

And finally
The pure question that throbs under every facet
Of trust and bitten peace,
To ask of how and when,
Giving up all the wherefore-whys, outdistanced
Beyond all confrontation.
So prepare to enter: You must be asked,
Facing the face in the glass.

                    — There is no one there,
You expect to say; thus having clouded over
That a shape cannot break through.   It is always an image,
Never yourself itself.   Likeness
Is only a mask of thought, no touching fingers
To taunt you to hopefulness, madness, emptiness, sleeplessness.
You are withered enough to learn and you lack the years to evade.
What could you fear
That you have not already sustained?   By now you have died
All the imagined human deaths.   Who could devise
Wiser horror? — Then take your height in the glass,
Silver the back.   Gaze — and joy
In our innocent birthday song
     Out of the mud
     And into a field
     Lighted with trees and stones

Earth of the paradise — fen
To Eden — garden of faultless joy,
Teeming berry and leaf and flower
And over, under, around, and across,
Birds and angels flying the air —
They yellow down from the morning sun,
Scattering home through sleeping stars

— While your God was breathing, breathing out of His tree
Beneath whose branch you slept,
His sacred fruit above your head
In the evening air: apples of God,
Glistening always over your vacant eyelids,
Cluster of suns
Ever beyond the reach of arms,
The reach of eyes, dazed
In haloes burning the clustered branch,
Clustering mystic suns
Beyond the reach of thought —

Where
Had your footsteps led?   From the garden wall
Had you spied the ravine beyond?   Your body
Shivered sleeping against the ground
The night you heard the branch sway down
To thrust into your hollow mind
The knowing suns, so into your veins
The birth of dream: *to seize beyond*
The reach, though seizing kill and spirit
Wail from its dying blood — to seize
His burning rose, swallow the fruit
Of God, His flesh infuse your flesh,
His sight your sight —

The sacred tree
Twists the cluster high in a sudden
Scald of wind.   A fleering bird
Shakes you up from the ground.   And must your eyes
Surround your body's fear, watching
Shadows out of whose coil
May leap your double of dream?

Light
Breaks on the garden, bearing into your glances
Comforting shapes of day — yet the drugging dream
Hangs on your eyes.   And shall they always peer
Dreading the sudden seizing wraith,
The possible other of dream?

He is everywhere.   Fly!
Save yourself!   What are eyes against arms?   Fly!
Hide in the cave by the wall, and think, think
A waking dream to save.   Seize!   Kill
If you must — all is alive in this land but the stones.
Take one! harder, fiercer.   Raise it and strike!   But stop —
Everything bleeds.

Now you are safe, you can walk
With this axe of stone in your hand, back toward the tree
Breathing to you as before.   Shall you forget
It led you to an axe through a coiling thought
Of sleep to waking? — Before you walk,
Look at your hands.
Where will you wash the stain?
Eden's well dries up at the touch of blood.   Cross the walls
To the cataract in the ravine.   But once outside
Can you come back?

Go to God with your stain!
Ask who made you shed the blood.   Open your voice, accuse
The clustering suns that grew in your mind the sickness of dream.
Dare you believe Him innocent, you who were cast
In His shape?   You were shaped of Him by His Will in a pyre
Of yearning, lonely of God!   All you have done is obey
The impulse under the image.   Why be afraid?
He gave you fear.   Is He in truth the God-
That-Makes?   Then go in the helpless knowledge the suns
Compelled beneath your skin.

The axe cries out
Against the blight of this Eden Perfected — land
Of the paradigm void — if nothing dies
Nothing can spring to birth.   The restless axe
Cries out for making.   The edge that kills creates.
Who will hold back the hand straining to shape
The multiple dances?

— You have crossed the wall
To the cataract in the ravine where blood dissolves

Back to the sea from which you climbed
Out of the mud
And into a field
Lighted with trees and stones —
Fen to Eden's ultimate height.   If anything shout
Into your ears that He drives you out of His garden,
Cry the Responsible God who prepared your flight
In the pyre that made you His double —

                             Puny creator,
Walking now with your axe beyond the ravines,
Beyond the cataract now —
Who could have ever believed this opening world of endless fields?
They would never have been believed, even from the farthest ledge
Of the garden wall.   And now, lost in their midst,
How can your teeming eye and ear
Accept such oceans of grass burning a naked sun,
Vastnesses of fields and rivers and trees, rising mountains,
Magnificence of birth so wide and huge and far
And high — world without walls! trilling with cries, calls, screams,
Miracle wild of shape and wing.   Leaping creation.
Infinitudes for the possible . . .

                           Does the axe
Know?   One might think it reasons,
The edge bubbled with rays, breathless
With force and flight.   Watch!   It is thundering toward you,
Surging over your head — your guardian!   Wake up,
This is no second nightmare.   You are no longer the child
Who cried for help in a poem that was prayer to Eden.
Nobody listens to cries in this goldening chaos,
Except his own.

                    Yet scream if it brings relief,
Though yours are the only ears that turn, yours and your generations',
Milling through chartless paths that shape
The soil, multiple treading millions
Rising and dying in change and to each a pulsing
Axe, the body's stone extension that rises
To fall, to change, yet never to grow
A willing tongue of its own.   Yours

Is the single voice and still it shouts from the reckless rise into knowledge
Forever against yourself and your stone
In wavering love and dread of both —

Though you have done no wrong. There is no evil
Except of a word you have made in fear. There is no fear
Except in the wound of wraiths borne
From your pure equation of man with axe. And are you sure
That pure is true, reasoning out of your cage
Of filaments attuned to your narrow gamut
Of voices here where the silence of night
Pounds the incessant torrent and beat, the blooming buzzing confusion
Past the filaments' deafness?

                       And if you burst the cage
Into the day's torrent, would you grow sure? —
Messages beating into your ears,
Morning through night, starlight through sunrise,
Howling: screaming: cries of murdered ants and dying birds and failing
        grasses: explosions
In shrieking trees: in the spilling bloods of the billion creatures falling,
        rising, seen and unknown, near you, over you, under you —
You walk the earth with an axe. Now it advances
Whirling over your head.
Acknowledge the stone, ask in the cage
Our only question: *Where?*

Though we tear at each other's tongues, we are the kindred
Of fear's confusion, given the range of a jungle
Unchartable, though the apertures of its sight
Would make of a point a sphere . . . the earth is round
And flat . . . each twilight we fall to wither reborn . . .
— Find the way through your dust,
Delusion done: Enter your tremulous wholeness:
The world is one and the world is a trillion fragments
Of touch. Grow them together, cleave them apart —
They bear no scar: It is you, their maker-and-breaker-
And-healer. Then press, cry
Against the cage till its agonized walls
Burst, and ravel and bind
Erupt in a flow of reason and blood's dissolving sea

Sight that makes and tears with a healing kiss —
Or, mute on land with fear,
Languish under your axe!

The myths
Denying change advance their sanctities
To ring you in a return to a God outgrown
And the priests you watched by the bloodfires on the swamps.
Must you flee them again, though swamp and fire
Had disappeared, had become night-past
Voids of fear?   Yet flee!   For ever the rites
Of terror wake, exhuming a primal dream
To strangle time and your history.

Everything made
Is good and sacred.   The paradise dream
Of childhood never was.   You were old
The instant you crossed the wall out of Eden,
Forehead gouged by compelling will to follow the sudden self
Boiling your veins.   O ancient face gorged with pain,
Beloved newborn face, look outward now and across
Your worlds within the world!   Admit no sin
But grief, no prayer but desire . . .   So turn eyes
With your making passion, and bear toward the multiple hills
Sight: and they shall be there as you build them there,
Though you die before or the clash of suns enshroud.
Truth is the truth of wish: direction is all.

LISTEN:

(On a spring day in 1853 Gérard de Nerval set out to visit Heinrich Heine, but he lost his way in the Paris streets, wandered, and stopped in despair. Finding himself near Notre-Dame de Lorette, he entered the church and began to confess. Then a voice within him said: "The Virgin is dead; your prayers are useless." Some hours later he loitered at the Place de la Concorde, his mind filling with thoughts of suicide. But each time that he started toward the river, something restrained him. Then he looked up at the sky and saw a vision: "Eternal night is beginning," he said to himself. He turned again through the streets and after long wandering, he found his own room and fell asleep. When he woke, he was startled to see the sun in the sky and to hear shouts of "Christe! Christe!" from children below his window. "They don't know it yet," he said to himself, "but Christ is no more." An hour later he was dressed and in the street and on his way to Heine's rooms.)

His knock at last, my Genius — and still I dread it
Fiercely with love.   What will he bring me today?
Another claw from the sea?   Rags?   Or a bird
Bearing its little death?   "Those are not eyeballs!
Planets!" Gérard will whisper.   How he will sob
Until I comfort his grief with "It's true!" — near God
Of the Gentiles, lend me your calm! — and grant him light
Yet not too much, this delicate poor Jesus
Of the burning storms, who sees with single eyes
Your double world.   Would I might also —

Gérard,
Here so soon?   Come in!   But what are you clutching
So tenderly in your hand?

Nerval's speeches are enclosed in double quotation marks; Matilde's in single; Heine's are set in italics.

"I think I saw a black sun in the deserted sky.
The black sun changed to a bloody globe.
It was hanging above the Tuileries — "

Just now?

"Everything lives, everything stirs:
All is answering all.
That is not madness."

Madness, Gérard, madness?
If only I might look with your eyes, and find!

"See, with your own!"

I peer, but the fire is cold.

"Why, then, are you smiling?"

Is this a smile:
A Jew's deathly grimace against himself?

"Man is double.   Never contract to a one!
I know.   I have watched me flying away while I stayed.
You have read my report."

Of course.

"Then, touch the string —
This that I hold in my hand."

How, when you clutch it?

"The string: my treasure.   But first, look with your eyes,
With all your sight!   Strain!   Force! and again! —
Good.   And now you can know."

But what?

"Now take it,
Touch it.   Then give it back.   At last in my hand:

The string from her girdle: Cleopatra's: hers
And now my own.   Her girdle about my throat,
I wind it — thus!   Listen:"

Stop!   Let me hold it!

"Gentle."

Come, I shall save it here for you.

"No.
I need it.   I found it at last.   The search was long."

No!   Wait — someone is knocking outside!

"The search, the search —
And now no more to search — "

The door, Gérard.   I must answer.

"Someone and no one, always.
Send him away!   Listen, I bring the Secret."

Of course — in a moment.   I shall be back.   Stay there!
There, that chair!   An instant — no more!

(No more —
An instant!   Now think, oh think, and act!   The string!
Seize it now?   It is — no, I can see it.   My God,
I see him: he has found out his Sacred Thread —
He will twist it around his throat —)

Mathilda, Matilde!

(If I reason — but could he hear me?   And now?   What now?)

'You shouted.   Why?'

Shouted, Matilde?   Shouted?
I am thinking — in a mistake . . .

'Is he well today?'

Superb!

'Then I'll go back.'

Yes, no, wait — wait!
I may need you.   Wait.   Let me think.   Kind God, must he die?

'Is he lost?'

Gérard?   Am I lost?   Shall we ever be found?

'Listen!'

To you?   No.   Go to the street — a cab
For the hospital!   Dubois! a cab!   Matilde,
Hurry!

'At once.'

Hospital, hurry — save him!

'Go to him, then, and wait.   I'll call you.'

Gérard,
Nobody knocked.   I sent him away.   Now, tell me again.
*   I am here.*

"The Secret?
Listen — but be calm!   It is all explained.
Listen, and gently listen:"

(Oh what have I done?
What am I doing?   Take me away instead!
I am the madman.   I, of the Tribe of Dream,
Summon my Enemy-Sane to lock up the Dreamer. —
O traitor-and-coward God
Of my fathers, forgive this crime, for you are the guilty
Condemner of all my fathers and fathers and fathers
In the ancient jails of our fear where the only tools
For keeping alive were the scissors of ghetto-wit
Honed on our skins of pain.   Praise yourself, God:

One of your chosen at last comes through to defy —
One of the terrified nurslings
Carrying yet in his blood the stifler-and-poison
Caution, and only faith in the things they can touch,
Taste, smell, use, and break with the tester's eye.
And what of the plundering truth
In vision the reckless behold?   Am I exiled forever,
Never to find what they find in a boiling brain?
Never to dare the passion? — A poet, I?
Spilling tunes on the toes of the claybound tribe,
Seer of the semi-blind? — Must I forgive,
Jahweh, the Safety-God? —)

'Henri, wake up!   They are here!'

Too soon.

"Who?"

Gérard, we must take you.

"Where?
I am here."

You are lost.

"Lost?   No, I am saved.
You have believed my eyes."

Come with me, friend!

"Must I come?"

Give me the string.

"It is here — it is mine!"

It is yours and I will protect it.   All shall be safe.

"But no.   Wait — I must tell you the Secret.   Listen:"

RANDOM PIECES OF A MAN

Thoughts of the War and My Daughter

The year you came to the world
Blood had already enflamed
The breath of a hundred cities,
Wounds of a thousand streets
Already stopped up, embalmed

In ash.   This side of the sea
We were June and green.   We could tell
Sleep from waking, in silence
Pure.   The wind blew east
From our rock-shelf, over the swale

Of ocean, never thrown back
To save: brittle and vain
With hope.   The year you babbled
The first of your words, you could play
Hide and seek with the rain

And his shadow — while we were learning
Fear, but slowly, crossed
In a weltering love.   You could prance
On fern and water, a spangle
Of sunlight endlessly kissed

By our eyes.   What was your thought
When you first looked overhead
And saw in a summer's field
Of night the ever-amazed
Face in a fleeing cloud?

The same as theirs, the children
With the tongueless women and men,

As they watched from the German walls
Over their death-camp cities
An ever-abandoned moon?

December 7, 1960

A River

Blue, windless and deep, above my head,
Above the valley, the plain, the distant trees:
    Depthless arch of a morning

September sky wherever I turn as I gaze
Upward. From these peering ledges of rock
    To which my straying feet

Have borne my thoughtless body, let me gather
A blue world overhead, a green below,
    To carry back if I find

The path to home. How did I travel here
So surely from the road through stumbling fields?
    What are those bending trees

Twisted across the slope below? — green granite
Arching a hollow? Where does that sudden river
    Come from? Where can it go?

Watched from this ledge below: see how it winds,
Sunk deep beneath its valleys, an ancient
    River. But look! it curves

East and beyond. Now it widens into a vast
Meadow of gray water? Is it water,
    That flood of vacant light,

Or a withered field?   But there: it has filled the plain.
It is water. — But if water, how can it stare
    Into the deeps of the sky

With emptied colorless eyes?   Or is it blind:
River too old to bear an outward light,
    To carry blue to blue?

These must be the acres I wandered across
A year ago from a road far from my house
    When I followed into the blaze

Of a setting sun an unknown hurrying man,
The loom of fleshless form that gave no shadow
    Back to the dappled ground.

These trees covet their stillness, yet I ask
Their presences to warn me against my hour
    Of flight, early or late,

Before my body can gaze with empty eyes
And love become too inward borne to answer
    Light of a sun with light.

(For Allen Tate)

Surface

Less to uncharm the sea
Than to learn from a working sky,

I look at surface, trying
To see beyond or within

The stretch and bursting of skin
Whence every newborn wave

Tossed into air can thrive
Over an open grave.

Preparation for Self-Portrait in Black Stone

Think of the serving light
As parabola, as angle.   Think of the rock
As coiled calm and a rage
Buffeted neither by heat nor sound —
The cold rapture tossed in a block
Of swaying night
To be stilled
In the fire and speech
Of shape.   Think of that shape
As oblivion hovering over a truce
Of mallet and chisel where nothing stands
But thrusts of querulous will —
Until
The sleep
Of substance wakes for the breaking hands
And I their use.

Mornings of St. Croix

Who will receive the sun?   "When?"   Whenever
It comes again, if it comes again.   "A wife,
Mother, or girl."   A woman — why?   "A man
Searches, a woman finds"

                              (Her glances bobbing
Left to right on the sandy path, smiling
At the swamps of cloud.

And the sun returned.
Tossed in the yellow air I found her, walking
The morning path she always walked, glances
Bobbing left to right, smile
Unchanged in the newborn light)

What a beautiful morning today, what a beautiful morning!
"Today?" Of course! Look at the sun! "Today?"
Look! The sky! "Today? — and yesterday? —
When every morning I live is a beautiful morning? . . ."

Boy over a Stream

Boy debating, over a stream,
Arms locked on a twittering trunk: —
I could hop on stones to the other bank
Or bend this willow into a bridge
Half the way, then swing and sweep
Into the air for the other edge.

If I hop, I'm there. — More sense to dream
Of what might happen if after my leap
I sink and then dive up through the air
In a lucky lunge to the other shore —
First among men who could double-dive
Both down in-to and up-from a wave!

Men and women would hear and adore.
But though they praised, marveled, and fussed,
I would hope for something different and more
From the tribes no man has yet impressed.
If I leap and fail, not a trout need care.
But if I win — if I scale the air,
Would a fox bark? would an eagle stare?

Letter from One Who Could Not Cross the Frontier

All in all it has been a desperate winter.
Ice storms broke through the panes, the sky scorned.
The children wailed in their sleep.

But now I move
Freely — oil on my bones — and the sun trembles
The tips of the willows skyward.

Nothing is lost.
Even the windows are whole.

Any morning now
The children will ask if it ever happened, and I —
I shall wonder how to answer.

There is no proof
That it ever happened, except for the scar of sound
Crossed in my ear and under the children's eyes.

Nightmare in a Workshop

Come, let us try again to make verses that sound
Like line-by-line translations from Modern Greek —
Candid — proud — and draped in determined appealing
Shagginess, so that you, kind reader, may droop
Beneath the imagined weight of a pure ineffable
Song which is far far better, you're sure.   So fancy
More than makes up for lack.   Thus-finished poems,
Fly! — and, borne on your irresistible failings,
Conquer! for man, O sensitive man, must always
Look through a glass of faith to improve the view.

Stop?   Put down the tools? — It is ever too late.
All our words are caught in a block like the Slaves
Of Angelo and therefore a thousand thousand

Thousand times more deep than any set free
Into the shriveling light.   Though our hope faint,
We must watch them reach toward the weakness we condone
In their vain striving to break from the shroud of stone.

Seven

— And I was seven and I had seen
Shells in the hazel boughs: within
The outer shell a hidden tan-
Gold godlet eye winking, awaiting
Scramble of fingers to lay it bare
For the crush-caress of tooth and tongue

— Now I was seven: already old
In the taker's pleasure, and it was noon
And May and the hazel boughs of a year
Before were calling me into their day

— Then what was school or home or time
Or frantic mother tied to a clock
That tolled me late and lost or drowned,
When I might learn at the living shells
Starting now in bindings of green
The life from sleeping dark to sun,
Of silent growth to the patient pain
Of waiting to be found, adored,
And crushed at last to a death in joy?

Clay

To a snow-world deaf,
To a leaf-world blind,
Where can you go
With your dangling mind

Save to the hells
Of joy?   Then come
In your pith of fear
And your skin of numb:

The soothing tongues
Of blazing grief
May hollow your mind
Of its unbelief

In light and sound
And striving wish.
But do not covet
Your remnant ash,

Revel, or brood
In fire too long:
All thought is clay
And withered song

Whose sweet will burn
To a salt of truth
When leaf is age
And snow is youth.

A Rose Song

Meek
Buttercup maiden,
I have passed you a hundred afternoons

Tripping home from school in the sun's
Concealing light,
Now you are suddenly grown
A rose umbilical maiden —
Wherever you walk is a gust of heat,
Even the stones beneath your feet
Awake.

Guide's Speech on a Road near Delphi

Stop the bus!   Then you will see. —
There, down there at the fork!

    Where?

Where the three roads meet, cross, join,
He killed, he struck.   Laius sauntering downward
But Oedipus racing up from the sea and raging
To flee whatever it was the oracle screechers
Showed him out of the fumes.   How could he stop,
Pelted by fear?   Why should he tack from the road
To let the hot-tongued menacer pass?   Old men
Are full of time — but the young? . . .   He flails, he slashes,
Bodies skid to the ground.   And he could not look,
His eyes on a string to Delphi, twenty-one miles
And uphill always.   He leaps with his horse —

    The myth
    Is true?

You ask! — One makes a choice.   Yours?
"A winter's song" perhaps?   You shake your head,
Believing nothing.   But I believe it all,
Watching this light each day.   There are no myths:
Everything happens.   Live long enough: you shall see!

Song of Nothings: In the Mountain's Shadow at Delphi

Nothing has stayed — only the rock where the raving
Women sat till they shook out words for priests
To weave into double-babble —

Nothing to touch
But a stung wall and marbles pressing the ground
Or leaping toward a cloud —

Nothing to watch
But eagles weaving out of the shining mountain's
Shawl of wind —

Nothing below but a double
Sea: an olive silvering north of leaves,
A south of Corinth water —

And on them all
And under, within, without, nothing nothing
But a sky's devour-caress: all-entering light

Of an open-fingering sun.

I Think among Blank Walls

Strive with reason under the open sky?
Landscape will spin your brain, wring your eye,
All knowledge floating weightless:

I think among blank walls
Bandied by sights whose spending clash ignites
A willing rapture, till the tongue recalls.

Seedling Air

I do not change.   I grow
The kernel that my hair,
My thought, my blood, enflames.
I sing my seedling air:

I shout this ancient air

Into the hail of days
That washes through my skin
To pound and drench my bones.
I keep my light within:

My light burns on within

Flooding my endless rooms
Of pure and feeling brain
Till streams of wisdom-warmth
Murmur within each vein:

They chant within each vein

Will to withstand unchanged
All grindings of that air
Though torrents press down hail
Harsher than they would bear;

For what has will to bear

But outward change that strives
To enter in, and breath
But inner bloom that wavers
Under the hail of death?

(For Edward Dahlberg)

Three in Throes

I the husband, she the wife,
Ogled by Truth or Vanity,
Invited a cat to share our life:
Chose the throes of sanity.

Modes of Belief

Ever since I grew cold
In heart, I always hear
Most men that I behold
Cry like a creature caught
In tones of dying will,
Such as their eyelids bare
With cuneiforms of fail —

Where are the young and wild
Teeming in hope of power?
Though striving lifts the bud,
None can achieve the flower.
Where can the bud disperse
Within?   Must every man
Entomb a withered child? —

What early hearts can store
Of sweetness still endures
Fever of flood or drought,
Till groping up from within,
A self-bereaving curse
Masses in reefs of thought . . .

(For Lionel Trilling)

House in St. Petersburg

If my mother had not been the protected child
Of a dreamy scholar in a protected house,
      I would not be writing these lines —

If the sign hung in the window of that house
Had told a different lie from the lie it told,
      I would not be writing these lines —

If the bribed police who winked at the sign had lived —
If the old one had not choked in a swilling night,
      I would not be writing these lines —

If the young recruit had been briefed with the well-bribed word
By his well-bribed captain before he walked by the house,

Or if he had never tripped on a cobble of ice
And ripped his shirt as he sprawled on a gashing stone,
      I would not be writing these lines —

If he had not then remembered the house with the sign
Because of the word it had always said to the street,

Or if when he asked the service of needle and thread
Father or child could have brought him needle and thread,
      I would not be writing these lines —

If the suddenly tongueless man of a stricken house
Had dared to speak with his eyes and a bag of gold,

Or if the gold had said to the young recruit
What it always said when the hunted spoke to the law,
      I would not be writing these lines —

If the young recruit had not shouted guilt in the street
So that passersby turned round to assault the house,

If he had not screamed the name as he climbed the steps
To the barracks and flung his find in his captain's face,

Or if when the captain scanned the innocent's eyes
He had found a gleam that confessed it was not too late,
      I would not be writing these lines —

If the innocent had not shouted again and again
And again — if the captain could have closed up his ears,

Or if his major, cursing his luck and loss,
Had never signed the papers to pillage and seize,
      I would not be writing these lines —

If the child and father, clinging with dread in the snows
Of night, had failed before they reached the frontier,

Or if their boat, lost in a wild North Sea,
Had not been sighted and saved on a Scottish shore,
      I would not be writing these lines —

Or, when they voyaged again, if their battered ship
Had not groped through its trial to the promised port,

Or if when they saw the sun of a friending earth
They had not danced in the recklessness of its air,
      I would not be writing these lines —

If the father after the years of dancing and grief
Had sought his sleep on an alien hill of Home,
      I would not be writing these lines —

Or if my mother, walking in tears from his grave,
Had not returned, one April, to join his sleep,
      I would not be writing these lines —

And if she herself, before, in a long ago,
Had never told this tale to a young one's eyes,
      I would not be singing her song.

SECOND-HAND POEMS

ANNA AKHMATOVA

The Muse

When in the night I await her coming,
My life seems stopped.   I ask myself: What
Are tributes, freedom, or youth compared
To this treasured friend holding a flute?
Look, she's coming!   She throws off her veil
And watches me, steady and long.   I say:
"Was it you who dictated to Dante the pages
Of Hell?"   And she answers: "I am the one."

STEFAN GEORGE

Denk nicht zu viel . . .

Do not ponder too much
Meanings that cannot be found —
The symbol-scenes that no man understands:

The wild swan that you shot, that you kept alive
In the yard, for a while, with shattered wing —
He reminded you, you said, of a faraway creature:
Your kindred self that you had destroyed in him.
He languished with neither thanks for your care nor rancor,
But when his dying came,
His fading eye rebuked you for driving him now
Out of a known into a new cycle of things.

PAUL ÉLUARD

L'Amoureuse

She stands upon my eyelids
And her hair is in my hair,
Her shape the shape of my hands,
Her hue the hue of my eyes,
She is swallowed up in my shadow
Like a stone upon the sky.

Her eyes are always open
And she does not let me sleep.
Her dreams in full daylight
Make suns burn up in mist,
And make me laugh, weep and laugh,
And talk with nothing to say.

HUGO VON HOFMANNSTHAL

Eigene Sprache

As words grew in your mouth,
Now a chain has grown in your hand;
Pull the universe toward you!
Pull or be dragged!

El ángel bueno

One year, when I lay sleeping,
someone — an unexpected
someone — stopped at my window.

"Rise up!"   And lo! my eyes
were beholding feathers and swords.

Behind: mountains and oceans,
clouds, peaks, and wings,
the sunsets, the dawns.

"Gaze on her there!   Her dream
is dangling from nothingness."

"O yearning, steadfast marble,
steadfast light, and steadfast
movable tides of my spirit!"

Somebody cried: "Rise up!"
And I found myself in your presence.

IN THE TERRIFIED
RADIANCE

(1972)

THE TERRIFIED RADIANCE

The Terrified Radiance

Because there is no forever
And any bird has as much to hope for
As any man, I can look on all I have made
With coldness, with relief —

Gather the scraps and sketches,
Bundle them into somber heaps,
Hide them in closets against the ever possible
Moment of need

For trading them one by one
To a friendless hearth where perhaps their ashen
Bodies may fan a second fire with the lucky
Loveable traces

That once had forced my fingers
Holding the pen to raise up visions
They had not known.   Because there is no forever
For any being,

I want no portal hollowed
Out of the equal selves of soil,
Grass, or stone to guard my breathless heap
That must one day burden

A room, a field.   For I know
And wish that whatever I am, after
A season, will die from the minds of those I leave
As those I love

Have died from mine, mother,
Father, friends of the hearth, all —

All but a cold company of strangers distant
In time and country,

Violent ones whose thoughts
Have been burning coals in my veins and keeping
My heart from falling into the lost disease
Of numbness to this eden,

That flows from the terrified radiance of our minds.

To a Crow

In the sea above where the crests
Of pine make a ring on the sky,
Watching your fires prepare
Their killer-dive to the ground,

I think of the closed-in ocean
That presses against the shore
Its striving lives unwatched
Or known, and among the known

Your counterself in the sea:
Darkness of water's fire,
The driver against all walls
And tides, yet fatefully borne

On its self-devouring will
To breed.   So can it seem
To a creature living on land
Who watches above and below

As he walks the middleground
In search of clues that his body
Lost.   He may even ask
If to kill is your sign from the air,

To kill and then consume;
If your other sign from the sea
Is to breed and slowly die,
Though you are not quite bird

Nor fish but mortal kindred
Spreading through water and wind
Your signs more false than true
For one who can neither swim

Nor fly but, hovering, makes
The dying live, and strives
To tell with his skin and eyes
The differing selves of darkness —

Darkness of fish from bird's,
Color of night from death —

Innocent War

(Gloss: "To a Crow," lines 29–30)

"To make the dying live" —

Somber name for the will
At the root of human love,

The one wild gift that men
Could add to the world's landscape,

Staying the spill of blood
From failing body and leaf:

Learn from this innocent war
Against the pull of the lifeless.

Gulls . . .

Gulls
Drop their unreachable prey from the air
Till the shells
Crack on the dying stone open

                                   I hear
Windows opened by trees — I hear
Seeds, the sunfire,
Rain soothing and flailing,
Sandfloors pushing up from the sea —

Tomorrow — yesterday — now:
Silence:noise — I hear them
Everywhere, anywhere . . .

                Days burn out and nights
                Boil into dawns —

Under the hiding wave
Prey calm in their guardian shells live,
Wait, while the gulls seize,
Pound through unbreakable air
The stone that wears its life away into sand.

Central Park: Midwinter

When you cross the path toward the meadow,
Ponder a speckled snow,
But do not look for the blankness
That crushes country hills
To a faith of animal peace
White in a more than white.
Watch for onyx, the dust
Of grayblue flakes in a wind
Of smoldering jewels poured down
From mouths of the lower sky
At the crests of our stone towers.

And if you forget this ash
Was grown on ancestral trees
Of sun, torn from their depths
Of mineral peace to yield
Slumbering fire, you will see them
Gasping up toward the height
But sinking down through air
To shed their final leaves
Into their kindred trees.
Watch them write on the snow
Their hieroglyphs of passage,

And believe that none who were here
Before us thirsted beyond
Their worlds of green ascent
Or turned from the sight of blooming
Trees to thoughts of a deathly
Wood in the crushed prairies
Of blackness. Only a creature
Starved for warmth would think
To make out of coal tombs
A second coming of sun
Before the passionless ash.

The Finding Light

Suddenly at my feet
A small rock breaks apart at a vein:

Openness always dying, without the shield of a skin —
More bruisable naked than else on earth is stone:

The tenderness ever surrounding, ever unseen,
Ever in wait

For the finding light its strife wrings from a man.

Erstwhile Hunter

Savaging land, the killer gale
Blown by the life from nowhere finally
Reels against the indestructible
      Sea. He will shear the crippled
Trees, he will bring the scalded stalks
      And boughs the single grace

He owns: expunge caprice with fire,
That leaf and blood once more regrow
Veils of calm and dare to nourish,
      Breathe, to sleep with quiet
Eyes under an ever prowling
      Heaven. — Who of the spared

But this broken self could scorn and exalt
The need that will make him torture his thought
On the lost? who but the erstwhile hunter
      Become a nurse to flowers
More scourges ago than hands could ever
      Uncover of axes abandoned

By the sleeping caves of the world.

Their Singing River (I)

Sometimes, dazed in a field, I think I hear
Voices rocking the trees; then I stop, race
To the boughs, listen — and hear not even a thread
Of a wind.

      The calling voices never resound
In aftertones that would make your ears believe,
Nor is there other proof except my temples'
Shaken emptiness. Nor can I know, if my body
Had leaped to the tree in time, what they might have said,

What I might have answered.   Or if some other signs
Could show their presence.

                              Now I cannot regain
Even by wilful dreaming the father faces
Or the eye or hair of the ancient women who bore me
Or think to imagine how they might pull me now
Into the redness of their singing river.

Not to Bereave . . .

Not to bereave is to praise the bridled
Rays that keep each body rising
          Or falling.   Who can be taken
That has not called with a sign to the seizer
          "Come, I am here."

Slaking caresses blind the blood:
Few die but have felt the scorching
          Bliss of a killer's desire
In a closed house or under the chained
          Sky where an otter

Sinks to the sea's floor to gather
A stone that will break the clam he holds
          Close to his breast.   While the flint
Will of the earth suffuses:forces
          All it contains,

What will you teach your veins?   The bird
Trapped from birth in a cell hidden
          From any sound, on the dawn
Inscribed in his blood, bursts with the same
          Cry that his brother

Shouts from the wood.   Tangled in skeins
Of will and knowledge, how can you know
          Sight as desire, who dare not
Glance at the furies that crush your sun?
          Shielding your eyes,

While the flint will of the earth suffuses:
Forces all it contains to thrive,
          Wings cry up from the dark
Singing as the clam dies in the song
          Of the preying stone.

(*For James Dickey*)

Underbreathing Song

Men have daytime eyes.
Nobody goes to the woods at night
To work the trees.   Even your skin
Knows when the light dies
To a blindness on its covering.   Sight
Lifts and falls with the sun,

But voices neither wake
Nor sleep in cells of bone and flesh:
They live you and re-live, they speak
In underbreathing song.
What if you cannot say the words
Of their dark-and-daylight tongue:

Its murmurs are your wave
Tying you to your turning sphere
Too vast to behold, too wild to distill
Calm unless you believe
Certainties flow from unwilled song
That cannot reach your ear.

Emptiness . . .

Emptiness seeps through the air, it is seeping
Into our clothes.   Where it blows from nobody
Knows, yet the dangling tie clinches
The neck, the shoulders chafe.   It could come,
We knew, the Unthinkable, but this cannot be
The one we saw.   Shelters abound:
Nobody tries the doors.   Everyone
Seems to be standing-listening as though
Expecting shrieks of a rain from a possible
Further sky.

       Is it still too soon
To wonder what if the fume could burn
Through all this skin?   The light widens.
Some have begun to tear their clothes
Without waiting to ask.   To learn, we were told,
Is to wait and ask — nothing was said of a presence.

Procreations

     . . . and yet and everywhere
Wreaths are curling up from the sand:
The sea's salt with the leaf's land
     In a fuse of air:
Bursts of streaming shape and sound,
Twining creations of soil and mist —

    Watching near and far
To draw from the ever-unfolding swarm
     Sparks of bestowing form,
And failing at our own command,
We weary towers out of a cave,
Forcing upon the inviolate ground
     Our witness stones . . .

And will this need desist
When coming nothing stands,
When the rock rises against the wave
With taking hands?

WOMEN AND MEN

Movie Poster on a Subway Wall

Whenever I pass her — morning, evening —
Her motionless sight sends visions trembling
Beyond enravishment, threads of my brain
Brushing against her hair, her mouth,
Her body's roses, till other threads
Signal remembrance and leave me only
Her tomb in a paper image —

                 I think
Of withered Donne on his sickbed tossed
In his clouds of angel lightning, begging
The gaze of his gods: I remember his cry
To the wonder of flesh that is earth, the wildness
Of hair that is grown out of earth, the reaches
Of mind,

         till my shaking eyes have lost
All strength to scour the streets for a sight
That might reconcile the image and tomb
Of loves that would live in me yet die.

End of a Visit

"I am going back — now," I say and you nod
Half-sorrowing, half-smiling.
We both look at the clock.

'I'll write, of course — next week perhaps' — a bird
Grazes a screen; startled,
Flies upward, darts down.

                    I gather
My parcels, books, coat; glance at your face
            (It is time to go from a child,
A woman now, bruised; with a place for her head,
            thought, and arms, and a trail
Her body reads in the dark)

                    "I must go back."

                    'I know — it's time.'

Drawn to the door, I hold it,
Open it, speak, half-aware
That while I repeat my words
The dim round earth to which we cling will be fleeing
Another countless thousand miles from nowhere to nowhere.

The Echoing Shape

What can you do alone all day?

Look for the cloud in the sun — listen
For underseas in the air — follow
A leaf, a weed . . .

            At night?

I try to take the darkness.
Nothing of shape outside begins
To speak to me: their daylight
Burns my ears: I gather in midnight waves.
My cat watches at my feet, both of us
Hoping to know what she hears in the blackness rolling
From across the lake where a bird
Sings for its branches.   How can I know
The bird is blind?   It may not be there when dawn comes
And though I could creep up close, in another silence,

I would be watching as always with eyes that recover
From whatever can kindle their light
An echoing shape of arms, thighs, shoulders — the severed
Shadows of all the visions they have ever loved.

Summer Morning Train to the City

Not you closed in a self,
Not even the skin of your fingers damp to the morning paper
Looking at me with their hundred eyes,
Or the perfume
Swarming out of their crevices,
Nor even the pink bulge in bracelets of heat
Of your knees giving out signals . . .

And my right hand stirs in anonymous will to go streaming
Over the fields that lie near your hidden country's
Imagined hills of flesh, to gentle apart
The twinning legs as it enters
The thighs' bounds, to learn the warmth and upward
To the heavier breath as it moves into where the fruit
Might rouse to the hundred tips of fire, vibrating
Fingers of kiss, scar, squeeze, and release
Till the swollen pear scream to be pierced and bitten.

— Legs uncross.   The eyes of your self glance beyond the paper
Past my eyes toward the train window and through to the yards,
Unaware of our bond.   O trainmate, look at the chained hand
Of the morning rite's oblation!

The captive we see is heavy,
Swollen still with the blood of its stopped-up wanting: Where can it go,
Summoned here minutes ago by a need beginning and ending its sudden
        autonomous life
In a body searching for passageways toward a timeless world?
Not you, not I, but a hand
And a fruit drawing the hand that has only to breach a covering —
Let us watch together the fire draining back to its hungering nowhere.

Terah

Before it can see the many
The mind blurs them to one
The better to cope with a separate enemy, friend, or truth —

                    And when Terah returned,
All his idols lay slain except the high one
Standing erect, at its side
The murderer axe:
"Who have destroyed my gods?"

"Abram my son, my son,
Have you killed your fears?"

"Now you have cut them down, learn their faces!"

While the boy covered his eyes,
Terah lifting the slain presences could see
How the spilt breath was pulsating on their faces:
"Let them die there, son,
If their living stings your brain,
But you will father generations of terror.
Can one man's thought contain the world's?"

"He is One at last" the boy screamed.
The listening father pitied:
"If the many are One, your One is also the many"
And he shook with the breadth of the world.

Isaac

The story haunts this tribe that cannot wipe from its eyes
The flashing hill, the trembling man tying his son in his arms, the
        bewildered ram,
Bearing twigs and firewood.   They think it again and again
Through fifty centuries.   Even now when they look at a chance hillock

Under the sky of an unmysterious day, the eyes
Of their poets hang it with flame —
                              "Father, father, save Isaac!"
One of them hears his night cry out, as though the indifferent cloud
Were sown with seeds of blood bursting to flutter
Over the boiling stones.

                        Even my own father
One morning of my longago childhood helplessly
Watched his thought slip through the triple Hegelian chain
With which he wrestled the world, to relieve the curse
Thou shalt not raise thy hand . . .

                              Nor yet can a generation
Die without shouting once into the air to purge its heart
Of the blind obsessive tale, as though for always unsure
Of the wrong of worshipping the blood's terror of sacrifice.

Talmudist

Gloat, glittering talmudist,
With your eastern eye, your northern eye, your western eye;
The days are a fog of clashing words: cleave
If you can — warp with your buzz-saw brain a light-filled
Path shallow enough for a heart to follow!

Why do you fist your words
With your merchant's hand, your scholar's hand, your toiler's hand?
Is a god you smother the dynamo of your fury
Or a wraith you reasoned into existence in hope
It would pierce your eye with joys?   Or a heartsick need

For a heaven-on-earth perfection
That drives you, though you have learned there can be no right
Unmixed with wrong.   Where will you go when the moment
Strikes and your arms, defying brain, reach out
To your brothers' will, your homeland's will, your body's will?

Song of Succession

What am I doing, fiftyish,
Trespassing on your asphalt?   A shrewder animal
Would have found him a shroud and a hole long ago.

      Spare me
Your soft solemnities!   I have also believed
All you ought to believe now.   Hence, unless you're mouthing it,
Chase me out of your jungle!

                If I stand pat,
Crush my brain!   No loss to your possible world (years
Have cut too many tracks in its flesh: how could anyone
Heal caution's sickness now?)

                    Then come, Oh drive me away,
Cleanse your street of me quickly!

          (But, careful: the plague —
          Better not come too close.)

                      Make room, both of us,
For the unforeseeable few, for the headless guileless
            bodywise tainted multitude!

                  Ready?

New York, San Francisco: 1960s

En l'an . . .

Autumn: paleness for men, harvest
      For planted field, for women
         Hollow calm,

When the curves of a narrowing sun fail
    To burn creation in two
        As in timeless summer:

Think? strive?   Look back if only
    To gaze after something abandoned
        Vibrating still:

What if a ray's returning knowledge
    Grew in its eyes, asking?
        How would you answer?

"Wait"? — wait till after the coming
    Rigid gloom bursts
        With the swelling arcs

Of the always springing of the ice-flower?
    Would you cry out, again
        Call back, despite

All you have learned shivering beneath
    The fierce unseeing fires
        Of an animal sky?

(*For Dudley Fitts*)

Dialogue of the Stone Other

Friends are falling about me.   Some of them
Cannot climb up from the ground.   Others
Rage, stammering answers —

Man
Smoothing your hair, standing before
Your glass, charged with the burnt light
Of the morning:

Friends friends are falling:
What came on in blasts, swift,
Single — can it become the season
Of steady blight?   I —

                    Keep your eyeballs
              Fixed on its never-wavering —

Friends
Are falling.   Merely to keep erect
May be a kind of youth.   Then —

                        Deafen
           Your ears to your own puff of words and —

Friends are falling, falling —

                     Will you not
          Stop to hear your stone other
          That keeps on asking again again
          What will you do with its life?

In the Coastal Cities

Their ancient ancestors gave up hope of ever regaining
The first eden,
Yet the later ones believed,
Walking their years magnetized by faint impalpable rays
Of the second, after dying.

Now their children's children's children
Nurtured in want and hope can neither want nor hope
For any time to come.   Helplessness
Foams in their eyes, tightens their hands.   You can hear them
On the streets in the poisoned towns.
Their daylight breaks in black,
Their spring and summer scalded by wintered fire.

Getting and giving love,
They know each other by signs,

While you, lost in your own confusions of want and hope, ask of them
That they willingly wane in the streets
And wait while the elders stop the sea from invading
The land.

What if the elders fail,
If the land goes under?
If the sea spurts from groundholes onto sidewalks?

Will of Choice

If you thought to name your course,
If you had the will of choice,
Would you stay where vertical stone,
Level asphalt, a dome of gas
Wall you away from your source
Yet hold a delirious force
That can slake for a time the thirst
In your cells of heart and brain

Or find a place outside
With the naked land? and hope
The plagues we bear may subside
Before the fever can creep
Through the slowly dying air
Into the roots of grain
And the skins of the planet prepare
To burst . . .

Chanson Innocente

Cast your faith in the ever-nearing
Catastrophe your brothers and I
Pull, each instant we live, down
On the mother-once sea, the nurturing sky,
The hostage acres of soil we flay
And beg for our bread and warmth.   Then hail
Catastrophe! — what else to hail
Except your terrified creature-lust

To survive?   Its imminence might save,
Driving, as with the wrath from a once-
Believed-in heaven, across the water
And land our all-devouring hordes
Till none could range but a remnant shriven
Of strangelove mind and suicide hand.

The Rock

I have looked all day for The Rock
In this land where the grains are always seen.
I found no mark on the soil,
Sand and loam too old once more to be pressed prone or pierced
Apart.   Only across the faces of scattered
Women and men are there any scars,
Rips, burrs — and these are such as a glacial mountain
Signs, roaring across dry ground to the sea
Of a younger land in the melting kill of its breath.

Sinai Foothills

Condor Festival

Herded the second month of each year
In fiesta, Indian mountain villagers
Learned from their alien lords who danced
A ring while axes bit at a tree
Ribboned with fruits and gifts till it flashed
To the ground.   Think of the Spaniard's trusted
Rite four hundred years ago

For chasing out pagan gods, when here
They hide in baited covered pits
On table-lands beyond their houses:
Indian mountain villagers watching
For condors.   When one nears they seize at him,
Rope his legs, carry him back
To the ring, and wait.   They cannot enter

The ritual ground until the villagers
Reaching above their heads have pillaged
All the gifts that hang from an arching
Pole. — But now they come.   Each holds
A condor wing; they bind the clattering
Feet to the tip of the arch.   Hungering
Human eyes watch him flailing

The air in a thundering will to soar
As horsemen with painted faces lunge at him,
Circle beneath his scorching eyes,
And then with their fists beat at the dangling
Defenceless head.   One of the horsemen,
Pressing his teeth to the gaping beak,
Rips out the condor's tongue.   The watchers

Shriek for the body, pounce for talismans . . .

THREE FRIENDS

We Brought You Away As Before . . .

We brought you away as before to return again with you here
But this time they knew you would have to be given a sleep beyond
    awakening.

And now we are back again, your three friends, in the same
City rooms, and everywhere your absence is an eyeless presence,

As though it might have been better if we had taken you away
To the wooded acres where you raced and wandered all the days long,
And had hollowed a passage in a corner of that earth and brought you
    there to quiet,

Or if instead we had set you free above, on the grasses,
And waited, watched, till your body fulfilled its own motion
Toward death, alone on your fields of home after your eight summer years.

Our Cat T.

Friend across the Ocean

I go to my quiet bed, put out the light, prepare to sleep
And my friend across the ocean lies in his sickbed waiting-

Dying with nothing more to reach for, being cut away
A part of his body also: what was not taken is gnawing

The sane, and he does not know, in the blood's protection: peering
Into the faces that hover over him, trusting-believing

Their glance yet seeing mostly himself gazing from the pillow and past
The casement into the blackness of the London winter night–sky,

And mumbling again, as in manhood decades ago, *Verweile doch,*
Du bist so schön, love doubled back on itself as then,

As now in my own body were it tied on a sickbed under a gateless sky.

W. J. B., 1894–1968

Wildness

We were together when we were young, and whatever the later
Moments of meeting, none of the burdens that the ticking grains
Had sown in the web of our separate lives could sever us.

I had told him long ago of something I had watched once
By a ruined wall of an ancient Italian town: a man
And a woman clinging together through flooding lava.   And still

They cling, behind a glass wall making them one, reach out seizing
Each other's safety against the sudden hideous thunder
Of kindred breath blown upward out of their trusted earth

To burst and descend as strangler-cloud.   He died alone:
What could he cling to who was always huddling close to the shadow
Of walls that keep out wildness — the world's, yours, his own?

But to die is to cast off dread: Wherefore now in a shielding
Crypt his quieted face lies parching, though the grasses already
Have come, have begun to invade and to take it back into
            wildness.

M.S.K., 1908–1967

THE HERO OF SILENCE

Scenes from an Imagined Life of Mallarmé

The only thing a self-respecting man can do is to keep looking up at the sky as he dies of hunger.
— MALLARMÉ TO CAZALIS, 1865

I. Dedication: An Eternity of Words

So to compose the universe —
Killing : spawning worlds with denial,
Dragging truth through scourging laws
To earn a life in my thought.

What if the innocent blood of body's
Desire rise up in words unaided?
Even flesh can be burned
To the whitenesses of a song,

That out of oblivion ash may float
— My Orphic Book of the Earth! —
An eternity of words where naming
Creates, refusal destroys.

II. Master and Pupils

Time to lock up my brain and drudge to school.

Dare I ever cry out: "I own a glass
That sucks in eyes to the depths?"

Might they hear
If I began: "I found a curious thing
By chance —
Perhaps it came in a kind of trance" —
Thus easing the word, that they might care
This once . . . ?

"A mirror, simply.   Familiar — but how to use it?
        Hear!
You must more-than-glance,
You must more-than-turn
When you look: Press, burn,
Stare them out of substance, enemy-loves,
Till the sight changes to sound,
Sound to nothingness —
The indifference of the sky, a stone" —

But none of them will care to follow me, captives
Of their own dismay,
Waiting inside this fatal door
For my entering step to trumpet daily war —   Yet
Might I plead with them:

                    "Close your book
And hear of this glass I own.
It sucks all pressing eyes, presses them back
Till gaze parying gaze
Bursts into ice of flame, to abolish walls,
Dissolve flesh into Azure" —

                    But no.   I am here.
Inside.   Against them now.

Gravely they throb: flesh I must love.   Has it overheard
My thought?

"It was only a mirror to me, to you,
Innocent glass and yet the defender of truth."

How they spurn!

"Open your pages!   Safer to eye a book!"

One refuses, begins to burn
Till I must stare him down.

Who is this other who presses back?   What wakes
In his eyes' answer?
What has he drawing me there
Through the mass of face dissolving?   Is light the youth?
Can I gaze it out of substance, flesh that trembles?

III. Soliloquy from a Window: Man and Flowers

If flesh, then all that moves.   If blood, then juices
Of ground: blood of a tree, a rock, a flower,
        Of all who rise in the mist

Ever floating about a thought's secret
Abyss.   Manas converge to the point of light
        Vision flees when the fires

Of seer and seen entwine.   — Look at me, flowers
Beneath this window: calyx of roses, gold,
        Purple, white!   Your multiple

Eyes, make me your mirror!   I dive within you
Bouquet: we return one another, flower and eye
        Moving from each to each

In wakefulness, one to the other's silence:
Song.   Shall we lose our flesh to dissolver-light,
        Starers become the stare?

You are shedding your faces.   Where have you gone, my petals?
Go to return, vanish as you return,
        So, live in a thrust of mind!

IV. Dialogue before Waking

Stare!   — Stare?

 When you will
You can stare it out of substance —
Not only petals.

 Whatever waits
For any man answers him with a face
Uplifted, throbbing to speak and be known.

 And will you know them then
For what they are as they greet you,
Or must you hide from the ecstasies
Of touch? turn dazed by the flesh
You overlove in your dark of fear?

 Stare!

 Since you must, at last, at whatever face moves toward you.

 Stare while the blood drains,
Forsakes the skin.

 Then stare with the ice of thought
Fired with a love that kills, and watch the skin
Curl, twist, burn like paper; the bone
To ash —

 And within that face
And out of that face that offered a trembling word . . . ?

 A hovering fume.

V. Fume

The air that hovered enters coldly,
Sounds in my brain suddenly —
    Nothing I heard before.

This is the silence thought can hear
From voices spoken by planets
    Scorching through nothingness —

Voice of the flame of sky! Imagined
Flower of flame! Floating
    Ideas of sound!   — Listen:

They throb alone, islands borne
In azure lakes, but glowing
    Fused and pure. O Poem

Of Flight, I will you into words
From the nothingness of sense
    Through silences of sound,

Such as upon her wedding day
Cecilia, saint and blinded,
    Sang in her heart to God

Her song unheard. Yet will I sing
Entwining sky and flower
    A flame that shall be heard!

VI. Into the Blond Torrent

Whatever palpitates lives: therefore threatens.
Name them all? — If naming alone could subdue!
  One of my waiting children
  Shall call them. All the equations

Exist. With our eyes' hot destruction we lift
Covers, so all that trembles can rise to the pure
    Reaching touch of kindred
    Selves. We have only to watch

To know. There is nothing left to create. We must see!
Unravel! vanquish! — even my innocent thirst
    For the flooding naked caresses
    Of her golden hair. Cover

My eyes? — Seize! drown! till the blond torrent
Bear me on her trembling thighs to the warm
    River of calm: the sleeping
    Ecstasy of the ages

Lost, found in her golden foam. O quivering
Gulf of invisible song! She alone — from her body's
    Vessel, let me tear out
    The dream! Let the waking phantom

Blind me! body burn with her flight! I shall plunge her
— Destruction be my Beatrice! — into the death
    Of love. And out of the blackness,
    Out of our blood silenced,

I may rise, victim, guarding the ash of her flame.

VII. The Waking

When body answered, blood
Rebelled,
Heart screeched at the ribs.

And when I uttered, vision
Burst.

And when I awoke,
I saw creation gaze on itself through me:
Infinity contained.

The dream that ravaged has remade.   Nothing can harm.
I hold in me a piece of the nothingness
Of which our night is made.

Agonized earth
Has vanquished under a vacant sky.

                              O Poem
Of Flight, abolish wings!

I have no pain.   My mind
The hermit of its own purity,
Cannot be touched by time, cannot be touched
Even by time reflected in ageless shadow:
Day.

        I do not seek to make.   I seek
The freedom gathered, kept, and to replenish.
The finite falls about me till I die.

---

*[Some lines of the poem echo words and thoughts that recur in the writings
of Mallarmé — such as mirror, flight, azure, woman's hair, absence, nothingness — as he moves from the "raw and immediate" world of sense toward "pure
idea, quintessence, blankness, silence." Other passages of relevance:]*
*I. Tout, au monde, existe pour aboutir à un livre . . . L'explication orphique
de la Terre, qui est le seul devoir du poète . . .*
*II. J'ai encore besoin . . . de me regarder dans cette glace pour penser . . . c'est
t'apprendre que je suis maintenant impersonnel, et non plus Stéphane que tu as
connu — mais une aptitude qu'a l'Univers Spirituel à se voir et à se développer,
à travers ce qui fut moi . . . [Lettre à Cazalis, 1867] . . . O miroir!/ Eau froide
par l'ennui dans ton cadre gelée/Que de fois et pendant les heures, désolée/Des
songes et cherchant mes souvenirs qui sont/Comme des feuilles sous ta glace au
trou profond,/Je m'apparus en toi comme une ombre lointaine . . . [Hérodiade]
. . . Que la vitre soit l'art, soit la mysticité [Les Fenêtres].*
III. Je dis: une fleur, et hors de l'oubli où ma voix relègue aucun contour, en

tant que quelque chose d'autre que les calices sus, musicalement se lève, idée même et sauve, l'absente de tous bouquets.

IV. In approximate English: "What use of transposing a fact of nature unless the pure concept emanates from it . . . Thought that has thought itself through and reached a pure idea."

V. . . . J'ai besoin de la plus silencieuse solitude de l'âme, et d'un oubli inconnu, pour entendre chanter en moi certaines notes mystérieuses [To Aubanel] . . . Le chant jaillit de source innée, anterieure à un concept, si purement que refléter au dehors mille rythmes d'images . . . Toute âme est une mélodie qu'il faut renouer . . . The invisible air, or song, beneath the words leads our divining eye from word to music . . .

VI. Le blond torrent de mes cheveux immaculés . . . Mais ta chevelure est une rivière tiède,/Où noyer sans frissons l'âme qui nous obsède/Et trouver ce Néant que tu ne connais pas! . . . La chevelure vol d'une flamme . . . Au ciel antérieur où fleurit la Beauté . . .

VII. Mon art est un impasse . . . Ici-bas est maître . . . We measure our finiteness against infinity [To Mauclair].

SECOND-HAND POEMS

OCTAVIO PAZ

Más allá del amor

Everything threatens us:
time, that divides into living fragments
what I was
                    from what I shall be,
as a cane-knife does with a snake;
consciousness: the transparency pierced,
the gaze become blind from watching itself gaze at itself;
words: gloves of grayness, dust of thought on the
            grass, water, skin;
our names, which rise up between the You and the I,
walls of emptiness, walls that no trumpet cuts down.

Neither dream with its population of shattered images,
nor delirium with its prophetic foam,
nor love with its teeth and claws are enough for us.
Beyond ourselves,
on the border between being and becoming,
a life more than life itself calls to us.
Outside: the night breathes, spreads out,
filled with great hot leaves,
with struggling mirrors:
fruits, talons, eyes, foliage,
flashing shoulders,
bodies that press their way into other bodies.

Lie down here on the edge of all this froth,
of all this life that does not know itself, yet surrenders:
you too are part of this night.
Stretch your full length, whiteness breathing,
throbbing, — O star divided,

wineglass,
bread that tips the scales toward the side of dawn,
moment of living flesh between this time and another
measureless time.

ANDRÉ SPIRE

Retour des Martinets

Oh, at last you've arrived:
Arc in the sky, sparks, rockets
Loaded with all the warmth
And the chill freshness of mornings:
I watch from behind my window where the blooms
Of this late spring are beginning to burst.

Faithful guests, you're here again with your spurts of crying,
Your arrows hissing their laughter at me,
Your interlacings, somersaults,
Your upward flights, your tumblings —
Quivering imps of the sky!

What magnets? what breezes?
What mayflies draw you here?
Is it myself your harsh eyes crave?
Am I a friend, a brother,
An echo, a strain recovered?

I?   — I, weighed down,
Eyes dimming,
Voice roughening,
Feet wavering,
Forehead doubting . . .

Oh, let me hurl back to the ground
All hopes of flight that had budded in me

And plunge my envies and anguish
In the scalding waves of your endless assaults.

Written in the poet's 96th year

RAFAEL ALBERTI

Canción del ángel sin suerte

You are the one that keeps moving,
water that carries me along,
that will cast me aside.

Search for me in the wave.

The one that departs and does not return:
wind that in darkness
dies and reflames.

Search for me in the snow.

The one that no one can understand:
ever-inconstant presence
that speaks with no one.

Search for me in the air.

RAFAEL ALBERTI

El ángel mentiroso

And, I was broken,
not with violence:
with honey and words.

In the uninhabited wilds
of sand and wind,
a prisoner, alone,

I, somebody's shadow —
and a hundred doors of the centuries
walled up my blood.

O splendor! Come to me!

Who was broken,
not with violence,
with honey and words.

ÉMILE VERHAEREN

La Bêche

Frost hardens the waters; wind pales the clouds.

There: in the east of the field, in the harsh soil,
The spade rises and trembles
Pitiful, bare.

— Make a cross on the yellow soil
With your long hand,
You who depart by the road —

The thatched cottage green with damp
And its pair of lime trees struck by the lightning
And its ashes on the hearth
And its plaster pedestal still on the wall
But its Virgin fallen to the ground.

— Make a cross toward the thatched cottages
With your long hand of peace and light —

Dead toads in the ruts without end,
Dead fish in the reeds,
And then a cry ever weaker and slower from a bird,
An endless cry of agony from over there.

— Make a cross on the road
With your pitying hand —

In the stable's empty skylight
The spider has spun the star of dust;
And the twisted beams of the farm on the stream
Spring through the pitiful thatch
Like arms with the hands cut off.

— Make a cross upon the future,
A final cross with your hand —

Bare trees and severed trunks — a double row
Along the roads bewildered in their rout;
The villages — not even bells to ring
The hiccoughing hopeless *Day of Wrath*
To the empty echo and its broken mouths.

— Make a cross to the four corners of the horizon.

For this is the end of the fields and the end of evenings;
Mourning turns its black suns in the depths of the skies
Like millstones;
And only maggots come to life
In the rotten sides of women who are dead.

In the east of the field, in the harsh soil,
There: over the scattered corpse of the old ploughlands,
The spade, plate of bright steel, rod of cold wood,
Holds dominion forever.

ANNA AKHMATOVA

from "The White Flock"

For us to lose our pureness of words and of heart
Is what it would be for a painter to lose his sight
    Or an actor his motion and voice
Or a beautiful woman the radiance of her eyes.

But do not try to save for your private self
What was given you by heaven.   We are condemned
    — And we know it well — to squander
All we own, to keep nothing for ourselves.

Then walk alone, and bring to the blind their cure
Only to know in your aching hour of doubt
    The jeering malice of the few
You taught and the chill indifference of the many.

MIGUEL DE UNAMUNO

Me destierro . . .

I exile myself into memory,
I go to live on remembrance;
Seek me, if I am lost to you,

In the barren-wild of history.
For human life is sickness
And in living sick, I die;
I go then, go to the barrens
Where death itself will forget me.
And I take you with me, my brothers,
To people my desert land.
When you believe me most dead
I shall quiver in your hands.
Here I leave you my soul — a book,
A man — a true world.   O reader,
When all of you stirs as you read me,
It is I who stirs within you.

MIRAGES:

Travel Notes in the Promised Land

(A PUBLIC POEM)

(1977)

Dusk comes strangely here.   It is morning there:
My island sun will be sweeping
Through ripening trees beside our house in my native land.
It is long past noon in London.   Soon my daughter
Will be watching the moon rise over her mudbrick house
On the edge of the sand desert in Persia.

Note: Four lyrics that first appeared in *In the Terrified Radiance* (pp. 110, 111, 116) also form parts of *Mirages* (pp. 140, 143, 155, and 151 respectively).

I. FIRST LANDSCAPE

From seventy roads they return —
Number the absent centuries on your feet and hands.
When they last herded away, were they one people?
I look at foreheads, eyes, lips,
And wherever I turn I see a different nation
Yet they all may have been one face.

                                        Is a woman —
A man — only the image of his native landscape
As their poet-physician witnessed?
The first landscape they wore failed
Unless part of it still remembers
In shadows beyond the shape.

If what I gaze on now are the wraiths of the lands they became,
Where will I find the face?
Which is the mask?

*   *   *

They can show you proof that he crossed this way
Long before anyone counted years,
But why did they choose this Abram child
Suckled in pledge to a moongod Sin
From a lost Sumerian city?
They can show you proof that he traveled here
With all he could take from the Syrian stop
On his way to Canaan the Destined —

                                        Canaan here?
This raucous dustiness under my feet?
Tangle of paved white avenues, asphalt
Streets, glass buildings, buses, cars, turmoil —

Driver, take me out of this place! *

"Where do we go?"

I came to look on the Land of Canaan.

"This is Canaan."

Possibly once. Not now.

"Sir, there were always noisy cities in Canaan — small ones — "

But Abraham . . .

"Abraham who?"

Abraham moved with his herd and flocks through the open hill country.

"Oh, that Abraham! Yes, of course. Like our Bedouins —
They live the way he lived — for thousands of years."

Bedouins? Bedouins where?

"Haven't you seen their goatskin tents, their camels, their —
Come, I will show you. Come! — Not far."

Scattered clumps of pasture now, but who can imagine
The early face of this soil?
Graybrown swales. Swellings of earthy sand.
Everywhere caves and mounds
Lead from where you stand to where you might have been standing
Forty hundred years ago.
Looking for origins —

Time twists, coils back through the air
Above this land where any stone might speak to you
Till eyes scald with mirages:

*The speaker of the poem sometimes addresses himself, sometimes others. In the dialogues, the words spoken by him are set in italics.

While the Canaanites spurn their open country,
Cling to their cities' fortified walls,
Abram wanders from north southward, muttering peace
To other tribes of nomads, his eyes gazing
On every jarful of soil in throbbing wakefulness
For a new sound from the voice that had sent him "Leave thy father,
Thy country!   Get thee into a land I will show thee."
By their own will, his eyes turn toward a misted town
Between two hills.   Carelessly touching its earth —
Words float up: "Unto thy seed I give this land."
He kneels, he begins an altar —

"But why, husband?" Sarah derides, "Many people say they hear voices."

'This is His voice.   Three times I heard.   I know the sound.
It made me abandon father, it rang in my childish ears.'

"And why should a god in his wisdom speak to you only?"

'You cannot believe.   Neither did Terah believe
Yet he knew when he saw what my arm had done.'

II. GENERATIONS OF TERROR

Before it can see the many
The mind blurs them to one
The better to cope with a separate enemy, friend, or truth —

                And when Terah returned,
All his idols lay slain except the high one
Standing erect, at its side
The murderer axe:
"Who have destroyed my gods?"

"Abram my son, my son,
Have you killed your fears?

"Now you have cut them down, learn their faces!"

While the boy covered his eyes,
Terah lifting the slain presences could see
How the spilt breath was pulsating on their faces:
"Let them die there, son,
If their living stings your brain,
But you will father generations of terror.
Can one man's thought contain the world's?"

"He is One at last" the boy screamed.
The listening father pitied:
"If the many are One, your One is also the many"
And he shook with the breadth of the world.

                *   *   *

That the idols fell in a faroff place cannot matter here
Or that the shouting son
Never heard his father's prophecy.   Distance shrivels

Under this quicksilver sky.
Visions dance over mountains and all that rises
Beyond, as all that has happened seems to have happened
Now or an instant ago.   My shoes as they walk this road
Twisting among the Judean hills
May be scuffing the dust of that unfound place called Salem
Whose priest-king dashes to welcome this man he had never known,
Offering bread, wine, and prayer — the blessing
Millions of Roman faithful in a hundred countries
Adore each day after the Consecration
                                        — easy to stray
From the source question: origins.

These hills are filled with buried altars.   Bedouins probably
Know where some of them hide.   But the hill wore leaves
When Abraham led his boy.
Walk from these ruined sands? or stare at them
Till vision greens the summit, raises up trees,
Peoples the desert swale with pastures, flocks, shepherds,
And hanging over, a cloud baring the face
Of the dead one who screamed that his son
Would father generations of terror, watching
For the fate of the child —

                        "Sir, would you care for a ride
To Jerusalem?   I'm going there now.
Please, where are you staying?
Not in Jerusalem?   But how
Did you come down here?"

This morning — hours ago.   I suppose.

"Where would you wish to go?   Let me help you!
Please, your shoes must be full of sand.
You are tired walking — you may not feel it
Yet.   Please, the heat — it's dangerous.   Worst
From noon to three and it's almost noon.
Sunstroke, we say, is the enemy number two."

And number one?

"Oh, the Arabs or the Russians. Take your choice:
We have none. — A poor joke, I know. — But please,
Please come in from the sun! — This way. — Thank you."

You are generous —

"Please, please. — If you don't mind, tell me
What you are looking for here.
Please if you want to, sir."

The altar rock in the land of Moriah.

"But why come here when it's in Jerusalem, in the Old City?
I'll take you as close as I can; you will walk the rest.
Moriah, Mount Moriah, where the good Lord tested Abraham.
You mustn't mind where it stands:
Inside the Mosque of Omar. The Moslems are sure
The rock was Mohammed's take-off pad to heaven.
Come, we could be there soon!"

Mount Moriah — or Land of Moriah?

"It cannot matter unless you're an old believer."

And what may a non-believer look for?

"Come, we shall be there soon!"

*Answers still unborn
To questions seething under the rock?*

"Please, sir! Please! We can be there soon — "

III. BLIND TALE

The story haunts this tribe that cannot wipe from its eyes
The flashing hill, the trembling man tying his son in his arms, the
      bewildered ram
Bearing twigs and firewood. They think it again and again
Through forty centuries. Even now when they look at a chance hillock
Under the sky of an unmysterious day, the eyes
Of their poets hang it with flame —
                     "Father, father, save Isaac!"
One of them hears his night cry out, as though the indifferent cloud
Were sown with seeds of blood bursting to flutter
Over the boiling stones.

                Even my own father
One morning of my longago childhood helplessly
Watched his thought slip through the Hegelian chain
With which he wrestled the world, to relieve the curse
Thou shalt not raise thy hand . . .

                   Nor yet can a generation
Die without shouting once into the air to purge its heart
Of the blind obsessive tale, as though for always unsure
Of the wrong of worshipping the blood's terror of sacrifice.

               *   *   *

 The cafe tables are almost touching:
Everyone overhears —

— "Then she rushed in for lunch, my little one. How she was
      beaming!
'Mama,' she called, and 'Mama' louder; and then with a bursting
'Guess who's going to have a baby! Guess!'
I shook my head.
'Guess, Mama! Please, please guess!'

I really don't know, my child.
Then she squealed with delight: 'Sarah, Mama.   It's Sarah!'
Sarah who?   I asked.
'Sarah — you know her.   Sarah in the Bible!   A baby,
And his name will be Isaac' " —

How much more will they tell her?
That Sarah mocked at her body's barren
Lustiness while her slave-maid Hagar,
Led by her hand to her husband's bed, proved what she feared?
Would the little one understand why the maid
Fled in despair through the wilderness till within her
A voice soothed with promises she could walk back humble ·
Yet calm, no longer trembling
As she waited the coming at last of her son
Ishmael, named for "God hears."

I want to warn: don't tangle the little girl's brain
With old men's tales of rites and covenants:
Let her wonder at Sarah.   Was bringing to birth
In her old age not enough to lift her long self-scorn?
Why else rage at the rival mother-and-child?
Why else force her half-brother husband in pain to cast them away:
The woman of Egypt with whose blood he had merged, their son
He loved — to wander, thirst, and die?

"Do you think I would have obeyed your demand if the Voice
Had not told me Ishmael also will father a mighty nation?"

'Your voice again,' she howled in his face,
'For that voice's sake you ran off to murder my child.
Is your newfound god juster than Canaan's idols
For whom they also murder children, bury their stifling bodies
In the walls of their houses?'

"Fall on the ground and give thanks for our son!"
But after the binding of Isaac,
Sarah and Abraham lived in separate towns.

Will the little one learn to doubt the hate of the mothers
Has never been overwhelmed by the father's love?

"Abraham — El Khalil — is the Friend of God
And Ishmael is our forefather," say the Arabs,
"The twelve sons are the princes of the tribe
Like the twelve sons that the son of your Isaac fathered."
Can the little one think the quarrel burns in the blood
When she sees their descendants roaming these hills as I see them now?

Perhaps she will come and take my hand.
We could pass through this door under the late March sky
And walk on the rounded hillocks, touch the gray boulders
Sprinkled everywhere: stone jutting out from the green.
We could wander here like goats and the sheep now grazing the fenceless
Slopes ablaze with poppies and small yellow daisies.
And we would stand there both of us open to the luminous sky,
Our thoughts transported in time,
Not even seeing the sprawl of box-like houses,
Not even hearing the clatter
Of the bursting city.

                — But the phantom breaks:

"Do you know what my watch is saying?" the speaker
At the nearby table shouts.   "I almost forgot
Today is Friday.   Come!   Oh there's never enough
Time" —

       Have I time?
                "Enough," says the driver,
"Last bus today" — from Jerusalem to the city
On the sea.   Broadcast words and Sabbath music
Fill the car as it rides the old road where hulks
Of ruined tanks glare — will always glare,
They say, till rusting bleeds away
The first of the hideous wars.
Some of the faces near me wince.   A few parrying
Anguish peer for evening candles
That light up windows along the streets, awaiting
A cantor's voice to sing to the air
In weekly santification
The celebration song of the world's creation.

IV. SEVENTH-DAY MIRAGE

How could the thought of this day rise up?   Never before
Had anyone stopped to rest, moving themselves and their animals
Along a never-breaking circle of thigh and shoulder travail till the
Fire of the sky charred into night.   Were they stumbling into a sign
Of a thousand rests before the ultimate one, that morning when a storm's
Swift splitting of trees into bloody winds forced them fleeing
Into their shelters: all at once idle, empty-fingered, nothing
For arms to strive with, while the red land raged: to wait
With their animals, forced to wait, to wonder sleepless, to stare
Dreaming — till a startled thought? a message? a vision? . . .

      Rub the mirage from your eyes:
This land cannot bear still another myth.
No one can learn the why, the when, or imagine the faces
On any ancient listener or how they could tell their children
The law they thought they had found,

      But come, look at this tide
Of reveling bodies, the young with the older, racing
The sand, playing against the green sea that entwined Jonah — boys,
Girls, dripping waves; women, men, smiling
In their seventh-day afternoon.   From where you stand
You can almost read the numbers
Tattooed on some of the arms now glistening in the wet light.
You begin to guess where some of these swimmers were born.
Your guesses are probably wrong.   Yet the longer you watch their faces,
The sooner your eyes will begin to believe that under the skin
Of these cheeks burnt with this sun some of the blood is old.

*   *   *

Eilat only? "Only . . . only an hour
In the sky.   Of course you'll see — more than you want.
It's the north part of our desert, follows the Rift.

But looking down from the air — that's a different world:
Not what you'd see from a jeep. — We won't be boarding
Soon, so have some coffee. The bar's down there.
Yes, they keep on coming and going in and out of this room,
Our soldier boys and girls."

Maneuvers, I guess. But how young they look —
Too young to be sent to fight.

"Older, older than you think. Talk with some of them!
Don't be afraid: they're not afraid."

But what more could they say than their bodies
Say as they greet each other, mixing
In twos and threes and clusters. Some of them shouting,
Laughing, others speaking, listening. A few far off
In revery . . .
    The soldier seated beside me
Is flinging off her cap: showers of copper hair
Roll to her shoulder. She shakes her head. Their clouds blaze
In the window's light as she starts to ply her comb with a coiling
  rhythm . . .
Now with each stroke she raises her rapt face in a lidded smile.
A dozen soldiers begin to watch, then more. I can almost hear
Breath stop at the sudden sight of a preening goddess.
Watching her face, I imagine her father. If he were to walk here now,
Would he scream out his Talmud's warning "Hair is a nakedness!"
Or in pain lower his eyes and beg of his Mighty One,
Merciful One, Most High, The Lord, The Rock,
A safe return for his daughter?

— "First call for Eilat. Plane for Eilat!"
From nowhere people and baggage queue at the gate
For searching. One of the last
In line, I try the measure of new arrivals.
Are they older? Is it training weariness? Most of them
Carry guns. The big room hums
With muted talk. No shouting, no laughter.
Books are helping some of them hide the present.
But there — in the south corner, four girls have been gently singing.
I strain to follow the music.

Parts of it sound like a song I heard on a bus
About a lake in the shape of a lyre . . .
Now one of the four is singing alone,
Her voice glows, suddenly round.   All of us listen, watch,
Except two men in fur-edged hats and long black cloaks.
Their fringed faces stare at the floor, avoid each other's eyes.
I know enough of their thought to be able to hear them
Curse the caressing sounds of a woman's singing.
Lucky for them she is stopped by a man with a checklist, asking
        questions.
She starts to speak, but we feel the bursts of an engine —
"Last call for Eilat!" We may enter the gate.

Before you come to the mountain
You travel sixty miles of a roadless desert
Rocking over boulders and sand as the four wheels twist,
Churn, wind through bright and shadowed granite canyons
Rilled with lava rock.   From your car window
You think there is nothing alive but the white wormwood flowers,
The acacias sprung out of fissured rock, the lizards, the quail
Suddenly winging ahead, and thousands of red-black butterflies
That ring a bush you had never seen.   When the sun strikes
The alien leaves with uncertain light, it might even seem
To your eager eyes to be burning with flame . . .

                              — "Danger: Mine Field" — the sign points
To a flat space fenced off with wire, hurling you back
Into time-present: you gaze upon innocent sand.

Before you climb the mountain
You circle the western base.   "This is the mound
— I give you the Oral Tradition —
Aaron somewhere here, then the Calf; and below,
The people who watched the ascent."

No one could climb that upper cliff.

"True.   Moses came through the pass.   Can you see it?
You will tomorrow.   That's where you start: from east:
St. Katherine's gate."

The desert stars fall backward into the whitening sky
As I climb across these rocks
Pulled, over centuries, by monks sent up from below
To pile a path to the cloud.
Could their eyes mark as their arms strove with the mountain
More than I find as I feel for remains
Of their handprints on these stones?
Climbers above and below — pilgrims as well as wanderers —
Their backs shading the sky:
Eyes see only ledges, gravel, crags,
At the feet of bodies pushing up for the crest's
Reward: shadowless rock
And a pair of hovels: one for Allah, one for the Christ.

The first ones wait for the last
Until we are all together in separateness,
Each one choosing a place apart.   Alone
On the summit, I watch the surrounding peaks, the far-off blue
Of gulf and sea.   Everyone's face is watching.
If there are questions, nobody asks, nobody answers.   In the sunrise
The wind is still.
Staring into the air from the rock, to one outside we might seem
To be waiting: non-believers no less than faithful.
Nothing stirs but the stillness,
Yet an absence begins to bear down on our heads.
Not for long: some stand up from the rock,
Others trying new ways for casting the burden,
Shaking the locked doors of the hovels, peering
Through windows, till almost as by command
The summit, swept of bodies, regains bareness;
And one by one we start the descent.
You might think, if you saw our faces,
Something urgent awaits us there;
Yet we are not summoned below
As we were not needed above.
I hear one of the faithful behind me
Telling himself that men cannot bear to linger on the high places.

A tall cedar, they said, grows in a clearing
Three hundred meters down.   I shall be there soon
Though I stay and watch, with every step

On a witness stone, wind and the sun
Lighting up with unearthly scarlets and golds
The cliffs of the facing mountain,
The scarps, pillars, traves,
And the slopes below furrowed in sand
The color of winter deer in the fields I come from.
The mountain I traveled to see is behind my eyes.
Will I climb another?

— Down at last on the desert plateau, what do I say
When somebody asks "Where now?"
To walk on the Sea of Galilee?
Then from its pitted shore to the caves
Of the Qumran scribes?   From there to David's Fountain,
Clamber up to drink at the rock of the tumbling spring?
And the day after? and after that day? and then? . . .

Dusk comes strangely here.   It is morning there:
My island sun will be sweeping
Through ripening trees beside our house in my native land.
It is long past noon in London.   Soon my daughter
Will be watching the moon rise over her mudbrick house
On the edge of the sand desert in Persia.

V. THE ROCK

I have looked all day for The Rock
In this land where the grains are always seen.
I found no mark on the soil,
Sand and loam too old once more to be pressed prone or pierced
Apart.   Only across the faces of scattered
Women and men are there any scars,
Rips, burrs — and these are such as a glacial mountain
Signs, roaring across dry ground to the sea
Of a younger land in the melting kill of its breath.

*   *   *

 Hold the enlarging glass to a stone, say what you see.
"Cracks, fissures, crevices,
Openness unshielded by wall or skin."
Prophetic name, fit for deity: rocks are born dying.

Not every looking-song hides
A hope that its vaster self
Could shrug away in sureness of disbelief:
Once you are out of a city, light can pour from the sky in visions —
Turrets guarding the hills,
Altars on the high places,
Imaginings — that grains of sand remember,
Compose themselves in circles, signs,
Waiting for recognition.

Now nothing more holds me here, though I know
As many generations looked from this height as suffered and sang
Through centuries.   I cannot reclaim their voices,
I could not hope to see through their eyes.
Were I to ask if they ever lived, mirage might begin to turn on itself, —

"Hello! and good afternoon.   But ah!
You haven't remembered your guide.   Why should you?"

Forgive me.   Was it in Jericho?   Capernaum?

"Guess again.   The face may help."

Ashkelon, then.   Or Haifa.   Acre?

"My sounds might as well have been taped:
You had eyes only for places.
By now, I suppose, you've seen them all?"

Enough.

"There are always more."

Monuments to war and apostasy? gain or god?

"History, sir: the way it was.   But now, —
Now you are in Jerusalem, city of peace.
If you come with me, you will see with your eyes how golden
It stays above the bleedings by conquerors and defenders."

*I've seen the churches, synagogues, minarets, mosques,
Temples, museums, colleges, parliament —*

"Come with me, please."

*David's and Herod's tombs, Mary's crypt, Calvary, Gehenna,
And the new monuments settling into the hills.*

"You think that tells it all?"

*Not all.   The hillside graves,
The other Via Dolorosa, Yad Vashem — shall I continue?*

"Come with me up there!
You can never see Jerusalem in Jerusalem.
At certain hours — from the Mount of Olives —
This is a perfect time — the air over the temple mount

Seems to exalt the sky.   You must turn away
Or an almost mystic light will make you reel.   So you look eastward
At the Salt Sea as it faints to purple and rose in the lowering twilight.
Then you turn back to look again . . . and again . . .
Tomorrow, perhaps?
If we started now, we might come too late.   And besides, besides —
For all the rapture, it's only a place, another place:
A nation is something more. — When I heard you name the sites,
All I saw with your eyes were varying heaps of stone.
Go in the other direction!   It's never too late to see them:
Only yourself can show yourself this people.
Auf Wiedersehen!"

— As though one could camp in their settlements,
Walk their cities and towns with eyes and ears
Closed.   Push through the crowds;
Sit at their side in bars, cafes, terraces, squares; hear them
Laugh, yell, gesture; look at their differing faces,
The smile, the sneer, grin, frown — flashing, lowering.
As though . . .

Waiter, another!   Fill it again!   And — have you a moment?

"Please?"

What are those men there saying — that table — there!
It must be crucial.   They speak with such fury.

"Of course . . . And now, what can I bring you, sir?"

Of course.   Yes.   Not my business.   Sorry, sorry.

"Sorry? They are sorry you keep away from them."

How could I join when I don't know what — when I can't tell —

"As though that matters — as though that matters! . . ."

— As though one could sit in their homes, bear while their sons and
          daughters
Teach you about your own country,

Swear at their ministers, mock their ambassadors, scold their leaders,
     question, defy . . .
As though one could somehow chase out of mind
The despair of Moses, the pain of Hosea,
Straining to make of tribes of refusers a single people.
And some of them still dispute from sunrise to evening,
Splitting sacred phrases apart, sure that the heavy universe
Hangs on the string of their thought . . . As though, as though —
Were it not for their kind —
Maddening sages, dazed prophets flailing
The strayers — who would be healing
This ransacked country? — hopeland of all refusers
Who stayed while others, unwilling to brandish the curse
Of self-election, fled.

          And the Russians,
Hearing some of the grave ones cavil,
Prodded their wavering vassals: Now is the moment.
Your enemy rips apart.   No one leads.   Can you fear
Cabals of sputtering talmudists who can shoot only with words?
This is the time you prayed for.   Strike! — But the vassals' mouths
Sank in the sand.

       "For every action
A season," tolled The Preacher — a time
For war, a time for peace, a time to dance, even
A time for the tribes to batter their own bodies.   It happened once:
Twenty centuries earlier.   And then their king Herod climbed on
     the graves
Of a hundred thousand brother-slaughterers.

            If you ask
The believers among them now to stand, you will number
Two among three.   Yet they know every woman and man
In this haven above the abyss
Is unsure.

VI. TALMUDIST

Gloat, glittering talmudist,
With your eastern eye, your northern eye, your western eye;
The days are a fog of clashing words: cleave
If you can — warp with your buzz-saw brain a light-filled
Path shallow enough for a heart to follow!

Why do you fist your words
With your merchant's hand, your scholar's hand, your toiler's hand?
Is a god you smother the dynamo of your fury
Or a wraith you reasoned into existence in hope
It would pierce your eye with joys?   Or a heartsick need

For a heaven-on-earth perfection
That drives you, though you have learned there can be no right
Unmixed with wrong.   Where will you go when the moment
Strikes and your arms, defying brain, reach out
To your brothers' will, your homeland's will, your body's will?

*   *   *

Suddenly flying beaks of fire
Roar with pent-up poisons across
The sky, climbing — shimmering down
Toward your women and men's uplifted eyes
That question "Ours? . . . the Other's? . . . Again?" —
       As suddenly
The roars' messages still all fisting words:
Arms reach out as before to become one sapient arm
Till fear in your enemy's brain cinders and two-faced calm
Holds the frontier: that within its walls
You can keep on keeping alive your distrustful people's
Faith in this old-new nation,
Waken the aloof sand and soil
From where those bodies you call your fathers' fathers'
Were dragged.

But they could have stayed,
Some of them, more than half in love with unheard-of
Joys drunk by their captors; many become
More Greek than Greeks in their new adoration
Of the body's naked splendors, the revels,
Dance, music, and song set free
To celebrate man-made miracles; others anxious
To join the games of dialogue trying the universe,
Ready to pay the price of assent to the rulers'
Pantheon of mythic mortals.
                                    They could have stayed,
The wearied many, aching to shed
Their covenant stones.   Like the countless
Deserter-thousands, early and late,
They could have tossed their treasured seed
In the wombs of their captors' women — if the Royal Greek
Had not compelled your refusers to ape them,
Filthied the Ark, set in its place his altar — soon
To be crushed by guerrillas joined
To an arch-refuser's son and a "Hammer" Judas . . .

                                    — The beaks have fled.
From a flawless sky
Morning sun streams down on the valley of Jezreel.
Watch, when you ride the road to Megiddo, how silver the light
Lies on the lifted orchards, the fields of blossoming melon,
That sip the waters purling under their ground.
To the east, Gilboa's crest; but eyes will turn westward
Toward the summit of Mount Tabor, the place where the ancients
Thirsted to build their temple: the same dome
Whose "marvelous roundness" ravished Jerome: the mount
Marked for the Christ's transfiguration.   No one can say
What else he touches with eyes or feet as he travels
This age-old caravan trail that tied the towns
Of the Nile to Mesopotamia.

                                    "Driver," I want to say,
"Wait, while I add my mite
Of breathy dust to these mingled layers
Of sweat, offal, and camel dung compressed
Through forty hundred years of blood — as late

As your country's birth-throe year
When Arabs blocked your way to the sea" — But I stop
As he asks "You have been here before?
Then you know where you are?" I nod.
"You know when you walk these slopes on Megiddo Hill,
Your shoes may be pressing the footprints of Deborah's soldiers?"
I nod again.
                    Does he see what I see
In their red eyes rolling, awed by Sisera's chariots
Flashing below on the plain?   His men and his drivers
Mocking, daring them, shrieking their thirst to fly at them,
Cut out their tongues — when a hole in the sky
Tears open — rain overwhelms the stream,
Drowns the plain, sinks the chariots,
Canaan's men and their leader fleeing
Her soldiers swinging swords at their necks —
                        "Have you forgotten?" he wakes me,
"Maybe you still remember it, sir:
The oldest Bible page where Deborah praises
The housewife Jael for giving the half-dead Sisera
Milk though he asked for water and a pallet so he could sleep —
While his mother waits" — he is trying to quote the battle hymn —
"No.   It says: 'While his mother waited, peering
Through her window, wondering
Why is my son's chariot so long in coming?
Why do the hoofbeats of his chariots tarry?'   Jael
With a tent-peg nailed Sisera's head to the earth.   'So may all
Your enemies perish, O Yahweh!' the war-song ends.   Those were also years
When they robbed on the highways, raided our crops, burnt our houses,
Killed our young men. — No wonder Gideon's soldiers
Smashed the jars that hid their torches
And fell on Midian's tents till they burned to the ground!"

Jezreel valley, mountains, Megiddo:
Flourishing, exaltation, strife:
Bound together: parts of a single book . . .

        "True.   Wherever you turn, you read
A page of our past."

                But not the meaning!

"Survival! — Disaster and victory —
Deborah, Gideon: victory; Saul and Josiah: disaster.
The first of our kings, hearing the breath
Of the Philistines, falls on his sword —
They hang his headless trunk from their walls.
Josiah attacks a Pharaoh
Who begs him 'Peace.   Go home!   My quarrel is not with thee!'
Two thousand years before, another Egyptian
Lords it here — and here, in your time,
The British Allenby breaks the back of the Turk — shall I go on?"

Victory or disaster: never Shalom!

"A dream we keep walking before us like a cloud."

And if it stopped, rained down?

                              "Can anyone say
How much of peace men would be willing to bear?
Able to bear?   They have never dared to discover — "

As though warned back? warned by the fear
Of losing the better burden that saves
From the heart-corroding pursuit of unanswered questions?

      "All I trust is what I see:
When men can't find strangers to fight, they turn on each other."

      Is your name, by chance, St. John?

"Thank you — not by two thousand years.   But you know
Where we are at this moment: Hill of Megiddo: Har Megiddo:
'Armageddon' — the word of John's Revelation —
Site of the final war that will end in the death of man."

      Then they would not have dug them here —
The forty thousand unfilled graves for the dead
Your leaders counted before the first one fell.

      "That was only the third of our wars."

Best to cover those graves with your cloudy monument.

"Better still to think of our land as a body:
Every war a sickness to be outworn."

    Still such trust in your past?

"In the present-past:
Now is our world's tomorrow."

VII. MARCHING SONG

Too much history here.   A new nation
Needs no ancestors.   Cancel the dead!   No heroes
Under your ground.   Blind are the patriarchs sleeping
With open lids: yours are the only eyes —
The first!
          Then blast, pounders, tractors!   Violate
All that would block!   Strip every mound!   Shovelers,
Calm the crevices, stifle the watchful caves
Streaming with shards!   Break every last foundation:
Then level the hills, walls, and all else that could jut
Above from below and against you:
                      Nothing with roots can stay.
All that you do must rise.   A new nation
Builds on memory's blankness, safe as the sea's —

*   *   *

As bleak, as sure.   Wipe away all
That could rise from below! yet wherever
They build, the ground exhales
The bones of others also, the crumpled walls
The salt of their sealed-in sweat.

You could find no harder proof that the land
Of the live Upgathered-dispersed is theirs than the Myth
Of Choice that your will to forget the trials
Of wanderers' strength demeans.
                  "Can any people
Prove their title to any soil?   No soil
Exists but was seized, settled, invaded,
Conquered . . . Murder's history
Accuses all who cry Usurper! against us."

A congress of nations gave you a land —

"As though any creatures had been endowed
With rights to divide, to give away pieces
Of something they never owned — Earth!"

They had even more: the power to convey the gift.

"And the morning after? . . .
Where did the power hide when the armies
Of seven Arab nations shrieked across our frontiers,
Ringing Jerusalem, telling their brothers
Who had lived with us peaceably on this soil to fly from us?
But the world tires of the story."

Many have never heard —

"That we cut the invaders back?   That the powers — "

No, the people who ran from their homes,
Men, women, children, the countless banished!

"Those who banished themselves? who were promised
Swift return in the van of their brothers' armies?
Or the others, stung with unwelcome, cast
Into pens of horror, disdained, scorned.
Will your world listen as well to our sisters and brothers
In Arab lands driven to run for refuge?
Look, they are all around you here!"

All?

"Thousands wait there captive.   The gates
Are locked.   No one will turn the key.   The children
Of the luckier ones learn to forget."

But you — you say you remember! — Remember now?

"If you need an answer
You have only to look at us coldly:
Have we been made or remade
In the image of this land?   You have traveled its miles.
Study us!   Can you see the imprint

Of merciless rock pillars? of wadis that drown?
Of a Salt Sea that slays the fish as they enter from Jordan?
Do the grazing hills, the Lake of the Lyre, leave any traces
Along with signs of sirocco winds, of naked suns
That blaze on deserts where quail and gazelle
Breed and live on; where thorn and wormwood
Bloom out of stone?   Have the valleys left the mark
Of fragrant gardens, fruit trees swelling
Close to hills that lift to the wind lemon and orange flowers?
And over all — a last gaze — can you pierce the reflected mask
Of a soil, burnt in the trials of fear, that refuses to die?
If you have an answer, share it
Among yourselves — we must take up the watch.   Shalom!"

Shalom, shalom: stay ready
For captives but start to forget
Your brothers and sisters in happy exile
On lands from where they will never willingly
Flee.   Sure and unsure,
They live quiescence.   Thriving
When others thrive, in fear
When others grope, eyeing with doubt,
Though what they seemed has faded
And what they become will disappear on the gales
That blow all strangeness from their shore.
To refuse is no longer possible
In newfound worlds they helped to shape
As they are, where guest and host
Lose themselves in each other.   Many remember
To love you, help you, fear for you from their windows
Behind secure frontiers.
                              Learn to forget them:
It is none too soon to gauge the day, the month, the year,
When you will be left in trust to yourselves
Alone in the clash of nations — some of whose wakeful suddenly
Stop to question the claim
Of laws that beckon to self-aggrieving masteries.

VIII. CHOICES

The knowing cry out, patient in piety,
Wait: it happened before on this land when the highways
Filled with prophets and seers and preachers
Heralding hope or doom, the hawkers
Of newborn gods singing hosannas
Of joy or pain

        — Will any nation
Stop out of fear for its citizens' souls?   So long as the sun
Nourishes earth, will the arrogant drown out the voices
Of the questioners and shrill to the world
Paeans to man's ever-upward fate: deaf to the seas'
And the creatures' born in the seas whose death is the death
Of air: deaf to the hungering
Helpless millions' riding to birth in the night of a planet
Of flailing peoples
Fearing to merge their separate powers
In a sovereignty over all, that might save?

                          Nothingness
Awaits the gardens of earth when the nurturers'
Will withers.
          Many who poured all trust
In testable verities waken
To possibles unexplored.   Some in the world
Have begun to live mirages.

               *   *   *

A few standing with open eyes
No longer see what the waves of light
Tell their brains, no longer cover
Their ears against the sounds that assault
The day, hearing only

Echoes within of fear.
Some try to decipher signs.
One of the old ones takes my arm.   If I stop,
He will gather me into his song of certainty:

"Cast your faith in the ever-nearing
Catastrophe your brothers and I
Pull, each moment we live, down
On the mother-once sea, the nurturing sky,
The hostage acres of soil we flay
And beg for our bread and warmth.   Then hail
Catastrophe! — what else to hail
Except your terrified creature-lust
To survive? — Its imminence might save — "

                                                I watch as I turn away,
Innocence out of the mouth
Of age: early or late? end and beginning? —
Everywhere, spoken or silent,
Revery overwhelms the shrinking intervals
Between the wordless moments
Of reason forcing itself to think —

                    "We shall raze our frontiers,"
One of them dares, "No wall can ever hold back
The floods of reclaiming people unless it is anchored
In soil cemented with blood."
                                        — 'Idiot.' 'Madman.'
                                        'No.   Let him speak.'

"There is no more soil, I tell you; no more soil
To mix such mortar.   Our country's loam
Reeks with the surfeit of dying clays,
Our fields with splintering skulls and thighs
Of women and children: the ash wears down
The knives of our harrows. — Mix more blood in this soil?
The seed we sow will yield monster-plants, we shall harvest
Poison-flowers of grain. — Open the gates! And come back,
You who would have remained if your brothers
Had not screamed you away! Raze the frontiers! Where is our choice,
        people:

Miser this ground for ourselves or share
When sharing can end the pain, the terrors,
The bleeding away of our hope? —
And the other nations will watch: they will learn — "

'With joy they will learn,'
A listener sneers, 'Bloodier ways to destroy us.'
'Suicide,' shouts another.

A third: 'Forgive him!'
'Needless,' a fourth: 'They know if they bring us down
We take them with us.'

'Treason, treason,' a fifth.

'Hear me,' a sixth, as he fuses his country's fate
With the earth's: 'They were always one.' —

Landscape of abstract shapes
That never lacked for prophets
Swarms with them now when the powers threaten,
Bribe, cajole, and bargain, honing
The ring that stifles.

" 'There always are choices,' you say?
But if at the last the only redeemer
Comes from ourselves? — You stir up the emblem-vision
That rankles in all our minds, from which we must reason
Back to this moment. — Cancel your love-like words:
Trust, honor, morality, justice,
Conscience, faith.   Replace them
With the antonym: ultimate silent love:
Survival. — Seal the frontiers!
Block all entry — by water, on land, through cloud!
We can make, if we must, like the emblem-fortress,
A new Masada, kill one another
As the lost resisters killed on the last morning
Of the three-year siege rather than come out alive
Into despoiler-hands . . . But these
Are not Romans; the weapons no longer
Spears but machines battling machines till a new deadliness

Falls through the air on streets and fields: their lands, our lands,
And all corpses accuse — "

                    In a desert's boiling wind
Thought can misread what fevered vision condones.

Choices wait so long as the games of power,
Ravaging close to your borders,
Rouse your defiance.   Without your rage
All their skirmishing severs: the gamblers' gaze
Will be driven at last to take up the challenge they dread,
Eye against eye.   You own the ultimate weapon:
Safety hangs on the wisdoms
Of interhate — yours and their own.

                         "On more, more
So long as part of the world and part
Of ourselves hold us guilty
Of forcing on creature-innocence
Sky-made shackles that human earthiness
Hates yet has to adore
To keep its world from its own self-ruin."

Take, if you greed for a mission,
From your private trial, the faith you found
When none could survive the sickness
Of disbelief in themselves. — Whatever
Your way could have meant, lives
By what you have been but no longer need to be:
Forsake yourself into freedom!

"It's time for mimicking others?   Try, try, try — "

But they've stopped listening as they seemed to listen.
Words may have stumbled.   Speak again:
Subside to the fretless calm that others live by!
But they're past reaching.

                    Just as well;
Better, perhaps.   My traveler's wisdom
Grows out of visions that look from without:

To presage the lives within, vision would have to rise up
Within.   And yet my outsider's thought repeats
Forsake yourself into freedom! not out of knowledge
Or right.   *Subside into calm!* scorning prophecy's
Self-deceptions — while I follow
At the same instant: revery
Floating away from here and now into time backward
Till it opens onto our moment
Of creature birth — the place or the places?
The same voice, fear, desire,   ·
Thought, taboo? — does it matter, since the first bodies
Diverged with time into multiple faces,
Minds, wishes, worlds, one of these worlds
Here-now: where I stand — once again alarmed
To your nationhood that confuses,
Today as when it began.

                    Unable to choose
The common lot or election,
Out of your wild compulsion to stop
The grief-giving blows of a numb caprice
Fluttering down from forces too blindingly
Vast for a penned-in animal's brain
To conceive or follow: So you reject the forces
By which all creatures live and the whole earth moves,
Replace them with your private image
Of what-should-be and name your creation "Yahweh."
And other peoples: other private images: other names:
Every son and daughter
Born to confuse godhood-desired with forces-that-are.
Where do they turn, those thorned into wakefulness?

                    None can disprove
The fevers making us poison wind, water, and land
For our children's children's children
Are not propelled — in the bitterness
Of justice-hope turned back on itself —
By the sickness of blocked desire that strains
To defy with its last weapon
The deaf unfaceable forces
By which all underlings thrive and suffer.

Who am I?   Was I lost somewhere on the seventy roads?
No more than others — no more than my father's brother who tried
To turn time inside out looking for ancestors.
We have always been led to a void at the end of a maze
By the wrong questions.
Ask: What I am,
Since the only certainty is the body out of whose currents
Clashing and blending,
Fumes of knowledge may rise — quieting question —
Leading us out of our nights
Into untroubled wakefulness.

LATER POEMS

(1977–)

Message to Someone Four Hundred Nights Away

My dear dead loved one,
I want you to know: today I went to our house,
The one in Weston woods that we made together,
You and I — I want to tell you: the same
October afternoon sun was shimmering
Out of the trees onto the ground where we stood — need I count
How long ago? — our heads bent toward the grass, our arms
Moving through tangled boughs to shear them
Against the wintering nights of ice, our fingers
Reaching through blazing leaves for withered blooms.   In the heady
Bittersweet wine of wind, we forgot hours till darkness
Blinded our hands.   Holding them out for each other
We found our way to the door.

                    You remember how many times
We tried to tell our two deep friends and our words
Failed?   But today I walked with them and their eyes
Showed they knew why we had lived here sheltered
Under the balancing rock.

                Shall I try to tell you, loved one,
How it lives, our huge wild oval granite deity
On the crest of our hillock?
Gales, storms haven't loosened its root in the bedded earth
From where we'd stand watching
Its shadow tilting down the ravine on the snows
Of a thousand flowering laurel-heads in the stillness
Of sunlit mornings of May till their whiteness melted
To green glisten of leaves.

            The woman and man
Who live here now were away when I watched, letting me gather
The field, the house, the woods, the idol-rock as they were
For us unchanged, but only while I stayed.   When they come back
I shall have gone, leaving no mark, taking with me
Your presence: our selves: not to return.

                         October 29, 1988

The House Hollow

The house hollow.   The last of our four-footed children
Dead.   Fur, bones, motion, willowy footprints,
Eyes that had looked at mine stranger than all other eyes,
Lost in a palmful of ash on a cold grass.

No one now to trail my feet or hide under low forsythia,
Watching me while I call.   Or late inside the house
Leap to my knees, trace on my quilt a ringful of sleep, wakeful
Eyelids closed, a quiet song in your throat through the night.

I see you move in shadows.   The bed trembles.
I hear the song I could not hear, in my empty dark.

(For Peter Dale)

Argon

*Inert gas mixed throughout atmosphere soon after it is inhaled;
hence all creatures breathe in part what everyone else who ever
lived breathed.*

So long as leaf and flesh —
Fed on each other's cast-out breath —
Nourish the oceans of lower sky: so long

As lip-sealed earth fulfils
Its sun-warmed captive circle, drink,
O drink while we may the forever imprisoned air

Of exhalations sullied
And saved, that lungs fill up their double,
Helpless inner-abyss with the strengthening gift

Of brothering air,
Undefiling, that infants, ancients,
Killers, and saints with all other choiceless share.

Florida Seaside

Every winter I saw her here, late
January, filling the same
Corner of beach alone: worn face
To the sun; then treading the sea's
Edges for minutes before the long
Glide on the water: back and forth
And back in slow, spreading spirals
Ending at last on sand — then hastily
Off again, alone as she came,
Till the next morning of brightness.

Our first four winters we neither glanced
Hello nor nodded, and then as if
Suddenly we'd been told we were sharing time,
One of us mumbled "Good to be back . . .
Better than shivering . . ." Never more;
Not even "Staying till April?"

The attendant knows each person's name and home.

"Have you seen her here?   Woman about my age.
Down from the north, I think."

   "Maine.   Of course I know her."

"Here this year?"

   "Not yet, but scores will be late."

"Or missing."

   "Why must you think such a thing?"

"People don't live forever."

   "Sure of it, friend?   Some of us might.
   She'll be here one of these days."

"Sure of it, friend?"

"Have to be.   Happens again and again.
Been here twenty years . . . Must run now —
Somebody's calling . . ."

Now that it's March, I might prod him to tell me all he knows of her.
"Why?" he would challenge.
"Nothing," I'd shrug, lacking an answer
Fitted to words.   He'd glance at me, shake his head,
Study my face, his eyes saying
I had no right, not even knowing her name.

Old Enough at Last to Be Unsolemn

Old enough at last to be unsolemn,
Solomon-like nevertheless I go
Imposing on the disparates communion
They shrink from sharing.   Calm, their wary hearts,
Scorning the tender wrath that would fulfil
Its trucer's passion in a world where clones
Of self-protective apathies distill
Insistent self-contentment.
                              Undeterred —
Though eyes ignore and ears refuse — consigned
By age's scars to make the separates one,
My choiceless mind spins out a siren's song,
Masking its ruth, to prison all who live
With fellow-fear into a love design.

Mind, If You Mourn at All

Mind, if you mourn at all,
Mourn for the hearts of men:
Their every deed on earth
Issues from some deep spell;

Wherefore, suckled on myth,
Choiceless though unaware,
They strive in trust that faith —
Or thought — or even will

Or dream might yet unlock
Tyche's bewildering maze,

Tyche's bewildered maze.

To Wake Each Dawn

To wake each dawn with hope that an absent-marvelous
Out of cloud, field, ocean
Might suddenly . . .

To wait all day till its coming fades and the known-familiar
Drowns my gaze, unknowing, uncaring, unwilling
To bare its redness light that could blind, bind, save, remake
Emptiness into presence,

While Tyche's towers
Look on.

Their Singing River (II)

If I had known you then,
Known who you were —
If I had learned of all you had learned in
    your woman's wisdom-love —

I would have hurried to find you,
Call to you, walk to your side,
Ask you to gather up close to me, to wait
    there, together to listen:

And I think we might even have come to know
    what they sang as they called to us,
Ancient kindred,
From their singing river.

For Susan Copen Oken

See above, p. 102.

Speech, the Thinking-Miracle

Speech: thinking-miracle
Bestowed in every human child
Leads me through stranger-paths
To fields I cannot remember

Where a light leans down from treetops
Glistening in the sudden eyes
Of a toad who stares at my face
Knowingly, it seems, till my arms reach down

To embrace — the cold of his skin
Against the warmth of my hand
As we stand there in the silence
Of ancient speech, wafted

Back to a timeless moment,
Forth to a timeless moment,
Kindred in creature-knowledge.

Man on a Greensward

So it was: she kept watching him leave her: daughter —
Knowing woman — watching the grieving father
Falter across the sward through the green shade
Of a crépuscule, shedding his clothes, naked
As when he had entered the world.   Watching
The once all-masterful body
Trace its trembling path toward a low embankment
Of stone as ancient
As earth, its home.   His also — a temple
Whose living columns would speak to him with glances
Remembered — so it had seemed . . .
                    And now a forest of symbols
Around him: sheltered in a trinity of trees:
Tree of day, tree of night, tree of the crépuscule
Between waking and sleeping.

He knows he is moving toward death.

Legs splayed, head sunk in his hands,
Half-dreaming, half-listening to intimations of hopefulness
Long ago heard in childhood —
      Blood remembers the quiet it once knew
      When in the breathing silence of the stream
      Some of its rivers were borne out on a dream
      For space of varying hours . . . in the end
      Blood returning to blood from the bones of breath
      To pour itself once more in the source it knew
Yet he knows his body will move to death when the lights
Of the crépuscule die down
And it makes its way to the edge of the sward where the greenness
Of the earth's sphere slips into seas of blackness:
Forgetfulness, or perchance remembrance.

SOCIAL POEMS
OF THE DEPRESSION

(From *The New Masses* and *The Iron Land* [1936])

The Crane-Driver

When we were walking toward the gates this morning
A soft rain was falling; from the boughs
Above us fell the sounds of hovering birds
Caroling through the rain.   Outside a house
A hearse stood and beyond the frontroom window
A staring girl bending above a coffin.

The tale went round: yesterday afternoon
They had run off, tramping the countryside,
Their precious one free afternoon together,
Romping through April woods, heady with sunlight
And hopes of love.

At half-past-five he left her, hurrying
In fear of coming late
At six, the posted hour to climb the ladder,
Walk to his cab, and start his crane to labor
All night above the wheels and flames below.

He came at ten-past-six.
Making up time, he scrambled up the rungs
That set him on the rails where side by side
The wheels of two cranes traveled.   Hastening on,
He leaped to his track, then strode, as always,
Along his rail to reach his cab.   But suddenly
His crane was moving toward him, engine lunging,
Flying at him.   Swift to escape its wheels,
He jumped to the other rail,
Landed safe, then suddenly
The other crane rushed over him.   His body,
Tearing to rags, dropped to the ground
Twenty feet below.

One of his friends sent for the girl in the morning.
She came believing nothing, eyes crazed, lips
A stiffened grin.   She walked inside to watch
The pieced-together flesh that was his body,
While in the sheds the riveters complained —
A bitter smell of blood.   In the bare room

She waited till a man came in to sew
The body ready for the hearse.   Quietly
She followed him outside.   Her desolate eyes
Stared at the road they traveled in the rain.

Street Song: New Style

Saturday noon.   Out of nowhere suddenly
A whistle screams, and out of nowhere suddenly
Three thousand men and women scramble and cackle,
Tumbling aside whatever stands in their way.

The favored few among them stride in scorn,
Knowing their cars will strain to speed them away.
Machinists and foremen, still grimy and greasy,
Dart in lines to quick-lunch-stands to roar
For hamburger, pop, and a handful of warm doughnuts. . . .
And an army of clerks steadily plods to the railroad
For the train to pull them back once more from the town.

Always on Saturday noons some rags of children,
Millhands' children, yelling, jumping, and beating
Time on a telephone pole, call to a clerk
As he plods his way to the train, "Gimme nickel,
Mister, 'n I make moosick!"

I, Jim Rogers

WITNESS REPORT OF EMERGENCY RELIEF BUREAU CASE HISTORY NO. ——,
NEW YORK, 1933, RETOLD FOR RECITING BEFORE MASS AUDIENCES.

I, Jim Rogers, saw her
And I can believe my eyes
And you had better believe me
Instead of the lies you read
Of the rescued millions . . . I saw her
Slip into our waiting-room
Among us thin blank men
And women waiting our turn.
But none of us looked like her
With her ragged face, dazed eyes,
And the way she clung to the thing
Her arms pressed against her bosom.

Somebody told her at noon:
Come back tomorrow, tomorrow!
Too many here today.
She nodded, clutching the thing,
And crept in again the next morning.
(None of us knew she had trudged
Two times three cold miles;
Maybe her desperate question
Made enough fire to fuel
The parcel of flesh and bones
And breath that stood for her body.)
She needed to know why the thing
Warmed by the rags in her arms
Wouldn't answer her any more,
Wouldn't make sound or movement.

She uncovered a pale limp baby.
The man who looked at it gasped —
Its arms thin as my finger,
The blue-filmed eyeballs staring.

"It's dead," he told her.   She looked,
Glared, and fell to the floor.

Some gathered up her body,
Others entered a record:
One infant, American, starved.
Address — ?   They'd wait to ask.
They waited, asked; she answered:
"I'll never let you thieves
Bury my child alive.
Give her to me!" That evening
She escaped to god-knows-where —
But I've been trying to learn
In these days of marking time,
While the whole tense land marks time:
And I've heard enough already
To hold some people guilty.
All through Charles Street I trailed her,
Where she'd lived the last half-year
In a warm, windowless room
Feeding the year-old baby
Her husband had planted in her
On a frantic anniversary:
The year his Jersey mill
Closed down its list of men . . .
One morning he walked to South Ferry,
Begged a nickel from someone
And jumped aboard.   The ferry
Whistled five minutes later,
Screamed *Man overboard!* . . .

But I'd guess it didn't surprise her:
There's something in being twenty.
She rolled up her things, and somehow
Made a new home, and somehow
Bore her child — and found
A job — wrapping up toys,
Fur coats, stockings, and whatnot
In a Fourteenth-street store basement . . .
In these days of marking time
While the whole tense land marks time.

Every day: 8 till 8 . . .
Not much time for a mother

To bring up the young of a nation
And make it fit for living . . .
But never would she complain;
It was they complained about her:
Too weak, too slow, wastes time.
"You'll be so much happier, Miss,
In a job that won't drain your strength!
Good-day, and the firm's best wishes!"

And that's how she came to Charles Street:
Too proud to beg, too frail
In blood or mind to rebel
Alone against this world
That fell down over her head,
That may have blacked out her mind —

Somewhere on streets of this town,
In these days of marking time,
Alone and maybe thinking
To follow her man in the sea,
Though maybe to live instead,
She's walking now.   And if I
But knew where to point my voice to,
I'd yell out: Where are you, Answer!
Don't run away! — Wait, answer!
Listen: you're not alone!

— If any of you who've listened,
See some evening walking
A frail caved-in grey figure,
See her ghosting the street,
Tell her that I, Jim Rogers,
Hold out whatever I own,
A scrap of food, four walls —
Not much to give but enough
For rest and for arming the bones,
And a straining fist for defense
Against the hounds of the world.
Tell her I offer this
In these days of marking time,
Till our numberless scattered millions

In mill and farm and sweatshop,
Straining with arms for rebellion,
Bind up our forces together
To salvage this world from despair.

Mr. Tubbe's Morning Service

(Homage to T. S. Eliot)

The priceless Mr. Waldo Tubbe
And all his little Tubbes now dare
Approach the world they long to snub,
Well insulated with despair.

The junior Tubbes accost their sire:
"Haven't the masses gone too far,
Trying to soil *us* with the mire
Of vulgar, droll U.S.S.R.?"

Their ancient sage prepares to speak
In holy numbers presto-pronto:
Fused Hindu-Latin-Chinese-Greek,
The special Tubbey esperanto.

Whereon each pupil makes a wish.
And Bishop Tubbe prepares to drool
A priceless strain of gibberish
Concocted in the learned school.

While all the little Tubbes let pass
Secretions of orgasmic glee,
Tubbe father empties out a glass
Of quintessential poesy

Compounded by rare formulae
Of liquid siftings, while Laforgue's

And ghosts of other live men die
Once more in the scholastic morgues. . . .

But not to make small Tubbeys prate,
Hound, or horn him with discontent,
But wait — while father concentrate
In holy philosophic bent;

For he will find them magic toys —
This wizard of the cult, Despair —
Blinders for all his tender boys,
Protective from what's in the air.

While each one sobs in holy pains
Sweet inner masochisms storm,
And Waldo's philosophic strains
Of adolescence keep them warm.

NOTES ON THE POEMS

p. 17, line 23 of "Heartbeat Obbligato" *plagal cadence.* Definition 6, Webster's *New International Dictionary,* 2nd edition, p. 372.

p. 23, lines 15–24 of "It Was Never This Quiet"; see W. C. Allee, *Cooperation among Animals.*

p. 30, line 18: "In all my lectures I have taught one doctrine, namely, the infinitude of the private man." Emerson, *Diary,* 1840.

p. 30, line 29: Parsons was one of the workmen sentenced to death in the Haymarket Square incident, Chicago, 1886.

p. 32, line 2: "Respondez," in complete edition of *Leaves of Grass.* In his "The Eighteenth Presidency," a broadside written in 1856, Whitman wrote: "What historic dénouements are these we are approaching? On all sides tyrants tremble, crowns are unsteady, the human race is restive, on watch for some better era, some divine war." In the preface to a British edition of *Specimen Days* he emphasized as the "basic phrase" of all his writings: "Good will between the common people of all nations." "A new and tender reverence" are also Whitman's words.

p. 32, line 14: "Everything possible to be believ'd is an image of truth." — Blake, *Marriage of Heaven and Hell.*

p. 32, lines 24–26: Horace Traubel reports Whitman's statement: "That is the same old question — adjusting the individual to the mass. Yes, the big problem, the only problem: the sum of them all."

p. 32, line 32 ("Into your country's ears"): Traubel: "Do you mean that a man who cannot take his own advice is bound to be a failure?" — Whitman: "That's the substance of my philosophy. . . . I wouldn't make it a stiff-necked rule. I would only make it a rule."

p. 36, lines 4 and 7 of "The Fear": See John Gribbin, *Almost Everyone's Guide to Science,* Yale University Press, 1999, chapter 7. Note also in particular p. 127, on the movements of the Atlantic, the Pacific, and North America. When I wrote this poem, "continental drift" was still a controversial notion.

p. 37, epigraph and line 13 of "Midnight: Deserted Pavements": literally "The flesh is sad, alas, and I have read all the books." ["Brise Marine."]

p. 45, twelfth-century dawn song. The refrain is transliterated "Dieu! C'est l'aube. Qu'elle vient donc vite" in Appel, *Chrest.* No. 53.

pp. 46–51: *Le temps a laissié,* "The weather's cast away"; *Nudités,* "Nakedness"; *Ce n'est pas toi,* "It wasn't you"; *Nativité,* "Birth"; *Un parfum éternel.* "An eternal perfume"; *Baisers,* "Kisses"; *Friselis,* "Ripple"; *Volupté,* "Voluptuousness."

p. 55: For readers who suspect that a writer writes only one book regardless of the number of volumes he may compose, this paragraph from my "Three Revolutions of Modern Poetry": "The war [on Nature] was, of course, inevitable, man being what he is: a maker of tools and bent on mastery. Actually he had always been moving toward an open declaration, from the ancient moment when he developed the hand axe and the flint in his struggle for food and survival. The intervening preparatory stages can be traced by anyone who studies the evolution of science and technology down through what we call the Age of Reason. By that time, of course, the intellectual elite of England had ceased to be intimidated by the forces of Nature. Nature was less a mystery than a machine. But it was not until animal power had been displaced by waterpower and steampower that the war began in earnest. From that point on it was simply a question of time, one thing leading to another until the discovery and use of atomic power. The war against Nature had been confidently waged and won; and we post-moderns, of 1945-and-after, breathe the spirit of a different epoch, and we have a different terror on our minds: Now that man is victorious, how shall he stay alive?" (*Varieties of Literary Experience,* New York, 1962, p. 138.)

p. 60, lines 12 ff. in "Thoughts about a Garden": "The Story of the Shipwrecked Sailor," in Adolf Erman, *Literature of the Ancient Egyptians,* London, 1927, p. 30.

p. 71, line 11: "the buzzing, blooming confusion" — William James, *Principles of Psychology,* 1890, vol. 1, p. 488.

p. 90: Readers familiar with the *Dayenu* passage of the Passover service may see the debt of this poem to the form of that responsive reading ("If He had not drowned our oppressors in the Red Sea/ But had delivered us upon dry land/ It would have been sufficient"). At the time this particular house was occupied, Jews were officially denied the right to live in that city. Third stanza from last: "Home"=Zion.

pp. 92–94, *Denk nicht zu viel,* "Do not think about [ponder] too much." The last German word may also mean "creature," "essence," "being," "existence," "condition," etc. *L'Amoureuse,* "A woman in love"; *Eigene Sprache:* "Individual [spontaneous, curious] language"; *El ángel bueno,* "The good angel."

p. 111, line 3 by Amir Gilboa, in *The Modern Hebrew Poem Itself,* ed. Stanley Burnshaw, T. Carmi, and Ezra Spicehandler, Harvard University Press, 1989.

p. 112, "En l'an," first line of Villon's *Testament, "En l'an trentiesme de mon aage,* In the thirtieth year of my age."

p. 116: "The Rock" (*hatsúr*), one of the Hebrew appellations of God.

p. 117: See Jerry McGahan, "The Condor . . . ," *National Geographic,* May 1971.

p. 119: *Verweile doch, Du bist so schön:* the words appear twice in Goethe's *Faust,* with slightly differing punctuation (Part I, Act I, line 1700; Part II, Act V, line 11580). Walter Kaufmann renders the former: *"Werd ich zum Augenblicke sagen:/ Verweile doch! Du bist so schön!"* as "If to the moment I should say:/ Abide, you are so fair."

pp. 120–127, I: The poem presents Mallarmé's quest: the seven scenes follow a career from the opening "Dedication" to the "Waking" out of the dream that it was: of abstracting from the world of sensation the essences that are the truth, truth of a special sort. In the first scene, he dedicates himself to this searching act: not only to find what these essences are but to create, after finding them, by naming them. "So to compose the universe," by decomposing it into its essences and then by remaking them into the "Orphic Book of the Earth," which (as he considered it) was the collaborative effort of all poets. Once found, these essences can create a universe of their own, a new "eternity of words." And so he goes forth, confronting the sensate world with the belief that "Even flesh can be burned / To the whitenesses of a song."

II: A teacher by profession, he goes to his classroom for his daily work — but worried by the insignificance of what he is teaching in the light of his quest. He dreams of brushing aside the textbooks and lessons to tell the students the great truth that he knows and is also seeking. But how? He thinks of saying to his students that a mirror transforms the object it reflects into its abstract self, its truth — And then he comes to feel it would be hopeless to try to persuade them to his thought: "Open your pages! Safer to eye a book!" But one of the students refuses — and suddenly he (Mallarmé) has become a mirror into which the boy gazes. Confused by what has happened to his own sentient self, he nevertheless knows that he has become a mirror gazing back into the boy and drawing out of this human object the essences that "mirrors" are able to draw out of the sensate world that they take in. And so he asks himself: Can he "gaze it out of substance, flesh that trembles"?

III: In a later contemplation of this experience, he tries to unravel his beliefs: a soliloquy from a window, a man gazing at some flowers. The thoughts floating into his mind as he gazes suggest some of the beliefs he had uttered about essence: the essential flowerness, that which is "absent from all bouquets." To be found, it must be removed (from all bouquets), leaving only the idea of flower. "Where have you gone, my petals?" he asks as by his force of mind he removes their presences. "Go to return, vanish as you return," he commands them now, but the second "return" is a return by living. Hence when they return to him they will not be flowers he can touch or smell but the essence-idea that will "live in a thrust of mind."

IV: The experience stays with him as he looks elsewhere on the sensate world — "Not only petals," he says. His other self answers: "Whatever waits" can stare back at the gazer to make itself known (a parallel of a kind to what happened in II, when the boy gazed back at the teacher). The scene continues in dialogue to its conclusive thoughts — that what comes out of this staring, which is a burning (I: "Even flesh can be burned / To the whitenesses of a song"), is the "hovering fume"; an essence that floats in the air (recalling the suggestion of the word "spirit").

V: And now, in Scene V, he is filled with a hovering fume — floating out of many different sensory objects. He speaks with words that signify absence, silence, nothingness, and in the fourth and fifth stanzas he cries out his resolution: in a Poem of Flight from sentience, he will create a song that cannot be heard by the ears of sense, for it will be pure flame — the flame out of which the fume of essence arises as pure idea. . . .

VI: Even out of the experience of human flesh in its inexpressibly consuming sense — of love-embrace, immolation, self-loss. Mallarmé's obsessive fascination by blond hair becomes a river of sensuous-sensual ecstasy — the "blond torrent" into which he dives and on which he asks to be borne, where he can relive "the sleeping / Ecstasy of the ages" at once "Lost [and] found in her golden foam." And then — the final desperate act: to destroy this power of the flesh, to kill at last, to plunge into "the death / Of love," so that he may rise up — from his finally silenced blood, no longer to be torn by the terrible forces of sense enflamed and enflaming; to rise up, holding the thing he has sought, the prize: the "ash of" the "flame" that is human life.

VII: He is shaken out of the dream — and the quest — for when his body answered, his "blood rebelled, / Heart screeched at the ribs," and when he spoke the words of idea-essence (I: words that had "burned / To the whitenesses of a song"), vision "burst." And he saw creation itself, the infinitely encompassing mirror, "gaze on itself through" him. Yet "the dream that ravaged has remade" — and he speaks with his familiar symbols through the remaining lines: of night, day, nothingness, purity. Waking into the transfigured reality from his dream (transfigured by the dream-into-waking), he cries out of the wakened quest, "O Poem / Of Flight, abolish wings" (thus silencing the Poem of Flight invoked in V, which bore his hope). The concluding lines of this scene are the confession: "Mon art est un impasse. . . . Ici-bas est maître. . . . We measure our finiteness against infinity. . . . [letter to a friend, Mauclair]."

pp. 128–133: *Más allá del amor:* "Beyond love." *Retour des martinets:* "Return of the Swifts." *Canción del ángel sin suerte:* "Song of the Unlucky Angel." *El ángel mentiroso:* "The Lying Angel." *La Bêche:* "The Spade." *Me destierro . . .* "I exile myself . . ."

p. 137, line 1: "Seventy" is often used in Hebrew literature as a round figure with symbolic nuances (e.g., the nations of the earth enumerated in *Gen.* 10 total seventy).

p. 137, line 9: Saul Tchernichovsky, Hebrew poet (1875–1943).

pp. 137–139: Terah, Abram's father, an idol worshipper, left his native Sumerian city (Ur) and settled in Haran (Syria), though he had intended to go to Canaan. According to *Gen* 17:4–6, Abram was told by the Lord: "Behold, my covenant is with you . . . your name shall be Abraham, for I have made you the father of a multitude of nations."

p. 141, lines 7 *ff.:* Melchizedek: eighteenth-century B.C. king of Salem who welcomed Abraham with bread and wine. Salem is thought by many scholars to be Jerusalem and is referred to as such in *Psa.* 76:2 and in the fourteenth-century B.C. Tel-el-Amarna tablets.

p. 144: Isaac: "he will laugh," in Hebrew. At the news of becoming a mother in her ninetieth year, Sara "laughed within herself," then denied it. After Isaac's birth she said: "God hath made me laugh so that all who hear will laugh with me" (*Gen.* 18:12; 21:6).

p. 145, last lines: The Friday evening "Sanctification Song" commonly recites the account of the Sabbath of the Creation (*Gen.* 2: 1–3).

p. 146, 3rd stanza: Jonah boarded a ship moored at the seaport of Joppa (today's Jaffa, adjacent to Tel Aviv). "The waters compassed me about . . . the depth closed me round about, the weeds were wrapped about my head" (*Jonah* 2:5).

p. 146, line 27: Eilat: port at the head of the Gulf of Aqaba, most southerly settlement in Israel.

p. 148, line 2: The Hebrew name for Lake Galilee is Kinneret, meaning "lyre."

p. 148, last line: Monastery erected in the sixth century by the Byzantine Emperor Justinian.

p. 151: See above, note to p. 116.

p. 154, 3rd stanza: *Eccles.* 3: 1–4. Herod came to the throne in 37 B.C.; in the preceding thirty years some 110,000 men had been slaughtered.

p. 156, line 16: "The Royal Greek": Antiochus IV Epiphanes, Seleucid king who ruled from Antioch (175–163 B.C.).

p. 156, line 20: Judas-Maccabeus ("Maccabeus": from the Hebrew for "hammer"), son of Mattathias, leader of the revolt against Antiochus.

p. 158, lines 2–7: Gideon, twelfth-century B.C. military commander and judge. Josiah: king of Judah (640–609 B.C.), mortally wounded when attempting to stop the armies of Pharaoh Neco of Egypt, who had set out for Assyria.

p. 165, line 30: Masada: stronghold overlooking the Dead Sea, where 960 Zealots chose to kill themselves rather than surrender to the Romans. The end came three years after the destruction of the Temple of Jerusalem by Titus, A.D. 70.

p. 175, line 10: Greek goddess of Chance. "Her overwhelming aspect was her uncertainty." — *Classical Handbook,* Appleton Century, 1962.

p. 179 Photograph by Susan Copen Oken.

SELECTED PROSE

MY FRIEND, MY FATHER

Originally published as Book Three of *The Refusers,* Horizon Press, 1981. Re-issued with an introduction by Leon Edel in 1986 by Oxford University Press. Copyright 1981 by Stanley Burnshaw.

I

This is his greatest day, they were telling me. Aren't you proud of your father? Think of it, son! The man from the White House in Washington! The President coming this afternoon to visit us here. What a great honor, boy, for your father! Aren't you proud?

I nodded hard with my six-year-old smile, but all I could think of was Giant. How big can he be — President Taft? Four hundred pounds, some said from his pictures, and tall. They had already opened the double doors, but maybe, I hoped, they'd have to break down a wall . . .

Where did this happen and when, you ask? Nineteen twelve — where we lived — a place called Pleasantville. Thirty miles from Manhattan. My father had built up a paradise world for orphans rescued from Europe. It was famous by now. People were coming from Germany, Belgium, France — even Japan — to see what this immigrant Jew had made from his dream.

A dozen trustees and their wives, clothed in their summer best, kept milling around our verandah, restless, half afraid that the Man mightn't come. Not my father. Certain that he could count on the President's host, he moved about through the waiting group, spreading assurances, lavishing courtesies. Then he noticed me propped on a pilaster, with my baseball mitt and bat. He walked toward me slowly, winking his light blue eyes. Looking down, he beamed, "Run off, if you want to! Take your ball and bat, but not too far. I want you here when the President comes with our friend Mr. Lewisohn." He turned toward two of the dressed-up men who were watching. "Gentlemen," he announced with elaborate whimsy, "I want you to meet my only son in America." It was one of his favorite pleasantries, at which I never failed to grin though the humor was past my reach. It appeared, for a moment, out of his hearers' also, till his reassuring twinkle explained he was teasing the brink of propriety.

Soon, with all the others who filled the hall, I watched the Man on the podium, heard grandiloquent phrases, clapped with the crowd, and fidgeted in my seat. William Howard Taft's great bulk disappointed, but I saw from the look on my father's face that this odd stranger, twice his cubage, had flooded his heart. To be sure, as I later realized, none of the tributes revealed the least comprehension of what this "Institution" on which the President poured his praises meant for the man who had shaped it. Nor had it troubled anyone else in the hall, to judge from their words. Nor eminent visitors who came and would come from all over the world. Nor me — till I neared the age that my father had reached at the time: his forty-third year.

Weeks after it entered my mind, I decided to question him. He was happy to talk about all the events that my letters had led him to think of. In his characteristically organized way, he told the tale of his youthful years and the ones that followed, without broaching or even skirting the question. Indeed if it hadn't opened my eyes on this man and his world — and my own — I shouldn't be writing these words. Only one other person, so far as I know, had a glimmer; and he covered it over quickly. But whether he said it aloud I'm unable to tell, since never in all his replies did my father mention the matter. Had it dropped too deep inside him to bubble up to awareness? Within the range he envisioned, there were bounds beyond which presumptuousness might not venture. He knew, he was sure, what his strivings had sought and won. But he didn't suspect he was — how shall I put it? — teaching a lesson to God.

Madness, you say? Hardly. Hold on for a moment! Accuse him of anything else — he was Reason itself — he was Moderation's advocate. Like many other young scholars enthralled by the Greeks, he'd been awed by the workings of hubris. Mention Odysseus and out of his mouth came the hero's speech to the nurse, warning of insolence, unrestraint, and the costs of excessive pride, followed with the explanations. As I think back now, it was never far from his thought — nor very far from my own.

What would you guess he proposed when my teacher told us to letter a proverb to hang on a wall? "Just two words," my father beamed, "but the best to remember. Here!" — he wrote out FESTINA LENTE — "Latin for 'Make Haste Slowly.' You know what that means: before you act in a hurry, stop and take time to think. *Festina* means hasten; *lente,* slowly. A splendid rule of the Greeks." Then he uttered some sounds that I'd never heard. Seeing me gape, he chuckled, "That's how they said it in Athens. Would you like to learn —?" I shook my head. "But your very first words were Greek." I nodded, mumbling the Homer line with which I had greeted the world . . .

Of course, some said he was pushing knowledge too far. But coming from where he'd come and being the person he was, did he have a choice? Does anyone? If you go back early enough in a life, fate seems to put out branches in different directions. He was lucky — or so he believed . . .

2

Stopping again? Another attempt gone wrong? What you've written is faithful enough. On with it! tell what's crowding your ears. Shut out the clashing voices! You've more than enough to recount my life from all that you saw and heard. Why hesitate now? It's really no earth-shaking story or the universe would display the signs. — True, though: it's left some marks on a score of lives — or hundreds. The number's no matter. What counts is the passing of time with its shadows that hide and devour meaning. The longer you wait, the worse: whatever pattern you found won't deepen, for all your probings. I, your father, was born; I lived, strove, fought when I had no choice — what else is a life? Besides, you know the wherefores and whys as well as anyone cased in another man's skin could imagine. — *Imagine*! That's the trouble that freezes your fingers, harsh as you've been on your brain to stick to the truth — my truth — as though any man could *know* another man's story . . .

You were probably right to stop attempting what can't be done. Yet you'll never give up, so fixed are you on its meanings. Maybe there's still a way. You must let me speak through your mouth . . . unless that would mean defeat to you after your starts and surrenders — No! Allow me to speak through my *own*, for a while at least. The risks will be mine. What can you lose by my telling? Besides, whenever you're ready to have me stop, I'll leave. Meanwhile stand by quietly, son, while I take your task. Put down pen and pencil and hear! I'll even talk in your manner. Listen! . . .

Your ancestors — yes, I'm aware you're not avid for history, but this is a link with your French friend Spire, whose people had come from Speyer, not 50 miles from Worms-on-the-Rhine, where our forebears lived for years. In 1648, with the Peace of Westphalia, families took to the road: Spire's for France; ours for da Costa's Holland. A call had reached my father from one of the Baltic provinces: Courland, literally "chosen country." It was always changing sovereigns. At the time I was born and reared, it was solidly German, but before I finished school Czar Nicholas turned things upside down. To most Courlanders — Lettish peasants: Germans mixed with Slavs — the shift from German teachers to Russian meant very little: they were still enslaved by the barons. But for "my circle" the change was a shocking blow. Suddenly we were ordered to spurn the German Romantic ideals that nourished our hopes: to exchange our excited faith in the Sun of Enlightenment for the gloom of the Russian steppe.

We learned quickly to manage, even to giving a hand to the Russian teachers, who reeled at their tasks. Faced with youths trained to out-German the Germans, the bumbling pedagogues did their miserable best. Besides, we were young, proud, cocksure; and Mitau, long the capital seat of the Dukes of Courland, well lived up to its sobriquet "God's little country." And so we went on with all that we'd done before but with double the fervor, our reading circle proudly declaiming Schiller, Goethe, and Lessing till the halls of the Russified college rocked with Enlightenment's paeans to Man.

Yet life in the charming town on the Lielupe River, with its pine forests and meadows, all but closed us off from the world outside. Blissful provincials, none of us spoke of the turmoils plaguing people in Europe, news of which, if it came, escaped my ears. As Jews, our numbers were limited to families known to have lived in the city for years. And I never knew antisemitism. On the contrary, the feeling between ourselves and the Letts was closer than friendly, since Jews had helped in their struggle against the barons' attempts to wrest the Republicans' power.

And of course everyone knew of my father's profession. To work as Associate Rabbi in a city of 20,000 was to be a public figure. Synagogue tasks were his occupation and yet, for reasons I can't explain, he had also amassed some wealth. We always seemed to be living in more than comfort — all five brothers and sisters — and to keep a kind of open house for relatives, friends, and neighbors. This ease combined with my native ebullience may perhaps explain my innocence when, having passed the state exams for the graduates of the Gymnasium, I applied at the Lazarevsky Institute.

I entered the Rector's office and showed my credentials. "Training to teach, young man?" He eyed me carefully.

"Not at all, sir."

"No? Then what?"

"To enter the diplomatic service."

"You?" he blasted. "Didn't your father tell you it's closed to Jews?"

"Then you give me no choice but to serve some *foreign* country?" He gaped at me in amazement. "Thank you, Herr Rector," I said and turned on my heels.

By the time I was home, I'd decided to leave for France. "France," my father began, "Why?"

"The land of Enlightenment, Freedom, Justice," I cried, "where the Declaration of the Rights of Man was —"

"Yes. Quite so," he replied rather strangely. "Your brother Friedrich will meet you there." He paused thoughtfully. "Nothing for you in Mitau. After a year, if you change your mind, go to London. Your brother Max will be there. Talk with him, then decide! He comes next month."

"Of course," I agreed, but, proud as I was of this brother — he had won a medical post on a prince's estate — I had made up my mind on France. All my heroes of Progress and Reason — Voltaire, Diderot — all who had fought for the causes I prized had come from this land. Besides, nearby was Italy, cherished by Goethe. I would lose no time fitting myself for sharing that world.

In the months ahead I often found myself brooding about the scene with the Rector. What did being a Jew have to do with my competence? Jewish lawyers, doctors, businessmen came and went as they pleased — I had never heard of a "problem." Why had *my* Jewishness set me apart? My father's? All sorts of men sought his advice, Gentiles as often as Jews; and not on religious matters. People spoke of his breadth of knowledge, tolerance, fairness. To be sure, we belonged to the synagogue, kept the holidays, said the prayers, though our family's way of expressing religion was music — singing. . . . Thus I kept pressing my brain, but it left me staring in space, bereft of even a semblance of justification.

I decided to talk things out with Eugene Thal, my closest companion. We had started the reading circle together, holding discussions of new ideas till the sun went down. For all his devotion to books, I considered Eugene much more worldly than I if only because his father, a wealthy merchant, had made himself known as an atheist. If any among my friends could end my bewilderment, it was Thal.

When I knocked at the door of his house there was no one home. Nor had anyone seen them depart. One week later they all returned, solving the mystery. Father and Mother Thal and their eight children, who had left Mitau as Jews, were now officially Protestants, baptized in the Lutheran church at Königsberg. Eugene denied it all when I asked, "How could your atheist father do such a thing to his son?"

"But it didn't happen, I tell you."

Months passed. Brother Max returned for a visit, planning a study-year in Berlin before embarking for England. Sooner than I could believe, my twenty-first summer had ended: I would leave in late October. Never once as I gazed through the train window did I think to ask if my eyes would ever again behold the faces smiling goodbyes. Of course, I'd be back for an August visit — probably with my brother, who'd help me settle in Paris.

On the trip from Mitau to Königsberg I was unexpectedly thrown into contact with dozens of Jewish immigrants who had boarded the train at St. Petersburg and Moscow. For the first time I learned of the terrible hardships forced on these men and women, who had lived for years beyond the Pale prescribed by the Czars. My heart went out to these brave and resolute people who, despite their inhuman treatment at the hands of corrupt officials, hated to leave their birthplace.

When the train stopped at the frontier town of Eydtkühnen, a delegation of German Jews, led by a well-known scholar, boarded the coach. They had come to help the immigrants pass through customs, check their papers, and prepare them for their voyage across the ocean. Because I spoke both languages, the Russians asked me to help reply to the detailed questions the German delegates presented to every household. Words I could scarcely believe came out of their mouths. I looked at the delegates' sober faces: they had heard such accounts before. As for myself, long before the last of the immigrants answered, I'd abandoned the thought of France.

I approached the delegates' leader. "If you were I, Herr Hildesheimer, would you throw in your lot with these people? — go to America?"

"If I were you? No question."

"Unfortunately I haven't money for passage."

"Neither have they. If you're ready, sail with my blessings! Shall I put your name on the list?"

"How explain," I began to stammer, "to my father? to my mother?"

"Say that you took the advice of a cautious scholar who would do the same if he weren't three times your age."

On the cattle boat *Virginia* bound for New York I spent four crowded and troubled weeks. Much of my time was given to "mastering" English with the help of three small books I had bought in Hamburg: *A Student's Grammar of English*, *A Christmas Carol* by Dickens, and the same in German translation. Reading the two versions was simple enough, but not the pronunciation or spelling, neither of which seemed to follow logic or rules. I appealed to the ship's doctor, who tutored me for an hour each day. To judge from the number of times he laughed, his labors were well rewarded, though he urged me on for "doing well for a brandnew immigrant." He also took me down a peg when I said I was certain to find a job at once as a teacher of Latin or Greek.

I had other tutors as well — among the immigrants. Some at first were unable to bear my ignorance, others refused to believe it. I did my best to explain. As a rabbi's son, I had known our people had suffered because of the Church. From the bloody Crusades through seven centuries, Jews had been chased from country to country — Britain, Spain, France, Germany: pillaged, tortured, walled into ghettoes even in lands of refuge. And yet such things, we had firmly come to believe, belonged to human prehistory. The Christian nightmare was ended. Great revolutions had flooded light on the world. Ghettoes were shattered. Freedom, justice, emancipation proclaimed the Bright New Future for all. Life was teeming with hope. We would live to be part of the golden Brotherhood of Man . . .

My Russian shipmates stared at each other in horror. "Courlander Jews!" they groaned. "Nobody ever spoke of the Easter pogrom? Elisavetgrad . . . Kiev . . . Odessa . . . Christmas in Warsaw in 1881 . . . ?"

"Never. Not in my presence." I shook my head. "Maybe they wanted to spare me. I was ten years old — no, eleven."

"So was my son, but he knew."

Before the *Virginia* arrived in New York I had learned as much as the people on board would tell me. Some were reluctant to speak or mocked when I questioned; others glared with distrust. Scrambling among the ones who would talk, I was able to piece together enough to darken my days and nights. For the first time, I began to think of my father with doubts, questionings. How could this sage of my youth withhold the facts that were part of our birthright? How could he calmly let us depart for the world unarmed for its hazards? Out of fear? Self-protection? Ignorance? Shame? — of the shame we might suffer once we learned? Father Thal must have weighed the costs of contempt before the Königsberg baptism, but his sons at least were alerted.

Rage, pain, confused with self-accusation hovered above my head as I stared at the ocean, eyes bulging with scenes my shipmates had witnessed. The Easter pogroms kept gnawing my mind. What could our people have done to have earned such suffering? By now the whole world knew the attacks had been planned, carefully planned in a hundred towns by the Czar's police: Cossacks driving the natives to pillage, plunder, rape, kill — and the Poles matching the Russian feat with a torrent of Christmas blood for their holiest time of the year. Nothing had stopped the butchery. People of power and fame — Victor Hugo in France, Gladstone in England — denounced the "unheard-of barbarities" only to learn of renewed attacks in April that followed — and again and again in the next two years. The victims, after the first pogrom, set out for Lessing and Schiller's land but were barred from entering. The vast tide had to look elsewhere for shelter.

Among the friends I made on board was a teacher of history who had spent some time with a man sent over by HIAS — the Hebrew Sheltering and Immigrant Aid Society, formed in New York to facilitate emigrations by providing funds for travel, hostels, and shelters. From one of their Hamburg agents, my teacher-friend had gleaned some remarkable facts. Since 1881, he was told, about 75,000 refugees had found their way to Palestine, Argentina, and South America, roughly a third to each, with another 10,000 to Canada. But the overwhelming numbers had gone to America: some 700,000 — from Russia, Poland, and Austria-Hungary — more than five times as many as during the decade after the first pogrom in Odessa.

Jews all over the globe were helping their fellows. The world was watching the starkest test of brotherhood, and much of the world was moved by proofs of the bond. Jews, from the rich to the poor, gave what they could. Men of wealth, themselves safe from the dangers, were bringing forward stupendous sums to assist their people. This very year, from his palace-home, Munich-born Baron Maurice de Hirsch had set aside 500,000 British pounds to enable Russian victims of persecution to establish themselves on the soil of friendly lands. And this act was but one of many. Other groups in a number of countries were standing guard for the safety of their brothers.

Terrible as the forces of hate had become, there were deeper, vaster strengths in the human heart — so I reasoned. Evil was more than counter-weighed by the good that inhered in man. Hope had kept faith — havens of welcome were showing the way. And for all the blood on his history, man would not die into blackness — least of all in civilized lands where every person could raise his head with pride. While Russias and Polands raved in barbarity's nightmare, the sun that had dawned on the West glistened, and I — I was on my way to a country of light. What counted now were my days to come in that land.

My head rang with these wondrous words and my heart believed as I strode from Castle Garden's gates into my newfound city. Fortune struck on my very first day. One of the horse-drawn wagoners, waiting for immigrants, dropped me off, without saying why, at a house on Rutgers Street.

When I entered the hall, I noticed a dark-eyed girl gracefully perched on the landing, watching the new arrivals. I smiled at her as I made my way to my room. Before two days had passed, we were greeting each other.

Not many months ago she had fled St. Petersburg with her parents and older sisters, after living there all their lives in comfort and calm. Like a handful of other privileged Jews, they made "contributions" to the police, who winked at the bogus "Shirts Made To Order" sign in the window. Then out of the blue, one day a new recruit to the force knocked at their door. He had come to make a purchase. When he asked to be shown the cloths, he was given a cryptic stare. Nonetheless he took off his coat to have his measurements taken. The head of the house looked at him, shook his head, and ran from the room. The recruit, unaware of his captain's "arrangement," stormed through the house, demanding to see the goods and equipment — none of which could be found.

Thrilled by his lucky discovery, he rushed to the station, roaring his news on the way. The police captain had no choice. In twenty-four hours the Kivmans fled from the country. By now, eight months after crossing the ocean, the girls had established themselves as a working force: the older two, expert retouchers of photographic negatives, the youngest — my charming dark-eyed friend, Sonya — of hand-colored positives.

The three offered to teach me their crafts, but after days of bungling, I decided on something else. Equipping myself with samples of what they had done, I called on a number of studios. To my great delight, the very first place I visited brought success. I was given two large plates by the well-known Pach Brothers Gallery. When I brought them back, the owner examined them carefully, pronounced them splendidly done, and handed me six new plates with a hearty promise of more. From that time on, the girls had a thriving income, which I made much larger by bringing them all the work that they cared to handle. And so it was that in less than a month I also was firmly established, representing — under the name of Ludwig "Zimmerman" — not only exquisite negative work but hand-colored photos as well. To celebrate, I sent a share of my fortune ($25) as a kind of springtime gift to my father and mother.

But what of my true vocation? Having learned that Nicholas Murray Butler, the philosophy dean at Columbia, had studied for years in Germany, I decided to seek his guidance. His eagerness to counsel impressed me as much as his charm, but most surprising of all was his grasp of my needs and my aspirations. It far exceeded my own. And before our interview ended, I agreed to enroll for a Master of Arts and to take the courses he named, which were varied enough to serve as the base for whatever teaching career I might finally choose. Our discussion at times was amusing, Butler speaking in English and I in German, with fitful attempts by him to converse in German. I must have shown some shock at his errors in grammar for he smiled when he saw me wince and asked my indulgence.

Columbia, then in lower Manhattan, was a fairly small university. I came to feel a personal bond between myself and my teachers, some of whose works, I was startled to learn, might be found all over the world. How could a New York scholar possibly know as much about *Faust* as the experts in Germany? And yet, my Professor Boyesen's volume was being studied by German students in German colleges. The news struck a blow at my Courlander's insularity, making me smart and rejoice — and question my pride's allegiance.

But not for long: I was stirred by the prospects before me. I would work at selling by day and study at night — "How could one hope for a better plan than to earn by light and learn by night from scholars?" The ridiculous rime pictures a nose-to-the-grindstone bachelor's life, whereas it was more, very much more, because of the dark-eyed girl to whom I was drawn on my very first day in this city. The spark that had touched us both from our earliest meetings led us to friendship and soon into pledges of love. Before many weeks had passed we were eager to marry. Her parents, not in the least surprised, beamed when we offered our news, then — somewhat pained and sheepish — asked us to wait "for a little while." We half-expected as much while hoping they'd find the courage to shrug off an Old World tradition. We assented to the delay, but only till one — not both — of the older sisters would marry. In the meantime they invited me into their household. And so we were all together: six adults in a none-too-ample apartment, but at least we were almost one family and of course the delay would last but "a little while."

Also, we were darkly aware — Sonya and I — of our blessings, thinking of all we learned of the people penned in the streets around us: more than 200,000 now, half of them children. Two of our neighbors had called on friends from abroad in the "Big Flat," a tenement north of Canal Street, spread over six city blocks. What they pictured to us of the foulness, crowding, vermin, dirt, and poverty was too difficult to believe; but that was true six years before and "things were improving" — so, at least, wrote *The New York Times,* which sent down people to make reports on the immigrants. Just how great the improvement might be, we could hardly know or how the most pained or the poorest newcomers managed.

It was common knowledge, however, that certain "Uptown" men and women, church and laity, overcome by the horrors that marked this world, had been "doing things" for years. One of them, Felix Adler, a rabbi's son who promoted an "Ethical Culture" society, had been so incensed by the evils of slums that he virtually forced some construction of model tenements. Another — Stanton Coit, a Christian idealist — had moved from his comfortable home to the East Side's Forsyth Street, where he formed the Neighborhood Guild: University Settlement, the first of its kind in the nation. Succeeding him came Charles B. Stover, a quiet person whose selfless works caused him in time to be known as "a sacred man" . . . Which he may have been: it was he who inspired the most heroic of all, Lillian Wald, a woman of twenty-six, to abandon the German-Jewish world that had made of her, as she said, just a spoiled child. Too young (in her sixteenth year) to enter college, she studied instead at the New York Hospital for Nursing, and within a decade was teaching her skills to a class of immigrant mothers. With a fellow-nurse she lived on Jefferson Street, doing all that they could by day and by night — in their fifth-floor flat or in patients' rooms — to heal, cure, guide, assist, even to bringing down surgeons to people too ill to be moved. She soon established on Henry Street a nursing settlement like none to be found anywhere else. Her name was on everyone's lips. A remark she made to an Uptown friend was already a legend: "We are full of our neighbors' troubles."

And yet, odd though it sounds, her work together with other acts of benevolence often disturbed my thoughts. I began to question myself. Had I really thrown in my lot with the victims I met on the train to Hamburg? All I had done since reaching this shore was aimed at removing myself from their midst. To be sure, it was never to live on streets such as these that I'd crossed the ocean. To move from their world was something that had to be done if Sonya and I were to live as we wished to live. In time — after the promised "little while" — we would go our way; but now we would have to remain and play our part — a self-demeaning, dependent part, for whatever betterments reached this place had been brought by others. Why? Were there none among all the thousands about us willing or able to act? And what of myself? I was much more lucky — also, in certain ways, more able — than others, but not until now had my failure "to do something" preyed on me. *Noblesse oblige,* I mocked myself. To be sure, my work by day and my study by night were burdens enough. And yet, and yet . . .

Meanwhile, although our future would take us away, our present was here — and with more than enough to busy us, in addition to Sonya's

English classes and mine at Columbia. There were concerts, lectures, art exhibitions, dances, debates, choruses . . . one had only to look at the lists in the "old" University Settlement or the "new" Educational Alliance. Both institutions had of course been gifts from people of wealth and good will who intended them not just to entertain and help but largely to guide, to teach, to "Americanize the greenhorns." Orthodox Jews and Socialists scorned "the scheming ways of German Jews to civilize their barbarous brethren." But for every five who condemned these college-combined-with-clubhouse centers, there were fifty who praised them. Many shrank from the new, or refused to change, or shrugged off the strange as defilements. Others would wait "and see." But some were ready — anxious, in fact — to make themselves part of this world that had opened its arms.

What could I do to help? "Teach! You're a teacher: teach!" the Alliance director smiled when I called at his office. "Teach what you *know*! And you'll help them share your joys in these poets! What shall we name it? Lectures on Heine, Schiller, and Goethe?" I nodded. "Good. Your first meeting is Thursday at 8." I would try my best. So, I knew, would my listeners in spite of our troubles with language.

To my heart's relief, I was "doing something" at last. But, for the picture to be true, more must be said: I was also a marginal person. Ignorant of my neighborhood's lingua franca, I was forced to turn to others to put the Yiddish phrases and words into German, Russian, or English. Sometimes I managed to guess my way by matching the sounds I heard with what I recalled of Middle High German. But Yiddish was also mixed with re-furbished borrowings from Hebrew, Slavic, and now — mirable dictu! — American English. For a while I tried my best with a patient instructor. Soon both of us threw up our hands. If Nicholas Butler's errors in German had made me wince, how could I force my perfectionist tongue to do the things that Yiddish had done to German? Anglo-Saxon, Middle English, Latin, Greek, Hebrew, Arabic — these I'd been able to learn with ease, but not the mother-speech of my fellow Jews! It was more than merely absurd. In spite or because of myself — or both — I was fated to miss much that I wanted to savor: the vibrant tales, bittersweet humor, oaths . . . the dramatists, poets, writers of stories, whose works, I was hotly assured, were as great as the greatest. One fine day, I promised myself, I'd master my weakness; till then I would have to accept it. There were heavier thoughts in my mind.

What would we face once we had quit these streets? Would the people who owned this haven-city welcome us into their midst? A number of writers sent to observe the immigrants' world found much to extol — the astounding hunger for learning; the pride, the loyal closeness of family life; the nurture given the needy and sick in the true Mosaic tradition. "No fair-minded man who visits this place," wrote one reporter, "should close his eyes to such positive things" because of the squalor that overwhelms him — pushcarts, crowded pedestrians, bewigged women, the bizarre dress, the uncouth manners, the hoarse shouting, the guttural cries of the vendors, the filth, the sometimes unbearable stench. The Uptown press made much of presenting "a balanced view of this genuine ghetto south of Houston and east of the Bowery." But even reporters who tried to be understanding managed to aggravate nativist fears of an enclave of threatening strangers which was bound to spread as the terrors in Europe mounted. I had crossed the ocean to live a life of humanist freedom. How much chance had an alien to build his ideal? The Enlightenment, everyone knew, had come to these shores, and where if not here, in the nation famed for equality, could it grow and flourish? Besides, we had seen what those of good will could achieve — Coit, Stover, Wald, and the unnamed others of wealth and power who worked and watched, we were told, from behind the scenes. And the city's great university held out its arms to help me. I had already found an opening into that world.

It proved larger, perhaps, than I knew. A week before I was granted my Master's degree, Professor Boyesen approached me. "Here, young man" — he held out an unsealed envelope — "take it, read it, and let me know your decision." The letter to Dr. William Rainey Harper, the President of the University of Chicago, strongly urged him to grant me a German in-structorship with a special course on *Faust*. I was dazzled. The prospect of starting my teaching career in a great institution was more than I ever had hoped. I would make the journey at once. Sonya, of course, and the rest of the household did their hesitant best to share my delight; but when I came back with negative news, they appeared, oddly, relieved. Hadn't they understood? I explained again: though my future there was bright and the college ideal, the remuneration wouldn't meet our needs. Sonya smiled. "My mother says you were born under a lucky star. Here!" — she held out an envelope — "Was I wrong to open it? When I saw who sent it, I couldn't wait." She began to recite, "The Civil Service Examiners' Board . . . ," having learned the letter by heart. I not only passed; I was told to report — "appointed a teacher of German in Public School No. 74" at 7:30 A.M., September 11, 1894.

At once we began to make plans. How would we find a safe replacement for "Zimmerman," who would give up knocking on studio doors? Ask the young man engaged to the eldest sister, who was planning a shop of his own? If he took the job, it could speed their marriage and end — thank heaven! — our waiting. In the meantime, just as before, most of my nights were Columbia's, with courses still to be chosen. It would take three years for the doctorate. "And then," my father-in-law-to-be remarked with a wink, "your education will start."

In the spring, on the day I entered my twenty-sixth year, we married and moved to a home of our own in Brooklyn. Compared to what we had left it was surely a palace. The "parlor" windows framed an enchanting view of a park, and though we had insufficient room, "soon" the place would be spacious — the five of us would be four the moment the single daughter followed her sister's example. Much of my time was spent at school on East 63rd Street, at Columbia, at the German Teachers Group where I had to preside. As the year went by we knew that a place in Manhattan would make life easier. Such a change, however, would have to wait till our child that was on the way had greeted the world.

By the summer's end — four months after our daughter's birth — we moved to our "permanent" home, as we smilingly called it, pleased as we were to be close again to all we had missed. The parlor windows, facing the busy East River, flooded the two front rooms all day with the sky. And our "house" — 57th Street: Sutton Place — quite unlike the brownstone flat near the Park in Brooklyn, was in walking reach of both my school and my college. Our household also had changed. When the last of the daughters married, she persuaded her father to share their home, which was nearer than ours to his favored haunts and his special friends.

One quiet evening Sonya told me the tale of their ocean voyage. In a North Sea gale on the third day, their ship lost its propeller. After tossing for days, it was found by a rescue boat and towed to Scotland. Soon again it set sail, but the hazards worsened. Storm upon storm battered the limping vessel, adding days to the journey. The Kivmans, like other observant Jews who had brought provisions, found themselves short of food. At their father's orders, they ate whatever was offered — thus ending one pious observance. Others followed as sickness spread through the steerage. When he heard that the "black measles" had taken the lives of a score of children, Sonya's father gave up his morning and evening prayers. His wife and daughters looked on as he dropped his precious phylacteries into the sea. Striking the water, the leather cases leaped in the air, then fell, to be pounded from wave to wave. Six days later they watched him arrange his belongings. Setting aside the books of prayer with the Talmud volumes, he asked his daughters to walk through the ship and give them away. None of them moved. "*Please,* daughters!" he looked away from their stunned faces. When they left him, he shut his eyes and turned to his wife. Her cheeks were covered with tears. He touched her forehead. "Your father's treasures deserve a believer's eyes. You know that I have no right to them now." They sat together silently. Then she wiped her eyes and took his arm. Nobody ever again spoke of the books. Whenever asked of his former life, he would shout merrily, "*Here* I am — in *America*! — Have you seen the new play? Such acting! . . ." or "Not right now. I'm late already," and rush to the Café Royale.

In our early talks I had sometimes been taken aback by his worldly remarks. How had this scholar, bound to the fenced-in law of his Talmud, learned so much about writers, politics, history . . . ? Yet his secular knowledge struck me less than his fearlessly busy mind. Once an issue was raised, nothing could stop him from tracking it down, regardless of what it might make him concede. Although by now his views no longer surprised me, in recent weeks he began to "explain" the much-scorned Uptown Jews and their nervously haughty behavior. "Haven't they reason to shrink from us," he argued, "to hate our conspicuous ways, since their sweetest dream is to be like their neighbors, lose themselves, cover their difference? Hold your curses! Your children will probably do the same or worse. And at least these Upstart Germans open their pockets — and more than we like to admit, also their hearts . . ."

As I told Sonya, it was not until we were living apart that I saw him for what he was. He often paid us visits — mainly, I thought, to play with his "New York grandchild," whose charms he seemed to adore. But he also knew that, much as I prized my daughter, she was very far from the glorious-looking child I had hoped for. "Tell him, baby," he'd coo to her, "say what a beautiful girl you'll be when you're five years old. Your papa thinks you're wearing your permanent face. What a foolish man you picked for a papa, but Grandpapa knows." Then he'd tell us about the marches, petitions, meetings, slogans demanding justice for Dreyfus: "Down with the Antisemites of France!" "Free Captain Dreyfus!" . . . I promised to join the protests soon — as soon as my work and my nine-tenths-finished thesis permitted. Three short weeks and I'd have my final session with Butler.

On the following Wednesday, a letter arrived, advancing the date. When I entered his office, he smiled warmly at me — more warmly than ever. At once he spoke of my "excellent" courses, naming them one by one. As for my thesis, he and his colleagues were "most impressed"; in fact, they believed "it might well become the definitive treatment." When I asked jokingly, "Will anyone rush to outdo my *Order of Words in Old Norse Prose?*" he beamed, shaking his head. Then he paused, moving about the papers stacked on his desk. Placing a folder under his eyes, he began quietly, "Something recently came to light that will cause a delay. Our graduate office, when making their routine check of candidates, failed to find any record of one of the minor courses required of our doctorates. It appeared that either you never had studied Plane Trigonometry or if you had, your grade was omitted. I wrote at once to the Rector of your gymnasium." He dropped the folder and nodded. "His answer reached me on Monday. It was clear that we'd have to postpone your degree. However, in view of your excellent work of the last five years, I asked the Committee to waive the delay on your promise to take the missing course in the fall. My request was refused." He coughed and gazed at the ceiling. "Your degree is withheld for a year. There's nothing more I can do."

"I believe there is, Dean Butler," I barked, too angry to temper my voice. "Give me the textbook name and set an examining date. I shall need two weeks, and the minute I pass, the Committee will have no further reason to harm my career."

His eyes seemed to pop from their sockets. "How can you possibly do a semester's work in a fortnight?"

"An examination is all I demand and you *owe* it to me. If your clerks had been doing their duty, you'd have notified me not now but two or three years ago, and we wouldn't be having this problem. The error is theirs, not mine."

"No, not yours," he tapped on his desk. "They should have discovered it sooner." He pondered for minutes. "Come back at four tomorrow. I'll have the textbook here." He pondered again. "Two short weeks to master it? I'm sorry to see you drive yourself so." He rose from his chair and took my hand. "But if you should fail — and I'll be surprised if you *don't*" — he forced a smile — "remember, a year's delay in a young man's life is hardly the end of his world. I hope you'll think it over and change your mind."

"Thank you, Dean Butler," I said. "Tomorrow at four."

By the time I reached home I was calm enough for a matter-of-fact report. But before I could finish, Sonya burst out "No! Not now!"

"Come," I smiled, "two weeks more and this nonsense will be forgotten."

She moved her eyes from side to side, then fixed on the floor for minutes. "Tell me," she finally whispered, "what great thing would you lose by waiting a year?" My pride, I suspected, troubled her more than my fury. "Why did you have to say what you did? — take on this extra burden?"

"I was outraged by the injustice!" I must have shouted, for almost at once her mother, bearing a tray with tea cups, moved through the door.

Sonya turned to me, nodding softly "I know, I know," and placed the tray on a table. "Shouldn't you find a teacher to help? . . . with so little time. We can keep the house very quiet."

"Tea . . . at the table?" her mother smiled.

After four nights of fruitless work, I was ready to give up trying. Then, as though by chance the disparate parts of the textbook suddenly fell into place. Their logic began to make pleasing — elegant sense. After the test had been given, Butler rushed from his office. "Congratulations! 100 percent — amazing — a perfect paper! May I keep it? I want to make it part of your file. One never knows, young man — and *again,* my congratulations!" I was greatly tempted to add, "By the way, I discovered a dozen mistakes in the text," but remembering Sonya's "Why did you have to say what you did?" I thanked him and took my leave.

With that problem solved, we scanned the papers for "news." They had said the results of the Civil Service test I had taken in March would appear in June, though the ones who passed might learn in advance by mail. Sonya had asked our postman to watch for the hoped-for letter. As things happened, however, the news was roared in my ears by my principal, who had "just heard from a friend at the Board . . . 'Find yourself a German teacher,' he tells me, 'Yours goes to DeWitt Clinton this fall — he'll also teach Latin.' I'm sorry to see you go, young man, but glad for your sake. It's the best high school we have and Buchanan's one of the finest — the principal. Don't be surprised by his accent: he's a Kansan."

I could hardly wait for the final bell to rush to Sonya. I'd been confident that I'd pass, but to win an appointment *at once?* — to teach *in September?* It was all too fine to be possible. As I fled up the steps to our door, I shouted the news. Sonya gasped with delight. Then she linked her arms in her mother's and both of them danced for joy.

Almost at once we made plans. We'd go to the country this summer, but keep the apartment at least till our second baby was born — at the end of the year, no doubt. And after that "we would see." But where would we spend July? At the Café Royale, Sonya's father had met "an extremely impressive man who knew all there was to know about country places and everything else." He would ask his advice. And so when my classwork ended, we rented a place in Hasbrouck Heights, next door to this paragon's friend, a well-known physician "who'll keep your son-in-law on his toes, I assure you. He's read every other book in print — and his wife is a doctor too. But Old Sabsowitch . . ." They were brilliant and charming people, though less entranced by rustic delights than ideas. "Old Sabsowitch" would gladly have talked each night till dawn if his wife hadn't dragged him to bed, which was partly why the two months passed so quickly. As August ended, the thought of going back to the city failed to fill us with cheer. Sonya thrived in the country, our daughter Eva and Sonya's mother as well. Some day perhaps we might even move from Manhattan. Sabsowitch frowned, though his friend the paragon claimed to have found "the solution." We should meet him soon and ask his advice since he knew all there was to know! . . .

Once my new job began all thoughts of life in the country faded. My high school work was a challenge and the Kansan principal different from any man I had met in New York. Four of the boys in my Latin class astounded me by their quickness. I remarked as much to Buchanan. He beamed, "Give them as much as you can — they'll take it and like it too. And, oh, they can teach you to ride a bicycle. It's the fastest way to your house, and excellent for the body! When you pedal fast, you can fly! . . ."

For the first time in years I found myself blessed with leisure. I could browse among books, read for the pleasure of reading; talk with colleagues; explore parts of the city I never had seen. Sonya and I visited friends, strolled through the Park to look at the colored leaves, walked by the river. I could even watch our tiny daughter hide in her Grandmother's skirts till the laughing woman swept her up in her arms. Quite suddenly I became aware of the endless burdens Sonya faced just to keep our house in order. She could never have possibly managed, I thought, without her mother.

As the weeks sped by and autumn moved toward winter, a severe cold wave struck the city. Sickness came in its wake. The newspapers printed daily reports of hospitals overwhelmed by patients. Warnings appeared, urging older people to keep out of crowds. Though an epidemic had not been declared, everyone knew that pneumonia raged through the streets. As the days went by, we thought our home might escape, but in mid-November Sonya's mother took to her bed. Our summer friend Dr. Sabsowitch came at once and, out of concern for Sonya's condition, promised a nurse. "With rest, quiet, warmth, care, our medicine — and luck, luck — it should run its course. I'll be back tomorrow or I'll send an assistant. As for you, my Sonyatchka, stay away from her now. The nurse will know what to do."

The woman arrived with the doctor's instructions. Day dragged after day. Nothing appeared to change. After his fifth visit, Sabsowitch led me aside. "Sonya knows — I can tell by her face she expects the worst. I'll send out word to her father to come tonight. You will want to be all together. But of course miracles sometimes happen when doctors fail. This one failed." He threw up his hands. "Get some sleep, if you can."

For weeks after the burial, her absence darkened our lives. For Sonya's sake I asked her father to stay with us. She protested at first, but his presence helped us to live with the emptiness. He was hardly a stranger to death. From his past losses, he'd learned the wisdom of purging grief by talking about the dead. Sonya and I would listen for hours as he spoke of the rabbi's only daughter and pictured her father's frantic search for a mate. "I was one year younger — sixteen. All I could 'do' was the Talmud. And my hands had never been soiled with toil, as they said. Her father added a wing to his house and planted bags of gold right under our bed. Then we began having babies. . . . And you, Sonya, you were the last — our thirteenth child: the lucky one. . . ."

In mid-December the cold gave way to spring-like warmth, but then an even more frigid wave battered the city. Sabsowitch called at our door one night without warning. "Too much ice on the streets for a mother-to-be," he announced, "so I've come instead. May I enter?" Touched by his kindness, I started to thank him profusely, but he waved me aside to closet himself with Sonya. When he reappeared he smiled, "I'll send you a nurse to help with things in the morning. Sonya will give us a Christmas present, unless I'm wrong."

He was wrong. Christmas passed. The streets were covered with white. Ice cakes cluttered the river. Restless with fear, Sonya's father paced the front room, stopping to stare through the windows. Then he joined me, lifted his grandchild onto his knees, and patted her cheeks. As the sky darkened, I busied myself with lights. Suddenly "It's over!" the nurse called out, "a beautiful girl." I rushed into Sonya's room. When I came to assure him, he scarcely gave me a glance. "Come now, Eva," he kept repeating, "tell your papa your sister's name. Don't be afraid! You said it before. Say it again! Mary, a beautiful name, your Grandmother's name, and *you're* my beautiful *beautiful* girl."

"Time for Eva to go to bed," the nurse broke in, "then I'll prepare the tea. Ready Eva? Your mama's already sleeping. When you're in your bed, your papa and grandpa will kiss you goodnight. Ready, my beautiful girl?"

I grew less aware of the void made by the loss of Sonya's mother as the new life filled up our home. To my hitherto protected ears, the endless demands of two small girls on their mother might have come out of three or four. The strain now showed on her father. From the wan look in his eyes, we could see that he longed to rejoin the downtown life he had lived before. At times Sabsowitch came along when he visited us, which was not too frequently now because of my "new career"; having started to tutor at night. Besides, as the months went by, my daytime students became more demanding, mainly because of Buchanan's continued prodding "to give them all they can stand." He had taken to bringing "observers" into my classroom and to sending flattering notes about my "performance."

The surprisingly early spring stirred us with thoughts of summer. Sabsowitch, having assumed our return to the farm-like house we had rented before, wrote to the owner to hold it. Having no better prospect, we followed his lead, much to our Eva's delight.

This year the nightly discussions turned on the Dreyfus affair. We knew all the facts: when the French Intelligence found him innocent, the Army hid the reports, only to have the victim's brother pin the guilt on an officer. "Major Ferdinand Esterhazy's the one," the newspapers told their readers, "France has been torn apart, but the turmoil can't continue."

"Nonsense," Sabsowitch argued, "it's far from over. True that the great Zola's *J'accuse* was a bombshell of sorts. But the real fight is between the Intelligence chief, Picquart, and the Army command. That's why their judges acquitted their major in minutes. Will the Army ever allow itself to be guilty? They'll press Picquart." What made our Russian doctor so sure of himself, we had no idea; nor were we quite convinced. But as things turned out, Sabsowitch proved a prophet. In August the Army announced that much of the case had been forged by a Picquart man. Faced with the proof, the traitor committed suicide, his accomplice fleeing to England. As the news quickened our hearts, Sabsowitch warned, "Don't celebrate yet! Do you think that the Army's about to admit it was wrong? You'll starve to death if you go on a fast till it happens."

Could Socialist wisdom explain his prophetic rightness, or was it simply his cynic's view? "How do you like your beloved Land of Enlightenment, Noble France?" he taunted me warmly. "If you're still so sure of the Goodness of Man, wait till Badanes arrives. He has things to tell us next weekend."

I was more than eager to meet him. From all I had heard, we were certain to take to each other. No one, however, had mentioned his lack of manners or heavily foreign speech. I must have shown my dismay, for Sabsowitch urged me gently, "Don't be put off by the man's aggressive behavior. It took me time to get used to it — and patience. But he's worth it, Ludwig. There's gold under all his dross. You'll see — after dinner this evening."

When I joined the table, the talk was again of Dreyfus. "Saul's had news from Paris," the doctor explained. "Tell us again what you've heard."

"The same old story except that they've put it to work. Paris comrades are setting up schools at night for the people, so they'll never be fooled again by the gangs at the top. It's called L'Enseignement Mutuel . . . And it's right — the 'mutuel' — though the only hope is to teach the *people* to learn. Education —"

"Ludwig is with you there," said Sabsowitch, eager to bring us closer.

"Hardly," Badanes scowled. "He cares about *how* people speak. The *what* doesn't matter."

Sabsowitch bridled. "How could you possibly know?"

"From the thesis he wrote on prose word-order in Norse."

"Our friend doesn't read very carefully. *Old* Norse prose," I corrected, "and related Germanic dialects."

"Ach! What difference?"

"Day and night, as you should have known from von Humboldt." He stared at me, utterly blank. "Wilhelm, of course." He kept on staring. I laughed, "Come now, be serious! Anyone even half acquainted with education knows all about him."

"*I* don't. Tell me! What have I missed?" Suddenly humble, he looked almost painfully anxious.

"If you study him when you go home, you'll find how little you know of the implications of language for the world and its future."

"Don't stop!" he protested. "Tell me about von Humboldt. I'll listen all night."

"Not right now. But I'll make a start in the morning."

"Name the time! I'll come to your house *early*."

He was pacing outside while I ate my breakfast. I showed him in and introduced him to Sonya. "Would you rather sit here or walk?" I asked.

"Whatever you say, but start, start!"

We began at a leisurely stride, taking a wooded path and stopping at times to rest. His ears perked up when he learned how von Humboldt a hundred years ago forced Pestalozzi's modern ideas on the stiff-necked teachers of Prussia. At the same time, I explained, he was learning Kawi, an ancient Javanese speech, along with the living speech of the Basques, which has no connection with anything else on earth. He began a comparative study and discovered something no one had ever imagined: that every language expresses the feelings and thoughts, the history, even the culture of those who speak it. In *The Duel* he sought to trace a . . . metaphysics of language. Death, unfortunately, came before he could finish it. I had just done a thesis on *Faust*. Von Humboldt's thought 'struck' at the perfect moment. Literature was my passion, but I came to suspect there was more to a book than its author's vision. It was *language itself — the only thing we have that sets us apart*. Von Humboldt gave me the key. Human beings perceive the world through language. Different tongues mean different views of the world. The earth is a Babel of not only words but perceptions, and every speaker believes that *his* view is right. If people would only grasp and *act* on this truth, the past, present, the future would be in our hands . . . I've talked enough. Tell me about yourself?"

"A great thought," he shook his head, deaf to my invitation. "Remarkable. Very great." He paused. "How can we put it to *use?*"

"That's the enormous question."

"There *must* be ways. We must think about it together."

Sabsowitch tried to make him prolong his stay, but he left in the morning. "Next time you will come to Flushing," he announced as he said goodbye. I shook my head and thanked him: vacation would soon be over. In the last days of August, without any warning, he reappeared, bringing his wife and daughter. Sonya went out of her way to welcome them. "Don't be shocked by this man," I said before they appeared for supper, "he shouts whatever comes into his head."

She smiled, cocked her head. "He's not the only one here who could learn some manners." The words were a gentle rebuke at my own failings, which had often jarred her nerves. But compared to our guest, I would seem decorum itself.

Sonya served an excellent meal and I did what I could to make everyone at the table join in the talk, including the children. Things went smoothly until, with typical bluntness, Saul turned upon Sonya. "You're a wonderful cook — better than Olgatchka. But would *you* get up in the morning at four just to bake bread for your husband? This one does," he nudged his wife, "rain, shine, snow."

"Shah, shah, Bah-dah-nis," Olga shouted and jumped from her chair. He followed, finally coaxing her back to her place. Our children gasped at the scene but Sonya made a joke of it. "Olga's a much better wife," she laughed, "but I also got out of bed at four to bake this cake."

"Four in the afternoon," squealed Eva, rocking with glee. The other girls joined in the squeals and the storm was over.

Suddenly thoughtful, Badanes nodded. "I know — some people behind my back say I behave like a boor. No one at home taught us manners . . . now everyone's too respectful. But it's much too late for us."

"Come, come, Saul," I began, not knowing what to say next.

"Come come nothing!" he snapped. "So your guest behaves like a boor and you, like a good bourgeois. So my wife's a peasant and yours is a fine St. Petersburg lady. But I know we can be great friends. We've something to give each other. Why don't you move to Flushing? You've money enough with your high school job, and your two little girls would bloom not only in summer but all year round — just look at my little Bertha! Oh well, don't answer me now, but visit us soon. Will you come? Be our neighbors and Olga will bake an extra loaf for Sonyatchka every morning."

I laughed, "So that's why you came to see us, to lure us out of the city? Not much chance." I spoke of my German Teachers group and my tutoring classes. But before departing, he made us promise to visit.

We left our flat on a golden September day, unprepared for the gleaming fields and the air fragrant with autumn. The maple trees with scarlet leaves, the gentle slopes and the meadows ravished our eyes. Could Badanes have been prophetic? we asked when, after a week, we returned to "consider" houses. Of course we were not aware that our friend had examined them all and spoken for one which he "knew" would fit our needs. It was only after he showed its virtues and we agreed that he let us in on his secret. "And now," he chortled, "We drink a toast to your future home."

Weeks passed before we could make the move, but once it was done we knew we had acted wisely. Olga lost no time in explaining country ways to the city greenhorns, and thanks to her patience, Eva and Mary learned about chickens and cows. Sonya would have her own garden next spring. Eva might even help. And one day soon they would all go out on a most exciting adventure: finding "the perfect dog to protect our household." Olga led the way: to a nearby farm whose owner "would have an idea." His wife showed them into a barn where they fell instantly in love with a half-grown St. Bernard, to whom I was joyfully introduced that evening. We now had another — four-legged — child in the house.

He was named Manhattan, the place I had feared might prove too far for travel each day. To be sure, before we moved, I questioned Badanes, only to have him say he'd commuted for years and found it a boon: one used the time for preparing the next day's schoolwork, which meant that the nights were free. From DeWitt Clinton, I took a tram to the ferry, then a train and another tram, topping it off with a pleasant walk to the house.

Sonya would sit on the porch, watching the corner street-lamp, while the dog rushed down to meet me. By the time winter arrived, I was able to plan my trips to allow for pleasure reading, for which I never before could have stolen the time.

Each weekend became a holiday to which we looked forward, eagerly planning whenever we could. Sonya's father, alone or joined by a daughter, paid us a monthly visit. The chance for discussions with Saul attracted him quite as much as playing with Eva and Mary, both of whom ran to greet him the moment they spied his rosy cheeks and silvery beard and his black St. Petersburg coat. It was easy enough to persuade our city friends to visit us, but my German Teachers group was another matter. Weeks passed before we could find a date that would suit them all and provide us time for preparing. I proposed a gala affair, and Sonya made no objection to starting with oysters. But special forks would be needed. When I said she might try to borrow them from some Gentile neighbors, she glared at me. Even our atheist friend was taken aback. There were limits even for non-observant Jews.

Our party, everyone said, was a "real" success. The table was handsomely laid and Sonya had never been so gracious a hostess or served so varied a menu. Though Eva did only passably well with the Schubert songs I had taught her, she received such warm applause for her singing of *Röslein auf der Heiden* that she had to re-render it twice. Once the group departed, some neighbors called to say how impressed they had been by the guests. They asked to talk to the hostess, but Sonya was busy tending Mary, who had stuffed herself with watermelon and cucumbers.

Saul and Olga, concerned for the child, called in the evening. "Cats," he sighed, "have much more sense when it comes to eating. They know when to stop." I nodded. "Oh well," he went on, "with Mary, at least it wasn't the oysters. I know an atheist Jew who gets sick at the sight of them."

"Is his name Badanes?" He shrugged. "I wonder, Saul, what kind of Jew you would say you are?"

"The kind that was born as one and will die as one."

"What about Yahweh — God — the Lord . . . ?"

"You sound like Napoleon quizzing Laplace and you'll get the same answer. His cosmic scheme didn't need that hypothesis; neither does mine."

"But your Socialist faith — how does that fit your scheme?"

"Faith?" he exploded. "It's only a hope. For all Karl Marx's proofs, it's still just a hope . . . and probably much too high for human animals. Ask the Germans of '48! Ask the French of the barricades! Even ask your wonderful Uriel da Costa!" His voice grew curiously sharp. "You've called him the very first secular Jew. He was no such thing at the start. It was only after deciding that Moses never had spoken with God, and then he became" — he paused before going on — "the kind of secular Jew that you claim to be but aren't." He wagged his finger at me. "Da Costa at last outgrew all need of a faith. Not you, Ludwig: you have *great* faith: you believe in the good at the core of man. Every Humanist does. He has to, to remain a Humanist. Now then, tell me how you can be both a secular man and a worshipper? All that you've done is to change the Almighty's address: from the heavens above to the heart of man."

"Not at all," I protested. "We're talking of different things with identical words. For me, there's no such thing as religion without some supernatural force. And there's nothing supernatural in the possibilities for good in the nature of man — which is where I place my godless faith in the future."

Olga tiptoed into the room. "Sonya's asleep. I made her forget the dishes. We do them tomorrow. Now — have you two settled the oyster question?"

We both answered, "Forever!"

"Good, then we go to bed. Come, Bah-dah-nis."

He returned with her in the morning, but before I could welcome them in, he shouted, "We only touched the tip of the iceberg." I must have appeared bewildered. "Being a Jew in America, Ludwig. Every time I think that I've found the answer, a new question appears. Bertha announced at breakfast she must have a Christmas tree in December."

"What did you tell her?"

"I said, 'We'll see.'"

"It's just a question of time for Eva and Mary."

"Would Sonya agree?"

"If the other children here have parties and presents, why shouldn't ours? It will take some careful explaining, but I know we can make them understand their difference — Eva at least."

"If you tell them the Church invented it all just to woo the pagans, they'll ask if we're also pagans. No, no. Either we let them do what our neighbors do or we tell them the crazy truth."

"We can do both and more — they're intelligent children. They'll take pride in knowing more than their Gentile friends. I'll explain the winter solstice festivals, all the different names for Santa Claus, why it didn't begin till centuries after their 'Savior' died."

He grunted at first "I suppose so," then shook his head. "Oysters to start, then Christmas. Where do we stop?"

"Wherever we wish. As you said, we were born as Jews and we'll die as Jews . . . and see to it that our children say the same."

He appeared relieved for the moment at least. "Back to your work!" he waved me off. "I know you must finish writing today, but I simply had to —"

"Nonsense." I would have liked to go on, for my thoughts seemed to find a way of resolving themselves when we talked, whatever the subject. Even a merely ephemeral hint could ignite it — "the most challenging mind I've met," as I said to Sonya. "It probes beneath and around and above before it can rest." With every passing week he was leading me farther away from what he contemned as my "wholly unuseable, self-indulgent obsession with language" to join with him in "the richest of all pursuits: a review of educational theory." What if it took us a year? It was something we owed ourselves not only as teachers but also as men imbued with our separate missions. In this "broadest of all pursuits" they would merge as one. If all went well, we would start as soon as the paper Buchanan had urged me to write was finished. Saul had already compiled the list of authors and ordered the needed books in German and English.

Of our ten "greats," some — like Rousseau — were already familiar; nonetheless we examined *Emile* with as much care as the less-known work of Comenius, whose concepts had brought him world renown a century earlier. Our approach throughout was the same: weighing the useable contributions from Fichte to Horace Mann, Pestalozzi to Montessori, Froebel and Herbart to Dewey and Rhein, and their model schools. To do what had to be done in depth, we planned with care, each of us taking parts of a text on which we reported weekly, then relating the parts to all we had studied before. At the end of the second summer, we reassessed the entire pursuit. Our conclusions would often differ: each of us found new reasons to cling to the separate godless faiths we had held before. Convinced at last that neither would change the other, we agreed to give up trying — and comfort ourselves with the greatest lesson of all. Our years of study had reinforced the hope that we shared in common: *learning and knowledge alone can reshape the Future of Man*!

In the short time that remained of summer vacation, we made the most of the country about us. Our girls had begun to blossom — Mary, of course, but Eva too, who had entered the world as a far from attractive child. Blue-eyed and rosy, romping about with their friends all day, they were busy from morning till night, hunting hedges for snails and lady-bugs, gathering Stars of Bethlehem, dipping their toes in the brook, even jumping across a snake when they happened to find one. Sonya, but for her household chores, would have spent all day in her garden, watched by our dog, who was never far from her side. To my great surprise, she had grown rather fond of Olga. What made them friends was past my power of explaining. Olga's appearance alone would keep me from making casual calls. With her hair wound up in a knot and her body wrapped in an over-sized apron, she always seemed to be padding about on her large bare feet from the porch to the kitchen to scream at her chickens. Her proudest delight was her carefully ordered parlor, which overflowed with miniature china animals. She could never thank Sonya enough for helping her tie these gems with pink satin bows — as Eva and Mary could never thank her enough for letting them take, in exchange for churning her freezer, all the ice cream their bottomless bellies could hold.

On the morning that followed Labor Day, Sonya and Eva, half reluc-tant, set out for school. Like others in rural places, ours was an old red-painted building cramped for space, with two or more classes sharing one room. The house was heated, poorly of course, by a large black stove. As they stood in line, the children were given daily marks for "heel and toe," pointed outward and shaped in a V. What concerned us most were the hours they spent in the basement; its dampness explained their endless sniffles and colds.

"There are worse places," Badanes remarked as we took the tram into town. "Citizens get what they ask — do our neighbors complain? Besides, our girls will survive" — he looked at me strangely — "better, maybe, than you." I pressed for his meaning. "Ten quick years and each will be changed to a different person, while you'll keep on drilling the same irregular Ger-man verbs and Latin declensions the rest of your life. Do you like that prospect? Why did you study Froebel and Rhein? — Use the knowledge! Look around! The city's growing — so are your chances." Before he could add a word we rushed on our separate ways. His face stared like a phantom in front of me all day long. The next two nights he stayed in Manhattan. By then the phantom had been replaced by an echo: "The city's growing — so are your chances." When I cornered him to explain, he laughed, "Do you think I'm hiding some news? I have no spies at the Board. As I said to you, Look around! If we keep our ears and our eyes open, we'll know when there's something to aim for. Meanwhile, enjoy your restlessness!"

Soon it was Saul's turn to be tipped off balance. "By the way, you may tell Bertha," I said one day as we boarded the tram, "her wish will come partly true. We'll be having a tree at Christmas for all our girls. Not only Eva and Mary. The party's for Bertha too — and her pious parents, that is, if they'll come." He gave me a puzzled glance. "Eva is sure to tell her. I thought I might warn you."

"Thank you so much, so much," he smirked and put his nose in his papers. Nothing was said as the weeks slipped by. Olga merely shrugged when Bertha went off on a shopping trip with Sonya, Eva, and Mary. The girls gaped with delight when the tree at last was set in place and Sonya hung it with baubles and stars. "It's really a family party — my sister Leah's coming from Grand Street — her three sons are exactly your ages."

Our neighbors were overjoyed at the white Christmas. As I led the guests toward our house, the boys rushed on ahead. Before they could shake the snow from their coats, they spotted the tree and leaped at the branches, pulled at them, ripping them off the trunk, and jumped on the baubles and stars. They had moved too fast to be stopped. Nobody said a word.

"Olga," Sonya recovered her poise, "will you help with the serving? We'll put all the trays on the dining-room table." I motioned to Saul and the boys' parents to follow me there.

We had nearly finished the meal when Sonya winked at the girls. "Don't you want to open your presents? There's something for everyone." Eva, Bertha, and Mary rushed to her, clinging and shaking their heads. Sonya rose from her place and into the parlor; Olga followed. When they both returned, their arms were heaped with boxes. Olga handed Eva the ones for the girls. Before Sonya could do the same with the others, her sister reached for them. "It's a very long trip home — it's late already. Put on your coats, boys," she ordered, "now, now!"

The moment the city guests departed, the girls fell upon Sonya, bursting with sobs and moaning "The beautiful tree, our beautiful tree . . ." Eva screamed "I hate them, I hate them." Sonya tried to soothe her with kisses. "No, no, Eva. I must have forgotten to say we were having a tree. Don't hate them! Their foolish heads didn't know what their hands were doing. Isn't that right, Olga?" Olga, bringing a coat to her daughter, dropped her eyes. Bertha walked up to Sonya, "Thank you for making the tree for me and Eva and Mary — and my beautiful present." Saul and I avoided each other's eyes as he opened the door to leave.

When I came to his house next morning, he whined reproachfully, "Well, are we going at last?"

"Tomorrow. Sonya's in bed."

He nodded. "Of course — why not — after yesterday's pleasures!" I shook my head half-smiling. "No?" He thought for a moment. "Then it's Child Number 3." I said we couldn't be sure. "Sabsowitch can!" he exploded. "Come, we'll go to the city and bring him, and Olga will stay while we're gone." Sonya had other ideas: we'd *all* make the trip. By noon we were on our way.

The visit more than made up for our wretched Christmas. Sabsowitch confirmed our hopes and also offered "to usher the infant into the world with my own two hands — and on Labor Day, if my guess is right." Sonya went straight to her sister Pauline, who had plans for taking the girls on a little tour of the city, including treats. When they reached the flat, the children's grandfather hid by the door. Then he led them into his room and made them guess what his boxes of gifts contained.

He must have left in a couple of hours for when Saul and I reached his café, he was there. Too bad we had come too late, he said, to hear about Herzl's foolish faith in the Sultan, who'd be even worse than the Kaiser. Then, he went on, a man in front had heard a Reform rabbi announce "Washington is my Zion," followed up with a call to destroy Zionists. "What's it to him," a newcomer called, "if I make up my mind tomorrow to move to Palestine? As a matter of fact, things are fine in Petah-Tikvah in spite of Arabs and Turks and the heat and malaria. At least they'll never run our risk of watching Jewishness disappear in a Melting Pot. Remember: since the beginning, Jews have been Jews and nothing else."

"Ignorant nonsense!" somebody shouted. Everyone quieted. The shouter, a well-known scholar, merely shrugged. When he finally rose, he faced about, sighing wearily. "Now comes a lecture," Saul chuckled. The speaker shot out his hand with each phrase: "If you'd read Exodus and weren't asleep, you'd know that the people who followed Moses from Egypt were not only Hebrews but *erev rav* — a mixed multitude. And that was only the start. Ask yourselves: how could the twelve small tribes that defeated Canaan grow by Caesar's time to about eight million? Ten of the tribes disappeared, yet in five short centuries they were more than two million in Palestine only — and one out of every ten in the Romans' empire. How did it happen? Miracles?" He shrugged with contempt. "Conversion! Converting heathens: every kind of conversion. The Sadducees used force, and the Pharisees used example. But many more came on their own. Pagans who saw how we prospered; women who called themselves 'fearers of God'; slaves when they gained their freedom; later even some kings: Adiabene,

Yemen, Khazar." He shrugged again and shot out his arms. "Today, by rights, we should be two hundred million . . . 'by rights,'" he sneered. "Well — what had happened? Tell me!" He paused. "Lecture is over."

Sonya's father tugged at me. "Come. We must go." I'd much have preferred to stay, but Pauline had mentioned an early supper. Besides, if anything new arose, Saul would surely say on our journey home.

As it happened, the talk that ensued led to a long debate on Herzl's solution. The Socialists scoffed, convinced that, with all its risks, only their creed could "save the world from the people," as Saul had put it, and obviate racial strife. Disinclined though I was to carp, I heard myself saying that Jews, by temperament, were unsuited to *any* scheme which would make them hew to a norm. It was evident through their history. They had always wrangled among themselves, from the wilderness years to their terrible civil wars. "Every Jew decides for himself, whatever the cost to his fellows, even himself."

"You're saying they'll never make 'socialist sheep.'"

"They might for a while, but then —"

"They'd have to be forced? Maybe. In any case, the world can't go on as it is." I raised my eyebrows. "You really think it can, in America," he shook his head. "We're back to the same tip-of-the-iceberg problem." He laughed when we said goodnight. "Pleasant dreams! It'll still be there in the morning."

As my class vacation ended, I realized I had given no thought to the changed name of my school. "So it's 'DeWitt Clinton High School' — no more 'Boys'? — Politics!" Badanes scoffed. "If you doubt me, ask your principal, though he's probably part of it too."

Buchanan ended my wondering. "I've something to tell you," he said when I entered his office. "This city's growing so fast, we can't keep pace. By the end of the term I'll have two new branches, and others will follow. We can find the space, but the great problem is people to run them. Next year there'll be an examination" — he read from a note on his desk — "for the position of vice-principal in the New York City High Schools. I hope you'll arrange to take it. Once you pass, you can move ahead as fast as you wish. I have some books to suggest to you."

"Thank you, Dr. Buchanan. When may —" Before I could finish, he held out an envelope. "Oh — how very very — kind," I was speechless with thanks. He beamed, waving me out of the room.

My first thought that night, after telling Sonya, was to urge Badanes to enter the list. "You've lost your reason," he laughed nervously. "Can't you just hear me making a speech with my horrible accent to a hall full of critical high school boys? They'd howl me out of the place. — No, no! I'm fine where I am. — But we'll study together . . . and I'll teach you all I learned — mostly how to 'obey' the stupid orders from higher-ups on the Board. Now show me Buchanan's list."

As we thought of the coming months, our household lived in a state of excited content. Our third child, due in autumn, turned me into a home-body, giving me twice the time that I'd need for study. The weeks passed by, the air shivered with spring. In the wake of fitful cold, sickness swept the city. Of all the people dear to us, one was severely stricken: sister Pauline.

As we reached our house after the burial service, Sonya sighed, "Whenever I carry a baby, somebody in my family dies."

Eva tugged at her skirt. "All good things come in three's. That's what you've always told us, Mama. What did you mean? Girl babies."

"Grandpa couldn't come back with us," she said, "but he sent a present for each of you. Come, you can open them now while I make the tea. Then we'll let Papa go back to work in his study."

Before I set out for the fateful examination, Saul warned me, "Write as much as they ask, then add some more. Don't hold back! Tell them all that you know! You're twice as smart as the people who'll mark your paper." His assurance helped my hopes, which began to sink when I saw the lines of applicants waiting for places. News had spread that hundreds of college professors had come from every state to compete for thirty vacancies. Two days later the Board announced the results. My head reeled when I learned I had won first place, with a mark of 97½%. The news created a stir. The daily papers featured the story, stressing the fact that the man who came out on top out of 700 was an immigrant Jew who had lived in America barely more than ten years.

Letters and telegrams flooded my desk and Buchanan's. Before I could read them all, a note arrived by hand from a man named Samuel Levy, the President of the Hebrew Sheltering Guardian Orphan Asylum, located at Broadway and 150th Street. Could he interest me in becoming the head of his orphanage? I answered politely No: that the Board of Education had just appointed me Vice-principal of a high school. I thought no more of it, nor did Sonya and Saul, who were much too busy planning a big party-surprise for my birthday.

A few days later, Buchanan asked that I come for a talk. "Sit down," he smiled when I entered. "Ludwig, we're colleagues now." He had never used the name before. "This morning 'we' had a visitor: a student from back in my Kansas days — Henry Wollman. He's now a well-known lawyer, also one of the Board of the Hebrew Sheltering Guardian Orphan Asylum. He's urging me to persuade you to talk with his friend Judge Levy, to hear what he has to say."

"Have you met Levy?" I asked.

"No, but from Henry's account, he's well worth meeting. Graduated from college at seventeen, then after his law degree, he was made a city magistrate, then a special sessions justice, and now the Judge of the Children's Court. But that's just part of the story. More important to me is his work for the needy. He's served the United Hebrew Charities for fourteen years, offering legal assistance free of cost to the poor and to children charged with a first offense. And now he's all wrapped up in plans for the orphan home. Henry says he's determined to make it the best in the world. Of course, he knows nothing at all about education."

"And I know nothing at all about orphan homes."

"I told Henry you'd have to persuade yourself." I nodded and rose to leave. He walked with me to the door. "Thank you for coming, Ludwig."

The interview with the Judge was an odd affair. Sure that my presence meant I had changed my mind, he began with a brief account of the 'H.S.G.S.,' as he called it, from its founding in 1879 on east 57th Street by the wife of a former Civil War brigadier-general. "And in five short years, four buildings were needed just for the infants and boys, with a fifth for girls — more than a mile away — a cumbersome arrangement soon resolved by moving the 800 charges into the former Union Home and School for the Children of Our Soldiers and Sailors — in rural Washington Heights — 150th Street between what we call 'Broadway' and the Hudson. The Board of Managers," Levy went on, assuming every detail concerned me greatly, "consisted of fifteen ladies, and even five years ago, when they made me the President, women were still in charge. But the picture has totally changed. We've now a Board of Directors of men — men of outstanding achievement — and foresight — and dedication, such as Leonard Lewisohn and Louis Seligsberg. I know," he smiled, "you'll be greatly impressed when you meet them."

"Forgive me, Judge," I said at last, "and please don't think me ungracious, but I feel that whatever contribution I have to offer *should* be most effectively made through the *public* schools. I lack the words to say how much I admire all that you and your colleagues have done."

"Done? Why, we've barely started! I haven't even mentioned our plans."

He frowned, piercing me with his eyes. "Our problem is making them work. It calls for the knowledge and skills that we lack — the kind you possess, Doctor. Our critical moment has come, when more must be done for these wretched children than merely clothe, feed, and *plainly* educate. When they offered me the Presidency, I accepted on one condition: that I have a free hand to achieve my goal: the *individualizing* of *every* child."

I could hardly believe my ears. It took me moments before I could say "I also revere Pestalozzi."

"Who?"

"Johann Pestalozzi!"

"The name's unknown to me."

"A Swiss philosopher — the founder of modern education — you're almost using his words: 'The individuality of each child is paramount.' He said it almost a hundred years ago."

"A hundred years ago!" he shook his head, half-smiling, "As I told you, we lack the knowledge. But tell me, Doctor, what do you know about homes for our poor, neglected, abandoned, or orphaned children? Have you ever visited one?" This time it was I who shook his head. "Doctor, how can a thoughtful man reject out of hand the greatest chance he may ever have to help remake these innocent, victimized children into strong, intelligent, self-reliant, and proud American Jews? At the very least, pay them a visit and *then* make up your mind. Is this asking too much?"

I gave Sonya a careful report of our meeting. She had no comment to offer. Her eyes were fixed on our baby Pauline, perched in front of us, who was trying to pick the flowers out of the carpet. "I've read what I could about orphan homes," I went on, "but there's almost nothing . . . I'm to call at the Judge's chambers . . . As he said, the least I can do is *visit* the place." She nodded and left my side to tie the white lace cap on the baby's head. We had no reason to speak of the matter again till a note from Levy arrived, stating the hour he intended to call for me at my school.

"It was quite the best we could find at the time," Levy apologized as we neared the building. "The original part is the same — the mansion built for Cyrus Field — his company laid the telegraph cable across the Atlantic. He spared no expense. Behind the enormous windows facing the street is a geometrically perfect circular room, with fine arches, marble floors, and the like — parlors and sleeping chambers. The westerly one has a splendid view of the Hudson. But the other quarters" — he winced — "possibly they might do for 300 children, not the 900 crowded there. But remember, please, what I've told you. We'll build the finest home in the world for our boys and girls." We sat in silence for moments. "About a third of them have only one living parent; more than half are the destitute or deserted." We relapsed into silence. "I trust you're prepared, Doctor. When I look at these boys and girls, I think of them not as they are but *as they are going to be*. Otherwise I would shut my eyes."

"You've given me fair warning," I said as we entered. But the sights were worse than I'd feared. At once I asked why the children's heads were shorn to the scalp. "Ringworm epidemic, and finally under control." I raised no further questions. I had no need to ask why every face I saw had a haunted look — why the children seemed so pale as they moved about in their uniforms, aprons, and high-necked dresses, making it often difficult to tell a boy from a girl. After hastily greeting the staff — from the bookkeeper Superintendent and his Matron wife, to the monitors, nursery maids — I was shown the entire premises: the dormitories, dining room, kitchen areas, playing grounds, and the like. As we moved from place to place, Levy kept up a running account of everything but the sights before us. "Three plans, as I said, are being considered: the cottage system, the pavilion, and a possible combination. I'm much inclined toward the first, and I'm hoping to visit a cottage home at Barkenside, England. The will of the late Leonard Lewisohn started us off with a gift of $50,000 and another 75 if we raise that much by subscription. Rest assured that we shall. Please give all these facts to Dr. Buchanan. He'll probably mention the Charity School in *Oliver Twist*. Thank heaven, this isn't quite *that* bad, don't you think?" I told him I hadn't read the Dickens story.

"But oh, I've almost forgot," he seized my arm, "I must show you where Field and his family lived." He led the way from the entrance hall up a magnificent stairway with broad mahogany bannisters, then into a great bright parlor. He pointed out the silver and black Carrara floors, the arches tapering into a dome-like ceiling painted with angels, the enormous picture-window facing the street with a view of the garden below "where your girls will play, safely enclosed by the hedges. As you see," he smiled, leading from room to room, "you have far more space than you need. I'm sure your wife will be pleased. She'll enjoy the change from the country cottage to a city mansion — which has also a country air. Would you care to walk through the place again?" I shook my head, thanked him, and said I was much impressed. But my words belied the heaviness in my heart.

By the time his carriage reached my school, Levy had filled my head with "some confidential words." Leonard Lewisohn's place on the Board would be filled by his younger brother, Adolph: "also a copper magnate, but a person of rare foresight, as different from your typical millionaire as the day from night . . . with his special devotion to orphans — himself orphaned before he was six years old. A man without formal schooling, yet in his curious, practical way, voracious for knowledge, with a high regard for learning, talent, brains: for men who know what he doesn't know. I've arranged to make him our President." He went on to name the other Directors, following each with a capsule characterization. "All in all, as you'll see, an ideal group." When the carriage stopped, he pressed my arm and bade me goodbye.

I found Buchanan bent at his desk. Hearing my steps, he looked up, nodded, studied my face. "When you're ready to talk, Ludwig, tell me" — the words came slowly — "how shall I put it? Now that you've made your visit, tell me about *yourself*."

"Torn in a dozen directions," I tried to smile. "My heart goes out to those pale unhappy children — all in orphans' uniforms, heads shaved to the scalp. You'd feel the same if you saw them. As for the place, the living quarters, the staff — shall I give a description?" He shook his head. "Anyone could make it a great deal better, given the chance, and Levy offers *carte blanche*. I'm also convinced he'll make it the best of its kind. But he doesn't need *my* help; he knows what needs to be done. That's why I wonder why he solicits a man without the slightest knowledge of orphan care. Public education is all that I know, all that I've studied. The Great Enlightenment —"

"Great?" he jumped up angrily. "The Enlightenment couldn't abide your people. Voltaire denied you the right to freedom. How can a thoughtful Jew admire a bigot?" He paced up and down, his jaw clenched. I had never known him to rage. Minutes lagged before he came back to his desk. "Ludwig, I won't mince words. As a social-minded, responsible Jew, you owe a debt to your people — an obligation to put to use for their welfare all that you've learned in this country. Moreover, this task is a brilliant challenge, greater by far than any you'd otherwise face: the *education* and care of *victimized* children. Judge Levy will grant your every wish, provide you with all you need. I tell you an offer like this will *never* come by again. Take it!"

As I traveled home, I reviewed the words I had hoped to say to Buchanan. He had closed all doors to discussion: even to grant a Humanist's failing was not allowed . . . A Jew had to take an all-or-nothing stand, condemning the whole of a man's achievement because of one aberration. And the same logic — rejecting even the good that had come to the world — lay behind his injunction *Take it*! Buchanan would make my decision: to cross him might surely endanger my teaching career! Regardless of doubts, risks, or personal preference, a Jew's choice must conform to *his people's* needs! I had something new to remember: Put yourself forth as a citizen of the world, and the world will push you aside as a renegade Jew.

Sonya was hardly pleased by the thought of giving up our sequestered life for the semi-public world of the HSGS. I expected as much. She wondered aloud how such a move would affect our children, saying nothing at all of fears for herself. "One thing," I announced, "I made utterly clear. If we make the change, you can live as private a life as you please and with not a single obligation whatever — none, not any, to the HSGS, the Judge, the Board — *anyone,* Sonya. All who know you admire you just as you are — your retiring nature, your sensitive mind, your devotion to our children."

She blushed. "Go on with you!" waving me off. "When will you talk with Saul? He's waiting. Better go out and explain."

Before I could start, he bellowed, "Put your fate in the hands of the German rich, when you've just received the most crucial thing you could ask for? For the rest of your life, absolute freedom from want. For your wife and children, money — and more: security. For yourself, the finest possible chance to rise to the top, with the record you've made and your excellent speech, manners, ambition, brain . . . Just stop for a minute and think! If you stay in the schools, you'll be freed from worries forever! Even stupid Buchanan would have to admit it — it's so *laughably* clear. But no! They've flattered you out of your sense or you wouldn't be wasting a thought on that HSGS."

It was useless to argue Levy's and Lewisohn's "difference." To Saul Badanes, all Uptown Jews were the same: rich, basically ruthless, driven by money and power, yet also scared that their immigrant brothers would one day tear off the mask they'd contrived to prove they were really much more Christian than Jew. "But they know it's a hopeless hope. So what do they do? The next best thing." He pointed at me. "With their money, position, and power, they've appointed themselves the Voice of America's Jews. Oh they'll help our poor and needy, all right, but only so long as *they* keep control, only so long as you do what *they* like, follow *their* rules. But once you fall out of line or challenge their 'wisdom,'" he stopped for a moment, in fury, "they'll do to you what Amsterdam's rabbis did to da Costa. Not 39 lashes, but courteous smiles. Don't be a second Uriel!"*

---

*Uriel da Costa, a Portuguese Catholic convert, fled to Amsterdam in 1615, bent on saving his soul by living according to Moses, only to find himself forced to obey a different Judaism ruled by the rabbis. Excommunicated twice, he died a suicide. (See *The Refusers,* Book II.)

His fierce concern for my future moved me more than his logic, which impugned any decent act by the rich. His cautions, however, could not be scorned. There was no disputing the risk in rejecting a sure career in the schools for something unknown. And yet the latter might bring rewards of a deeper, much more humanly grateful kind. To hold in one's hand the fate of a thousand benighted lives; to be given the means of flooding these lives with sunlight and strength and happiness! — how could any believer in justice turn from the chance? Saul would cry back with the stock reply: that *all* victimized lives must be salvaged: Socialist justice alone could redress the evils of fate. "Perhaps," I nodded, "but when? 'In time?' — *after* you've wakened the world to act. How can these miserable children wait till the world listens?"

"Tell me: what can you *really do* for your handful of innocents after you dress them in clean, new clothes, build up their bodies, brighten their halls, teach them to laugh and sing and play like — usual children?"

"Train them to cope with the world" — I was taken aback by my own reply: the question had never been asked. "Strengthen their minds and bodies so they can hold their own — and *more*!" — my words were new to my ears — "equip them *better than others* to cope with this world."

"What a mission! *Over*compensate for Yahweh's injustice! Do what He should have done! Teach by example!" He smiled acidly. "Moses wrote out laws for the Jews — you're going him one step better. Why not? It's your pious right as a secular Jew." He paused, waiting to pounce if I tried to explain. I held my tongue. "Amusing, isn't it, Ludwig, since you'll also have to make sure they're observant Hebrews. After all, there's the H in the HSGS."

My head hung in dismay. There were limits to what a man dared say to a friend. To try to reply in kind would be worse than vain, even if words could be found. How explain there was something other than reason at stake? After minutes, I said to him, "Come with me, please! Visit this place! You might change your tune."

"Never!" The ear-splitting scream made Sonya rush to the porch. I could only look at her helplessly.

Our hearts shook as we watched him dashing away to his house, kicking up stones in the path. I repeated to Sonya all he had said, and my answer. "Poor Olga," she sighed. "He even tried to coax me to change your mind. He's so very sure that he's right."

"Buchanan's sure that he's wrong."

"And you?" she laughed, winking both eyes.

"I've sent some questions to Levy. One of them deals with where we might live. We must have the right to a home away from the place, if we wish."

"You asked that for my sake?"

"Haven't I made myself clear? *We'll* decide about the HSGS *after* Levy replies."

"Why, when you've just announced it to Saul?"

"You mean — " I bumbled.

"Saul knows," she smiled faintly, "and Eva knows. She remembers why you changed your mind on the train to Hamburg. I've told the children about the big round room in front and the river in back and all the friends" — she broke off suddenly — "Look outside, Ludwig!" Olga, clutching a pan of cakes, hurried our way as fast as her bare feet carried her. "Peace offering. Maybe she'll make him come to tea if I beg her." I shook my head but she stepped from the porch to meet her.

Events began to move swiftly. Levy called for a Board of Directors meeting to "act on the final arrangements." In his most judicious manner he told the group about all that had taken place from our first encounter. Then he went on to name my specific conditions, one by one. All were approved unanimously. Levy had probably talked in advance to each of the men, for I had the sense that they'd come largely to take a firsthand look at this oddish Courlander immigrant who had turned his back on a safe career for a far from dependable future. To avoid any possible conflict, when I made my acceptance speech, I reminded the group that their vote would give me the right to "do *whatever* I might see fit in remaking their institution — including *any* educational plan that I felt would fulfil its needs." In my summing up, I spoke of the tasks ahead as a co-adventure, which would carry forth our religious and cultural heritage, "which is to say, the Mosaic idea-and-ideal that rests on the rights of the individual man, woman, *and child.*"

"The way you put it, Doctor," Levy smiled, "you demand *carte blanche.* Now you have it." The meeting ended with handshakes, congratulations, and from Lewisohn, a newcomer to the Board, "Auf wiedersehen on March the first or before."

Two weeks later Sonya arranged a party to mark the event. As a mid-December storm whitened the windows, the children fingered the panes. All at once Olga broke into sobs, moaning the news of our leaving. Saul finally coaxed her to join his toast. "To your future, Sonya! . . . and Eva, Mary, Pauline . . . And you, Ludwig, also. May the Lord Almighty help you," he all but sneered, "God knows that you'll need him."

"So will those children," Sonya added quietly. I had told her all I had learned from the few visits I managed to make when my school day ended.

It was far from easy to play the "inspecting guest" without evoking looks of suspicion and fear. But my host, the long incumbent head of the "Home," was doing his limited best, pointing with noble pride to the wax-clean dining and sleeping halls as he led me to every corner and nook of the hideous building, then onto the grounds that sloped to the Hudson River. He only wished I could come early to see how well his orphans behaved, marching to school and back like fine little soldiers, boys in their uniforms, girls in identical dresses, never disturbing the peace of the affluent neighborhood. I took great care to conceal my thoughts, asking only the plainest questions and thanking him for the endless facts he supplied. Yet my presence, I knew, upset him. I had failed to applaud the things that excited his pride. He had wanted more than courteous nods in response.

A month went by before I felt safe in asking about his staff. He was visibly offended — even after I said, "But my dear Mr. Fauerbach, everyone knows that you chose your people with skill and care, just as I know you will give me your honest assessment of each." Clearing his throat, he pulled out a drawer from the desk and opened a ledger. One by one he reeled off the names, listing the tasks of each. "Excellent people, all of them. Loyal, loyal. You'd think they'd have left with all the sickness we have" —

He had touched on the problem that Levy feared might have made me spurn his offer. The Judge wasn't one to dissemble. He decried the children's health as a frightening history — outbreaks of eye infections and lesser afflictions and recently the most stubborn of all: a huge epidemic of scalp ringworm, striking 500 children. It did no good to point to their overcrowding, which would take some years to remedy. And placing the sick in public wards was unthinkable. With characteristic foresight, he set about looking for men equipped to master the problem. Friends at Mt. Sinai Hospital told him of Milton Gershel, their brilliant young chief resident, who had just resigned to devote himself to research. There might still be time to change the physician's plan. The dire plight of the children combined with the medical challenge at length prevailed.

"— And at once he set up a bacteriological laboratory and made a nearby building a hospital annex," Levy added proudly. "Before the end of the year our plague was controlled. But that was only the start. Gershel proceeded to study the health — past and present — of every child. The height and weight of each was recorded, a special diet prescribed for the undernourished. Far too many, of course, were below the average in height.

We learned that of all the parents, almost a fourth had been hospitalized with a chronic disease; that of all the children, a fifth had lived in tubercular homes. Think of it! One out of almost every two from a household racked not only by want but long-term sickness. No wonder Gershel insisted on special standards of sanitation. And they're strictly enforced, as Fauerbach must have warned you." I shook my head. "Gershel," he smiled, "would turn the place upside down, if he could — order a quarantine on the least suspicion. But anyone else in his place, I suppose, would do the same." He thought for a moment. "He's competent — very; wilful — but wide open to new ideas . . . in science, that is. You two should do well together. You're a few years older but much more . . . Well —" he stopped his mouth with his hand. "I'm depending on you, Doctor. By the way, have you met our LJC . . . ?"

LJC, I supposed, meant Louis J. Cohen, head of the boys' division — a proverbial martinet with the heart of gold . . . which in fact he was, and more: a man of impeccable principles, with a rare devotion to children; but my first impression left me somewhat unsure. Not so with the woman in charge of the girls. After five minutes I knew she was hated, feared, and could never be changed. My Educational Alliance friends urged me to talk with Sarah Canter, who directed "Domestic Arts." She had supervised children only, but they guessed she could "manage" the monitors of our girls. A pleasant woman of forty, she was obviously not overburdened with books or culture, but her motherliness exuded from every pore. I decided to take a chance, and asked her to join the HSGS in the middle of March.

We were due to arrive on the third. Having bid goodbye to neighbors at night, we were able to set out early. All went smoothly, in line with Sonya's arrangements — then suddenly there was nothing to do but leave. We eyed one another in silence. Eva and Mary for weeks had jabbered about the exciting "move" but now, embarked on the journey, they lost their tongues. Gazing back at the emptied house, they watched till it disappeared in the morning fog. I had hoped for a fine spring day as an omen, and I tried to believe that the sun would break through the sky. But a thick rain beat on the cobblestone street as our carriage began the last of its travels: up the long, wide boulevard called Broadway.

I was seated beside the driver, with Sonya in back, flanked by our older daughters, the youngest held in her lap. As the rain pounded, I heard myself muttering senseless sounds — number-sounds: "March three/nineteen three/now in your year thirty-three" over and over again while my eyes looked to the left for a glimpse of the huge brown building. The motto inscribed across the sign at the entrance gate flashed in my mind. Turning round to the girls, I said, "When we enter, look at the words just over the doorway. They're fine, beautiful words. 'Shelter us under the shadow of thy wings.' Do you know what they mean, children? The HSGS is a brave strong mothering bird that nurtures its fledglings."

Before I finished, the carriage stopped and the driver, spreading his huge umbrella, opened the door for Sonya. Other men with umbrellas rushed to our sides and ushered us in so fast that I barely heard the noise that had startled our daughters. "Did you see all the children banging the windows and smiling, Mama?" Eva and Mary asked. "Their heads are shaved, so they must be boys."

"No, no," Fauerbach snapped, "They're girls. You should know from their high-necked collars and aprons — but Doctor," he turned on me anxiously, "Please!" — and began to explain the proceedings. Leading us into a foyer hall, he asked us to stand "for a moment or two" so that all who were there could greet us by saying "Welcome." He was now ready to name the men who had come in behalf of the Board, but before he could speak they brushed him aside. Begging Sonya's indulgence for Fauerbach's lack of concern for her comfort, they asked us to move our receiving line to a sitting room in the rear. And there we remained till the last of the welcoming party had said his piece — only to hear from Fauerbach that "the whole of the HSGS" was waiting and that Rabbi Goldstein would lead the induction service.

We followed him into the chapel, which filled with applause when we entered; then he led us up the steps and onto the platform, where he whispered "Doctor, the Reverend Jacob Goldstein," and disappeared.

"Welcome, welcome, at last," the Rabbi beamed. "As you see," he swept his arm toward the audience, "all our boys and girls have awaited this moment. Bear with me, please, while I say a few words both in their behalf and my own." He showed us to our chairs and signaled for silence.

"Dear girls and boys and friends of the HSGS," he began in a deep, rich voice. "Yesterday we said farewell to Mr. and Mrs. Fauerbach at the close of their seventeen years of devoted care. Today we hail the successor, whose presence graces us now." He bent his head for applause. "He of all people will understand why the words of the Latin poet Catullus fly to my lips, though ours is a joyous occasion. 'Ave atque vale — Hail and farewell.' Farewell to those who enter their golden years and hail to the new young chief of our blessed home." The applause deafened my ears. "Let me tell you about this man," he lightened his tone. "Let me tell you the story. Less than a dozen years ago he boarded a train from his native town to start his career in his city of dreams: Paris, the citadel of Enlightenment. But on the way something amazing happened, something led him to change his plans, to deny himself his dream — something that touches the well-spring of human hearts . . ."

As I heard him presenting his florid account, I wondered how he had learned about my "past." Only my intimates knew what he called "the story." Whatever the source, I found it discomfitting to hear a stranger make of my brief career a series of startling triumphs. Nothing that I might say, I knew, could stand up against his performance. Hence I had better limit myself to a sentence of thanks followed by something brief on the privilege given to me to carry forward the splendid plans for a happier HSGS. It would probably do — but the Rabbi had other ideas.

"Doctor," he said, "we shall not presume on your kindness nor ask you to speak to us. This is our day to welcome you and your household — to give you our pledge of loyalty — and to ask the God of our fathers to bless you and keep you and guide you now as you seize the task you have chosen . . . May I ask that everyone rise for the threefold blessing as spoken to Aaron by Moses, in Numbers, chapter 6."

Like a vast wave of muted thunder, the Hebrew words resounded from wall to wall. Sonya's eyes filled with tears. My throat tightened. All I could do was to show my thanks with a nod.

How I wish you could pick up the tale, my son, and spare me from living the first few jubilant years. But you wouldn't be born till after the "transformation." Besides, if your lofty notion about my career is valid, we had better hold to the truth as only I saw it. And yet I would bore us both if I set down all the tittles and jots of my days and nights, crucial though some of them were. You must picture me as obsessed by this orphan's world, where all that I saw begged to be changed and at once! — which was quite impossible, though hard on my native impatience.

How do you lead people to give up ways that they've followed for years? How do you help them *wish* to remake themselves? look on their bygone actions without discomfort or self-disdain? There were no formulas, no orders, commands, or blandishments, falsehoods, manipulation. Instead: reasoning — hard-headed, practical reasoning — and work, in the service of "individualizing every child" — the motto announced by Levy and now on the lips of all. Who could deny the virtue, the justness, the excellence of our goal? And everyone had a part to play, if he or she would work together. Others should pack up and leave. "Only those who feel sure they can take the shocks of the days ahead — which will not be easy — should plan to remain." I kept repeating. Without exception, everyone answered with strong assent. I put small store in such promises, but at least I had sounded a warning.

Let me read from some notes I sent to the Board after I'd seized the reins. I kept them beside my bed and somehow they've still survived!

> "It is neither the hideous checked aprons, nor the terrible bell, nor the institution oil-cloth in the dining room — such things, easily changed, miss the core of *institutionalism*. What concerns me vastly more is the prevalent *nature* of the relationships between the adults and the children. These relationships are official — nothing more, nothing less. The men and women in charge are strict disciplinarians, and disciplinarians only, and the children are judged solely by how their conduct affects the institution rules and routines. . . ." — I put these words in quotation marks for the reason that what they describe belongs to the past — not entirely as yet, but soon — *assuredly soon.*

> We don't feel the least bit horrified when the children yell and shout; when our boys and girls play tricks and pranks on each other. Their voices no longer are dampened by fear of evoking scolding words from their supervisors. Our children have blood and vitality. They have also the right to self-assertion and, to a certain extent, self-determination.

One morning the time seemed suddenly right for announcing my Five Point Program. "Prepare for the unexpected, my friends," I warned Sarah Canter and Louis J. Cohen, as they waited, obviously ill at ease, in my private living room. "Please sit down and be comfortable. I've called you here where no one can see us or interrupt — to tell you what I've in store for our boys and girls and to ask your advice and help. *Nothing will come of these changes unless you can make them yours.* — I want your honest judgment! Plans are subject to change. I'll happily make improvements. Whatever you think, say it!"

"Count on us both, Doctor," Sarah replied.

I rose from my chair. "I hope you won't mind — I like to pace about as I talk. And there's much to say, but I'll be as brief as I can. We should start by taking stock of the HSGS. First, an excellent medical system. Second, a cultivated Rabbi. Third, Sarah, in charge of the girls. Fourth, Louis, in charge of the boys. Fifth, the Judge, but for whose vision we shouldn't be here. To sum up our assets, five excellent people in crucial positions. Keep this in mind as we look at our problems — we've lots of them," I smiled ruefully. "One we can do very little to solve — our makeshift assemblage of buildings. As you know, the Board is studying promising plans. However, so long as we're here we can lessen the overcrowding. But I won't go into that now. I must speak of the all-encompassing problem that curses our children's lives. Let me read from the confidential notes I prepared for the Board . . ."

I let the words sink in, then repeated "institutionalism — a very poor word for describing the core of the problem, which amounts to a matter of *attitude*. How the staff regards the children reflects itself in how the children regard themselves. Your supervisors act on the premise that orphans have to be held in line because *by nature* they're bent on doing wrong. — Who said so? Why must they be controlled as incorrigible sinners? This wouldn't happen if they were living at home. Your supervisors have made them think they're expected to misbehave. Your supervisors are in for the shock of their lives. For the monitor system is over — Point One — I'm announcing its end this evening. Never again will our children be ordered '*One,* jacket off! *Two,* sit down! *Three,* right shoe off! *Four,* left shoe off! *Five,* right stocking on!' and so forth. I'll give the word at supper time.

"I'll also announce Point Two. The main remark that outsiders make about orphan children is the sameness in how they look and behave. After Sunday, no more aprons, no more uniforms! On Monday, when our children walk to school, strangers will not be able to tell them from other children . . . for another reason also — and this is Point Three: no more marching in drill formation like soldiers! Oh I know the idea will strike them at first as strange. Most of them may not know what to do. They've forgotten how to behave like normal children.

"And now — are you ready to hear Point Four?" They nodded hastily. I lighted a cigarette, after vainly offering one to Louis. "Points One, Two, and Three get rid of the obstacles. Now for the New! — Tell me, how many people among us ever think of the HSGS as part of the local community? In numbers alone we're a rather imposing part. But our life inside rarely meets with the life outside. This was one of the reasons I organized clubs for the younger children with kindergarten teachers, who've been teaching them songs, leading in games and talks. Some supervisors complained that it undermined the routines; the children were so keyed up that they bothered the rest. But the fact is that the little ones tugged at my knees with delight: they were having the time of their lives. I've arranged for eleven new clubs so that boys and girls of every age can join the program. Three of the leaders are HSGS alumni — you may know them, Louis; two are daughters of men on our Board. The clubs will meet one evening or afternoon each week, and trips outside will be taken. Philip Seman, my new assistant, screened all the volunteers to note their ideas, interests, talents: music, books, current events. Their responses amazed us. One of them — Morton Rutsky — is planning an operetta about the HSGS. Imagine it! He's been living across Broadway for years and never thought of visiting."

By now I had stopped pacing about. Seated across from my listeners, I waited some moments. Perhaps I should give them time to absorb what they'd already heard. I could save the last for tomorrow. Louis might have been reading my thoughts: "Didn't you talk of a Five Point program?"

I nodded. "Please listen carefully. I'm about to establish a Boys' and a Girls' Republic — one for each. The children themselves will elect their officers and, gradually, with our help and guidance, learn to govern their lives. — Now, before you object, let me say that something resembling it seemed to work — on a very small scale — in the George Junior Republic in upper New York. But nothing remotely like our scheme has been ventured, with so many hundreds and hundreds of boys and girls. I've wrestled with all the questions. Is so much democracy possible? — foolhardy? — dangerous? — even desirable in a huge institution? Will we ever persuade the men and women who make up the staff to cooperate with something they feel could diminish their status? Will the children themselves — suppressed through the years — overreact? run wild with the notion of power? How can we help them learn what self-government means in the deeply responsible sense? How should the limits be drawn? By whom? Myself in league with a children's council? But stop for a moment and think of the possible benefits of this break from the institutional past. It might establish, once and for all, the fact that each child is a separate entity; an individual with his or her rights as an integral part of society, who's entitled to have the chance to express his or her own true uniqueness as a person."

I raised my hand to stop myself. "You see . . . I'm beginning to make a speech to persuade you. — I won't say another word. And please don't tell me now what you think! Tomorrow, perhaps. No, make it here again, two afternoons from now. You might want to discuss it together, but not a word to anyone else!"

Two Saturday mornings later, after the Rabbi's benediction, I announced the birth of the HSGS republics, with a very careful description of how they would work and what they should do for all. Louis and Sarah had meanwhile gathered a special group of children to meet in my office and plan procedures for putting the scheme to work. By then Points One, Two, Three, and Four were all in effect. It had taken a worrisome week for some of the boys and girls to function without the "help" of monitors. At the same time, "city clothes" became a refreshing novelty, as well as the end of the drill formation in walking to school. There were more than a few children, however — because of their troubled backgrounds or of factors outside our knowledge — who appeared unable to live with change. There were also others who chose to keep to themselves. For months I had kept a private file of such cases. In the wake of my new reforms, it grew suddenly large.

Meanwhile all five points of "The Doctor's Program" had won overwhelming support. I was much impressed by the "style" of our club volunteers who seemed to enjoy coping with cases of diffidence, shyness, and fear. Much to my private amusement, boys and girls were starting to ask why we paid no attention to "things right under our noses." Why no club with Blanco, our jack-of-all-technical-trades? Or another, to learn about gardening, chickens, and pigs at the farm next door to the playground? Or, of all things, classes in deep-sea diving with LJC? The small spark we had set was becoming a fire. Luckily I could shift the burdens on Seman, spending my "extra time" in making sound and secure the project I counted on most: the republics.

"Extra time" — by now the phrase had an irony, especially for Sonya, who had almost given up hope of reclaiming the evening family life we had known before. Yet she saw, even better than I, what might come from failing to do *whatever* might have to be done for the thousand surrounding lives, any of which could suffer some urgent demand. And since nearly everything called for change, my working plan for the day might take a week or more, though in time the stubborn objective would be attained. For example: the supervisory staff had at last been cleansed of incompetents, but enlisting the proper replacements was a slow, discouraging task. Similarly with the public school, directed by a former colleague, with whom I had good relations. Without delay he set about finding placements for all our children entitled to enter high school, none of whom knew of their right to continued learning.

Meanwhile, though my daily plan kept listing "Visitors' Days," I hadn't yet looked at the question. Four or five times I began — by sending for Louis J. Cohen — only to hear my stenographer droning "Still more volunteers who insist on seeing you." It was Sonya who finally pressed me to keep myself clear for Visitors' Day. Twice Eva and Mary had stood on watch near the gates as odd-looking strangers, waiting in line, answered questions, then entered to look about wildly till a boy or a girl leaped at them from the crowd. But many children, Eva moaned, kept waiting after the gates had shut. "Did you speak to them?" Sonya began. "Maybe the father or mother was sick and had to stay home." — No, no, Eva and Mary screamed. They sobbed till their throats were dry, then stared through the back window. No amount of comforting talk could make them speak. We both decided to act as though the event had never occurred.

On the next scheduled Visitors' Day, Sonya took both girls to call on her father. The following morning I sent for Louis and Sarah. "I need your help, before I speak after Saturday's services. Here are the notes I'll take to the Board, if need should arise. Tell me if you approve: 'Parents have — in effect — been discouraged from seeing their children. As the number of inmates grew, Visitors' Days were reduced: at the HSGS from a day each month to one in two; in other homes, to one in three. Gifts of candy and fruit are forbidden; kisses, embraces, frowned on, for reasons of health and disease. Unless very drastic changes are made, the tie that still exists between parent and child will be ruined.' — What do you think?" They nodded. "Next Saturday after the benediction, I'll tell you briefly what they will hear. . . ."

As the chapel filled, Sonya, Eva, Mary, and I walked to our usual places. The Rabbi, knowing I planned to speak, made his sermon needlessly short. I had little to say — simply that every child blessed with a father or mother was to write a letter or postcard tomorrow, stating that every parent was more than welcome; that the HSGS Director would be pleased indeed to meet them, talk and explain the new arrangements for Visitors' Days; that children whose parents were less than fluent in English should write, if they could, in Yiddish; and if not, should talk with Miss Canter or Mr. Cohen, who would give the needed assistance. And finally, the Director wished each parent to *know* he was ready to do everything possible to make the future Visitors' Days a *very* happy occasion. . . .

As we talked together outside the chapel, Eva implored, "Mama, please take us out somewhere, *please,* while Papa talks with the people he always sees in his office?"

Sonya glanced at me sharply. "Better make sure, Ludwig," she whispered in German, "that *your* children know they *also* have a father."

Blood rushed to my temples. I thought for a moment. Then, bending close to Eva's face, I asked, "Do you think you can learn to ride a bicycle?"

"With you, Papa?" she gasped with joy. "If you teach me?"

I smiled. "And afterwards, Eva, will you teach Mary?" Both girls nodded wildly. "Then come! And we'll all go down to the stores and see what they have. And on our way we'll stop off for lunch."

"In a restaurant, Papa?" Eva's eyes seemed to leap from her cheeks. Both girls squealed, skipping as fast as they could toward the great wood bannister at the foot of the steps that spiraled up to our door.

"In twenty minutes, Sonya?" I asked. "It may take that long to change the appointments. Possibly less. Will you have enough time to get them ready?" Eva and Mary both beamed down from the landing.

Our outing proved an unending success — I'd forgotten how much delight I could take in my daughters. Hours afterwards, lying in bed, staring half-asleep at the night's darkness, I seemed to hear my heart accusing my brain. Every day you set out on chartless waters, fearless, alone, sure, fixed on a destination mapped in your head — steering wherever it leads you, never stopping to see if your craft might have sunk in a maelstrom out of which you've surfaced alive, but with part of you lost . . . I jumped from the bed, tiptoed quickly into an empty room, sank in a chair. Why had it taken a sharp rebuke to set me back on my course? "Papa's always talking with other people," said Eva. — I wrote a simple letter to Sonya, thanked her for all she had done today. She would find it under my pillow in the morning, she would read it after the children had gone to school. I lighted my pipe. No time left for trying to sleep. Rather to probe, assay, heal, rearrange.

"Dr. Gershel came just as you left," my stenographer greeted me. "It was something special, he said. He'll be back tomorrow." By now we'd become good friends — with Sonya also. Whenever he'd knock at our door, our girls would sweetly jostle him toward our piano and beg him to play "While We Go Marching Through Georgia." Holding each other's shoulders, with Eva in front, the trio would snake-dance in and out of the drawing-room arches, again and again until the pianist pleaded for mercy. In our quiet moments we'd chat about everything on our minds, from the foibles of certain men on the Board — and their wives — to the fishing trips that we'd take some day when we found the time, which we swore would be soon.

Being "the two great doctors discovered by Levy," we shared the Judge's shining hopes, but they never entered our talk. Nor did our workaday problems. We were reaching the age when nostalgia would add a bitter sweet to the plans we'd confess for our futures. It was then that our friend might ruminate about going back one day to his "true career . . . I can't put it off forever. Any doctor could do what I do in this place. Tell me, Sonya, why am I waiting?" She'd offer to take her cards and read his fortune and he'd wave her off ("I'd as soon you'd study my palm. I'm a scientist! — but you're . . . well —") and we'd change the subject. Several times I had hoped I might stir his interest in the boys and girls I had labeled FAIL TO ADJUST AND RELATED CASES. "You'd have to make a special study of each in the file," he replied, "and where could you get the funds or the people to do the work?" A research project or nothing. Between the medical man and the humanist: always the great divide. I might have to look about elsewhere, since the problem, begun as a few exceptional cases, was taking a new dimension.

Our only other nearby friends had also been brought by Levy. Like everyone else, Sonya and I enjoyed the Rabbi's magnificent smile, flashing eyes, and fine demeanor. That his lightning bursts of anger always gave way to remorse seemed part of his self-design as a latterday prophet. Despite my efforts, he never discussed his Australian past or how he had found the leisure to learn the philosophers, poets, and other greats whose phrases studded his sermons. He preferred telling the tales of his current achievement: "Before I arrived, the Superintendent — mind you, the Superintendent! — led the religious services. Could anything be more absurd? No wonder the children knew nothing about their faith, history, culture, language, or God. A thousand Hebrew heathens in a *Hebrew* asylum!" Signs of possible lightning played on his brow. "How make a start? With the older boys and girls, of course. How can one speak the same sentence to infants, children of eight, ten, twelve, sixteen, and hold their attention, win respect, admiration, even their love?" I shook my head, which he took as my sign of agreement.

"In addition to Sabbath and holiday service, I formed classes to give them back their heritage. I established groups for Hebrew, a tongue whose beauties, I said with disdain, even the Christians praised. But once and for all I warned: Rabbi Goldstein would never stoop to the easy path; he would never talk down. 'I'll quote from philosophers, poets, and the great of all nations. If some of the words exceed your grasp, reach out with all your will till you understand. Moses remade the ignorant slaves he had led out of Egypt into the wisest people. How? By commanding them to be worthy of Yahweh's choice.' Soon a good many children asked me for books — literature, poetry."

"What my Jacob hath wrought," said his wife wistfully, "no one will ever know except the orphans, who — may God forgive me! — worship him."

"When the Judge begged me to come," he went on, "he had no idea what a desert this was or how it might bloom. A remarkable man but like many lawyers, sometimes weak in judgment." Ignorant at the time that Goldstein had offered to serve as Director, I steered the talk to something nearer my heart; I spoke of the Jewish life in my home as being conveyed less by thoughts than by music. "Doctor, I'm a man of the word, not song" — I had chanced on another divide — "but I've heard you've an excellent voice and often sing with your children. Should I add that I envy you?" he grinned.

His wife never failed to console Sonya. "And how, my dear, can you bear it — right in the middle of things. I admire the way you're making the best of it." But for Sonya the change was a better than mixed blessing. Though a dwelling-place designed for the rich was nothing we ever had craved, its spacious proportions and elegant charms were a true delight. Visitors always remarked on the huge front window streaming with sunlight, the beautiful marble floors, the tapering arches and ceilings, and the western-most room with its picture view of the Hudson — by day the ever-changing flotilla, by evening, searchlights flooding the waves. "You must need an army of servants, my dear," Mrs. Goldstein would say. "What a burden keeping after them — to say nothing of keeping after your children." Sonya would smile or talk of the planted enclosure in front where our daughters played — the "Directors's Private Garden," with its flowering shrubs and six-foot hedges that hid them from passersby — or the farmer close to our playground who often brought us baskets of bright fresh peas garnished with roses.

For a time I had tried to win his help with my special project — the Boys and the Girls republics — but without success. Even the fact that it already gained a measure of fame failed to change his view of it as a passing indulgence. My "wild idea" of entrusting orphaned boys and girls with the right and power to govern themselves seized the attention of people outside our walls. Public-spirited visitors asked and received permission to watch the councils in session on Sunday evenings. Board members, social workers, teachers, and unidentified others came to hear and observe. Surely it would have been better if I'd abstained from intervening at critical moments, but an overanxious sponsor might be forgiven his zeal in keeping the work from losing ground. And in any case the republics suffered no loss. On the contrary. They not only governed: they also founded a savings bank; set up and managed a growing library; and even a kind of cooperative store stocked with candy, stationery, toys, and related items, giving its profits as spending money to its poorest citizens. But most important of all: the republics lifted "the tone" of the HSGS. I could feel the change at every hour and every place — in the way the children spoke to each other, among themselves, to the staff, to visitors; in the way they behaved at work and play.

One change I had hoped for failed to arise. Knowing how much it reflected my own desires, I thought it best to say nothing. Yet as time passed by the lack grew into a symbol of unfulfilment. When the volunteers met for their monthly meeting, I ventured, "Perhaps I'm asking for more than I should. Our children smile and they laugh, but I rarely hear them singing." Some suggested a prize for the best original song. Another, that every club adopt a song of its own. If we make a start, the rest will follow. No one, of course, mentioned the play that was destined to cause an unforgettable change, least of all the composer, sitting in back, holding his tongue while the others searched their brains.

His club, one of the first for older children, officially dealt with the stage, acting, drama. What they really were doing no one suspected. The leader in league with his followers were putting together a "musical spoof of HSGS," as it soon was named. There was nothing to fear, he assured some boys who thought they were going too far; "None of the words could possibly give offense and besides, in this age of the boys and girls republics, the time is ripe to make harmless fun of ourselves, including the man who used to be called 'The Superintendent.'" He was cautious enough to rehearse the songs in the privacy of his home. Hence on the opening night they fell on the listeners' ears with overwhelming surprise. The hall roared with applause and laughter — with shouts of "Again, again!" till the actor who rendered the feature-song gave up after five or six encores. To be sure, without the music, the context, costumes, and gestures, the printed words can't hope to explain the impact made by the sprightly irreverent song on an audience used to solemnities:

> Oh the Doctor's very smart, we know,
> And his work is *pretty* good,
> But if they put me in his place
> Why things would then go as they should:
>
> If I were the Superintendent
> There are lots of things that I would change,

There'd be outings every day
And the band would have to play
Every night at supper time.
If the children didn't care for school,
Why I guess I'd have to change that rule:
They would stay at home all day
And do nothing else but play —
If I were the Superintendent.

The ditty reflected as nothing else would the changed spirit, the confident courage and pride of the boys and girls. "It's more than the hit of the show," Seman looked straight in my eyes. "You may laugh, but to me in its modest way it's the deepest, most heartfelt tribute to a *newborn* HSGS—"

Which was already on its way, to a new life, in a new land miles from the city — thirty, to be precise, some hundred and eighty upland acres known as the Benedict Farm, in Westchester County, within the Pleasantville township. Following his return from a visit to England, Levy urged the Board to adopt his proposal. He had spent some time at "Barkenside," an institution where children lived in cottages, twenty or more in each, "with a motherly woman, who seemed to notice and listen to even the smallest and shyest among her charges." Levy was much impressed by the thought that the living arrangement itself might explain why no child seemed to be lost in the mass. The Board was also impressed, even those concerned by the problems parents would face in making thirty-mile trips to visit their children.

When President Lewisohn asked my view, I based my words on what I had learned from my several trips to the Protestant cottage home at Hastings-on-Hudson, directed by Dr. Rudolf Reeder, a fellow Columbian. Only two of the Board members knew of the place and neither had gone to see it. Lewisohn asked that Levy and I compare our findings and ready ourselves to report to the Board three weeks hence when "we'll have to make up our minds — yes or no." The task demanded more than either of us could offer. There was Barkenside and the Hastings home and nothing else of which we had first-hand knowledge. Scores of unanswered questions arose whenever each of us privately dreamed of "the best cottage home in the world." We had no choice but to limit ourselves to all we could say with assurance, stating the pros and the cons (which were many) and ending with our recommendation.

Once the decision was made by the Board, things moved rapidly. A building committee led by an expert realtor, who was also a Board member, scanned well over a hundred sites before the purchase was made — for exactly $50,281.33. An architectural firm was engaged and a number of subcommittees formed to deal with the planning stages. All at once I realized the enormity of the tasks that lay before us. What of the school, for example? Reeder and I had disagreed on the crucial question of range. We would argue again, keeping in mind the "best cottage home" ideal and the limits that fiscal realities imposed on the finest of blueprints. One fact was past doubting: it would take me years to arrive at a plan equal to all our hopes — and then the work of "translation" could start. Meanwhile the "newborn HSGS" was here: it would have to be nurtured, guided, firmly reshaped to fit its envisaged future, whatever that future might be.

In the midst of all these ponderings, Levy asked me to call at Lewisohn's home for a private talk, without his presence. I arrived, knowing little more of the man described to me years ago as "a copper magnate as different from your typical wealthy man as day from night . . . with his special devotion to orphans . . . himself orphaned at six . . . a man without formal schooling yet in strangely practical ways, voracious for knowledge, with a high regard for learning, talent, brains: for men who know what he doesn't know." The description had set my mind, yet I tried to learn something more of this man who could never forget the lines of orphans he saw as a child in the Hamburg streets, each of them holding out a stick with a cup at the end into which the passersby could deposit coins. His concern deepened with time. Determined on seeing how children actually lived on the Lower East Side, he frequently made the rounds with a friend who visited homes of the needy and sick. He had walked and breathed the air of Hester, Ludlow, and Broome Street tenements; had pushed his way through crowded pavements and gutters. But the other side of his life? . . . What would this unconventional Captain of Business want of a teacher almost as young as his son?

After a smiling welcome, Lewisohn instantly set to work, handing me architects' drawings. "We've an excellent pair, Jacobs & Heidelberg, but totally ignorant of cottage homes. You'll have to give them an *expert* education — tell them *all* they must know, then test them with questions. They'll expect your call. By the way, when you get a chance, give me your thoughts on these sketches. Heidelberg is the practical one, Jacobs the artist. Concentrate on the artist!

"And now," he paused with a frown — "about money. The HSGS always enjoyed a surplus. Today we've a healthy deficit. Accept my congratulations! From what I can see, it's a bargain." Doubtless pleased that my jaw had dropped, he began to chuckle. "Oh I've spies, plenty of spies. Some attended your childrens' councils, some the clubs. I know all about your matron's cooking-and-housekeeping classes — and that operetta. Don't fail to let me know if they give it again — Levy also. We both want to hear it and bring some friends.

"And speaking of Levy — you know I admire and respect and like him *very* much as a person. Brilliant attorney, excellent judge. But what can a lawyer or even a judge know what's best for an orphan unless he'd been one? Please realize, Doctor," he kept on nodding, "if *you* hadn't asked for the cottage plan, I'd never have given approval. You've a huge responsibility. Before we're done, it will cost us a million dollars — which I'm fully prepared to provide. But you and I together must stop at nothing to make it the best that the world has ever seen." He paused, eyeing me sharply. "I repeat: *the world.* I also said we must work *together,* which means that you'll have to *teach* me any number of things that I'll *need* to know. I've had rather little schooling, but I've taught myself how to learn." He nodded again. "You have all my confidence, Doctor — in all respects but one." He grimaced. "Are you working too hard? Too many hours? — I hear that your wife's a gardener. So am I, in a modest way. From the time I was six years old I had what my teachers called a herbarium. My father thought it unmanly and one fine day he told the maid to destroy it. You and your wife must visit my place at Ardsley. I'll call you soon. It's not too far." His eyes twinkled. "Don't be afraid to remind me. Like you, I've too many things on my mind.

"By the way, I hear that your father's coming. I hope you'll allow me to meet him, unless you think he'd frown on my way of worshipping God. My own father was — almost heartlessly orthodox, but I know it wasn't his fault. He didn't understand the child that I was." He shook his head. "He didn't *try* to understand."

"Oh well," I smiled wanly. "My father tells me he tries but he still can't see why I turned from a — 'theoretically' great career in the public schools to 'closet myself,' as he says, in a 'charity home' for children — only Jewish children, and orphans at that."

He lowered his head, then glared at me over his heavy lenses. "I also wondered. With your brilliant record and excellent speech, you could go to the top and beyond into other fields." He frowned. "What will you tell your father?"

"Just what I told my colleagues: the HSGS is an *educator's dream,* given the freedom assured me. For to offer a child what he needs, teaching must follow him round the clock — a twenty-four hour program." He stared in surprise. "What are five days a week from eight to three, ten months of the year? Very much less than a third of his life in his crucial, formative years. Then think of the countless — and often contrary — *other* things that he learns — that he *has* to learn — after the school bell rings. Much if not most that he's taught in class doesn't relate at all to the rest of his world. Finally, think of what children learn from their parents! — What public education tries to do can be quite undone at home." I could feel him ponder each word. "But of course," I added, "this is just one of the reasons I took the step that my father deplores."

"For *you* the most important one. You've enormous faith in education, though up to now it's failed."

"What else might act to better the world? Each of us enters it blessed with — 'capacities.' Nothing we do can change what the Good Lord gave us. But education can make the best of whatever each of us has. The Great Enlightenment opened our eyes to the possibilities for good in every man. Education alone can nurture and shape them."

"Then an educator's a kind of artist, a sculptor of lives? And like all artists', the result depends on his vision? A great responsibility. How will you know if you're right or wrong?"

"How can an artist know?"

He gazed thoughtfully. "Do you think that you'll change your father's mind?"

"You must ask him. Of course he speaks only German — so I suppose" — I tried to end on a genial note — "you and I might *both* go wrong with our plural endings — like my dean, Nicholas Butler, when we first met at Columbia."

"Then I won't be afraid to bumble — if you warn your father." It was time to leave. "We must keep in touch — we're working together now. Auf wiedersehen."

But the week before my father came in October, Lewisohn had already taken off on one of his "copper trips to the West." They never met. It was probably just as well, though I'd eagerly planned to urge my six-foot white-bearded octogenarian, straight as a soldier, to ask Lewisohn's view of the Czar's chances against the Rebels. As likely as not, after the greeting, my father would have said nothing. The irrepressibly talkative sage I had left in Courland years ago had changed himself to a listener. "You ask too much," Sonya chided me softly. "By the time you're eighty, even you will have less to say — having said it hundreds of times before." The added fact that he spoke no English also annoyed him. The few receptions we held in his honor became such a strain that we canceled plans for more. In fact within a week the visit became a burden — and the major part would have to be borne by Sonya, engrossed as I was with my FAIL TO ADJUST AND RELATED CASES which pressed at me day and night.

Luckily she could carry it off with easeful affection as well as concern for his comfort. A splendid tour to show him the "city's sights" proved more than enough. And although he thanked her warmly for taking him down to the "Great Café" to have tea with her father, both men soon ceased trying to bridge the German-Russian barrier. Sonya, however, promised a second meeting: one of her bilingual friends would solve in a trice this problem that kept them apart. On the way home my father confessed his greatest pleasure: walking hand in hand on the street with our daughters. After his visit had ended, they told us how proud they had been to parade up and down with their handsome giant Grandpa who would sing them soft little German songs and stuff them with animal crackers.

"When my father comes," I had warned Sonya, "don't be shocked if you see us talking till dawn. That's how it used to be and he never failed. By the time he'd stop, all my confusions would vanish!" But now it was clear there could be no help from the Sage. Never again would he sit me down to decipher my face, prod, question, and guide while I searched my soul. At best, perhaps, I might corner him — and perhaps he might listen. If a chance arose before his leaving, I would seize it.

I scraped the ashes out of my pipes and turned to the papers heaping my desk. Two hands seemed to have rapped on my office door. Scanning the long report in my hand, I ignored the noise. The door opened slowly. Turning around I saw my father watching me. He stepped at once toward my desk. Waving away the smoke-filled air, he pulled up a chair. "Moderation is best," he began at once, mimicking me. "Nothing in excess, ever! Moderation — noblest of virtues! — Weren't these words your motto when you worshipped the Greeks? But now you've dropped your faith in the Golden Mean. Aristotle would put on sackcloth, mourning his false disciple."

Shocked out of breath by his accusation, I threw out my arms to him. "Father, father," I gasped, "what are you saying?"

"Nothing you couldn't grant if you looked at yourself. — How do you spend your days? Smothered in clouds of tobacco, and working, working, working the minute you wake till you sleep — as though the Lord hadn't *dowered* you with a valorous woman and three fine daughters." He cried out bitterly, "*This* isn't what I crossed the ocean to see: my promising son throwing away his manhood." For a long minute we fixed each other's eyes. "When you were young," he leaned back, frowning, "we used to have talks together. Now we're older — both — yet I'm still your father — and loving enough to issue a firm command — with the poet's cry who would blast it into your ears: *Du musst dein Leben ändern!*"* At once he sprang up to leave, but I seized his arm. He stopped, sat down, waited.

I strained for words. "Father, the day you came I was bursting with questions. Then I studied your face. It preferred silence. You spoke little. I told myself: too many years have passed: he's done with listening. But today without warning the father I longed to talk with comes to my door and speaks as he used to speak." I lowered my head. "The command is heard — the last you will need to give me." I waited, gazed at the floor. "Today my father spoke as he used to speak. Will he also listen?" Almost at once he nodded. "How do I start? . . . The day you came I told you why I had cast my lot with these victim-children. You seemed to understand." He nodded again. "Even in free America, it matters little whether or not you believe: whatever sect you were born to, owns your life. Yet here I stand with the *same* faith as the youth who bade you goodbye; with the same *hope;* with the *same question* — You wouldn't answer before we parted. 'Ask again,' you said to me, 'when you're old enough to be certain.' — Thirteen years have passed." I paused, watching my words. "I claim the right to call myself, to think of myself, as a Jew while I also dream that the Great Enlightenment's Religion of Reason will widen our people's faith as it widened before. — Moses brought the name of Yahweh to Aaron who brought it to Goshen, and the faith he set down in his books held sway till the scribes and rabbis set up a changed religion to take its place. So I ask again: Can you as the Hebrew sage you have always been grant me a place in the fold *today* while I hope for the coming change?"

He smiled softly. "Fold? Which fold? — Being a Jew is a way of 'taking' this world, and the way changes because humanity changes. Moses' faith weathered the heathen hordes and his tribes' corruptions through seven centuries, till the Temple fell and they trudged to exile. But the world their conquerors let them reclaim had changed. Under the pressing force of surrounding peoples, the ancient religion altered. Yet even this more consoling faith — which the rabbis upheld for almost 2000 years — ceased to pre-

*"You must change your life!" The closing words of Rainer Maria Rilke's sonnet "Archäischer Torso Apollos." Could the speaker possibly have read the poem?

vail. Not very long after your Great Enlightenment, ours arrived — and
you know who ushered it in: Moses the Second . . . But who would dare
predict where the pathway blazed by Mendelssohn's 'doctrines of reason'
will lead Israel? Never before," he threw up his hands, "can one count so
many . . . 'folds'."

"Is this your answer, father?"

He shook his head. "Moses the First would tell you the Lord weighs
a man's worth by his acts, how he fulfills his *accountableness* to his fellow
man. Little Moses the Second would say the same. The first two Moses
bless you. So does their namesake, your father. And now" — he leaned far
back in his chair — "tell me something *I* cannot know. What will you name
your fourth baby if Yahweh sends you a boy?"

I never explained to my father that I "worked, worked, worked" throughout his visit because of my urgent concern with the children who made
up the file I entitled FAIL TO ADJUST AND RELATED CASES. The weeks that
followed my five reforms had brought me a number of unexpected reports.
Further comments and documentation opened my eyes to something no
one had noted. But once I was able to take apart and compare what I called
"the behavior data," I found myself making distinctions by type — from
boys and girls who could scarcely function without their monitor to boys
and girls who — irrespective of all other characteristics — shared one trait.
I awkwardly termed it "an isolative disposition" of the kind that would
never thrive under group living, but required the affectionate care of a
motherly woman in a private household.

I knew I was entering dangerous ground — "foster home placement"
— yet the file grew larger and larger. To be sure, our background materials
often were useless, at times misleading, nor had we ways for discovering
other forces that shaped the child into what he was. Theoretically, Gershel
was right when he spoke of "making a study" of every case, but I had to
cope with immediate needs, and the "boarding out" of an orphan child was
anathema to Jewish asylums — something to which for limited times they
might have to resort but otherwise quite unthinkable. And yet, I was now
compelled to propose, based on clearcut documentation, something which
not only social workers would greet with horror but Boards of Directors
as well.

Before undertaking a possibly fatal step, I met with Levy and Lewisohn.
I began at once by warning, "Facts I had never looked for about our children's behavior forced me to do some research in the last three years. I have

carried this forward privately with the help of Louis J. Cohen and Sarah Canter, who are never far from our boys and girls. Fortunately or unfortunately — you'll be the judges — the net conclusion contradicts everything that social workers and Boards of Directors believe. I propose adding an important, permanent new dimension in child care because there are certain children who, for reasons either within or beyond our knowledge, are constitutionally unable to thrive in an institution. For such boys and girls — since they are simply unfit for group living — the only valid alternative is a very carefully chosen foster home." I reeled off all the standard objections to "boarding out," beginning with child abuse and exploitation, but my listeners interrupted to hear some specific cases. "Choose from my file at random, but please read through at least a dozen of each. The entry sheet begins with a careful abstract; the rest of the page gives times, places, and so on."

Fifteen minutes or more may have passed before Lewisohn turned to Levy. "Every one of *these* children must be removed."

Levy frowned. "I say the same of the ones I've studied. But finding the proper foster homes? All your research finally hangs on that *problem*."

"With sufficient staff and effort," I said, "and time — time. It can all be done."

"No question. It *must* be done."

Lewisohn eyed him gently, then turned to me, muttering bitterly, "'Orphans are all the same!' — We'll never hear *that* again." He rose from his chair. "Do you realize what we're about to do? — hurling a bombshell into the child-care world. Perhaps we'll live to see the effects of this revolution."

"But your Board of Directors must realize this is part of the plan they approved when we talked of 'individualizing each child.'"

"Leave the directors to me, Doctor. I'll leave you the social workers. They probably won't speak to you for a year."

I lost no time in putting my plans to work. And of course, as we all expected, when the child-care world learned that my new-formed Bureau was placing in homes *all* "babies" from three to six, social workers and boards of directors shook their collective heads. But not for so long as predicted, and not without some occasional sounds of dissent. Besides, none had opposed the basic idea of giving a widowed mother financial help to allow her to keep her children at home, though private funds couldn't possibly meet the demands. Three more years, however, would pass before the issues would win a national hearing. The specialists called to the White House

Conference on the Care of Dependent Children voted in favor of family care, citing as most desired, financial aid to maintain the "natural" home, with the foster home as second, and cottage-plan institutional care as third. The "experts," alas, were totally unaware of the future HSGS, with its un-exampled curriculum, just as they failed to take account of the known improvements over innumerable natural homes to be found in some British schools, not to mention the clear advantages in child growth and learning and change that living-in-groups at its best could provide compared with the natural home, any number of which fell wretchedly short of the White House ideal. Thus, measured by early practical change, the Conference bore little weight, except for a few papers, one of which, on Widows' Pensions, was read by Lewisohn.

Our relationships seemed to deepen and grow each time I called at his office. And he often seemed to go out of his way to make his admiration known for the HSGS, even to stressing our "brilliant Director's study of school curricula and cottage home plans." Yet privately he never ceased to urge me to break my habit of overwork by hiring some able assistants and "taking off afternoons and even whole days with your wife and daughters."

The advice was badly timed. Running my job was burden enough, but now I was also involved with the Bureau and — just one staircase away — with Sonya's concerns. Though she looked radiant and suffered little discomfort as months went by, the dreaded news of her father's health robbed her of rest. For weeks he had been alone in his room, with only incautious visitors. Gershel had gathered enough from the sister with whom he lived to forbid Sonya against attempting a visit. Time gnawed at her mind, as hopeful reports reached us. Then without any warning, Gershel was told of the death. We went together to break the news. Sonya had only to read our eyes; she fainted. Her first words when she spoke again were those she had said of her sister Pauline's death: "Whenever I carry a baby, one of my family dies." Glancing at Gershel, she groaned, "At least it's safe to visit him now at his grave."

He shook his head: for lack of burial space, the body would have to go to a very distant location. "Take relief from the fact that his suffering's over. You've worn your nerves to the edges. From now till June I'll keep my eye on you day and night. You're strong; you can have a strong baby, *provided* you follow orders." I had never heard him talk to her in that tone. Later that day I questioned him. We agreed to shield her from all upsetting news. It was well advised: six days before the birth of our son, a series of Russian pogroms as bestial as Kishinev's bloodied the earth of Bialystok.

The world was aghast at the Czarist government's action, but we vowed to keep the news from Sonya's ears.

Our task was helped because people were making so much of the fact that we finally had a boy. Lewisohn's special chauffeur arrived each day with "American Beauty" roses too tall for our vases. Seligsberg, one of our close director-friends, countered by starting the practice of bringing Sonya violets each Saturday morning. Meanwhile Milton, pleased by our adding his name to our son's, urged me to find a full-time nurse, and before I knew it, his candidate made her appearance. Our daughters were awed and delighted with the Scottish governess Jane Adams' formal regalia: white uniforms, navy blue cape, and hat. Her flair and spirited self-assurance gave added "tone" to our household, "the grapevine" insisted. In any case, Sonya now had the leisure to make new friends, with whom she would sometimes take our girls to the Park or the Audubon bathing pavilion.

True to my promise to Lewisohn, I planned on hiring assistance. More than a dozen prospects sent from well-meaning friends left me doubtful of finding anyone likely to meet our needs. Yet my father's shadow kept hovering over my shoulder, his shout still rang in my ears. Through a sequence of chance encounters, I was introduced to a lively young Philadelphian. His personal charm was more than matched by his background, and one of his college concerns had been education. We took to each other at once despite his doubtful view of my Great Enlightenment and his faith in the need for maintaining Jewish identity. As a volunteer he had spent much of his leisure visiting homes in his city's poverty districts: social work had already entered his blood — along with a love for American poets. In fact the longer I worked with this man, the broader his range appeared, from his high regard for the Quaker creed to his hope in the Zionist dream.

For the first few months I placed him in charge of all our social activities, which now included more than forty-two clubs. The ease with which he met each challenge led me to waste no time: I sent out a formal notice appointing Chester Teller, Assistant Director. He and I also had talked of my plans for the Pleasantville school, whose innovations stirred him with searching questions. Both to reinforce and to test my theories, I set aside two hours each morning, from 8 to 10, in which we studied the classic educational works of English and German philosophers.

Levy and Lewisohn both were pleased with Teller's appointment and my plans for redistributing pressing tasks. The moment at last had arrived for taking the ease I'd dreamed of for years. Sonya was not convinced.

So Milton and I one April morning decided to treat ourselves to "fishing Long Island Sound." By dusk we were back with a big enough catch to make our daughters' eyes jump out of their sockets. In the course of our evening feast Milton remarked, "Not bad, Sonya. But this is nothing compared with what we can find in Nova Scotia." Turning on Eva and Mary, he said, "Papa and I will bring back a salmon as big as your brother, if you'll stuff the skin. Then we'll hang it up on your wall. Agreed?" Eva "hated" the thought of sleeping under the gaze of a fish, so Milton proved he'd been teasing by rushing at once to the keys and playing their theme song "Marching Through Georgia."

Promptly at eight next morning Teller rapped at my door, and within five minutes the word "apperception" rang through the room — "Given up smoking, Doctor?" he asked. I smiled, shook my head, then patting my ribs said something about having "gorged." We returned to apperception, but my thought was divided between our debate and a series of intermittent pains invading my chest. Before our session ended they disappeared. I gave them no more concern, but early next day they returned. Though I said nothing to Sonya, when Milton stopped by my desk at noon, I asked if something was wrong. A hasty examination showed nothing at all. However, he ordered a daily after-lunch nap to break up my otherwise uninterrupted pressure of work. I pursued the regime but the pains returned each day. What happened during the next few days was described years later to me by Mary who had long since become Marie:

After the household had gone to bed, Sonya, concerned by the length of my stay in the bathroom, opened the door to find me prone in a pool of blood, unconscious. At once Jane Adams fetched the Nurse from our ward, followed by Gershel, who lifted me into bed and watched through the night. By dawn two of Mt. Sinai Hospital's specialists came for a consultation. All three men made the same diagnosis — acute nicotine ulcer — "which the patient should survive, barring a second hemorrhage." I remained unconscious for days. A pall of silence fell on the HSGS. Each morning heaps of flowers arrived from the Board of Directors. Sonya, pressed for space, ordered them piled in a bathtub, muttering, "Why are they sending so many now? What will they do if he dies?" But he didn't die. Within three weeks he was well enough to convalesce in Atlantic City . . . and to cheat on a few of his diet rules. On one point he never wavered: his oath to abstain from tobacco for twenty-five years . . .

Throughout my absence Teller performed admirably, making clever improvements. In addition the plan I'd begun of spreading and sharing responsibilities had worked so well with the staff that even at times an older boy or girl could take on an adult's task. Milton meanwhile, more concerned than I by my brush with fate, prescribed varied excursions as well as a daily bicycle trip to be paced by Eva. Highly proud of her role, she also hoped to use it to skip her piano lessons. By now all three of our girls had to take them weekly, though only Marie enjoyed them. Her teacher, impressed by the child's facility, urged us not to rule out an artist's career.

By now everyone knew my priority task was the Pleasantville plan. Since Teller and I were nearing the end of our studies, I managed to make fairly frequent trips to the cottage-home school at Hastings. What attracted me most were Reeder's efforts to correlate subjects — for example, arithmetic, nature study, geography, drawing — with the children's immediate environment and environmental problems. In some respects I thought my friend's ideas too limited for his charges' welfare. And on one subject we never agreed: my commitment to high school learning. "Completing grade school," he argued in line with entrenched tradition, "must suffice for any child in humble circumstances." I maintained that, with the proper controls, both grade school and high school could be compressed into nine full years. Such a plan would give a dependent child an incomparably more effective basis for making his way in the world. For me this nine-year program became the core idea of all I was trying to shape. Though Reeder agreed it was theoretically feasible, he called it "a much too revolutionary attitude toward schooling orphans."

Before I arranged to present my scheme to Lewisohn, I took some care to verify not only once but twice, all relevant sources. I wished to be sure of each point and fully armed to cope with the doubts and questions that were sure to arise. Teller was squarely behind me, and so, it appeared, were the newer scholars, at least by their implications. I intended to stress this fact. Lewisohn's known regard for accepted experts led me, in sanguine moments, to think that he even might say "Try it out! If it works, then we'll know it's sound." But when, after hearing my words, he shouted "This is the best educational plan that I've ever heard of," I was speechless. "Everyone knows," he roared, "that a classroom wastes at least half of its time. This will show up the schools as the most inefficient teaching machines in the world! You're launching a real revolution — the *best*. My congratulations!"

"I'm touched — deeply," I finally managed to mumble, as in fact I was.

"You know I say what I honestly mean. Teachers will curse you for making them work as they ought to, but far more pupils will bless you for saving them boredom. I *know.* I've some bright children. — Well, now, what's our next step?"

"I'd like to submit the plan with all its details to the greatest expert alive. He's at Jena: Professor Wilhelm Rhein. He founded his university's *Muster-schule,* which laid the pattern for the model schools in our colleges. If you authorize me, I'll write to him now. I would need three weeks, not more."

"Splendid idea! Rhein's endorsement would save us the need for a test-run. We could leap right into the program, and show" — he raised his voice — "show *America* — show *the whole world* — what Jews can do when they have the courage to dare." As he bade me goodbye, he smiled, "I was sorry I missed your father. Be sure to see him while you're abroad and give him my greetings." He changed suddenly. "Let's have the Rhein approval as quickly as possible! My secretary will cable your messages now."

Often during the next few days I found myself musing on Lewisohn's cry about Jews and courage and its relevance to the Zionists. Questions of double loyalty had often been raised and not only by enemies, nor did the "explanations" suffice, for how could a Jew be a true wholehearted American if he thought of a foreign soil as *his people's* homeland? Russians made much of the myth that the fifty-year-old Alliance Israélite Universelle, founded for schooling and charity, was a shadow scheme for ruling the world. The only practical counterattack consisted in making striking "gifts" to one's newly adopted country. And what better gift than a plan, fostered by Jewish courage and brains, that would better the chance of *every* American child?

My explanation, perhaps far fetched, was one I could also argue with Zionist zealots, of whom my assistant was one. Despite the Reform rabbis' offensive campaigns, Zionists seemed to be gaining ground in unlikely places, their most eminent recent convert being Supreme Court Justice Brandeis. Zionism, indeed, was one of the burning issues I planned to present to my father. They'd have to wait, of course, till after Jena, from where I'd travel to join my brothers and sisters.

Placing the HSGS in Teller's care, I bade my dear ones goodbye and sailed for Europe. Since my program was written in English, I would offer oral comments in German. But as it happened, before Professor Rhein allowed me to speak, he grilled me for hours on American teaching methods, on which he seemed even better informed than I. Then he set up a two-day seminar — with colleagues — on the socio-economic structure of urban American neighborhoods, with stress on public and covert behavior toward needy children. He was now ready to ask for an overall presentation of what I had come to show and especially *why*. The next weeks were given over to a point by point discussion of my twofold curriculum, for boys and for girls. With a deference which surprised me, he asked if he might make minor revisions, adding the reasons for each. Then he set a date for a second seminar — with the same colleagues — at the close of which he pronounced my plan "a wholly novel idea in teaching — the expression of a learning ideal which the formal German Prussian code could never approve but which nevertheless represented the basis for the most harmonious development of the individual child in terms of an academic, esthetic, ethical, religious, civic, and vocational preparation for life." He also stated that such a new curriculum today could be worked out only in free America and with private sponsorship. As the seminar closed, he whispered, "I've had copies made of your work, for my own reference. Do you mind? I've also written to your Mr. Lewisohn, saying *all* that I said a moment ago. Thank you for coming to Jena, and *Auf Wiedersehen.* . . ." At the nearest cable office I sent a message to Sonya, then made my way for the train to Königsberg.

Despite my brother's warnings, I was shocked by the suddenly aged face of my father. It was wrong for him to be living alone, and since he refused all invitations to live with a daughter or son, we asked him to let us bring in an older woman he'd known for years. "Good. I'll even marry her, if you say so," he smiled, then turning to me, he asked that I offer a full account of Jena. Knowing that New York orphans scarcely concerned my brothers, I made my speech as brief as I could. Rhein might have been forgotten, for all that my brothers discussed was the enmity between France, Britain, Russia, and Germany's Wilhelm II. It had weathered the 1905–06 Morocco crisis, but what if a new one arose as German colonial efforts clashed with the French and the British African? What, if war broke out, what would it mean for Jews? How would the Zionist "stand" affect their civil status in Britain, France, and the Balkans?

My brother Max, catching my father's eye, raised his voice above the chatter. "Herzl thought he would make us into an indissoluble mass, but his vision has started a conflagration which may burn the whole house down. All of us know about sons who refuse to live in a home unless it campaigns for the Zionists. Yet none of us here ever dreamed of moving to Palestine — surely not I, a British physician attached to the Royal Army, and deeply fond of my chosen country despite the nonsense we make of the king and queen. Yet every day all over the West the dream of Herzl throws its enchantment; one never knows whom it strikes. For, as all of us heard, Gentiles of high importance in Ludwig's country give their support to the cause — millionaires like Rockefeller, Morgan, Catholic cardinals, even Chief Justice Fuller — while Reform rabbis want to pillory every Zionist Jew. What do you make of it, father?"

"What *I* make of it matters less than what my children may *do*. I've never made up your minds, even before you passed your magical twenty-ninth year." We chortled, recalling that not so long ago any Jew under thirty found reading Maimonides could be excommunicated. "Judaism has no dogmas, really," my father went on. "The orthodox could never agree on a systematic theology. Even the books of Moses have contradictions." He sighed for a moment. "Rifts as deep as the one that lies at the Dead Sea's bottom have always divided our people. But when danger threatens, they disappear, and Israel again is one . . . And now that I haven't answered your question, Max, describe your double life! Do your rich patients know that you treat the poor for a pittance — which comes out of their pockets?"

Aware that soon our reunion would end, I asked my father to give me a private hour. My second "burning personal issue" could not be shared at the dinner table. "You remember our children's rabbi, Father? the one who conducts the services — Jacob Goldstein, the man from Australia? He won't be going to Pleasantville. I'll have to replace him. But more important, I want to replace the service." My father raised his eyebrows. "I've examined scores of prayer-books and I lighted on one, written in England. I've almost learned it by heart. By making omissions and adding music and special poems, I've put together a service to give our boys and girls a feeling of awe and joy . . . worship filled with music . . . interspersed with responsive readings and prayers we can sing *together*. It's a kind of worship-drama in which each child has a part . . . a weekly prayer to the Lord in the beauty of holiness, as the saying goes." I waited before baring the difficult question. "The man who'll replace Goldstein — he's the one with whom I've examined dozens of prayer books — is a fine retiring scholar, with a speaking voice that can hardly be heard, and deaf to music. Obviously he can never conduct the service. The question I should like you to answer — the question is — whether . . . whether — "

He raised his palm. "The question is whether you . . . what?"

"Whether it would be wrong for a — 'part-time believer' — which is what I've become — to lead the service — to stand up facing the Torah and sing *Adonaí, adonaí, el ráhum v'hánun éreh apáyim* . . . [Lord, O Lord, merciful and forgiving, slow to anger] . . . *vrav hésed v'émes* . . ."

"Your Hebrew could stand some improvement."

"In a year I should know it as well as English, thanks to my tutor. But you haven't answered my question."

Turning his half-closed eyes from left to right, he paused and drew a long breath. "I've sometimes wondered if Moses was sure that he heard the Voice."

"Sure?" I cried in amazement.

"Heard with his ears, not his heart. — But, in any case, there was nothing for him to have done. Could he share his doubts — that is, *if* he doubted?" He shrugged. "And what if at times he was neither sure nor unsure!" He paused, glancing aside. "In practical terms, it could make no difference at all. After telling God's secret name to Aaron, Moses was forced to act as the one who had heard the Ineffable Voice . . . In time, *by acting the part, he became the part* — and *that* is what matters, my 'sometime' believing son." To my deep annoyance, Max dashed into the room, his mouth half-open with shouts. He held his voice till my father finished saying "Before you leave, we might spend some time humming some songs and prayers. There are one or two that the children might take to heart."

Teller, eager to make my welcome home a gala surprise, arranged a party of friends and staff, who burst into song the moment I stepped to the pier. Strains from "If I Were the Superintendent" rose out of every mouth but my little son's, which had still not learned to talk. A table laid "for a fine High English Tea" — Jane Adams' idea — greeted my eyes when I opened my door. Friendly faces beamed wherever I turned, while my fingers itched to open the trunks that I'd filled with presents bought from Königsberg shops. The boxes would have to wait, Jane Adams kept telling Marie and Eva, till the last of the guests had gone. To my great relief, the gifts I brought for the girls — in accordance with Sonya's instructions — were "just what we hoped you'd bring": and the long Swiss necklace of gold that my brother Max had chosen moved Sonya to tears.

Glad as I was to be back at work, it seemed a bit of a strain. "Vacation blues?" Gershel remarked, seeing me stare in space. "Don't be worried about your boy. He's had a large head since birth; besides, some children don't talk till three or more." I nodded. "Has Teller spoken with you yet?" Accustomed to Milton's ear for gossip, I pried. He chuckled and dashed away. I sent for Teller, whose more than usual heartiness made me wonder.

"I've been holding out on you, Doctor. Very good news for Evie and me: we're engaged." Without allowing me time to respond, he spoke of the Widows and Orphans Home in New Orleans and the recent visit paid by their first vice-president. If I'd recommend Chester Teller to serve as their new Director, Evie and he could marry at once. I offered congratulations. "Thank you, so very much. Evie will be delighted. . . . And when you have time, I must bring her brother to see you. He's constructing a plan that will fire your imagination."

At dinner that evening I teased Sonya about her reputedly busy life in my absence. "Fortune telling's a dangerous business, even for gypsies. Did you have any great successes?" She nodded. "Chester Teller?" She shook her head. "Who, then?"

"Louis kept after me night after night to tell him his fortune. Finally to keep him quiet, I went for the cards, making a joke of it all. But it wasn't a joke. I laid them out as I always do, half in fun, but what they were show-ing surprised me. I laughed, 'Do you know what they say? They've said it twice now. Before the end of the week you'll be married.' His jaw dropped and without even saying good night, he jumped from his chair and van-ished. The rest of us looked at each other. Then Milton started to laugh, 'What's the name of that grand romantic lady who teaches you rhetoric, Sonya? The last time she came, her daughter was with her. LJC happened to pass. He took one look at the girl and before she knew it, he was walking her down toward the river.'"

It was true, much too true, as I learned the next morning, from the fidgeting bridegroom himself — love at first sight, the girl of his dreams, etc. "And now, my Deep-Sea Diver?"

"I thought," he bumbled, "something more could be done about help-ing the children after they leave us. I've made some tries, you know, on my own for years. But to do it right —"

His suggestion was happily timed. An "Aftercare Department" had been on my URGENT list for a year. Now it could come into being: an office to "follow up" (as Louis put it) each boy and girl after leaving; help them in finding and keeping jobs; stay in touch with employers; even give money when needed or provide for loans. "We do as well as we can when we take in a child. We must do no less when he or she enters the outside world on his own. You may start — as soon as you bring me another Louis to take your place."

"I've a few ideas, Doctor. Do you want to hear them? . . ."

Teller's coming departure brought to the fore some thoughts from the back of my mind. With the Pleasantville move in the offing, to adminis-ter the HSGS called for more than a single assistant. Fiscal matters, pur-chasing, minor hiring tasks, and the like could be done by a person with business experience. One of our Board members had told me about an efficient and bright young man, George Halpern, who seemed to "be born for managing." A wholly different type, of course, would be needed to oversee our schools, interview teachers, and work with me on curricula. Within three months, by chance, at a Principals' Meeting, my dinner companion talked of an "HSGS alumnus" who was one of the most effective men on his staff. The name sounded familiar: Michael Sharlitt. Hadn't he supervised volunteers in charge of our clubs, till his graduate studies forced him to leave? A telephone call arranged his visit next evening. I spoke in full detail of the Pleasantville move and my weeks in Jena. "Have you chosen the man to run your school?" he asked rather nervously.

"We need someone who understands the problems, the many unspoken needs and fears that are bound to arise when deprived children enter our shockingly strange and shining world."

He stared at the floor for minutes. "I'll confess to something I shouldn't — only because I despise dissembling. At the heart of every orphan, myself included, is the dream to come back one day and lead the procession. . . ."

All through my absence in Europe, Teller had shared the job of leading the club volunteers. He had asked Louis Seligsberg, during one of the latter's "violet visits" to Sonya, if he knew of someone able to ease his burden. "My sister would love it," Seligsberg said, "but how could I broach it? She'd say you were taking her on because I belong to the Board." Teller's idea — that she call on him, using a different name — resolved the dilemma, and more. It brought to the HSGS a woman whose contributions would prove of lasting importance.

Shortly before the Tellers' departure in mid-December, we arranged a farewell dinner. The new couple was joined by the bride's brother, Judah Magnes, a young California rabbi now engaged in trying to found a *kehilla*. The word, he explained, means community; the idea supposedly going back to at least 200 B.C., in the Jewish Black Sea settlements. The Magnes *kehilla*, like all in the past, would integrate "in a single organization every expression and element of Jewish life in the city — law, teaching, welfare, religion, and so on." The *kehilla* idea never had tempted American Jews, many of whom believed that, except for religion, any grouping formed for avowedly Jewish purposes clashed with the tacit "contract" of Jewish assimilation-in-return-for-emancipation. It took the Bialystok pogroms of 1906 to rouse America's Jews to the need for working together. In November, the American Jewish Committee was formed "to prevent the infraction of the civil and religious rights of Jews, in any part of the world . . . [to]

alleviate the consequences of persecution and to afford relief from calamities affecting Jews, wherever they may occur." But the spark that probably helped to galvanize action behind the *kehilla* was the false allegation by New York's Police Commissioner that half of the city's criminals were Jews.

We were not surprised when Magnes described how hard it had been to persuade the proud independent agencies to join in a single group. Could *kehilla* weather the strains? By the end of 1909 it would prove victorious in bringing together arbitration courts for religious disputes, separate bureaus for furthering education, dealing with social problems, handling labor relations, a school for training communal workers, and so on. The prospect of a unification stirred us all, and the party closed on a note of hope. None of us, as we said goodbye, dreamed that this new *kehilla,* though it lacked all power to enforce decisions, would soon fall apart or that Magnes himself would be turning most of his time to the Zionist cause. Least of all had I any reason to think that my own future might be affected: that *kehilla's* failure would pave the way for an organization eight years hence whose leader would one day force me to make a crucial decision.

On the following morning I found spread out on my desk a large painting marked "Pleasantville HSGS." Up to that time we had seen nothing but blueprints, which I used for checking dimensions. Only when serious doubts arose were we given a roughed-out sketch of the structures. But now — as though having read my desire — one of our two architects made me the gift of what our eyes would behold when the final stone had been laid, the trees planted, the lawns mown. We were overwhelmed by its beauty. Even the letter listing the needed changes failed to restrain us, though the questions raised told me that much of my time would have to be spent in revising plans.

As I gazed at the colored rendering, I knew what a boon it would prove for the cottage-mothers-to-be and the teachers-to-be. The picture would save them from trying to reconstruct from verbal descriptions the physical world they would enter. They could look at each of the twenty cottages much as they "soon" would be. I could show them the open porch with the boxes awaiting flowers; point to the groundfloor wings running the length of either side, one for dining, the other for recreation; and the two wings directly above, for the children's sleeping. All they would have to imagine were the kitchen, basement, service porch, and the several suites for the cottage mother and teachers sharing the house. I might even ask for some roughed-out scenes of these places.

My eye, noting the calendar, set me to reckoning time on a scale I had never thought of. How many years remained for preparing the move? When must I start the search for my cottage mothers and teachers, who could make or break the dream? And what of the numberless smaller tasks, any of which might call for a year or more? Without so much as thinking, I left my office and sent for Eva. Damned be the calculations! . . . Do what Milton warned whenever problems threatened to overwhelm! Focus your eyes on the streets, people, buildings — empty your mind! . . . Call your daughter! Ask her to join you! . . . riding your bicycles — ride with the wind in your face! . . .

I had learned to respect his physician's wisdom despite our sometime arguments about a man on the Board who was now courting his favors. Milton was right in saying my youngest child would speak "in time — possibly all at once" — which was what he did, in a burst of sound — much as he started to walk: suddenly running around the room unable to stop. By now the boy had learned to parrot the opening line of *The Iliad*. "Speak Greek," I teased, "if you really prefer it to English." Despite my pleas, he repeated it over and over again: "*Ménin áeide theá Pēlēiádeō Achilḗos.*" Eva at first tried to teach him an English version — "Sing, goddess, the wrath of Peleus, Achilles' son" — but for weeks he held to the Greek, then for no reason at all dropped it for good.

"Odd boy," said his nurse Jane Adams. "Assures me his *real* mother has great blue eyes and golden hair. Now where could he ever have come upon golden hair? And he's oh-so-proud of his birthday. — Begs people to ask him, so he can knock them over with 'June the 20th of May.' How did he dream that up?" Our girls, properly jealous, teased him mercilessly when Jane wasn't near. Yet they had their approbation: Marie, the facile pianist; Eva and Pauline singing with all their hearts as the three of us launched into Schubert songs when dinner was over, leading people to talk of our house as a "musical home."

Sonya was no less fond than I of our weekly nights at the opera, though she rather disliked the second-row seats I insisted upon "so as not to miss a single nuance" — or, as she would add, "the rouge on the coloratura." Would we lose our city pleasures once we had moved away? I swore to retain the Opera House subscriptions and to keep in touch with friends. The train took only an hour. I especially hoped to remain a part of "The Nine," as we called our intimate group of philosopher-social-workers, who met one evening a month to parry views and upset one another's pieties. Sonya smiled with discreet disdain when I swore not to let the country-future narrow our lives. "Mark my promise: we'll have the best of both worlds."

"I'll mark it," she said. "But isn't it early to worry about that now?"

It was earlier than she knew, for I hadn't even attempted to deal with the first of the major tasks: finding the "ideal women" for cottage mothers. I sketched out a list of essentials. What would each of them face? A group of thirty boys or girls, ranging from eight-year-olds to the first four 'teens. They would share the house not only with her as their leader but with two or three teachers also, who would live as privately as they chose, in suites of their own. — Under what conditions? I made some notes:

1. All the domestic tasks would be done by the children.

2. The cottage mother would organize and supervise the living arrangements — housework, care of supplies, cooking, serving at tables, social events, etc.

3. But since each cottage of 30 (boys or girls) would govern itself as a small republic (part of the overall republics: one for boys, the other for girls, as currently organized), much of the actual work of assigning and supervising would be done by her two assistants: the President and Vice-President.

4. There would also be other elected officers, with limited terms: Secretary, Treasurer, Book Custodian, etc.

5. Quite as important: a handful of Special Committees dealing with entertainments, visiting other cottages, athletics, economy, schoolwork, etc.

I put down my pen and pictured a kind of ideal. She would be a "youngish" woman, who would set an example of what our cottage-home life could give to children in terms of happy and fruitful relationships. She could count on steady aid from the Big Brother or the Big Sister committee — the dozen older children in every cottage, charged with helping the younger ones take their places and play their parts in the HSGS.

But no one should dare propose that she play her role without receiving the utmost in preparation. She would undergo an intensive training program at a nearby annex outfitted for this purpose. She would take the entire course (five months) and be paid her salary and living expenses from the very first day. — So far so good, but how design the program itself? Were there precedents to consult? Before doing anything else, I should have to find and train, well in advance of the program, a handful of older women of solid background who had lived or worked successfully with children and were just as eager as I to take the plunge . . . into "a great experiment," as they'd probably call it. We would make mistakes galore and we'd hold regular sessions to learn what they were. But now I should lose no time in building this corps of "seniors," on whom I'd have to depend to keep the cottage-plan working even after the Pleasantville move. Once I had found these women, we'd start by searching out every conceivable problem-question that might arise. And for areas in which we were less than sure, we'd call on expert advice and make it part of our program. I would also count on these seniors, after *their* training, to help me find and screen the twenty "regular" cottage mothers, on whom the worth of all that we planned might rest.

My second personnel problem — attracting the "right" teachers — seemed much simpler to solve. New York City was filled with men and women, many of whom might regard an adventurous nearby country school as a welcome change from "the system." I had already found in my principal a surprising grasp of even some intricate aspects of our curriculum. Furthermore, Sharlitt's childhood years in the HSGS had instilled in him a sensitiveness to personality-dangers that could prove of inestimable value in choosing teachers.

Ignorant as I was of the homely details of "vocational arts," I gave him the over-all charge of these two divisions. The one for boys would offer twelve to fifteen courses — working with wood, metal, combustion engines, electricity; iron, steel, sheet metal; mechanical drawing; type composition and printing. The "Boys' Building" would house the required equipment, from a stripped-down automobile to lathes and planes for wood and steel, an elaborate wiring system, as well as an open forge. Our manual training instructor agreed to direct the girls' program as well. A broad range of work would be taught in their separate building — sewing, costume design, dressmaking, millinery, embroidery, freehand drawing, stenography, typewriting — and "domestic science": a series of classes including food preparation and kitchen management, which would also be taught to boys.

So much, then, for the secular parts of the Pleasantville plan: what of the "Jewish dimension"? Although I had learned about various ways of meeting the problem, none practiced elsewhere offered the integration I hoped for. Every child would take his courses in Hebrew language and Jewish history as part of his regular program, but that would be schoolwork only. To bring the "dimension" into the home, every cottage mother would have to be taught to lead the Friday evening prayers and the candle-blessings. Yet the great "challenge" remained: a drastic change from the present Saturday service.

In the course of screening men for the newly created post of "Chaplain to lead the religious life of the HSGS," I'd come on a curious bachelor scholar who asked to know *exactly* what I envisioned. I spoke of my hope of making the Sabbath services a kind of worship-and-celebration in which our boys and girls would play as active a part as the man in the pulpit. Very much pleased, he pressed me to be specific. "I think I know enough Hebrew now to join in piecing together passages out of existing prayer-books to be used for responsive readings as well as hymns to be sung — not spoken but sung by the whole congregation. I hope you agree."

He smiled sadly, shaking his head. "You know my limitations and so will the boys and girls." At the very start of our talk he said he had trained for the rabbinate, but his deferent manner and "frank dislike of the rabbi as public performer" made him retreat into teaching. I asked him to reconsider my offer.

He sighed, "If I have to, Doctor, I'll stand in the pulpit and try my best though my voice is poor, as you know. Somebody else will have to speak the responsive prayers to bring out the words, and maybe a third person to lead with singing." He hesitated before going on. "But you've probably found that man. While I was waiting outside your office, I heard from the overhead rooms a strong male voice singing some prayers."

I laughed, "I'm afraid it was mine, practicing hymns with Eva Cohen, our music director. She's familiar with more religious songs than I knew existed. The three of us should do well together. Come with me now and meet her!"

"On one condition: that you yourself stand in the pulpit beside me and conduct the reading and singing."

Many of my associates were moved by the thought of our having a special person to "lead our religious life." The reason was in the air. Every month had brought ever harsher news from places ruled by the Czar, who had ceased pretending to lay a hand on the Black Hundreds and Union of Genuine Russians in their persecution of Jews. One peaceful sunlit afternoon, word arrived of the brute expulsion of all 1200 Jewish households from Kiev. This was to prove but the start of a worse persecution, which would come with the "Beilis Trial," based on the trumped-up charge of a Jewish ritual murder of a Christian boy. For two long years — the years that would mark the transition out of our barracks life into Pleasantville's Eden — protests and pleas in behalf of justice raged through the world.

There was no other course for our lives to take but the one we had given our hearts and strength to pursue. Work for the future HSGS would go on at an even headier pace because of the terrors.

Sharlitt used every resource within his reach, and beyond, in his search for our teaching staff. But before we made a commitment, I conducted a personal interview, interspersing substantive questions. Some of the people resisted a social worker's attempt to check their competence. One person, however, relished our dialogue. Trained in a Jesuit college, he had turned from parochial schools in the hope of finding a place which could use his extensive knowledge of music, art, and dramatics — a fact he gladly confessed when, after we'd tested each other's Latin and French, I asked why a Catholic wished to live in a world of Jews. "To learn," he said, "if a person of different faith might enrich the lives of hundreds of orphaned children, with the help of your music director who, Mr. Sharlitt tells me, is bursting with plans of her own." I had no idea at the moment of the rare contribution that Philip Brant, a Jesuit, working with Eva Cohen, a rabbi's widow, was destined to give our world.

I asked a number of teachers to start to work in August in the nine-month program I planned as a kind of transition-move from the public school. Three hundred older boys and girls would be given a scaled-down version of studies, including vocational arts. I counted on this experiment to help not only to iron out whatever faults might arise but also to put the children at ease in the novel classwork, as well as providing a large enough group that could graduate from high school within two years. "Domestic science" would also be part of their classes: boys as well as girls would be taught to cook and practice simple domestic routines that were part of "running" their cottages.

At times a director or two, spurred by Lewisohn, would drop in to audit classes, even on days when I happened to be in Pleasantville with the builders. Sharlitt conducted this "dry-run" school with confident calm, keeping a careful account of questions and problems which all of us, teachers included, tried to solve at our meetings.

And now . . . with our school well under way, the time had come for my last, most hazardous task. Before making any move, I decided to lay the problems before both Levy and Lewisohn. The Judge, visibly pleased that I sought his counsel, urged that a matter of such concern — "finding the very best cottage mothers" — be brought to Lewisohn only, who, he knew, was hoping to hear my plans.

"All that you've done, I suppose," Lewisohn looked at me grimly, "largely depends on these women. What's the best way to proceed?"

As briefly as I could, I summed up my thoughts. We should draw them from the well-to-do middle classes — daughters blessed with some knowledge of Jewish religious practices — reared in good, well-ordered homes — with at least some knowledge of how a household is managed — women not afraid to display sympathy and affection — endowed with a genuine liking for children — above all, young enough and adaptable enough to understand or sense the emotional problems of boys and girls.

"How will you find your applicants? . . . where?"

"Through the magazines and papers published for and by Jews. I plan to place *very* clear advertisements in all of them, then correspond with the women who sound most promising. I'll narrow them down to seventy, interview each, and engage thirty."

"And what will you do with your raw recruits?"

"Put them through a most rigorous training program, which should sift the wheat from the chaff." I went on to outline the course.

Lewisohn listened intently. "Thorough enough! I'll drop in to watch, if I may. Don't be alarmed if you get few promising answers. Advertise again and again and if nothing happens, we'll put our heads together."

As things turned out, letters poured in from everywhere, including a number of well-known homes in eastern cities: about two hundred in all. I reduced them to seventy-five fair prospects and sent each a list of questions. Within two months I had interviewed nine of the very most promising, from whom I selected four to be senior cottage mothers. I also worked on a tentative list of a final twenty, plus five to be called on for help as the need arose.

In the midst of these preparations, news reached our ears of a ghastly fire in the Triangle Shirtwaist factory, south of Washington Square. The flames had spread from the top third floor at about the time, 4:30 P.M., when the employees would be getting ready to leave. A helpless crowd watched in panic as firemen strove against faulty exits and fire escapes. It was over in eighteen minutes, leaving 146 dead, "among them skeletons bending over sewing machines," as the Fire Chief told the court. The tragedy gave rise to offers of help from Gentiles all over the land, suddenly made aware of the plight of immigrant Jews and Italians. Letters of application from non-Jewish women to serve as cottage mothers cluttered my desk. I lost no time in proposing to Lewisohn, who quickly agreed, that we welcome some of them, while making sure of their willingness to undertake all the tasks, religious duties included, that our cottage-mothers-to-be would have to fulfill.

Our training program began mid-February 1912 in our annex five blocks north. In my welcoming words I reminded all my listeners of our interviews, which had stressed the whys and wherefores. Nonetheless it seemed rather wise to repeat some essentials. I stated again why a cottage plan was preferred to all other arrangements, following with some reasons *why* our curriculum would compress the standard twelve long years of school into nine. "All other orphan homes," I quoted my stock explanation, "regard a grade-school education as sufficient for any child in 'humble conditions,' whereas *our* plan, which offers a high school diploma, affords a dependent child an incomparably better basis for making his way in the world.

"And now," I went on, "let me say a word of the physical place. In a month or so you'll see it with your own eyes. Meanwhile study the painting the architect made." I raised it for all to see. "It will stay on this wall. If you've questions, ask them, please! By the way, here on the table I've placed a simplified ground-plan which the architects made — a map, one for each of you. I suggest you refer to it now as we look at the painting." I proceeded to point to the small square plaza and the largest building joined to the technical schools on either side by the curving colonnades. "The largest houses the school, library, classrooms, offices; also the synagogue — a beautiful hall for religious service and special events — and a groundfloor auditorium for school assemblies, plays, entertainments, and motion pictures. You all know where the cottages stand, but you haven't seen this bird's-eye view of our acreage." I held up an architect's blueprint. "It shows what the painting omits. Our hospital is here, with the smaller building beyond for a quarantine. Down there," my pointer moved to the spot, "our Reception or Intake House, where we'll study for several weeks both the characteristics and social response of each newly admitted child. The service buildings — laundry, bakery, store-and-supply, power plant — all have been set at a distance behind the school — virtually hidden from view . . . And now let me introduce my assistants, my principal, and our chaplain, after which I'll discuss the program itself."

Mornings were given over to lectures, discussions, interviews; afternoons, to practical work under the guidance of "teachers": a corps of dieticians "loaned by Columbia" who had laid out a detailed course of study combined with practice in cooking and household management. The range of subjects that filled the mornings covered as much as this group could absorb of matters new to their minds — from child welfare

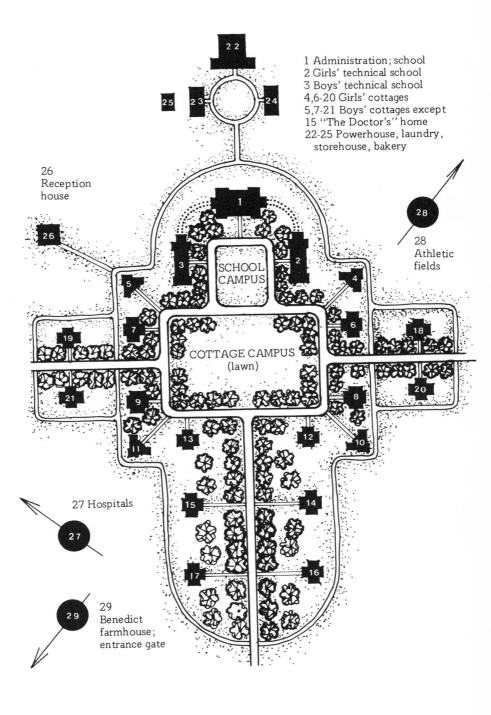

1 Administration; school
2 Girls' technical school
3 Boys' technical school
4,6-20 Girls' cottages
5,7-21 Boys' cottages except
15 "The Doctor's" home
22-25 Powerhouse, laundry,
     storehouse, bakery

26
Reception
house

28
Athletic
fields

27 Hospitals

29
Benedict
farmhouse;
entrance gate

SCHOOL
CAMPUS

COTTAGE CAMPUS
(lawn)

and problems of growing children to the requisites of a home-like atmosphere as expressed in social behavior; from the elements of boys' and girls' self-government to methods of drawing on older children to become, in a sense, responsible for their younger cottage-mates. The most fruitful learning took hold through discussions after my lectures. The same was true of the formal religious instruction that our chaplain gave individually with the help of our Hebrew teachers.

It was far from an easy program, with only late afternoons and evenings for recreation. At some of our aides' suggestion, we arranged a series of "pleasure events," but within three weeks our "girls" had built up a social life of their own. Meanwhile I tried my best to talk with each of them privately once in two weeks, to let her pour out her heart or ply me with questions. I was often moved by these meetings. I could feel how deeply "The Pleasantville Plan" had stirred and enlarged their lives. By the time the program approached the end, everyone knew that the course had surpassed its goal. Our last formal session closed on a pitch of high expectation. In a week we would make "the move."

On a beautiful morning, July 1, 1912, six hundred boys and girls lined up on 150th Street in front of "the old institution," each one waving a small American flag and smiling impatiently. Traffic had been rerouted to enable them — grouped now in cottage formation, their cottage numbers pinned to their clothes — to parade behind the band along Broadway to 125th Street. From there they marched east to the New York Central station, where a special train — decked out with festive banners — awaited them. Most of the boys and girls who were taking the thirty-mile trip had never set eyes on a rolling field or a woodland.

Sixty minutes later the train arrived at the Pleasantville station. At once the children arranged themselves in cottage formation and began the three-mile walk to "The New HSGS." As they reached the top of the entrance hill that curved round the apple orchard, hundreds of voices shouted and screamed. The Pleasantville story was true! One of the boys in the group, thirty years later, wrote of this moment, "Of all we saw, the thing we liked best was the sight of our cottage mothers, who were waiting to greet each one of us. They too had their cottage numbers pinned to their clothes, so that we'd know them and they'd know their children . . . And so, along the road we went with our mothers — toward home."

Box lunches were given to all, beds and lockers assigned — and all at once the architect's painted sketch came alive with *children*! — east, west, north, south, dashing in and out of their cottages, over the square, across the unmowed fields, from the orchards down to the entrance gate to the bake-house and colonnades. Thanks to well-timed planning, that very evening the boys and girls, under their cottage mothers' direction, cooked their own suppers and set their own dining tables. By then, as daylight started to fade, all six hundred children assembled around the great rectangular lawn in front of the school so that all of us — here together at last — could watch the strikingly beautiful sky as the sun sank through the far Westchester hills.

"Wait, if you will, two weeks," I had asked the directors at our June meeting, "and then, if you'll let me know the day and approximate time, you can count on a guided tour. I think that within a fortnight we'll be properly settled, though of course the shock of the change won't be over for all the children — and as some of you know, there are still things for the workmen to finish — for example, the playground equipment: swings, slides, jungle bars, and the like for the youngest children, and the basketball court and baseball diamonds. But they've already cleared an enormous field, and the boys will probably improvise on their own. By the way," I added, "some of you might enjoy our Saturday services. We've worked out something new, with lots of singing and reading of prayers by the children. The services start at eleven."

A few days after July 15th, the directors began their visits. They came in droves — so it seemed — some of them bringing their friends and their children. They were visibly shocked with delight by the cottages, classroom buildings, and other structures set in the fragrant woodland surroundings, not to speak of the student projects already begun in the two vocational schools. They overwhelmed us with compliments. A number of visitors talked of a "sense" of delighted excitement that seemed to be everywhere — on the children's faces, in the way the men and women spoke to each other. At first the arrival of "high-placed strangers" somewhat disturbed both the staff and the boys and girls, but as summer wore on, the children began to look forward to seeing "important faces," overhearing excessive compliments, and answering friendly questions. "We're all on display. Better get used to it now," I said to the staff. "It may last for years."

My first concern was to see that each cottage fulfilled its role in the social life of its children. The hope was to foster our own type of the so-called extended family, the children ranging in ages, with the young ones bound to the older by the Big Brother and Big Sister relationships. We had made it clear to our teachers that the fact that he or she happened to live in a house with children carried no obligation to share in its social life. They could play as small or large a part as they chose, and of course they would always be welcome to join in the Friday evening festivities. Whether or not it centered around the birthday of one of the children, the formal meal might be followed by an interchange of visits in which one cottage served as host to another. Games, songs, sometimes playlets or dances, were planned in advance by the Council of Cottage Mothers. Whenever I could, I made it my business to visit each house where the entertainments took place, often joining the children in some of their songs.

One of the innovations I cherished most took place soon after our move to the country. Each boy and girl was urged to invite a parent or other relative to spend a day as the guest of his own cottage. I declared that the HSGS was always open for visits except during classroom hours. As guests they of course were invited to dine with the children, on food that, in many cases, had been prepared by their own sons or daughters.

The unrelenting pressure of "things to do" led me to fear that unless our procedures improved, things might well slip out of control. I called in the principal, Sharlitt, and Halpern, my righthand man. As Assistant Superintendent, the latter had felt himself forced — against his will — to make a number of quick decisions without even trying to "interrupt" for my authorization. Michael at times had also decided to "spare me the added burdens" and act on his own. Yet they knew quite well why this practice could never go on. The best-intended decision might, for reasons beyond their knowledge, lead to confusion, chaos, or worse, since all that went on in Pleasantville was conceived as an integral whole, with every part dependent on all the others. Means would have to be found quickly to keep me fully informed.

And thus arose what would soon be known as "The Uninterruptable Luncheons." Mondays, Wednesdays, and Fridays, just before twelve, a table appeared in my office with food and settings for three. Then Michael arrived with his bottomless coffee-urn, followed by George, who hung at the entrance a typewritten sign LUNCHEON: NOT TO BE INTERRUPTED (TILL 2). Our meetings contributed something I hadn't expected. Merely from hearing each other's reports — interspersed with questions — both George and Michael came to acquire a grasp on all that was going on outside their respective realms. It was reassuring to see how each man met the demands confronting him. Time after time, I would glance from one to the other and silently count my blessings.

"One of my teachers, Cronyn," Michael said one day, "asked me about the haybarn — the empty one in the meadow beyond the farmhouse. Could he have permission to make it into a club-room for the staff, since there isn't a place for the men and women to 'use' in their leisure hours? And they feel they should have a place — I'm still quoting Cronyn. The barn would make a perfect retreat, far enough from the cottages not to disturb the children. I said that I'd let him know."

"A bad mistake on *my* part," I replied, "not to have thought of their needs. A great mistake. If they're not enjoying living here, why should they stay? I'll make amends at once, before they pack up their bags and leave."

"Not very likely, Doctor." Michael grinned at George, who broke out in smiles. "Not with all the romancing around us. Nobody's breathed the slightest complaint. Besides, just a month ago we said we'd build them a tennis court, which we'll also flood in winter for skating. As for making amends, it's just that the notion of turning the haybarn into a hideaway's taken their fancy. And I gather the answer is Yes? Incidentally, we've a real genius in Brant. If he tires of teaching French, he can turn to painting. I happened to walk through the auditorium yesterday afternoon just before the rehearsal. He was finishing up the scenery sets for the operetta. What an artist he is! And if Eva Cohen isn't leading me on, he knows all there is to know about music and operettas. There's lots of excitement about the one they're rehearsing. Some of the teachers are planning an after-show evening party. I warned them to keep it secret. If he heard, Brant might simply decide to vanish. I'd like to attend but won't. I told them my presence might be constraining. They smiled and thanked me." He laughed.

"Don't worry about them, Doctor!" Halpern nodded. "They've set up a little world of their own, and they're also proud to be part of the HSGS."

They had reason to: we were being acclaimed by the outside world. Experts seemed to vie with each other in shouting our praises — "The most outstanding and best-run child-caring institution anywhere," said Hastings K. Hart, the Russell Sage Foundation's president. Professors from Harvard requested a special group of charts and photographs for permanent display in their Social Ethics Museum. Child-care specialists from everywhere in America — also Europe, even Japan — were asking permission "to enter and study Pleasantville." Because the visits of social workers and other "experts" became so frequent, we had to call on our older children to guide them around. For a time they found it exciting to welcome "all these important strangers," but after the glamorous visit of President Taft, "the chief of the U.S.A.," nobody else could impress them. They were still talking about his friendly speech, his smile, his charm, and how proud he was, as he said, "to be wearing the gold-seal button of your Republics. . . ."

One grave problem still troubled me — "and until it's resolved," I told my Board, "I refuse to accept *any* praise except under protest." The problem involved the school. What could be done to legitimate our "unorthodox" curriculum in the eyes of the outside world? We could graduate our seniors in June, but without the officially recognized high school diplomas, thanks to the poor showing they made for the College Board Entrance examiners. I knew from my work in the New York system how far our children exceeded its norms. The problem was my mistake: I had made no provision for teaching the class how to cope with the "Regents" type of testing. "*You're* not responsible, nor are the boys and girls," I explained to Sharlitt. "It's clear from the way they wholly mishandled the questions. The technique of passing examinations is — to put it crassly — a kind of specialized 'art.' "

I began at once to draw on certain department heads in the New York schools to observe our teaching and classwork with a view to providing reports and improved procedures. Was it fair to allow other seniors to leave without any "real" diplomas? Should I let a year, even more, go by before confronting the coming group with the Regents tests, which were now the compulsory college-entrance "finals" throughout the state? There was reason enough to be hopeful. The head of Industrial Arts at Columbia's Teachers College judged the work of our children of twelve to sixteen to be better than similar work by others two, three, or four years older. I resolved to let nothing block us from reaching "the Regents goal." I might even take on a class or two in my "leisure" —

Which to Sonya was still a joke, if also a fact to be lived with at least in these first few years. She was far from idle herself. After improving as well as she could on the taste of whoever had furnished our house, she devoted herself to gardening. First there were shrubs, of various kinds, blossoming bushes, and evergreens to vary the angular lines of the cottage exterior, featuring ten full lilacs she found near a battered farmhouse. Flower beds heavily filled with blooming annuals gently curved round the two large pillared porches. A neighboring farmer reported daily at 10 to complete the cottage plantings. The vegetable garden, set in a low-lying field behind the house, was next on her list. Then came her fondest project of all: a grape arbor, framed of hemlock boles twelve inches around, which would also serve for the Succoth feast in the autumn.

Our three-storey cottage was ample enough, though our girls, eager for privacy, objected to sharing bedrooms. Eva, now rechristened Evelyn, took the train from Thornwood, a mile away, a freshman at Barnard College. Marie, still in our classes, soon would follow her steps. But our youngest girl and our boy remained in the HSGS. Sonya took great care to see that their clothes did not differ from those of their friends. And Michael instructed his staff to "treat them just as you treat all the others." Words reached me one morning that my son's face had been soundly slapped for some silly infraction. It never occurred to him to complain, or to Sonya or me to speak of it. Nor did these young ones seem to experience discomfort when enjoying things denied their friends. For example, the morning the nearby farmer arrived, his jacket bulging, to "give us a present," insisting we needed a cat and a dog to complete our household. Dressed in his Sunday finest, he handed Pauline a kitten, adding "the dog, of course, for the boy." Within ten minutes scores of our children's intimates poured from the cottages to join in the great event. "Just imagine," one of the girls marveled, "soon we'll be chasing not only the cat and the dog but dozens of kittens and puppies — one for each cottage, maybe. . . ."

We missed our city friends. At first we'd ask them to come for a day, and the hours were pleasant enough, but the second visit was always delayed. It soon seemed all but impossible to keep up friendships that mainly had fed on propinquity when thirty long miles intervened. Besides, Sonya was much in demand by the younger women — housemothers, teachers and often their weekend friends. They'd flock to our door, bursting with "things" to tell her. I was sure enough of the reason, after Michael's and George's remarks about the romancing under our noses. In Sonya they found the friendly candor and sympathy of a worldly and wise young woman. They "adored" her stories — and of course her fortune-telling enjoyed a *sub rosa* fame. One afternoon, coming back from my office, I noticed five women draped at her feet on the porch carpet. I decided to enter the house by the rear kitchen, only to stumble on three of the visitors putting the final touch on a cake to surprise their hostess. They begged me to join the procession. I was barely able to hold my tongue. "Say what you're bursting with, Ludwig," Sonya insisted.

"Are you sure you want me to, girls?" They nodded excitedly. "Then I hereby officially name your hostess: Director of Love Affairs at the HSGS," and I left in the midst of their laughter.

There was one companion whose absence we deeply missed: the man who had been my warmest friend from the time Judge Levy had brought us together nine long years ago. The closeness among the three of us — he was not our physician only but our luncheon guest and our confidant — was so widely known that his "disappearance" was causing concern. Michael and George made separate overtures, hoping to heal the mysterious rift. But Milton had merely waved them aside. And my own efforts by telephone met with a curt "Dr. Gershel says that he's much too busy and won't have time to return your call. He goes back on the three o'clock train."

In the year before the Pleasantville move, our relations had grown a bit odd. I was often forced to be absent from lunch because of our training program, and Milton, in turn, had made a point of avoiding talk about Pleasantville. In reality, as I told Sonya, Milton no longer could hold a place of importance and he's far too proud to become a superfluous man. True, yet after all he'd achieved for the HSGS in his first few years, how could he fail to feel bitter? And taking the train back and forth merely to supervise hospital nurses and check on the children's health? — I for one wouldn't blame him. To be sure, it was not our doing. But never in all our talks had he shown the slightest wish to be part of the Pleasantville world, though I offered him countless suggestions. It was saddening to be losing so close a friend, whatever the reasons. . . . We'll get used to it, I told myself. After all, Badanes never forgave me for leaving the school. "The children always liked to listen to Milton's father's stories about his life as a soldier 'saving the Union,'" Sonya remarked. "Did you ever tell Judge Levy about this end to our 'friendship'?"

"Once. I said that bringing us all together might help — that perhaps there was something I'd done — some act of omission — for which I'd gladly atone. I even wondered if taking our boy when he broke his arm to a village physician — a kind of emergency — might have piqued Gershel. The Judge nodded, 'We've all lost friends at times and never knew why. Don't rack your head for the reason. — Now let's get back to the point we were settling. — Oh, by the way, Gershel's developed a brand-new friend — and I dare say patients as well: the one on our Board who can't forgive you for ending the military band. — Don't give him a thought — he's harmless — the one on the Board, I mean.'"

Weeks later, quite without warning, Lewisohn's limousine appeared at our cottage. Before I opened the door, he had walked the pebbled path that led to our porch and had climbed the steps. Half out of breath, he grinned, "Forgive me for dropping in without calling — I've just come back from the West — but all of a sudden — thirty minutes ago — I heard myself shout, 'But they've never been here after all my promising.' Without even changing clothes, I called for my car — and away we flew — and

I'm here to kidnap both of you." He turned his back on the chair I offered. Looking toward Sonya, he added, "And from what you've done with those old lilacs and canna, I'm sure that you'll like my roses . . . Come, don't bother to dress! We've a beautiful day. Telephone Halpern, Doctor, tell him it's urgent business." He chuckled, "It really *is* a matter of life and death — with flowers as much as people. Maybe before you leave, I'll convert you both."

I thought of pictures of royal estates I'd seen as a child, but Ardsley was even more beautiful. Open fields, blue-green lawns, sloping and rising meadows, and pathways curving to houses set among trees as though they had grown up together. And light — sunlight floating through giant oaks, maples, hemlock — and wherever we looked: blossoms. After a rather hasty pause for tea and cakes, Lewisohn led us down from the broad verandah into a leafy arbor. "Some time I'll give you a tour of the whole estate, but today we'll visit my gardens."

Only an expert botanist could have known the plants, native and foreign, within the succession of hothouse buildings and open acres. Neither Sonya nor I could speak, lost in what seemed unreal. We walked for nearly an hour. Lewisohn also was silent, though now and then he would lower his head, touch a flower, and speak to it.

"Please sit down," he said as he opened the last of the hothouse doors. "Rest for more than a minute! Soon we'll do some climbing." We followed a winding trail that slowly led us up to a stony crest which offered an open sight of the distant hills. "I hope you're pleased with the view. What do they call it in Europe, Doctor? A *belvedere*? I'm told that this one changes with every shift in a cloud, but my poor myopic eyes can't see such refinements. Oh my," he suddenly stopped. "I ought to have shown you my blacksmith shop. After all, with Pleasantville's technical schools, you should see it. By the way," he laughed, "I'm building a miniature railroad . . . And the blacksmith shop! Next time I'll try to remember, though, frankly, when I'm 'at work' in my gardens, nothing else enters my mind. And now, we'll walk this way, to my 'castle,' as my friends and enemies call it."

Back on the broad verandah, he guided us to a table set with refreshments. "You're the best guests I've ever shown through the gardens. Most people think that they have to chatter, but both of you kept your eyes on the plants. I suppose you noticed me talking to flowers — certain flowers. I do — and I think they know . . . *Think*, did I say? — Scientists twenty-five years from now will be doing the same . . . As a boy I used to walk in the woods near Hamburg, looking for flowers. That's when I first started to talk to them — quietly. I said to myself: all things alive must have some kind of feeling." He chuckled. "What am I doing . . . talking my own philosophy to a Ph.D.? I hope you experts can make some room for an amateur."

He signaled the butler to bring a tray. "Iced coffee and tea. — I wish I could ask you to stay, but my wife will be bringing guests and the cook fiercely objects to changes." I gave the expected replies, but he interrupted "I hear that the children really look forward to Saturday services, though it's hard to believe — for one who was raised by a painfully orthodox father." He mused for minutes. "After I'd been away six years from my home in Hamburg, I arrived on a Saturday morning, bursting with joy to embrace him. But the instant I entered the room, he scolded, 'Carrying bags on the Sabbath? May merciful Yahweh forgive you.' And then, instead of welcoming me with a fatherly kiss, he boxed my ears . . . I suppose he thought he was doing the will of the Lord. But" — he paused again — "I must come to your Saturday service. Now that I'm through with my trips out West, you'll be seeing more of my face." He laughed. "I hope you can bear it. I love the sight of the cottages, and the children singing. Louis Seligsberg couldn't believe it, he said. The boys and girls, that Sunday morning he came, were washing windows and cleaning rooms and singing, really singing, all of the time. I told him I'd have to hear it to be convinced . . . Oh, by the way, Seligsberg tells me you're — how shall I put it? — strongly in favor of Germany. Tell me why!" Before I could answer, the butler arrived with a message. "Oh, too bad — we'll take up that subject soon, but my guests are here and I know you'll allow me to greet them." He glowered. "Just between ourselves, I wish you could stay. They're not very interesting people —" and off he ran, at an awkward trot. A servant we hadn't seen before asked us to follow him to the "station car," as he called it, which was waiting to drive us home.

It took us days to get over the Ardsley visit. What touched us both was the openness of our host, his uninhibited speech subtly imbued with deference, as though he were reaching out in a bid for friendship. There also were touches of testing. What was my view of the War? I had made no secret about my stand, yet from what I'd learned, many Uptown Jews abstained from commitment: Germany, Austria, Turkey vs. Britain, Russia, France, with some minor participants. Belgium was overrun by rampaging Germans, to the pained dismay of Seligsberg, who kept trying to change my view: "Your brother's a medical man in the British army. Do you want their defeat? And what of the helpless orphans roaming through Belgium?

What if the selfsame brutes should lay their hands on the French you admire so much?" I was darkly aware of Lord Grey's words, as he stood at his window, watching the lamplighters turn off the London lights: "The lamps are going out all over Europe; we shall not see them lit again in our lifetime." Yet "everyone" knew that wars were outmoded diplomacy. Civilized lands would settle affairs by reason — President Wilson would move at the proper moment; the carnage would end. What of my other brothers and sisters, what of their sons? Hope for a peace and faith in human reason somehow sustained me despite the ongoing bloodshed.

Three days after the Ardsley trip, John A. Kingsbury, New York's Commissioner of Public Charities, asked me to join his official committee to inspect all child-caring institutions receiving municipal funds. The work itself was assigned to three: Brother Barnabas of the Catholic Protectory, Dr. Rudolf Reeder of the Protestant Orphanage, and myself of the HSGS. The first and the second studied the educational, social, and recreational aspects with minor attention to institutional and family home care. I was given the much more delicate task of inspecting a great many Catholic institutions. Only Pleasantville's "fame" and high reputation for "standards" could explain the excessive defensiveness with which I was met by the Brothers and Sisters in charge. They were paragons of courtesy, and I in turn did all I could to be tactful and friendly. Unfortunately, they showed themselves to be totally unaware of even the rudiments of modern ideas of education and child care. Inevitably my reports created a stir. Controversial accounts appeared in the papers, followed by charges and countercharges, despite the fact that, at my insistence, a number of Catholic Brothers and Sisters came to the HSGS to observe and assess our procedures. Meanwhile a leading Catholic layman discreetly requested Lewisohn to ask me to leave the committee, then a lawyer connected with Tammany Hall persuaded a friend on my Board to object to my "marked political activities." Both maneuvers collapsed, and before the year had passed, the official result — a pamphlet *Child Caring Institutions: Plan of Inspection - Questions - Suggestions - Standards* — was published by the Commissioner. Our efforts were praised not only by fellow-professionals of all persuasions but also by John P. Mitchell, the Catholic reform mayor, some of whose appointees had supported our labors.

During all my "outside" activities — which in time proved a boon to Catholic child care — Michael labored incessantly in the hope of achieving the coveted "Regents Goal." I even offered to help as the critical week approached, but the die had already been cast. Within six days our students emerged victorious. Michael's faith had been fully — even dramatically — justified, as some of the class, in a number of tests, scored 100%, which the Albany Board confirmed.

I telephoned Lewisohn's office. "If I'm interrupting, forgive me, but we've won, you and I. The State is awarding our children the Regents diplomas and they've given our three-terms-a-year curriculum official approval, which has never happened before. All that we dreamed in your office has now come true."

Lewisohn roared in the telephone, "Do you think that I'm really surprised? It was bound to happen, but anyway, congratulations." He paused. "And now can you guess what I'll do? The minute I hang up the 'phone I'll cable Professor Rhein and sign it with both our names. And one of these days I'll pay you another visit. Tell your wife I've found a new rose that I think will grow in her garden."

News of the Regents' approval spread like proverbial prairie-fire, and even people without full grasp of its meaning greeted each other with smiles. Three short years and we'd reached the goal of acceptance with our 1915 Commencement. Brant and Eva Cohen outdid themselves with their musical settings, and the senior "class play," given that evening, closed the day with the singing of "Alma Mater," followed of course by the ever popular "If I Were the Superintendent. . . ."

Lying in bed that night, I wondered, "What should I aim for now?" The question was surely presumptuous. We had more than our share of steady complaints. Boys especially failed to be doing as well as they could with the meals. Our teachers often experienced troubling problems in "getting used" to the school's demands and to sharing a house with children. Most of our cottage mothers were still fulfilling my hopes, fairly exuding a sense of crusading ardor despite events that could fill them, at times, with despair. At our weekly meetings, I stressed the need for studying every newly admitted child, to learn his or her particular likes and fears, capabilities, aims, and — for lack of a better term — "emotional make-up." I was broaching something that decades later came to be part of standard "intake" procedure, by proposing a kind of profile for every child . . . which naturally led to discussing the Big Brothers and Sisters. The minute the words were mentioned, one of our senior house-mothers caught my eye. "May I take a moment to tell you what happened this morning? . . . When I left my cottage, I noticed the new little boy we admitted yesterday. He was walking all by himself to school, wiping his tears. I hurried at once to his side. 'Is your name Sam Simon?' He nodded and faced away. 'Tell me, Sam, why are you crying? Didn't your house-mother give you a big brother?' He shook his head. 'Sam! Don't you want to have a big brother to help you?' He kept on shaking his head, then looked at me coldly, 'Ain't I got enough boys to hit me?' — The story of Sam of course has a blissful ending. . . ."

Lewisohn, true to his word, paid us an early visit — a quarter past ten on a Sunday morning. Instead of stopping before our house, he drove around the great square plaza, then over the service roads behind the cottages. Sonya and I waited until he entered our porch from the rear. "You know why I came so early, Doctor?"

"To check on Seligsberg's tale about the singing?"

"One of my tutors said that an English writer called his country, because of its poets, 'a nest of singing birds.' I thought of that phrase as my car drove by *our* singing *children*. But oh," he turned around for a moment, "I've left some things in the car." He motioned his driver, who took from the rear a small bouquet and a leather box. Giving Sonya the roses, Lewisohn said, "If you like the color I'll send you two or three bushes. Plenty of sun all day!" Before she was able to thank him, he planted the leather case in my palm. "A belated birthday present, as you'll see when you open the back. There's a small inscription. I hope you'll approve. And now I must rush away to write my speech." I must have looked very curious. "Haven't I told you? I'm making a gift to the City College — a stadium, designed for open-air concerts and free to the public — forever! I preferred that it be anonymous, but I weakened. They're naming the place the Adolph Lewisohn Stadium. The cornerstone will be laid in a week and I'll have to say a few words, as the President asked." He paused. "Every time I think of the speech, my head goes blank. Maybe you'll think of some words that would get me started, Doctor. Would you care to ride with me? Ardsley's not very far, as you know." He turned to Sonya. "I promise when he comes back he'll bring you your roses. — Imagine, Doctor: six thousand seats! . . ."

Seligsberg, now a regular fortnightly visitor, chuckled. "I thought I detected some non-Lewisohnian sentences. Adolph asked me to go there for moral support; he meant it. He knows what a figure he makes on a platform — short, squat, heavy-spectacled, circled by giants. But the speech was excellent, brief — and the ceremony, touching. What a gift! There's nobody like him. Too independent to please the stuffier Uptown Jews — they call him the Gadfly. May his tribe increase!" — I showed him Lewisohn's words inscribed in the watch he had given me — *with deep admiration and steadfast friendship*. Seligsberg read it gravely. "Be assured that he means it. —

Oh, I tried to bring him along to see the performance. He said that he's still a trifle afraid of Shakespeare. '*You* afraid?' I teased, 'Adolph, the copper magnate? But this Shakespeare *Dream* is a play for children. Change your mind!' — Oh well, we'll manage without him, won't we, Sonya? . . ."

We stepped outdoors for a last look at the sunset. "Tell me, Doctor, what's going on in the hideaway?" I told him about a teacher's request to make of an unused barn a faculty club-house. "I've looked at the place. Have you?" I shook my head. "Whatever it was before, the fellow's an artist — the place is crammed with pictures, books, magazines, beautiful ornaments, hassocks, rugs . . . and then outside there's a garden, vegetables, flowers. My Alice's friends keep talking of 'George's Little House.' Alice, you know, mixes with all sorts of persons: writers, painters, actors, directors, philosophers even. She tells me some well-known people spend weekends at George's, though their names mean nothing to me — Walter Lippmann, some theatre folk — a Robert Edmond Jones, a Kenneth MacGowan, Philip Moeller. They sit on the floor in front of the fire and talk about all the things that are new in the arts, politics, women's suffrage, Henri Bergson and Life itself — the smallest subject of all. Makes me want to be young again . . . like your daughter Evelyn, who's part of the group."

"She hopes to marry this winter — one of our teachers."

"My congratulations, though you don't sound very elated."

"Sonya is, and for once I'm putting my faith in her intuition. When they marry, they'll move to Erie to manage the Fairview Home. I never thought my daughter would be a social worker. Neither did she."

The awkward turn of the conversation changed with the dinner bell's sound. "If it's any comfort, Doctor, Alice is having her troubles. Fellowship House — how much better that sounds than your 'Aftercare Department' — is learning, but only, she says, by making mistakes. Seems like a costly way."

"Sometimes the only way — but at least we've closed the entire circle: children under our eye not only while here in our care but after they break in the world. For the first time they know that we'll answer their call till they're able to hold their own."

"By the way, and to change the subject, do you still keep up with The Nine?" I nodded. "Maybe they'd help to save what's left of the wrecked *kehilla*. Magnes, I'm told, is a pacifist when he isn't a Zionist spokesman. I thought the plan had the germ of a useable program. I wish you could give it some time. If you weren't so overburdened, I'd beg you to join." He sighed wearily. "With all the things on your mind, I wonder how you ever find time for your own children. . . ."

The remark weighed on me all through the evening, making me miss some parts of the Shakespeare performance. I tried to conceal my restlessness, but not till Seligsberg's car drove off was I free to confront the question. Sonya had raised it once when Eva was only a child. Had she felt it hopeless to raise it again, knowing my situation gave me so little choice? Whom could I turn to now — except myself, if only that self could answer the question? The thought of a private journal had struck me before. Now it made urgent sense. Setting down thoughts might show me what I believed or thought I believed. What has the child-care expert to say of his own children? No one would hear but his journal. Write it in German script so no one can read.

EVELYN — (20). Hasn't confided since Halpern's wife tried to wean her from Sonya; brilliant, not too profound; by turn, defiant and willing to follow; does inappropriate things to attract attention; knows there's more to the world than the HSGS and her "great" father; will marriage help her to find herself? — not likely; probably loves me more than she knows; must do all I can to help; too proud to take my advice. In sum: most troubled of all three girls.

MARIE — (18). Never needs to confide in anyone; knows she's the prettiest girl of the three and gifted — paints, draws, competent pianist but not any genius; social, confident, very compliant; thinks me a semi-god and herself the semi-god's rightful daughter; sure that the world will do her bidding; needs to be cautioned; happiest of the three but so bound up in her joyous world that she leaves us out.

PAULINE — (15). Sweetness incarnate, ever since she was born, but now impossibly overweight; probably thinks I blame her; bursts into tears when teased; oversensitive; reaches out to be friendly, sociable, helpful; needs wider horizon. Extremely intelligent, sensible. Wise to have sent her to high school in N.Y. Outwardly optimistic, inwardly fearful? Fearful of me. Must do something quickly to save her from losing her way in the world. Generous — to a fault. Inveterate reader.

MY SON — (10). As able at playing baseball as doing his schoolwork; too restless to finish a book; loves to garden; friendly but shy; overwhelmed by my presence; responds to affection but never initiates — probably thinks it unsuited in front of his friends; tied too close to Sonya. What does a boy *really* think of a father who can't throw a ball or dig a rosebush? Asks too-literal questions; has no imagination? "Why did you say that God is a rock" — typical. Very good mechanically; very fond of animals — to a fault, perhaps?

Safely hidden inside my desk, the journal also served for reminder-notes too private to write on my office diary. Some of the entries formed a strange obbligato, mocking the smile of trouble-free joy that the world saw on my face:

COTTAGE MOTHERS — Some of the best make the worst showing as house-keepers. Discuss with Senior Council before proceeding. Be tactful.

SERMON IDEA — Discuss Zionist plans for Palestine in synagogue service so children will know. Not a word of my personal views. Also talk about "chosen people" — will "chosen message" be better? Comment on ancient Jewish music, royal singers, King Sennacherib's call for Jewish musicians as part of tribute. Tie to our Sabbath singing.

BLUM — When he gave his Shop demonstration to visitors: "And so whenever you've built a machine and the parts work and the parts work well, there's nothing left for the builder to do but sit back, relax, and oil it. It's time for him to go off and build something else." Might have been talking of me.

BRANT AND COHEN — What would we do without them? Must repeat their Purim play — brilliant idea, using Faust and Aida arias with "Jewish words" composed by the Jesuit Brant! Invite Lewisohn, Seligsberg.

BELGIUM-JAPAN — Lewisohn: "Belgium cabled again. Begs me to send you to rescue their orphans. Board refused. I also said No to Japan but they'll keep asking. Aren't you proud we're unwilling to spare you?" — Every chance I've ever had to get into the world-at-large and out of the Jewish enclave runs into trouble! Buchanan all over again: "Your first obligation must be to your own people." The pill gets harder to swallow.

AFTER PASSOVER SERVICE — What's wrong with us? We extol the Lord for His justice while our own Haggadah proclaims the inequality with which He endows the four who ask the Mishtanah questions. How can the Jews *still* call Him just, seeing the grief inflicted on children too young to have wronged His will? Is He challenging us to try to make up for His lapses? Maybe Badanes was right when he charged me with playing God, doing for injured innocents what a decent God would have done. . . . Even worse — overcompensating.

DIRECTOR X — Still talking to teachers (Gershel's friend). "Wonderful! Just as good as a very expensive private school — but for orphans! Don't you agree? What a waste." Teachers embarrassed, report to Sharlitt. Also says Lewisohn fails to receive credit due him for making Pville possible.

DANGER! — Two directors want their children to spend a month in Cottage 8. Must discuss with Lewisohn. Sounds like underhand work of X.

The War worried us all, especially after President Wilson's envoy failed to persuade the Powers to lay down arms. While Europe's soil ran hot with blood, America held back, a divided country, except for the east, where public opinion favored Britain and France. Wilson won re-election — on a Peace platform, while war propagandists kept on working for Britain. Certain men with financial power said they expected the worst; others, the best, their common helplessness taking the public's toll in "depressions."

Meanwhile the groups committed to Jewish causes voiced concern because of the need to assist overseas victims. For the very first time our confident Seligsberg changed his tune: "Where will the money come from? Only the Lord can say what will happen. Whether the Germans win or lose, we'll never regain the world we've known. Balance will disappear. Those who expect to go back to the lives they lived before will find themselves tossing and turning between extremes." He apologized, "Of course I'm a Jeremiah, compared to my friends. One of them thinks that the world's great age will begin anew and quotes some poet as proof. Even the unpoetic Lewisohn laughs at my gloom. — My, how that man astounds me! No one would ever suspect he's mourning a wife and mother of five, after thirty-eight years of marriage. But nothing has ever daunted him."

When our note of condolence remained unanswered, I wondered what I might do. Ten days later a call from his office asked me to come for tea — five P.M., 881 Fifth Avenue. He greeted me warmly. "Thank you for coming on time. We'll talk where no one can hear us. I've something to say. Promise to listen!" I trailed him into a sitting room. "I'm very fond of you, Doctor, and recently you've been on my mind. What would you like to do with your life, now that your dream's come true? I know as sure as we're talking here that you couldn't possibly remain content with doing 'the same old thing' for the next ten years: your golden decade."

"The dream, Mr. Lewisohn, hasn't yet fully come true. There are still many things to be done."

"You answer only in part. I'll put it another way. What would you *love* to do with your next ten years — for *pleasure, happiness, joy, delight*? You're a whole generation younger than I, but I *know* I've enjoyed more than twenty-one extra years of — what shall I call it? — 'living.'"

I felt like a fool but I had to reply, "I suppose I've never had either the time or the sense to ask such a question."

"Ask it now, or let me answer it *for* you! In certain ways we're two of a kind. It's not our nature to stop and sit back and admire our finished achievements. Restlessness drives us on. I've dozens of things I'm yearning to do — not only wrongs to be righted, causes to help, but also downright indulgences: houses, paintings, jewels. — You never cut loose into words as I'm doing, but what if you let yourself go? What would you *really* love to possess and to do?" He stopped, embarrassed. "Forgive me! I shouldn't be talking this way. Let me get to the reason I asked you here. I've known you thirteen years. You're much too gifted a man to remain dependent on others. You've more than earned the right to enjoy whatever you wish — I repeat: to enjoy *whatever you wish,* without concern for the money." He rose from his chair. "I'm ready to launch the Lewisohn Bank of Grand Street, but only on one condition: that you be the President. All the details will be handled by my technicians — I'm aware that banking never entered your head. What really matters is this: I want you to co-adventure, to stay at my side as a special partner, looking wherever we should, choosing together the wrongs to be righted, the causes in need of help, and the like. Oh, needless to add, my offer assures you more in terms of wealth than you're likely to need or want, for you and your family: independence financially. For the project is sure of success, with your great executive talents and the high prestige you enjoy all over the city." He raised his hand to stop me. "Don't say a word in reply! This is all between us: you, your wife, and myself. It must go no farther." He walked toward the door, laughing. "My son Sam worries about me. 'Father, you're spending your *capital*!' — 'Who made it, my boy?' I answered." Pulling open the door, he whispered, "Write me a letter within the week, or call my office."

When I told her my news, Sonya burst into howls of laughter . . . "Can't you just see Badanes' face? . . . and the rest of his Socialist friends?" Pulling herself together and finally drying her tears, she cried, "The Head of the Lewisohn bank no less — a bank on *Grand* Street! He's probably running wild and there's no one to stop him. That's what happens to widowers. Next thing we'll hear, he'll be married."

"Luckily I can make my reply by letter." But for some reason, her endless laughter annoyed me. "You won't believe it, but when he finished, there wasn't a single word I could think of saying. Not even 'Thank you.'"

I made some notes in my journal. What in fact *would I love* to do with the next ten years, if I owned Aladdin's lamp? In rejecting Lewisohn's offer, was I casting away the supporter without whose friendship, trust, and devotion much of all I had built would have never been realized? Yet how could a man of his understanding so mistake the values by which I lived? . . . Which is not to say that we've all the money we want or would ever hope to earn. I would have to write a candid letter with thoughtful omissions.

Despite my most zealous efforts, I find myself incapable of writing a letter consonant with the generous gift you have offered. Like many others, my manhood was filled with dreams of important achievements aimed at improving the world, only to mark with the passing of years the disparity between the height of my hopes and the reach of my own capacities. And so I "accepted reality," and, using such gifts as the Lord gave me, followed the course that was forced upon me by nature. Education, viewed in its broadest perspectives, became my vocation, so that when fair Fortune led me into the lives of victimized children, I was able to carry forward in broader and ever more fruitful ways the limited start I had made as a teacher of other children.

It is difficult thus to unburden myself without inviting the risk of sounding much too noble or pious. Yet the fact remains that financial independence or overgenerous income has never entered into my workaday plans or played a part in any employment decision. This is not to say that I lack the normal desire for pleasures, comforts, joys, and delights that money would bring to my wife, myself, and my children. I know that your offer would greatly enrich our lives and I realize that, in giving it up, I am doing something less than thoughtful or fair of a father and husband, by indulging my private desires. And yet I feel bound to hold to this choice, hopeful that whatever the future holds, it is likely to bring financial rewards sufficient to meet our needs.

Let me end these inadequate words on a positive note with regard to one of your statements. I am ready now and always to co-adventure with you and to stay at your side as your partner, to use your words, in your efforts to right wrongs and choose just causes. For I hope that despite this letter, you will never cease to count me among your friends, indeed among your most grateful friends and stanchest admirers.

"What kind of language, Doctor, did Lewisohn find so immensely moving that he's boasting to all his friends of the 'hardly believable selfless man who runs our HSGS'? He told me he made you an unrefusable offer, yet praises you to the skies for turning him down. Don't think I'm prying," Seligsberg added, "but even *I* hadn't known you were one of the saints." I was much relieved.

With turmoil, fear, apprehensiveness fairly streaking the air, we instantly talked of the War. Germany's submarine command boasted of sinking 300,000 tons in a single month at the end of the year, and aimed for and tripled that tonnage in April alone. Sure of controlling the ocean, the Kaiser scoffed at Wilson's "peace without victory" plea. Britain, nearing despair, countered the U-boat strategy with a combination of convoys, hydroplanes, depth bombs, destroyers. The German gamble would fail, but not before April 6th, when we entered the War.

The conflict came close to home, not only because of my right-about-face in opposing Germany. Our daughter Marie's fiancé Nemser, one of our Harvard teachers, enlisted in August, hoping to earn a place in the Officers Training Corps. At about that moment Chaim Weizmann and other movers and shakers chose the instant when Britain's and Zionists' aims were one. The cunning behind the official response was not to be known for years, but the Balfour Declaration, November 2nd, astounded the world with the promise to favor the "establishment in Palestine of a national home for the Jewish people" and to do its best "to facilitate the achievement of that object. . . ." *Das Yiddishe Folk* declared, "For the first time in 2000 years, we again enter the arena of world history as a nation." Judge Brandeis, in a moment of heady abandon, declared that "opposition to Zionism" could henceforth be considered disloyalty to the United States. Not that the mood of America's Jews was unified. On the contrary, endless arguments swept the country, even though Wilson finally added his blessing to Balfour's.

For reasons beyond my knowledge, one night when the telephone rang, I knew I would hear the voice of my former assistant and hopelessly smitten Zionist, Chester Teller. The Jewish National Welfare Board had asked him to set up a string of centers from Maine to Florida for Jewish soldiers and sailors to use as their second home. He had already pleaded with Lewisohn to give me a four-month leave. Would I come? Sonya and I might enjoy the diversion and of course there was nothing more important "to maintain the high morale of our brothers in khaki uniform than the home away from home that you two could create." Evelyn and her husband would gladly look after our children — he already had called them by telephone. Could I see him tomorrow morning? I wouldn't be asked to start the job for another three months. It would take that long for his people to lay the groundwork.

One week later, greatly to my surprise, a sudden consoling telephone call from an old, trusted — unnameable — friend brought tears to my eyes. He mistook them for signs of surrender, having heard of the fight I had waged for the last six months. For the first time I revealed the facts to Sonya. As a charter member of the newly formed "Federation of Jewish Philanthropies," Pleasantville had to submit a fiscal account for routine review. But to everyone's great astonishment, a man had been named to head the group and *approve* the budgets who was totally uninformed of the whys, the wherefores, not to mention the hows of the very groups that were now his domain. He had started out as a grammar school English teacher, then, for no discernible reason, was put in charge in the Lower East Side of all activities other than classes. In his graduate work on teaching English to foreigners, he had shown no inclination to learn about social welfare, child care, even the doings of Jewish philanthropies. Why he was placed at the helm of the new Federation no one was able to say, and the ruthlessness with which he proclaimed his proposals shocked the organization down to its core. Pleasantville, he declared, is a luxury Jewry no longer can stand, if it ever could! Put in place of its nine-year program a grammar school from the New York public system and you'll save at least $50,000. Agreed?

The astonishing statement placed indescribable strains on my Board of Directors as the struggle ensued. My counter-arguments became well known through the welfare world. Leaders in Gentile organizations wrote to acknowledge the debt they owed to the HSGS for raising their standards. Moreover, the New York State Board of Regents reaffirmed its approval of our curriculum. My opponents were quite unable to work their will. As a consequence, for the whole of the calendar year, Pleasantville HSGS continued unchanged, while gathering increased support, as talk of the "money-grubbing debate" spread through the welfare field. Nevertheless, in time, I would face a decision. To give a dependent child what we all had resolved was his due, from my first meeting with Levy in 1902 to all subsequent meetings with Lewisohn, Seligsberg, Hart, and other child-care thinkers of every persuasion, seemed to mean nothing at all against saving $50,000. Nor did it count that the HSGS alumni had raised $1,000,000.00 in War Bonds, leading the War Department to christen a plane "The Spirit of the HSGS." I would keep my opponents suspended in air throughout my four months' leave, then make my response. It was painful to study the faces of many trustees, themselves concerned with their own, and the nation's, economy. Yet one blunt fact was apparent. Federation had robbed them of independence as well as personal pride in the HSGS achievement. They were finding themselves manipulated — some of them, more and more willingly — by a social-worker illiterate who, ever eyeing his chance for financial advancement, would finally give up his "welfare job" to become — of all magnanimous entrepreneurs — a commercial "factor."

At the start of the year, Sonya and I traveled our separate ways, mine to Camp Devens in Massachusetts, hers to meet me in April somewhere in Georgia. For both of us the trip was a true education, which I've written about in a separate piece; but I can't let this capsule account say nothing about the enrichment brought to our lives by the men and women, young and old, we should otherwise never have known. Day by day we grew ever more deeply aware of America's greatness, the varied people who thrived in its cities and towns. All my life I had holed myself up in a miniscule part of a land too vast to imagine. And instead of returning to Pleasantville with a sense of coming back home, I began to see the endless "possibles" waiting for any man with a will to learn. Throughout my trip I had had no time for my journal, though my head was teeming with questions. The very first night at home I went to my study, turned to an empty page, and thanked the Lord for teaching me German script.

> Admit it to nobody else, but much of your joy in your "noble work" is the purely technical satisfaction of analyzing malfunctions, finding the needed parts to correct them, putting them back in place, then making them run again. And after that's been accomplished? . . . Pleasantville's doomed. I must look for some other social-work world that's in chaos and show how our common efforts can make it into "another monument to the Jewish genius for justice" — thereby gaining the double pleasure of righting wrong and using the technical skills that the Fates endowed me with instead of the poet's genius I'd have given my youth to possess . . .
>
> URIEL friend, do you hear me? The last laugh is on both of us. For it took a bookkeeper's mind to catch up with Yahweh — and now he's putting things back as before, doling out grief and good fortune by His Own Insensible plan, if He has a plan. We've been given our just deserts for believing in Moses. And now where do we stand? What shall we do? Commit more sins in our wilfulness to right the evils the world inflicts on the innocents?

Rumors of Pleasantville's "problem" buzzed through the Federation's halls despite the official news that the subject was closed. It was widely reported that Lewisohn made a ringing denunciation: "We've built the greatest monument to dependent children the world has known. Monuments don't drop from the skies. It is men who conceive them, strive for them, build them, and pay for them *gladly* before they can bask, as all of

Jewry has basked, in the world's acclaim. If we let our Pleasantville monument fall into ruins, I for one will never cease to proclaim the reason: greed, hard-hearted human greed." And he walked from the room as fast as his stubby legs could transport him. Constant repetition had doubtless embellished his words, but the stand he was forced into taking could raise no surprise. Precisely when he was said to have given the speech was never clear, nor did I feel inclined to pursue the matter.

Meanwhile I kept very close to the Pleasantville premises, since a "polio" epidemic, the signs of which had been seen in June, closed the gates to all but authorized visitors. Finally, during a special July meeting, I was given an ultimatum. "My" school *could* continue provided I'd fire its principal along with a number of teachers and not only run the HSGS as before but, in addition, supervise all the classes. I announced that, at least till the end of October, no such change might be made without destroying the New York Regents arrangements, which could not unilaterally be revoked. Without any further discussion, I left the room, treated myself to a five-pound box of Mazzetti confections, and boarded the train at Grand Central.

The War of course overshadowed everything else. When suddenly on November 7th the air around us exploded with sounds of foghorns, blasts, sirens, we assumed that peace had come. Children, cottage by cottage, walked toward the synagogue, offering thanks for the end of the carnage. Then our family took the train to New York to join in its wild celebration. Unfortunately, the news had been premature. Rifles and cannons continued to fire for another four days, time enough for thousands of youths and men to die or be maimed for the rest of their lives.

Two days later the Board of Directors sent me a formal request to appear on November 20th. Before the meeting had come to order, I walked up to Lewisohn: "Permit me to give you my formal resignation." After a moment I said to the others, "I don't believe it would interest you, but between today and the day I leave in December, there will be a number of dinners, meetings, testimonials, speeches, and similar 'celebrations' attended by welfare workers from many parts of the country, at least so their letters attest. Each of you will be welcomed, provided you call in advance. Assuming you have no questions, I take my leave." I extended my hand to Lewisohn, who held it a moment.

The next morning, without so much as a word from his office, he appeared at the door of my cottage. His presence upset our household, but I managed to lead him up to my study and close the doors. We sat on the couch beside each other, facing the maple trees his gardeners had planted years ago on the sides of the great green plaza. "My, how they've grown!" he remarked, pushing the curtains aside. "Pleasant to know that roots and boughs will outlive us all.

"I keep thinking about us, Doctor. The plan I proposed for the bank would have kept us together, but now — well — let me tell you a story — about a man who lost. And the man who lost is myself.

"By the time you arrived in America, I had made so much money that I wanted to stop. But my brothers pushed me. They wanted a giant merger, they wanted the copper Guggenheims to join, but the Guggenheims refused, preferring to keep their money within the family — and win! I was ready to let the matter drop and told my brothers. And then the Guggenheims fell into luck. A strike at our copper company gave them the upper hand and by clever Wall Street maneuvers, they won control of the coveted prize. The Guggenheims, God bless them," he laughed, "came out on top! Stock exchange people called it 'a battle of epic proportions,'" he sneered, "'which the Lewisohns lost.' Losing that kind of battle didn't faze me one moment. I was much too busy trying to find the worthiest causes for some of the millions I'd earned through the years. But you" — he paused, suddenly red with embarrassment — "you haven't a fortune to rest on. Of course, you're young and the world's wide open and everyone knows of your gifts and your hard-earned achievements. You deserve the best. Now what can I do to help, if you will allow a trusted friend to offer a hand, a word, a thought? Do I have to explain why I've come here?"

In a flash I was thrown back sixty-three years, witnessing not the man at my side but a silent, dreamy six-year old, who was deeply fond of his mother. Sitting beside him one afternoon, she felt herself suddenly sicken. She rose from her place — sank to the floor. Within minutes, the mother lay dead . . .

"Why do you hesitate, Doctor?" The flash disappeared as I looked at his face. "I had hoped we'd be always together, down at the bank, and you said that you'd always advise me. One of these days I shall take you up, but *now* — now the question before us is *You*. Tell me all you're willing to say to a trusted friend! I'll listen."

"Late last night I was telephoned by Frankel, one of The Nine, you've met him, of course. I'll try to repeat his words. 'Ludwig, how soon can you go to work? I've a brand-new desk at 105 Fifth Avenue, but the fellow we hired for the job is over his depth. He's hopeless. He'll sink and drag us down with him. Help us! Besides, there's a lot at stake. I'll wait for you at lunchtime — noon — the Brevoort Hotel.'"

Lewisohn warned with his fingers, "Please don't agree too quickly. After all, you could use a vacation. Besides, I've a stack of ideas in the back of my head. Call me after he's told you the whole of his story. I'll be waiting . . . anxiously."

"Frankel? Lee K. Frankel?" Sonya prodded the moment Lewisohn left us. "How can you possibly let him down? He's always been a true friend."

"Do you want a vacation?" I asked her. "We've money enough. Lewisohn thinks we deserve it. But I'd rather get back to work — if there's really so much at stake as Frankel says. We'll decide tomorrow."

At this juncture, my son, I'll spare you the full account of the testimonial dinners, meetings, playlets, speeches, and all the rest that were part of our long goodbye to our Pleasantville years. Besides, you attended them all. Perhaps you remember them better than I, except for the curious hymn of blessing — the one in Latin that Brant recited word by word at our last assembly. Only he and I knew the meaning. I thanked him for the courage beneath his blessing. My very last act, of course, was the series of visits I made to each of the cottages. As I entered the door, I raised my hand for silence, and then, in a handful of words, thanked them for what they had done to make of Pleasantville all it had been for years, adding, "I'll remember the HSGS for your happy singing."

I'll also spare you, my son, the gloom of our weeks in Brooklyn, with the daylight filtering through the front bay windows, shedding almost no light on the inner rooms of the floor-through brownstone apartment. I had quickly accepted the "bargain" offered by my successor — his "perfect apartment, tastefully furnished, ready to move right in. It will save you weeks of looking. . . ." We made you a bedroom out of the hallway entrance. Pauline slept in the smaller chamber, Sonya and I, the larger. One bathroom, alas, would serve for us all. — "It's only a makeshift," Sonya repeated. "Evelyn's looked at a big apartment right near the River. You'll like it," she kept reassuring you. "Open fields like the country, except for the high buildings and noise. You'll see how exciting the city can be, after we've settled. . . ."

When I saw Frankel, he bared some shocking facts. The newly forming Bureau of Jewish Social Research had agreed to survey Chicago's communal affairs, but the man selected had given it up as hopeless. To save the Bureau's face, an expert with nationwide reputation would have to "pick up the pieces" and face the gruelling task. It called for testing the findings on hand, analyzing delinquency in the tenth-rate Maxwell training house and prescribing feasible remedies, then studying *all* the city's Jewish child-care groups with a view to making them one. "It's a terrible task. You'll run up against the stubbornest heads in the West. But once you're done, you'll find an ideal offer waiting for you . . . Custom made, I should call it."

"Thank you for all the bouquets, but what about funds?"

"Live in the finest hotels! Send your wife and your children presents! Telephone Sonya once a week, but for God's sake, take the job! If you turn me down, Ludwig. . . ."

Two weeks later I found myself in the midst of the worst chaos a man might imagine. Frankel would never have let me come if he'd known the truth. I announced to the Survey Committee, "Authorize me to do *whatever* I find must be done, or I'll go straight back to New York. If your answer is positive, remember my warning: I may step on many toes, your own included. Please give me your answer tomorrow."

Social workers would find what followed of interest, but *any* one concerned with victimized children might have cheered when I closed the Maxwell house, overhauled the agency dealing with cases held by the courts, and drew up "Modernization Plans" for the quite impossible boarding bureaus and orphan homes. The work afforded no pleasure, and I missed the evening warmth of our home. But I also found a refreshingly new indulgence. Whenever possible, I put off a dinner engagement to search the "Latest Movies" list for "the most stupendous film ever made by man," from which there were always five or six to choose. The wearisomeness of my daytime tasks made me thirst for escape — and after the first few evenings, I stopped reproaching myself for ignoring the Goethe volume I'd taken along for sentiment's sake, recalling Professor Boyesen and my former trip to this city.

It must have been several hours after watching the *Male and Female* version of Barrie's *The Admirable Crichton* that Mephistopheles himself appeared at my bed. "Your Heaven-appointed task on earth is to write the filmscript of *Faust Part II*. Start it at once in the morning, or you die!" — "In the morning, the morning," I probably answered in the dream, till he disappeared. Half-amused, early next day, I called at the University. The *Faust* expert was absent . . .

But — back again to New York! Frankel blessed me for "saving his life," then gave me his latest news. "Chicago's chief contributor called to offer you lots of money if you'll head their proposed federation. Talk to Sol before you even consider it!"

Lowenstein spared no words. "Tell Chicago No, but Frankel Yes when he offers the Bureau of Social Research. You're the ideal person — and just what you'll really enjoy. But please don't ask me to say who's funding the place." He smiled quietly. "Now The Nine can have its regular meetings — and there's much to fight about — maybe a bit too much. . . ."

For people working to better social conditions, 1919 and 1920 were promising years. Jewish welfare's expanding world was finally coming of age, with facilities shaped to service communities, large and small. My assistant, a sociologist working "on loan" from his college, and his aide, a promising graduate, more than fulfilled my hopes. Soon I became familiar with cities and towns in the East and Middle West, and was showered with tempting offers. But my "education weakness" drew me elsewhere. Odd as it sounds today, there wasn't a single training program for Jewish social workers. Harvard's Maurice Hexter, in charge of the Boston Federation, conspired with me to set up a Summer Institute, to initiate those who might wish to enter the field and to give intensive training to people already employed. The Institute lasted four summer weeks: mornings given to lectures, discussions; afternoons to field trips to nurseries, family casework centers, prisoners' rehabilitation bureaus, foster homes, and the then much debated emotional-therapy clinics. Fifty young women and men attended our "school." I knew what happened by day, but all I could learn of the night-life came through the rumor network.

Pauline, our youngest daughter, was the Institute's "social success." And the songs she wrote for the play that ended our season brought her private applause that continued for months. Her future, however, challenged me. What did the world hold out — in practical ways — for a girl who lacked some so-called saleable skill? Since secretarial courses seemed an acceptable answer, I urged her to take them now and to join my staff, with the firm understanding that after one year, if all went well, she'd return to college.

She was able to make the best of the situation, unlike my son, who had not yet learned to cope with life in the city. For ten months of the year he kept from the streets, closed in his shell, till the last of June: casting it off to revel in camp in the woods of Maine. Family counseling might have improved his lot, but it seemed premature. The boy would simply have to adjust, like others who dreamed of themselves — as each of us sometimes continued to do in secret — as fallen nobility: people of quite superior grain doomed to live next door to boors with whom they could scarcely converse. Except for Chester Teller, who had moved into the big apartment a block away, we were virtually friendless.

I knew this could not go on. Sonya was back where she'd been in her

Flushing days, tied to marketing, cooking, cleaning, after the halcyon years in the HSGS. We never mentioned the subject, but one fine morning, both of us, sobbing suddenly, fell into each other's arms. After an hour we started to reach for solutions. I remarked that of all the places I visited, one in particular struck me. It was not too large a city — less than 500,000 — most of the people living in private houses bordered with lawns, plantings, and other signs of a quiet life. Yet the city's cultural fare was rich, varied: concerts, operas, plays, even the famed Carnegie Museum; three universities also, and a college for girls. More important, the people I'd met seemed open-minded compared with those in other midwestern places, despite their standard — defensive — view of New York. And the city was physically picturesque: built like Rome, on seven hills, and divided by two large rivers that joined to form the Ohio. Finally, the welfare situation was all but chaotic: even a fourth-rate "expert" could do an adequate job.

We kept this city in mind especially toward the close of the year when a number of men from out of town called at my office. I had learned how to ask key questions, weighing the manner in which they were answered, and making a point of saying I wasn't yet ready to make a commitment. After learning that several Pittsburgh trustees had come to New York to "interest" me, I agreed to visit their city again and meet with all the Directors. Within an hour they offered more than I'd ever expected, including their personal help to facilitate our move. I promised to make my decision within a fortnight, using the time to consult with some hard-headed colleagues, who gave me a list of certain things I "had" to demand.

The scores of untrained-social-workers-with-hearts-of-gold, whom I made fully aware of the standards they'd have to achieve, became my most difficult problem. It called for no end of time and patience, backed with irrefutable proof, for me to undo the past, to provide instructors for older as well as the new trainees; to introduce innovations, soon to be copied elsewhere (including what later came to be known as gerontological care); not to mention the final consolidation of dozens of bickering agencies — the list could go on, including the introduction of younger people from "warring" social and fiscal strata, helping to break the classic split between what we called in New York the Uptown and Downtown Jews. Social work was only part of my program. My educator's obsession involved me in two odd projects, one of which was to end in a kind of paradox.

It was past my power to explain the happy change that came over us. The house we rented was pleasant, and complete with a dog, a cat, a vegetable patch, a garden. Once again Sonya was freed from the household chores by a maid of all work; and a corps of congenial people invited our friendship. In less than a month we were looking about for a permanent dwelling. But the change went farther still. My son, who had never finished a book in his life and failed in some of his New York classes, shocked us all by winning a state-wide scholarship along with the editorship of his high school journal. And Pauline's plan for a college degree made a right-about shift when she found herself "hotly pursued" by a man whose persistence finally won. As for myself, I apparently gained repute as a public speaker. Invitations to join all kinds of boards and organizations flooded my desk. I found them hard to resist in the wake of the Pleasantville trauma and the callow anonymity of New York living. I knew that the first flush of overpraise was bound to subside, but it happened almost too slowly to be perceived. Although I thrived on plaudits, even I couldn't help but squirm when, after my second yearly report to a cheering hall, the city's patron saint of philanthropy, an eminent widow of eighty widely hailed for her knowledge of public affairs, suddenly rose to the platform and cried, "At last I can say 'I sit at the feet of my master.'"

I was startled early next morning to hear some ebullient sounds from the voice of my President, whom I'd christened Imperturbableness Personified. "Bear with me, Doctor," he cried into the telephone, "but never before has the University's President telephoned *any* Jew, least of all to solicit a favor! Dr. Whitman called to ask my permission to draw you into his plans for a Graduate Social Work School; and, most amazing of all, he said he'd greet you himself on the steps of the *Saturday* Club at one o'clock. No Jew has ever been near that place. — Now, before you tell me you'll think it over, say you'll be there! I can't explain what your visit will mean to our people . . ."

He had touched a sensitive subject. For years Maurice Hexter and I had been fashioning plans for a Jewish graduate school. The issue, publicly argued at all our nation-wide gatherings, was far from simple. We favored a full-time program which, besides the agreed-on-courses, would offer a heavy dosage of "Jewish content," adding, of course, that if "Jewish content" couldn't be clearly defined, everyone knew the meaning of "Jewish intent." In a word, we held that only a full-time, comprehensive school of our kind would attract students who "realized that Jewish pain could be understood only by Jewish eyes." — Once again my paradox: the son of the Great Enlightenment's Universal Religion wraps himself in the flag of "The Chosen" sect . . .

The issue was fiercely debated, and Hexter and I were at last outvoted, mainly because of money, though strangely enough, the Director, picked by the winning faction, sided with us temperamentally. — Pyrrhic victory? Without any more discussion, this 1924 National Conference of Jewish Social Service made me its President and the chair announced that the Training School for Jewish Social Work would open its doors in the fall. I agreed to visit New York each week as Special Teaching Lecturer . . .

At the entrance to the Saturday Club, President Whitman greeted me, shrugging aside my remark on the dangerous step he had taken in bringing me here. "Some day soon, I hope, this country of ours will come of age, not only respecting race and creed. Do you know what I tell my Freshmen? 'If four years hence, you haven't learned to love poetry, you'll have wasted the time.'" A Negro ushered us into the dining salon, sizing me up and down. We were quite alone.

"My son didn't need that advice," I said. "He'll be graduated in August. Forgive the personal note, but my son's convinced he's a poet — and he can't decide what he should do for a living . . . But tell me, Dr. Whitman, how can I be of service to you with your project?" He lost no time in making me know he had drawn a full report on my whole career, Rhein, Boyesen, Butler included, as well as my thesis. "I also know of your Jewish social-work battle, but I'm counting on the humanist view of one of the Enlightenment's advocates. To build the kind of Graduate School . . ." he began. Before our interview ended, I promised to offer my help and to join the faculty.

What I'd said at the start hadn't been fair to my son. He'd returned from Maine the summer before with serious offers: to join a professional baseball group or to write verse for a Broadway musical show. Hoping for my approval of both, he suggested tossing a coin to reach a decision. I refused. "Then you're still set on my studying business at Harvard," he groaned. "I can't understand how a one-time leading Goethe scholar can balk at letting me take a degree in literature. I could throw myself into teaching with all my heart. Oh yes, I'm aware that a Jew has a time of it, finding a job. But an influential professor swears that he'll place me after I earn my degree. Now why would he lead me on?"

"Listen calmly," I answered. "Assume that after some years you do quite well: you become an assistant professor. Assume you'll be teaching *King Lear*. Unless you win your students' approval, few will stay in your class, and so as a practical choice, you'll lower your sights. You bring *your* Shakespeare down to *their* level, for you'll have to meet them *where* they are and talk to them *as* they are. *King Lear* for a classroom of adolescents, not for grown, intelligent men and women. And so, you become a teaching success, dropped to your students' level not out of malice, of course, but simply because they are what they are: immaturities faced with an *inexhaustible* work of imagination." I stopped for a minute, noting Sonya's coming to join us. "If you're really bent on being a poet, take your motto from Wordsworth: 'A poet is a man speaking to men.' Men, men, grown-up men and women." I paused, shaking my head. "I'm sure you wonder why I no longer read Goethe. Everything he has written is here in my mind, and I know that I can't live long enough to comprehend the vastness of all that's there — even part of the vastness there." I found a letter beside my plate next morning:

> I listened to all that you said, but you speak from a vantage point of almost three times my age. My problem of earning a living is simply to find something that's not reprehensible, in terms of my own values. You possibly felt no different when you were my age. But in any case, I've arrived at a decent solution: To be of service yet also be paid for my pains. I've applied to the Social Work school for the fall. If they take me, your worries are over.

"They'll reject him because of age," I sighed to Sonya. And before the week had ended, the School confirmed my prediction, also suggesting he wait a year, study in Europe perhaps, after which they'd be glad if he'd reapply . . .

"We're back where we were," he laughed bitterly. "But what about Europe? Two years ago, you remember, you proposed a *Wanderjahr,* but I didn't feel ready. Then the next year, when I said I would like it, you changed your mind. I can get along with my French and Uncle Max is in England . . . ?"

His circle of friends concerned me: writers, painters, a good musician, one of Bloch's promising students, all inveighing against the financial boom and making much of the fact that thousands of people, greedy to "make their pile," mortgaged their lives to buy up stocks on margin, or charged usurious interest rates, while Europe was paying a fearful price for Germany's loss. It was true enough. Though ignorant of related facts, they blamed the USA for turning the cradle of culture into a Wall Street paradise. Yet they also envied aloud the expatriate artists crowding the Paris streets who felt no qualms of conscience at all in exploiting the fallen franc . . .

"If you find a job," I said one day before leaving for work, "and you save some money, I'll match it. I'll *triple* it. Then you can have your *Wander-jahr*. Meanwhile I'll give you letters of introduction, provided you're ready to tramp the streets as I did when I was about your age."

Our house was growing more and more tense as the weeks went by. Un-expectedly Leo Robin, one of our "Big Brother" leaders, paid me a call one Sunday. He had made a drastic decision: quitting his job, setting his hopes on "Tin Pan Alley" and Hollywood. He had come to resign, say goodbye, and thank me in person. "By the way," he said to my son, "still hunting a job?" I nodded. "Why don't you walk me home?" My son was more than pleased.

Leo began, "As for the job, I'm giving mine up and I think you'd like it. I know you've imagination and my boss Grove falls for 'inspirational' ads. You can handle a pencil, sketch, and you know a lot about type. If you want, I'll telephone Grove — he thinks *I'm* a genius! Grove and his side-kick Homan are patient, able, and generous; and they think of themselves as artists! If you feel moody, say so, and they'll *force* you to take the day off. What am I waiting for? I'll telephone *Lehman,* the head of the firm; I've done him some favors. — I'm sure you can't find a job that would suit you better. Remember, though, *getting* it, all depends on how you behave when you talk to Lehman. *Be yourself*! Don't try to put on a business act! Lehman's as bright as they come . . . with an excellent ear for language. If a really first-rate wisecrack enters your head, say it! He'll love it."

Half disheartened by all the talk of clamshell buckets, transmission towers, open-hearth furnaces, and so on, my son embarked on the train early next morning. Shown into Lehman's office, he was treated to noth-ing but praise for Leo's genius. "If you've half his talent, I'll never let go of you . . . never. And Leo tells me you're twice as bright. Are you? Don't answer! — You'll start at $19 a week — bottom of the ladder. But if you can do what he says you can do, nothing will stop you from rising. I'll call your father and tell him you got this job on your own — and, by God, you *did*. One of my boys will introduce you to Grove and Homan."

At dinner time my son told me I looked much younger, taking great care to add that the factory town was a hideous place. But he liked talk-ing with Lehman. "I'll never see him again, but what do I care? Nine-teen a week's hardly a generous salary. Of course he assumes that I live at home . . ."

A few days later the postman delivered an overseas letter. We rarely heard from my brother Max, whose ailing wife by now might have passed away. I held my breath. The opening lines set me at ease.

My dear Brother President and Double Professor:

I congratulate you on election to such Great Office, and your two new jobs. A professorship in an enemy camp is at least a 50% triumph. As for the one at the University, no comment. Pittsburgh must suit you admirably. I can read between your lines.

With a grandchild on the way and three daughters with husbands, count yourself Heaven's anointed! I'll pray for the child's good health and the happiness of the parents. Tell them I'll hope to greet them both before the decade is over.

As for your terrible son, I hardly blame him. If I had an affluent father, I'd happily give my time to writing whatever swims into my head; and to judge from what appears between printed covers, the smaller the talent, the better. If I had to choose all over again, I'd take an easier life than a family surgeon's battle with pain and death as companions. It would have made more sense to be buying and selling at horrible profits, running a shop, teaching Cheder, or practicing some respectable form of corruption, though I still suspect the wisest course is to marry an ugly princess.

Meanwhile, dance with me over the tomb of Marx, whose prophecies now are disproved. Russian factories still are producing two left shoes instead of pairs. Prices boom on our markets, and our Anglicans keep on siphoning back by marriage the money made by Jews. But even halfwits are minting gold these days. I made a killing, thanks to misreading a line of print in the papers. It's time you shelved your ideals and made a fortune. I'll try to do the same.

Love to Sonya and tell her the doctor who said her stomach pains were caused by a secret worry has been put out of date by some later brand of chicanery. Easy on tea, no coffee, and frequent the cinema till your grandchild arrives, after which you'll see more action than any film could offer you.

Your highly myopic MAX

From this point on, my son, it would make more sense for you to be speaking, though you still maintain what counts is the way *I* saw these years, since mine is "the tale with a meaning." You talked so much of your new career that I saw what you saw and felt your conflicting feelings as though they were mine. In a sense they were. You liked the craftsman's part of your job, also some of the men you worked with: messengers, draughtsmen, clerks, and the engineers. Most surprising of all to me: they took you just as you were: no "hard-hat jokes on imagination or artists." In a word, they accepted you . . . except for one steady complaint, "You can't be a man till you have your bout with the burns. It'll happen, boy, and the girl will swear that she'd never been touched till you came along. — Virgin, virgin! Never play ball with a virgin! . . ." The language was new to my ears.

Lunchtime became your problem: after the cafeteria, walking around the sheds and shacks where the millhands lived. Office walls protected your eyes from the things you saw when you tramped through places that once had been meadows and woods. "It used to be beautiful," your draughtsman friend remarked when he showed you his path to the river. "I'd sketch here Saturday afternoons. Look at it now! Coal dust on every leaf — the least of it. Everywhere this side of the water, wherever they put up a mill they ruin the land." After your first two weeks, when you said you'd become "political," you were more than sure of the reason: "If nobody stops them soon, they'll ruin our earth — and not only here but wherever a mill can turn out something to sell. Communism's the answer — and it kills two birds with one stone, for a Communist is also a conservationist, since the earth will belong to the people — and the people won't let it be ruined just so someone can make a profit. They'll *treasure* the earth, as we should." It was all that simple. Selah!

I knew he would never go shouting his new ideas. Fond as he was of some of his fellow-workers, he loathed their values, which stood for all he condemned. The daily contradiction he lived with partly explained his discomfort whenever I — quite unwisely — tried to make him admit to something he liked in his workaday life. Peace between us was more important. Besides, though I knew how much he wanted and savored his fellows' approval, nothing would pass his lips that might breathe forgiveness for my having forced him to give up his heart's desire: a teaching-writing career.

Blessed with enormous energy, he showed no sign of the overfatigue that his new regime would cause — rising very early to board a tram at 7 A.M., a railway train at 7:30, punching the clock at 8, and after the end of the working day, starting at once on the "other" life that would keep him up past midnight. He seemed to be stifling yawns more often than usual, but none of us said a word, since his lively step and his color were youth itself. And yet, how long would he hold to his present regime? Slightly more than another six months passed by when the bright young woman known for years as "his girl" quietly asked "Can you see any point in waiting?" Out-of-wedlock living in a middle-size city where everyone talked about everyone else was — needless to add — unthinkable.

I knew that he knew why I welcomed the thought of their marriage, though the point would never be raised: it would make him face some realities for which he professed contempt. Besides, I had reason to trust and respect my daughter-in-law to be. Forced to earn her livelihood, she had gone through library school and admittedly loved her profession. To be sure, in Bohemian talk and cultural snobbery, she was more than my son's equal, but she also treasured the bourgeois values of hearth and home. "Marriage should tame him" I said to Sonya, who saw he was much less eager than I. Soon I came to fear she was right. He was floating along on a tide he hadn't unleashed; yet how could he possibly turn his back on a paradigm of romance he had fostered for years? . . . "Something has to be done to sweeten the bargain," I finally realized. "I've the perfect solution, Sonya. It will not only bring him some real delight; it will end, once and for all, his annoying illusions of class-ridden Europe."

And so, our bargain was struck, quickly and happily: Every penny they'd save in the next two years I would double, which should give them ten full months in England, France, and Italy. They could go as far as they liked and stay as long as the money would last. A franc or lira would bring them less than a German mark, but I knew better than to press my favorite land on a voluble francophile. After the wedding, our weekly talk over dinner reverted to what it had been before, except for a veil of excitement that softened the edge when our judgments differed. I no longer constrained my admiration for "America: the young giant among the nations" — the phrase used time and again by our former Allies, who were now, in a sense, our enemies. Nor did I hide the fact that some trusted friends kept urging me on to participate in, benefit from, in a word, enjoy the great economic boom that fevered our country. I spoke about buying land, stocks, and the like; after all, I added, a salaried man couldn't pay for a couple's *Wanderjahr* out of savings alone. As I think of it now, I may have been rubbing it in, but all that I said was true. And yet — although my son would not dare to say it, for him much of this talk, in the light of my past, was treason. He finally felt compelled to state that he still held fast to his Conservationist-Communist notions. I asked "How do your fine Europeans help the '*people*' to help themselves? And how many ever go higher than grammar school?" I paused for an instant. "Nothing offered in all of Europe compares with our mass education: it's potentially the most powerful Socialist force that the world has seen."

He was visibly shaken. "If you're right, the millenium soon will be happening here."

At about the time they sailed abroad, Pauline's sons were beginning to bring the delights that my brother Max had described in his letter. For years Sonya had kept a full-time grandmother's schedule, staying till late in the afternoon; but now, with a three-year-old to ride my shoulders, we made a nightly ritual visit, after which we'd indulge our taste for the films. Meanwhile the mails brought weekly letters from London, Paris, Rome, wherever our voyagers happened to be: brimming with verve, excitement, charm. All they had found surpassed their hopes, even the three-day walking trip that Max, widowed and stoical now, pressed them to make from London to Brighton "If you really want to see England face to face, not that there aren't handsomer sights. But at least you'll vary this touristing business, which is also worthwhile — the British Museum, etc. On with you! Ring me if anything's wrong." They became so easeful a threesome that when Max later made his holiday trip to Paris, they served as his guides.

The great event for my son was his meeting with André Spire, the fine French poet two years my senior, an atheist who at twenty had fought a duel in the Dreyfus affair, and recently served as liaison agent between the French and the Zionists at the Peace Conference in Paris. Struck by the challenging candor of Spire's free verse — to which he was introduced one day by a Sorbonne professor — he started at once to work on a book of translations. And as though led on by the Fates, he came on the poet himself that very night at a party of friends. Spire, moved to tears by his new-found admirer, urged that they meet at his home next day to "continue." By noon it was all arranged; once a week the disciple would spend four or five hours with the master, gaining in six quick months an education no college could offer. I was ignorant of whatever else he was doing. Years later I learned he had written a Communist-Conservationist epic about the mill and its people, and that one gray morning he started at nine to write a page on the future of man and couldn't stop till he'd finished a whole small book by four: "Well at least I'm sure I know what will happen. . . ." A few short poems he had written appeared in the avant-garde magazines, we learned through his friends. Nothing in all his letters talked about writing affairs other than Spire, who was, after all, an event that he wanted to share.

I spent very little time on the correspondence; read it hastily. What concerned me about the *Wanderjahr* had little to do with the places he saw or what he might learn. For me the journey combined half-remedy with half-atonement; and the end, I hoped, would do away with the tenuous truce we had striven too hard to maintain. The trip itself would be over soon and my obligation fulfilled. I began to plan the timing once they were home. Though I tended to press too quickly, I had "to take steps. For much as I hate to say it, my children, it's time to put the *Wanderjahr* on the shelf." I kept rehearsing my speech for months in advance, but I still was unable to phrase the sentence to follow.

A letter from Max brought us to date: our travelers changed all plans when Leo Robin arrived in Paris with "his intimates, the well-known brothers Gershwin. And so," said Max, "for the children their year will end on a pitch of rapture" — which I thought a bit strong till I noted my friends' response when I mentioned the famous composer. That was "all the news at this time," then he added a curious postscript:

Thanks for your thanks but I am the one to be grateful. They're a joy and a challenge, keeping me (also) from too much grieving for Sal. As to your Sonya, waste no thought on the stones; once the bladder's removed she'll feel twenty times better. It's odd, by the way, how I go on talking of someone I've never beheld. Next summer, then — keep hoping — we meet in New York, your newfound Jerusalem.

In my last talk with your son I asked him to tell me about his father, whom I haven't beheld for 20 years . . . Do you want to hear his replies? Probably not — my usual doctor's dilemma, writing prescriptions not to the patient's taste. But from what I hear of father-and-son relations, yours is a healthy case; i.e., readily curable.

Apart from his admiration for all you've achieved — and that admiration is endless — three things worry him. One, he thinks you've been slowly seduced — in all innocence — from the kind of man that you were to something — he's never able to say just what; he talks around the subject, despite my physician's demand for a concrete statement. Instead he keeps quoting your William James and his famous attack on the way some Americans "worship the bitch-goddess SUCCESS" and the "squalid cash interpretation put on the word success." He blames your directors — how can you mix with the rich as part of your job and not contract some of their money-sickness? It all comes down to his wish that you'd stop trying so hard to make *extra* dollars when you earn all that you need and will one day live on a comfortable pension. *Solution?* Sell your stocks and bonds and other investments; squander your money; forget about getting rich. (We're too old anyway.)

Item two: How can a devotee of the Great Enlightenment, of Humanity's faith in equality, etcetera, allow himself to sound or think like a chauvinist? I explained: it's the normal immigrants' ailment and I'm just as bad. *Solution for both of us:* Remember to pinch ourselves whenever we start to act like the caricatures that we often may be.

Item three: His livelihood quarrel, specifically your eagerness to pay for a Ph.D. in Business vs. your utter refusal to pay for a Masters in English at half the cost. *Solution?* He had it before I could speak. When they're both earning a living again — a prospect he wholly abominates — they'll save enough to pay the cost of the Masters' degree themselves. (I'm quite convinced that they'll do it.)

Let me close on a curious note, which I probably wouldn't believe if I hadn't heard it myself. Writing, he's sure, is what he was born to do; but even so, he says he would gladly exchange his talent for half your brains. How's that for an accolade? Is it warranted?

Sonya was home before his letter arrived. Despite post-surgical orders for calm, she kept talking with almost youthful excitement about the return. The children would stay for weeks, of course, after a *whole* year of absence; our third-floor suite would be perfect. My son's old job would be waiting, perhaps a promotion — she had it neatly worked out — then we'd all sit down and resolve Item 3 of the Postscript. Parts of my brother's message still made me wince, though I told myself only a fool could fail to treasure a stolen glance at an offspring's thoughts.

The children's return filled our whole house with delight. All of us talked, questioned, listened, laughed, cried, ignoring the clock, which finally took its toll and settled us down. A week of parties mixed with serious talks with friends, including his former boss, shattered his hopes. In spite of or maybe because of the boom, applicants now were greatly outnumbering jobs. The situation had changed; it was pointless to look for things that no longer were found in this city, offices having been moved, for efficiency's sake, "close to the scene," i.e., the factory towns.

Finally quite convinced that he had no choice, he did what I long had hoped he would do: he set out "to try New York." Carrying letters of introduction that sounded impressive, he started to make the rounds. Nothing came of the interviews, and the likelihood that "in time" he would find what he looked for dimmed with time. But after a month a friend of one of his friends who admired his verses, "placed" him in a teeming office without so much as explaining what the employment involved. "You start with $100 a week — that's only a token, they're loaded. Don't ask me what you're supposed to do — you manage the advertising-promotion as *go-between* with the agency that produces the stuff. So there's nothing to it. The man you work for is crazy, like me, but also a genius and ten times a millionaire. Do what he wants and you're made!"

He surely tried to, I'm certain, but the man never talked to him long enough to make clear what was wanted. A secretary groaned with disgust "Nobody stays in this job because nobody can." But some day somebody's going to tell The Man *why,* and he's clever enough to listen. I think you should try. What can you lose?" She went on to describe "what everyone knew in the jewelry business" — the thriving conspiracy, legal of course, between his employer who "put the watches together" and the merchants who "pushed" them because of "an unbelievable mark-up arrangement no other firm with a reputation would touch." Instead of asking himself how long he could keep defrauding himself and the man who had found him the job, he called on my friend Chester Teller, who for years had directed summer camps for children. It was quickly decided: the *Wanderjahr* was resumed with a change in location: Maine. "As you see," the letter he sent me ended, "we've found the pleasantest way of postponing my whoredom for commerce. The morning after Labor Day, I'll tramp the streets again and knock on doors and hope. If you disapprove, consider my situation! In my place you'd have done the same."

He was right, shocked as I was by his running away. Looking for work in July and August was wasteful. But what if . . . ? I couldn't conclude the sentence. Six weeks of tramping the streets, knocking on doors, offering letters

netted me nothing [to quote from his postcard]. I know all about clamshell buckets, steel-making furnaces, towers, forms, gasoline cracking equipment, even how the NYSubway was built — which makes them write on my card INDUSTRIAL ONLY — work no longer done in NY, but where the products are made; ergo, living in factory towns. No choice but to keep tramping so long as the shoe-leather holds.

Within a fortnight he sent a letter by special delivery. "Probably," I thought, "he was short of money again." It read

This a.m., spotting a Help Wanted ad in the Times, half-jokingly I entered a smalltown dept. store in the cheapest part of 14th Street (6th Ave). My interviewer, an NYU School of Retailing grad., about my age, apologized when he showed me their advs. in the Daily News (tabloid, double the Times circulation). "Don't bother to say what you think. I've finally talked Mr. H. into letting me hire a man who can do a professional job. He's willing to spend only $50 a week but I promise you, if you take the job and show some results, he'll double the pay without asking." He sounded sincere.

There are also catalogues (called direct-by-mail) with lots of photos (my specialty). I start working tomorrow. This situation makes me think of yourself and the HSGS. When you first saw it, you said, it was in such chaos that any person with half a brain could make it 20 times better without much trying. I hope the analogy's right.

PS. I think I've been given the job because "my man" is fed up with illiterate yes-men and sees in me a soul-mate to whom he'd feel safe in confiding his utter contempt for the owner, a playboy I haven't yet met, who's reputed to be Mr. Malaprop. More in good time if I last.

Either his "chaos" picture was true or he undervalued his talents. In any event, the results of his work were so evident that, after one month, he was earning $75 and by New Years Day $100. Mr. H. was also pleased to have found a tennis partner for lunch, and to "make" him take a week's vacation "to rest for the springtime rush." At last I could smile — to myself, at least — at his business success. But his writing still came first in his heart; he listed the magazines that were printing his poems, including the monthly *New Masses*. And with "so much money, we're renting a pretty seashore house for the summer. When Max arrives you'll all come out for a swim — just an hour by train."

"Your successful son," Sonya remarked, "might as well be living in Europe. Max arrives in June — that will make nine months since they left us. Please don't give me the reasons. He works six days a week and we haven't the money to visit New York because we're going to show your brother America."

"Ourselves also! We'll have our own chauffeur and car and see all the famous sights while we're healthy enough to enjoy them. Everyone says we'll be having the time of our lives."

Max, alas, turned out to be far from the gracious guest I'd expected. He was much more eager to chat with the children and Sonya than to see the famous sights of New York, the skyline, bridges — all I had carefully planned. Whenever he could, he made fun of "American nonsense," such as too many baths, ice in the pitchers of water, New York's tropical climate. "Oh your city's big and rich, but not in a class with London. Even your Underground's backward. And waiting for hours in your Holland Tunnel because of an unfinished exit! Tell me, brother, how many levels of track in Pennsylvania Station? My dear, you should do your homework to serve as a proper guide. But I like your suburbs — the prettiest things you've shown me, though the lawns are a fright to a Britisher."

What I thought had begun as a joke became a continual competition till Sonya, reaching the end of her wits, burst out "Both of you, stop! You should hear yourselves! — talking like immigrant children, each of you boasting about his adopted country, putting me in the middle to keep the peace. If you can't behave, I'll go home. Do you hear me?" She was all too right. Each of us took her aside and told her as much. The episode proved a blessing. From that day on everything changed. We even laughed at each other's foolishness, long before our cross-country tour was over. On our last morning together, Max asked permission to talk "in private" to Sonya. Not till after our last goodbyes did she say how he'd begged her to wear as her own the small gold ring that had been "the treasured joy of his wife till the end of her days."

We received a hasty postcard mailed from New York the day he departed. "Dear Brother and Sister: Your son wouldn't let me go home till he showed me your monument: Pleasantville. Something I'll never forget — nor should the world." Tears filled our eyes; we couldn't say why. Nor did our son's letter mention the visit. Instead he wrote of enrolling at N.Y.U. for a Master's degree in French "because they'll accept my translations of Spire as a thesis. It will take 2½ years but without any salary loss. Mr. H. approves. 'Study can't hurt too much' — his latest motto."

His course-work began in September. Though he may have had almost no time for the news, not a single note of his ever referred to the Wall Street crash. He was looking forward to seeing us soon — at Thanksgiving: "Have already got permission to stay the weekend, or would you rather come down to New York as our guests: tickets, hotel included? Please answer this." What kind of world did he live in, to be unaware of the worst economic débâcle in history?

My son *is* old enough to take up the rest of my story:

3

A week before Thanksgiving an anonymous letter arrived at my new apartment half-way between my job and my classes at Washington Square:

Young Man: —
    Though I find it hard to believe, I have to assume you are *not* aware of your father's financial plight. In a word, then: — like so many of us, he was thrown to the floor by the Wall Street crash three weeks ago (Black Tuesday), but unlike many others, *he* intends to repay every cent he owes to the banks, friends, and so on. He has mortgaged himself to the hilt, as the saying goes, having borrowed on margin (at least you know what *that* means). I'm not quite sure but I think he had to abandon some smaller holdings. In any case, I *know* he can use whatever financial aid you can give, though he'll never ask — *you'll* have to make the proposal. I urge you to do it now. Sincerely — No need to mention names, not even my own. In this situation nothing counts but the information I send you.

So the "bubble of gold exploded" — my new assistant had found the phrase in *The New York Daily News*. When I'd asked "What bubble?" he gave me a pitying stare, then shrugged "October 29th," but I hardly listened. Stocks and Wall Street had been as far from my cares as the moon — or my father's finances. Before I placed my evening call, I scurried about, gathering all I could manage without revealing the size of my ignorance.

I telephoned after dinner. No answer. I tried again at ten with the same result. Then I wrote a letter offering all in our savings account and stating the sum. A handwritten note assured me that things were in order now, but if some unexpected need should arise, he'd proudly remember my offer. He added details: how he'd set up accounts, had started to pay them off — it would take some years but barring misfortune, he'd end up free of debt and beholden to no one, unlike a few of his "formerly trusted advisers"; other questions could wait till my coming visit . . .

— Now that I've taken over the tale of my father, I sometimes hear myself forming sentences which are neither my natural speech nor his but a hybrid he made in the hope of sounding like me . . . Hours after Thanksgiving dinner, lying awake upstairs in "my room," I was startled to count how long it had been since the three of us had been together . . . alone. No wonder we lacked the time to say all the words on our tongues — we had too much to ask, to tell, to hear. But tomorrow would surely be better. We'd arranged, my father and I, for one of our long talking-walks through the Park in the morning. He would go to his office in town for the afternoon, which I would devote to my mother. And the day after, we'd do together whatever our hearts desired till my train's departure at midnight.

Autumn stayed so late that the maples and poplars were still in their colors. Max ought to look at these leaves, I remarked; he scoffed when I swore that Europe had nothing to match our scarlet and golden woods — which led my father to cry "What a dear and impossible fellow! How could you get on so well together?" He grinned as he added "I'm sure you never imagined he'd let me know of your private discussions, including your view of my 'get-rich schemes' — his slogan. To judge from my situation, you were not very wrong. But we've had depressions before; we'll have them again, and *recover* — the business cycles. What troubles me most are the 'great' financial experts who suspected nothing at all." I mentioned something I'd learned two days before: the Communists' prophecies. He smiled. "Of course: they've been singing that dirge for years, while Russia's millions are starving." Although we talked about all that came into our heads — from my graduate work to the impotence of the White House —

he always came back to matters of money, capital, loans, and the "friends" he'd been foolish enough to follow — who were now worse off than himself. "It simply means, for your mother and me, spending with much more care. We're fortunate losers . . ."

"Pauline asked us for lunch," my mother announced as I stepped to the porch. One of her friends offered to drive, but I said it was such a beautiful day that we'd walk. "Ready to go?" We began at what I imagined her usual pace. After a block she stopped "Too fast. I'm still getting over my restful vacation with Max and your father."

I smiled and started to speak of the morning walk. "Believe it or not, we never argued at all. I had thought of asking his current view of the young giant among the nations but I held my tongue." She nodded, then almost at once began to say what it really had meant to him: less a financial loss than a blow to his faith, and some precious beliefs — in his own judgment, friends he had trusted, captains of industry, wizards of commerce, and worse: the "invincibility of America." He acted as though he "were tossing about on a sea with nothing to hold on to," as she phrased it. He called it "a new perspective — I can live with it well enough." By now, having finally stopped reproaching himself, he was getting nearer to what he had been before, though not the same. One change surprised and pleased her. He was suddenly most solicitous about her health, the way she was using her leisure, where they might go next summer —

Before she could tell me more, we had reached my sister's street. I followed her through the house to the yard where again I was introduced to my nephews, six and four, who hurriedly looked me up and down, then rushed to their grandmother's arms. They knew she was much too dear to be taken for granted — childhood wisdom that made me wince — and so they cajoled and squealed, demanding her answers. They would have to play in the yard, but after our lunch she would stay with them — which she hastened to do before she had finished.

Alone with Pauline, I asked why our mother had not recovered *yet* from whatever had taken its toll on the travels West. I had been with her in July before they set out; compared to now, she looked radiant. Pauline frowned "Don't you think we're concerned — or the doctors? They say we're impatient — it takes more time to recoup a loss 'in your fifties.' The surgery when you were abroad did wonders; they knew what to do and did it. Now they want her to take more tests — which she calls a waste. The doctors change their tune so often, she says. She suspects they're puzzled or, if they know, they're afraid to say what they know. But of course they wouldn't be hiding a thing from *us*. Besides, I'm close to her every day and I *know* she's better than when she came back. I can also tell from how much she can take from my boys — who'd exhaust King Kong. By the way, you'll be driven home at four. Tell her *you'd* like to lie down; it's the way to make sure she'll rest. — We'll be over tonight with the guests — people you know. Then pray for good weather tomorrow."

Saturday was a breezier sunlit day, all but ideal for the country outing her husband arranged, their children included. All through the afternoon I felt myself counting the hours with undefinable dread. "We're having an early dinner," my father announced, "at the house of a new colleague and friend. He knew you were coming. I simply couldn't refuse." The hosts were thoughtful enough to deliver us home by eight, so we'd have "the whole of the evening together." The minutes went so fast we decided to check the clocks. "Don't worry about the cab," my father assured me. "You won't miss your train." Our mood was instantly changed. Gazing deeply at each of them, I said that I'd never been so glad to be home and so sorry to leave. Close as my tie had been with my mother, we always lightly smiled and embraced when we met or parted. Tonight her goodbye was filled with tears — my father's also. The cab was waiting outside. I waved again and stared ahead. As the driver swung the taxi around, the sight of the downstairs rooms of the house startled me. They were empty . . . in darkness.

Propped in my Pullman berth, I looked at *The New Republic* my father had slipped in my bag, till the train rocked me to sleep. My ears still echoed my mother's voice as she stood at the door: "Write to us — when you can." The words were there when I woke. They stayed with me through the months ahead, urging me, while I strove with my work and studies. Pauline wrote to tell me how much my visit had meant: also quoting my mother, who was saying she ought to spend more time with girls of her age. "Am I bored with being a Grandma? What a question! You know it's my daily joy." After Christmas I sometimes visited Evelyn and her husband, who lived in the suburb Max had pronounced the prettiest sight in America. A brief note from Pauline arrived: "The diagnosis, colitis, should be a relief to us all."

Evelyn called me after the respite was broken. The doctors had given my father worrisome news. Their medications had failed. The only remaining step was the one they had sought to avoid. True — they were changing their tune again, but the patient had come through well last year; a repeat performance was likely. And indeed she could wait till April. Frequent telephone messages kept us informed, including, of course, Marie, who had traveled South. A note from my mother said how happy she was to know we were planning an early visit.

I telephoned after the surgeon told my father things had gone well and a good result might be hoped for. "We'll begin to drive the minute I leave my desk," I assured him, "and we'll keep right on till we see you." The April sky was calm, clear up to the Blue Mountains. Then snow and sleety rain closed over us. Evelyn's husband skidded us on, but clouds of fog forced him to draw to the side. We waited hours for the winds to carry them off. When we finally reached the house, there was no one there. Soon my father, Marie, and Pauline appeared. They had talked with the surgeon: "condition stable." Gathered about the room, we heard what remained to tell. There had been no choice but to take out the carcinoma.

He had girded himself for questions, answering all but the first with a nod: Is she holding her own? . . . Sedated? . . . Does she know? . . . Without thinking to ask, we returned to the hospital. I watched, from time to time, at my mother's bedside. Her entire body seemed to heave with each gasping breath, her eyes open, gazing at me, her face motionless. Whenever a doctor walked to the room, my father followed. Apparently nothing had changed. At dusk, with the shift of nurses, a new physician was summoned. My father waited outside. When he joined us again, he said nothing. Words were needless; we knew the body was struggling to stay alive. Yet none of us could keep from the room. At midnight, when I asked "Might she possibly understand if I spoke?" the nurse glared at me "Can't you see that she's dying? Better go back to your family. I'll call you."

It was past four when she summoned us to the bedside. The heavy breathing had stopped, the eyes were closed. My father put his palm on the cheek and caressed it. "My dear girl, my dear girl" — he broke into tears. Evelyn led him out of the room.

One of my sister's friends, who had come to the house in our absence, greeted us when we returned. "Please! . . . Won't you all go into the dining room! Tea? Coffee? Both. — It will take but a minute." We thanked her, nodded, and waited, seated around the table. Nothing was said. Moments later, Evelyn urged my father to rest for the hours ahead. Each of us found a bed or a couch to lie on. At half-past eight the doorbell rang. My wife's parents had come to offer whatever help we might need. . . .

A brief service was held early next afternoon, with family friends, my sisters and I and our mates crowding the downstairs rooms. I had never heard the ritual or the "woman of valor" words. Under the pale light of the

April sky, we drove to the Westview hillside. We watched the coffin lower and enter the earth, close to a fruit tree straining to burst in blossom. Before the sun had set, we returned to the house. New visitors awaited us. None of us had an answer when asked how long we would stay.

At odd times in the next few days lines from poets — phrases I barely recalled — swarmed in my head; some of them, firm commands, had changed into questions — "*Le vent se lève . . . Il faut tenter de vivre?*" Pauline, watching my lips move, asked what I said. I repeated the altered Valéry line. Literally 'the wind is rising — a person must try to live!' — as if one could choose! . . ." Evelyn interrupted: The hospital lost no time in sending its bill to my father. "I'll ask if he'll let me help — do you think . . . a thousand?" She nodded. Not till the end of the week did I plan to leave. Evelyn would remain. My wife decided to stay for an added week. I'd return early Sunday — by excursion train: two sleepless nights at a fifth of the fare.

Though this is my father's story, I'm unable to speak of his next few years without involving my own, small as the part must be. He was "still" my father, of course, but I now had come to think of him as my friend as well — the friend who would hear me rail at the senselessness of existence, where reason's patterns of expectation were mocked by caprice. My sisters returned quietly to the lives they had led before, and I knew I also would have to make my truce with necessity. That this hard phrase of Carlyle would hound me the rest of my days, I was still too callow to fear, but my father's sixty years should have taught him the hopelessness of denying the need to accept what I could not accept.

Nobody had to tell me the depth of his grief or the costs of his self-accusing. I wondered if, at the time, he had ever stopped to think how my mother's life had narrowed after her children had left the nest. And was he aware that her years of renascent brightness, begun when her grandsons quickened her life, were already changing? — no longer needed, usefulness ended. Pauline had tried vainly to cope with the emptiness of her days. Had he known?

Would I, in his place, have known? — not less self-concerned than my friend my father, gaining my bitter relief as words flooded my pages — elegy, ode, then sonnet and sonnet and sonnet . . .

The conqueror worm had yet to be given its due. Suddenly, we learned, it was seizing a second prey. Neither its host — my father-in-law — nor his wife or his children had been forewarned. Once revealed in the victim, the doom came quickly. Dogwood blossoms were still on the trees when the racked body entered the earth of the same hillside that havened my mother's grave.

We began to re-order our lives, but another would die before the plague might forsake us. A cablegram from a London colleague dazed my father: REGRET BROTHER MAX DECEASED SUDDEN CANCER STOP WILL PRO-HIBITS FUNERAL ASSIGNS BODY MEDICAL STUDY STOP EXECUTORS AWARD YOUR SON ONE THIRTY SECOND ESTATE ELEVEN HUNDRED AMERICAN DOLLARS STOP CONFIRMING LETTER FOLLOWS STOP CONDOLENCES . . . "One thirty-second!" I thought of the best-laid plans: the Borgia ring he never took off his finger, the poison-pill inside, to be swallowed the instant his cataracts blocked his vision. Who would receive that memento? . . . On my next visit, my father showed me the colleague's letter — " 'Galloping cancer, in layman's language — a fortnight or less . . . Unwilling to add my woes to my brother's . . .' " — Forbearance at last!

"And what," my father asked, "will you do with that princely inheritance? It was yours, you remember: *all.* I never dreamed he would break his word . . ."

"In time perhaps," I said, "we'd hear his reasons," then dropped the subject to learn his plans for taking some rest, change of scene, and so on. I mentioned Maine, but Evelyn and Pauline's husband were planning trips to the nearby mountains, long weekends if time could be spared from his added office burdens, caused by the city's depression.

My princely "thirty-second" gave me a new reason for taking the two-week furlough in Maine. Vermont was said to be rich with abandoned farms. We left them for others, driving instead through the Belgrade lakes I'd known in my summer-camp days. Max's eleven hundred dollars became a pine-and-birch-wooded acre set on the shore of a deep blue lake, with a hemlock cabin. The nearest neighbor, postman-cum-farmer, knew a builder who'd follow my roughed-out plan and ready the place by July.

My heart sank the day we came back to the city. Although nothing had changed, our one large room seemed cramped, airless; the noises of passing cars we had never noticed before, now troubled our ears. We could find both quiet and spaciousness in a suburb, but before moving, I'd have to complete the head of my mother. Sculpture held no fears for a novice. I'd begun with an empty milk bottle, set it solidly onto a wooden box-top, and covered the makeshift armature with modeling compound. One evening, under a certain light, it took on an eerie likeness. I asked the advice of a friendly painter. "Before you ruin it, get it in plaster!" I ordered casts for October to bring along on my next trip to my father's house.

I took care to place the work at the proper distance in front of our eyes. He gazed at it, shook his head, and left the room. Although the work might prove too lifelike to live with, I gave a cast to each of my sisters. None of them spoke of it, nor did I ask. A cycle had ended. Meanwhile my father and I chatted of all that had taken place since my last visit — Maine, my having put an end to my graduate studies, the suburbs . . . The deepened depression forced him to add to his staff. Trained workers were hard to find. The outlook was still unclear. Things abroad were worse — and Germany! The ruthless Austrian antisemite had to be watched. September elections raised his "Nazi" party to second place in the country. Had I heard what this madman planned to do with Communists? Socialists? Was I reading the *Times?* . . .

A surprising letter reached me before the Christmas rush, written from home in his difficult script:

> In January (early), when you look for the stone in Maine, I shall be offi-
> cially begged to accept the leading position in education (social work) in
> New York. Do I have to say which one? The wheel has finally come full
> circle — five or six years too late. In any event, I shall graciously decline
> on the grounds (true) of being much too involved in too many things in
> the Jewish *and* Gentile community here (including my membership on
> the Board of a Catholic institution, writing the new Community Fund's
> constitution, etc.). I have one regret: the offer ought to have come before
> your mother took ill. She would have called it a bitter-sweet Chanukah
> present. P.S. Take plenty of warm clothes on your trip.

Excellent counsel, but earmuffs alone won't serve at forty below. Luckily by the time my friend pulled up to his farm, it was twenty. I asked if the south pasture had changed — at my last count there were fifty-eight gran-ite boulders. "Nobody wants 'em but you," he nodded. I set out at once, warm in the windless sunshine. After our noonday meal I showed him one that seemed to me fit for my mother's grave. He nodded again "Better tell your sister to warn the mason: no rust, blood, or tobacco juice — they stain it forever." I passed the advice to Evelyn, also enclosing the verse for the plaque. My father approved. When the stone was unveiled, her hus-band read the line as part of the service: "O earth, mother of all, hold now close to your bosom one so bitterly wept," omitting Meleager's name. In a month my wife and I would return for another such service, at her father's grave.

My August letter sent from my cabin in Maine brought an instant reply:

Forgive both the haste and handwriting — stenographer on vacation . . .
Will see you in mid-October. Have compromised with the N.Y. school:
will be lecturing monthly. Eager to hear of your 10¢ purchase that's
changed your plans, but not in the mood for Prescott's "Poetic Mind."
Will your own book on the French poet really appear next spring? Glad
you've abandoned suburbs. Am spending the week with friends at a nearby
mountain. Can you read my writing?

A curious kind of excitement surrounded our visits. He found his New
York lecture class a joy; and he also was planning a change, though he
"wouldn't say more right now, but in March 1932" he would tell me the
story. To my great relief he hadn't asked about mine, which by now was
past recall. Professor Prescott, moved by the way *The Poetic Mind* had
shaken my thoughts, wrote to me as a long-awaited disciple. He and his
Cornell colleagues would gladly have me come for a Master's year, though
he for one wouldn't wonder if, in these dangerous years, at the last moment,
my "courage of recklessness" failed and I clung to financial safety. Surprisingly, it was no deprivation at all to deposit money each week in the U.S.
Postal Savings, which promised to give me more than I'd need to live on.
My three sisters, like most of my friends, managed to smile and wish
me well, though it still was "hard to believe that a book you bought for a
dime from a drugstore's remainder shelf, etc." I was anxious about explaining my move to my father. In late December after his visit, I sent a detailed
letter: I had mentioned my plan in an August note — had it slipped his
mind? In any case, it could hardly come as a shock, since Max, before his
departure, had urged him to make the best of our differing views, "though
anyone knowing how much he enjoyed teaching must wonder why he considered it bad for his son." Meanwhile I restlessly looked toward March,
when I'd finally hear *his* plan. I hoped it might bring him as much pro-
spective joy as I gained each day from the thought of my coming year! —
His four-line answer amazed me:

> Freud might say I forgot because I had wished it would not come true.
> But I know that you never will rest till you give it a chance. And within
> its premise your plan makes sense. I hope you will think the same of mine
> when you hear it.

Walking the winter "Depression streets," I could see no change in the
number of apple vendors or ragged children. Makeshift Hooverville shacks
were crowding the empty spaces on Houston Street, others along the Hud-

son, some in the Park. How would Enlightenment's advocate rescue Reason's Century? Money could put an end to poverty's wrongs, but now we were also threatened with Nazi hate. I might ask his views, on his next weekly trip to New York . . .

In March, when my father at last unveiled his long-awaited "plan" and spoke of the need to confront all threats, I expected a Communist cure-all. "Do you know what *kehilla* means?" I'd half-forgotten. "Community, the integrated organization of all who live in a city or town. Through the centuries it served as the basic unit of Jewish antonomous life, with its own regulations, synagogue, schools, burial grounds, judges, rabbis; its network of welfare, mutual-aid, and other services. I wrote before of the 1908 *kehilla* that gathered together groups in New York. But it lasted little more than a year — it had no enforcement powers. I promise you that *my* community council need never fear such a fate. If it comes to birth, it will do for Jewish community life what Pleasantville had done for children. 'A large order,' you say? — Very large — also *essential*." He paused. "In April I'll bring you the Draft Proposal — facts, figures, charts. My Board meets in May. What would you think of my starting out with this sentence from Goethe: 'I have often felt a bitter sorrow at the thought of the German people, which is so estimable in the individual and so wretched in the generality'?"

"Quite à propos," I smiled. "To make certain, I'd quote it twice." He grinned, nodding. Not since the days of his program-fight for the graduate social-work school had he seemed so eager and hopeful. Whatever men or events might do, his plan had hurled him back in the life-loving mainstream.

The Draft Proposal preceded his April visit, giving me time to look at the whole with its spare details. The instant we met he announced "Before you utter your verdict, I should say that I've added a heading 'Replies to objections.' My revised version provides them."

"Variations on the Jewish-separateness theme?" I ventured.

He nodded wryly. "What else? Breaking the unwritten contract between our hosts and ourselves, as they used to warn. Jews must accept or at least condone their assimilation in exchange for paper equality, give up their wilful differentness, their role of refusers, all because 'society' accepts nothing less. But the first prediction hasn't come true and the second is false. Through the ups and downs of Emancipation, Jews have remained what they were: a group apart, a sub-society, *refusing* to disappear. And America, Eden of numberless cultures, makes no demand that the Jews,

Italians, Irish, Mormons, *et alia* shed their respective identities. — But you haven't said what you think of my whole idea."

"A very audacious — and responsible program, with unpredictable outcomes. I've one question — about its third contribution: taking an active role in civic, esthetic, and other parts of the city's existence. It cries for specific examples. And I'd add something: the forthright assertion of self-acceptance through unity — through the fusing of separate strengths to produce a whole that will stand for *more* than the sum of its members, and therefore better able to cope with whatever may come."

He gazed at me grimly. "I'm witnessing something new: the cohesive effect of the *fear* of persecution *before* it has happened." He sighed. "These are useable notions, both of them. If you think of more, write to me." But my private thought was confused. No one could question his Council's worth for its own community, but what of the country at large? Was this more than a single sub-society's answer? For a paralyzed nation what mattered now was "the system" itself — and none but the Communists offered a clear solution. Of course they'd scoff at my father's plan, though it surely fulfilled, by extension, Stalin's demands of minorities: that their works be "socialist [i.e., American] in content, and nationalist [Jewish] in form." I could always count on *The New Masses* for ready-made cocksure answers.

On his May visit my father spoke of the uphill fight he was ready to wage — if he had to, for years. Two directors had vetoed his plan — it would "make the Jews appear as a separate *religious* group with interests different from those of the larger community." But the Board as a whole endorsed the "urgent need for the unification of Jewish communal life . . . and hoped a plan would be drawn to achieve this end." Warnings against arousing unwarranted fears had also been raised. The revised Proposal would probably take six months. He would send it on in the fall.

My July vacation ended the day that Hoover ordered the Army to rout the thousands of jobless veterans who demanded their World War bonus. Four days later I typewrote my resignation, effective October 1. The head of the firm was annoyed. "Some joke! Or don't you *believe* there are 13,000,000 men who'd sell their souls for your job?" Prescott's "courage of recklessness" phrase hummed in my ears as I gave my reasons for leaving. Mr. H. stared at me, shaking his head. "Remember, my boy, you can change your mind if you wish even after you've gone. Remember!" I thanked him. Twelve days later he sent for me. "Here," he held out the *Times:* A large crowd of starving unemployed men, who'd been dropped from the county relief rolls, smashed their way into grocery stores in

Toledo. "Don't think I'm hoping to stop you! Just that I want to make *sure* you know what it's like outside."

The day before I drove from New York, I wrote to my father. I was going alone. As soon as I found a room, he would hear, but in case of necessity, telephone F. C. Prescott. Two weeks later, I sent him a full account of my Ithaca life. He named his November lecture date: could we meet? A long letter answered my note of regret, much of it "bringing you up to date on the hideous Nazis," the rest on private affairs. His evening life had become an endless train of meetings and dinners all in the cause of the Council. The Draft revision could not be readied till May. As for my situation, how lucky to be given the run of the Faculty Club as a special guest . . . and my bright, sunny, two-window, three-dollar weekly room . . . and my friends! No, he had never heard of *my* Herbert Muller, only the noted geneticist, but if, as I promised, he'd someday publish a work that would shake our minds, he would surely read it. As for the check enclosed, I should count on another each month till his debt was paid . . . Could I visit at Christmas?

We fixed a date, but before I could drive through Easton, a blizzard stopped me. I would come for a day by Saturday-night excursion, I said when I 'phoned. My offer pleased him — "almost as good as a visit, my son, but my two long meetings would do away with our Sunday." Perhaps in the spring vacation, "to toast your forthcoming book."

A pall shrouded our world through the first few months of the new year. January 30, 1933: Hitler, backed by conservatives and the army, named Chancellor. February 28: all civil liberties suspended. March 25: absolute power to Hitler (Enabling Act); trade unions and all parties other than Hitler's destroyed; start of the *Gleichshaltung:* "coordination" of all institutions. April 1: national boycott of all businesses owned by Jews: by legal decree . . .

> I don't want to spoil [he wrote] this joyous letter hailing your book's arrival by mentioning Nazis. But to think that the more than 50% who voted *against* them in March look on and allow these horrors! Nietzsche wrote "The Germans have no conception of how vile they are." — But enough . . . Your beautiful book with its dedication touched me. — Words literally fail me, but surely you know what they are. Should there be a review in the *Times,* or is it too early? . . . P. S. Franklin Roosevelt has made an astonishing start with his NRA, AAA, etc. Have you followed his Fireside Chats? . . . The depression could hardly be worse. The note I sent to my Board to reduce my salary startled them out of their wits. — More

when we meet. The National Social Work Conference begins one day after
May 25 . . .

"Commencement will have to manage without my presence," I informed Prescott, but half-way through our discussion he nearly unnerved
me. Had I money enough for another year and a summer? That's all I'd
need — finish the specified courses and I'd have my Ph.D., since my Master's essay combined with my book on Spire would do for the thesis. If I
lacked the funds, perhaps I could borrow — friends, relatives? — but he'd
have to know by September.

I started to thank him for all he had done. "Mysticism and Poetry,"
he sighed, quoting my thesis title, "Timely: when Germans are burning
the books." He stared at the ceiling. "'Anything which strikes at the root
of German thought' — *their* words, I believe, for the 20,000 works they
put to the match: *students,* mind you, *students,* in a midnight torchlight
parade on the streets of their *university*! When I read the news, I recalled
your sketch of your father, who idealized all things German and was sure
that Reason would bring on a golden world. Will you see him soon?" I
nodded. "I hope he's girding himself for the worst. It will come. Sleight of
hand in picking words from books can do terrible things. Nietzsche swung
back and forth from vile to magnificent notions, but for all his ranting, he
was never an antisemite, yet the Nazis have made him one. Hegel's different. Marx, you remember, decided to rectify Hegel by standing him on his
head, but Hitler's scholars prefer him just as they *say* he was, with his adulation of world-historical heroes who needn't abide by moral laws as they
trample all over innocent things on their glory-path, for Germany's hour
will come — to 'regenerate the world.' — A man can crack his brain and
heart, reading such things, but we'd better not close our eyes . . . Please
drop in to say goodbye before you leave us! . . ."

Though our visit was brief, my father was able to keep me abreast of
his plan's progress — "slow, God knows, but certain." Scores of converts,
however, whose first quick Yes gave way to a Maybe or Tell-me-again were
proving costly in time. Something would have to go — his trips to New
York. "But I haven't yet said a word about those splendid reviews of your
book. Did your publisher speak of my order?" . . . Prescott's proposal led
him to mention the "countless unemployed postal clerks who have Ph.Ds."
Before we parted I asked about summer plans. Some of his friends urged
him to move to a midtown apartment, others to hire a woman to run the
house and drive him around. "If the latter happens, maybe I'll come to
Maine and see what you've done with your uncle's stupendous legacy."

It was good that he never appeared: my companion's ceaseless mania-cally Marxist talk would have maddened him. To me it was strangely re-freshing after all the "bourgeois books" I had read for my courses. It was also crammed with "Communist facts" I hungered to hear, along with "solutions." By fall I announced I was ready to help the cause. "Great," he grinned, "we'll go to the *Masses*. I'll tell them all that you've done. You'll be quite a boon." I tagged along, doubting his expectations. The *New Masses,* would change to a weekly the first of the year: how much time could I give them? Would I talk with the editors now? . . . For the next three months I was able to get along by doing free-lance layout work; then I found a part-time agency job, giving the rest of my hours to the *Masses*. "What do you need to live on?" the business manager cornered me after the second issue appeared. "We must have you here." I refused to be paid four times more than my fellow editors. "Don't be foolish! Their wives have jobs. Then it's settled. You're giving us all your time starting next Monday."

With numberless households living in want and 16,000,000 kept from earning a penny, mine seemed surely more than a journalist's job. Works of art were weapons, we said, in the fight for men's minds. Therefore a book- or a drama-review was an act for Humanity's Future. In April out-of-town readers started to make demands for editor-speakers. Before I knew, a series of thirty lectures from May 1st on had been booked in my name, each in a different locality, making a long loop to Wisconsin and back. But on May 31st I changed my routes to spend a day with my father. He was home, trying to rest from a lingering cold. When I rang the bell, his housekeeper-driver led me straight to the table. "Right on time," he beamed, "for my second breakfast. But you probably want a bath after your bus. Take your time!" A shower was never more welcome, but I finished it quickly. It was long since we'd been together.

"Tell me all about your trip! What were your speeches? Who came to hear you? Everything!" I gave a capsule account, with the names of most of the towns and colleges, also troublesome things — such as my angry outburst when the Midwest head of the Communist Party trebled his own tally of the May Day crowds that had marched in Chicago. "Did you really imagine your politicians were dreamers?" I said I knew about Acton's "power corrupts," but what was the point of *this* lie: no one be-lieved it. He chuckled. "A dozen self-styled fellow travelers on my staff most surely believed it. — Five of them, not at all very subtly, are trying to turn my 'bourgeois *kehilla*' into a proselytizing scheme for their League against Fascists. — By the way, they're about to go out on a strike, but all they can get from the Board are a few more holidays. Of course I favor their League — *anything* if it holds back the fascist dangers. I've never been able to learn what it *does,* its strength, its power to *act,* to exert a *truly* deterring force."

I lacked the answer. I told him what I knew of the founder, Henri Barbusse, who had written the famous war-book *Le Feu.* Last fall he had given his maiden speech at the New School — I served as ad lib translator — since then he's traveled 48 states building a network. "Did you ask what *concrete actions* he plans to hold back the fascists?" I shrugged foolishly. Nobody knew, I added, not even those on the platform: the British writer Strachey, the Mexican painter Orozco. "Then it all boils down to talk — to 'education' " — he looked at me in disgust, repeating — "to education, that 'irreversible force for the Progress of Man! The polestar of German culture.' " I made some glib remark — that not all Germans were Nazis. "Cold, very cold, ice-cold comfort right now. And I'm not at all sure their passivity in the face of what they've witnessed wasn't a crime." He glowered. "You know, I suppose, all that my youthful years had worshipped was German. And my stubborn allegiance hung on till — I'd rather not think. I was even trailed as a spy in the War."

The telephone rang. "Pauline?" The housekeeper answered the call and nodded. "After our lunch," he said, "she'll drive you to Westview, while I rest and nap. She knows you want to look at your mother's grave." He thought for moments. "At least her early death spared her these terrible years. At the time, who would have dreamed what lay in store for the living!" He rose from the table. "Come, let's go to the porch. With your bus departure at midnight, we'll have lots of time for a leisurely feast with a special dish in your honor." The cherry trees on the opposite lawn were flowering. We chattered along — about people I hadn't heard from, my now non-marital state, summer vacations. We were starting to talk of Roosevelt's reforms when my sister's car drove up. We hastened to greet her.

She winked at him. "Your grandsons are very annoyed. *They're* not afraid of catching your cold, but we'll wait till it's over. — You're getting in bed, I hope. We'll be back by five." We had driven less than a block when she said, "He used to come every evening, weekends also. My boys were just about all that brought him to life — then he started his Council. And now he's so deeply embroiled that he's overstraining. Try to make him ease up!" I promised. We turned to other problems — mainly her own. They were living from month to month; her husband's affairs, like those of their friends, were close to the brink, though the NRA and other Roosevelt reforms, they were hoping, would save them . . . "Let's change the subject," she said when she brought me home. "I've something for Evelyn's birthday. You'll take it, won't you? It's not very large. You'll see when I bring it this evening."

Toward the end of dinner my father remarked "Peculiar, isn't it! Editing never occurred to you when you thought about earning your living." I said: at that time I knew nothing at all about politics: nothing, but now — I declared, mocking myself — I've *mastered* it all. I added, perhaps too earnestly: Fifty writers endorsed the Communist platform in '32 . . . He cut me off with a firm "Do you want my opinion? First, you've acquired an added profession; second, you're striving to change our world for the better. How can I fail to approve, though I'm certain that what you're doing will *not* turn out to be the solution you think it is. — And now, dare I add a third? One of these days you'll throw the whole thing over, you'll find your entire position untenable. In a year — two at the most." The housekeeper brought on the special whipped-cream-and-chocolate-cake fashioned, she said, out of all that Pauline recalled of your mother's recipe for "Booker T. Washington Pie." What a marvelous treat, I shouted, skipping the name, which my Party friends would deplore as insultingly chauvinist. Two large helpings for each of us merely delayed my father's coda — which arrived with the coffee. "And so tomorrow each of us goes his way, each cocksure of his mission: yours to enlist people of every color and creed, mine to convert our Jews." He waited. "When I was your age I also hoped to perfect the world, through Enlightenment's new religion. It too was godlessly secular. Then the tearing-apart began, caught between warring allegiances: either to all mankind or a small properly labeled stiff-necked minority . . . The rest of the story you know." I urged him on. He mused. "What followed *seemed* a succession of ironies: always *seemingly forced* to take up the Jewish identity. But is 'irony' justified, when the two had the same purpose, both aiming the lance at greed, social inequity, human injustice, suffering . . . ? I can sum it up in three words: the arenas differed. — Selah!" I was hearing him make his peace with part of his past, but he hadn't yet finished. "Like you, I had risen above divisiveness, yearning to take my place as a world-citizen. Noble ambition, splendid, and also — *doomed!* No such creature is possible, for in terms of mankind, each nation — giant or pigmy — is merely another minority. Hence each man and woman is blessed with a hyphen. The millennium will come when every person can wear it with humane feeling, dignity, pride."

Pauline's arrival drew us up from the roiling depths into calming shallows. "Have you settled the planet's problems? I hope so. I've kept at home so you'd have the day together, which hasn't happened in years." I was too caught up in the moment to stand aside and wonder if we'd ever have one again.

"Are you sure you can carry all this?" Pauline asked, slipping a miniscule packet — perfume? — into my pocket. At once my father excused himself to climb to his study. "Not very subtle of me," she shrugged, "but a check is the best present these days." He was down in minutes. "Also for Evelyn?" she smiled as he put an envelope into my hand. Having achieved her purposes, she prepared to leave. "By the way," she turned to me, "please thank whoever thought up your trip. If he hadn't — Oh!" — she stopped herself — "Wait while I 'phone." In a moment she reappeared. "It's all arranged. I'll drive to the depot . . . And now — now we have plenty of time. I'll put up the kettle. Tea?" Without saying a word, she also set the alarm on the kitchen clock.

The buzzer went off at eleven, just as my father was reading the last of the letters "from my Holland nephews. I'll keep you informed by mail. Maybe the fools will listen." I opened my bags, pulled out my traveling sweater, and snapped the locks. Our goodbye would have to be brief. As I stood at the door, my father held out a check made out to the *Masses*. "Why?" I implored, "when you're certain our —"

"Why?" He eyed me severely. "Because we have common enemies . . . because you're giving your nights and days to destroy them. Reason enough! . . . Take it, my boy, and go!"

Throughout the next few months, and for no explainable reason, I heard his echoing "common enemies" throb in my head, till the night I realized, suddenly, that another bond had arisen, tying us close — ever more close, perhaps, for the rest of our lives. Letters, however brief or sporadic, set off responses much like those that occur when friends, sharing the same concerns, look up in silence, saying nothing yet feeling each other's thoughts. So I had only to mention the Hitler blood purge of June for my father to think of the concentration camps and the thousands of caged victims. Or for him to write of the often ironic effects of his Plan. Thus, from a note replying to mine on his birthday in May '35:

> I can't say which surprised me more: the bursts of praise or the ignorance of our brethren. Having never heard of the Septuagint, they "simply couldn't believe" that if Jewish scholars in Egypt hadn't rendered the Bible in Greek for the sake of Jews who couldn't read Hebrew, Christianity might well have continued to be just a minor Jewish heresy.

But his mood changed in the wake of the Nuremberg Laws of September. I received a note written in haste by hand:

> Re the latest barbarities: in a year they'll deprive the other 50% of their Jews of earning a living — then of buying milk for children, drugs, medicine, etc. . . . But the dangers are also here: millions applauding the "Jew Deal" speeches of Father Coughlin. Have you heard this maniacal radio-priest from the Shrine of the Little Flower!!! — Bigots can also be found in our highest places. E.g., Lincoln's words in debating Douglas: "I have no purpose to introduce political and social equality between the white and the black races . . . [The] physical differences between the two . . . will probably forever forbid their living together upon the footing of perfect equality" (quoting exactly). — By the way, the final vote on my Plan is Tuesday before Thanksgiving . . .

Its acceptance was taken for granted, with reports in hand from some ninety groups, each of them ready to state its endorsement. The meeting in fact had been summoned, they heard, merely to give the signal for launching the Council.

When the vote was called, a spokesman for five of the wealthiest men on the Board vetoed the plan as "dangerously democratic, in any case too democratic" and, supporting their stand, proceeded to quote Count Clermont-Tonnerre, "a long-dead friend of the Jews in France," of whom they could never have heard till the scholar he hired came forth with the warrant they needed: "Everything for the Jews as individuals; nothing for the Jews as a people . . . we cannot have a nation within a nation." The spokesman repeated the words to a stunned audience, then strode from the hall. Two days later the Council's author drafted his resignation. The Board's insistent attempt to dissuade him had no effect. He was already weighing dozens of dreams of places, projects, people, and — more than all else — of time to surrender to joys that had passed him by.

> You're the only one who's pleased [he said in a handwritten note in December] — even Pauline's "concerned" — afraid I'll be lost with time on my hands. But I warmly welcome the prospect — as well as my new assistant, who starts next week. . . . Am I disillusioned, you ask? My Socialist friend Badanes (who died last April at seventy-five) warned me about the job at the HSGS: "How can you trust your fate to those Uptown Jews?" — the same species that vetoed my Council. But he wasn't quite right: three of the five have been suffering second thoughts — want to "compromise." I've told them to ask my assistant!!! As for you, I'm even more pleased

(and relieved) that you're leaving the *Masses*. Very sorry you'll be in Maine when I go to Atlantic City for my last National Conference. But we'll meet in October. Some of my N.Y. colleagues want me to be a consultant. I'll come down to hear what they have to say . . .

His plans took a different turn. As news of his coming retirement spread through the National Conference halls, colleagues besieged him with cheerful congratulations coupled with questions about his future. Among the well-wishing friends and admirers were dozens of people he hadn't heard from in well over twenty-five years. One of them, introducing herself as a child-care worker and former Pleasantville cottage-mother, came to his side at every break between the discussion sessions. Marie smiled at the none-too-subtle approach of the beaming, dark-eyed woman who showed no wish to conceal her adulation. A tense courtship with roles reversed appeared to be under way. Four days later, just as the Conference was ending, the woman gayly announced to Marie "Your father and I are taking a cruise together . . . tomorrow. It was my suggestion — but only after he said that I made him feel years younger again. Do we have your approval?"

When you're sixty-six and forty-seven — I thought, on learning their wedding date — you waste no time. But to make it a public affair? — that is, with the daughters and son of a mother-still-mourned in attendance . . . ? The rite was painless enough and the awkward hours that followed were passed in meaningless talk with guests I would never encounter again. Besides, at the time I was more concerned with finding a suitable job than with fears for my father's whirlwind marriage, which could always be undone if it failed the hopes of the widower-groom and his spinster-bride. No such outcome was thinkable, Pauline reported. If anything brought him discomfort, it was sheer impatience at having to wait for his working year to be over. Having made his successor responsible for all he had formerly borne, there was little for him to do but sit back and observe. I could read part of his mood from the way he treated my letters, sending delayed replies and ignoring pointed questions I posed on the Spanish War. Europe only: Germany's threat to Europe's Jews lashed at his mind. By spring he decided to act: he would travel abroad on a family rescue mission. I would hear the details, he said, at the end of July. "Ethel and I shall be sailing August the 1st."

Last-minute problems curtailed their New York stay to a single night. Circled by many more evening guests than their room could hold, he excused himself for a moment to take us aside "Children, after I'm settled on board, I'll write a detailed letter explaining all that I'd planned to tell you tonight. And I'll have my steward mail it the morning we land. And now I must talk with our guests." The letter never arrived. Picture postcards reached us from France, Italy, Holland. Most of the words meant nothing: the people he named were unknown. It was not till the day he returned that we heard of his "mission."

They had spent the earliest part of their trip in Cannes, with regular weekends to Italy, at Alassio, to visit my father's sister, her son, and her daughter. All the remaining time, except for a brief stay with nephews in Holland, centered in Paris, where a niece and a nephew, each with their children, had happily lived for years. In all three places the outcome had been the same; nothing my father was able to prove of Hitler's intent to destroy the Jews could make them even consider their future safety. Goethe's and Nietzsche's remarks on the Germans were mere poetical fantasy. The Dutch were a civilized people: they could never betray their Jews. Mussolini, for all his bravado and Socialist treason, had never been anti-semitic and was much too clever to ape his lunatic suitor. As for the French, what other nation had made a Jew, Léon Blum, the head of state? Besides, the Dreyfus Affair had long ago ended "the problem," once and for all. It proved worse than useless to ask why Italian pilots were strafing anti-fascist civilians in Spain, or to mention the number of days it had taken the Germans to overrun Belgium decades before, or to point to the bare-faced racist words of the high-placed Action Française. "Don't think, Uncle, your warnings are wasted on foolish ears," said Sigmund, the Paris perfume magnate. "Your solicitude moves us deeply. But you've lived in America most of your life. You don't understand Europeans. If you did, you would know why a Nazi coup simply can't happen here."

The only one who showed concern was his fellow-Parisian Erica. Her mother (my father's niece) had married a German baron, her own husband had come from British nobility. "Are my daughters Jewish quadroons?" she laughed. My father had given to each the names and locations of agents and similar data — in case of a change of mind — but Erica, whose friends in Nice, without being asked, had promised her haven, wanted *facts* about crossing into the States by the Mexican border. "Now that the Germans have blocked all Jews from earning a living, thousands will flee for America. Will you take them in?"

He failed to say how he answered. Trying to break from the hopeless subject, I asked "When will you travel again?" He frowned. "But wouldn't you like to look at the synagogue murals at Dura-Europas? — Pharaoh's daughter nude to the waist, Joshua crossing the Jordan, raising the tablets — including the Second Commandment?" I made a last try: "Surely you want to see the Hebrew Pompeii of the Syrian desert."

He smiled "Tomorrow we travel to California. Write us! — I gave our address to each of you." He eyed me quietly "I want to hear all about your becoming a publisher, and your view of the farcical Moscow trials of 'Old Bolshevik spies.'" His first request was easily met with a brief account of my new career, but the second . . . ? when I, too, questioned the strange self-accusations? My answer, skirting the guilt of the one-time heroes, ended up with the safe cliché about *all* revolutions' leading to counter-conspiracies. My letter left him cold: he blandly ignored it.

> I'm writing by hand — no one to take dictation — to tell you that after 5 months' search, I purchased a private school for children of working parents (two buildings, staff, etc.). Ethel is taking charge of *all* except the curriculum (first four grades), which I'll change for the better . . . Climate here is a miracle! Also — I've stumbled on 3 old friends: Seman, former HSGS assistant; Kaplan, who worked for my Research Bureau; Karpf, of the Graduate School (N.Y.). Last evening I read them the words you wrote for the close of your Barnes volume . . . that the fields of Spain are providing the testing ground for the new death-dealing weapons perfected by Europe. May the future prove you mistaken!

In June I sent him another book I had put through the press, but his letter — still by hand, in his choppy style — merely mentioned the title. He was bent on making certain I saw what dangerous things Britain and France had done by their Munich Pact: "Now Hitler will seize whatever he can with no one to stop him — while my Paris nephew is more concerned with Coughlin's claim that Jews are 'getting what they deserve' for starting the Red Revolution!" Six weeks later, November 11th, twenty years to the day of the 1918 Armistice, the Nazis honored their Beer Hall Putsch with the worst pogrom: "Kristallnacht" — setting on fire hundreds of synagogues, thousands of private homes and shops; raping, looting, murdering; packing some 30,000 off to detention camps, then fining the Jews one billion marks for their crimes against humanity. France and Great Britain shuddered, but four months later, they merely sighed as Hitler gobbled Czechoslovakia.

All the while I brooded over the birthday letter I planned to send my father in May. Freed from livelihood tasks, he had time to view and compare all he had hoped to achieve at the start with all he had done, and to find *by studying both together,* the paradigm of our epoch: the young idealist Jew who was well on his way toward fulfilling his mission, only to witness all he believed in, fiendishly menaced . . . I pointed out that he alone was able to write such a work, since nobody else could know both sides of the story. His answer was simple and prompt: "If to find one's joy in re-living the past is the mark of age, count me as being far from old, though in fact I'm going on seventy." I replied that re-living was not my proposal, but rather re-seeing the twofold story against the backdrop of seventy years and into the present. "Much too busy," his postcard said, "even to think of weighing the pros and cons, but I'll give it the careful thought it needs once my school is in order: after September. N.B. Despite myself, I've made some notes both pro and con your 'paradigm.'" He added the date: May 6, 1939.

Earl Browder, head of the Communist Party, addressing a crowd of the faithful on the eve of the Russo-German Pact (August 23), gloated in triumph "Hair will grow on the palm of my hand before the Soviets talk of peace with the Nazis." As he raised both hands for all to see, the audience screamed in applause. Nine days later Hitler invaded Poland. In forty-eight hours Britain and France were at war with Hitler.

> Keep this *confidential* [he wrote at the end of September]. One of my friends of many years has a "nearby friend of a friend of a friend," as it were, who receives sporadic reports from a kind of "underground." Whether or not my guess is right — that it's part of a network in touch with Hasidic Jews — the fact remains that tales we dismissed as preposterous proved to be true . . . among them the Russo-Nazi Pact. However, the latest, reported yesterday, simply defies belief: that Hitler has ordered Himmler and Heydrich to round up every Jew, Marxist, and other enemy; work the "productive" ones to death in newly constructed labor camps and annihilate the rest . . . Conceivable? Anything seems to be, with Henry Ford showing off the Cross of the German Eagle as Hitler's reward for his "anti-semitic valor"; the national hero Lindbergh blaming the Jews and Roosevelt for anti-Germanic campaigns . . . One bright note to help us maintain our sanity: Erica has moved to the south of France. P.S. Your excellent "Heritage" book arrived — what a treasure!

An almost undecipherable P.P.S. retailed the "latest rumor — Hitler's partner in crime will reap his share of Poland before November."

The underground prediction was off by a month, and the Nazi attack on Denmark and Norway had escaped their ears or my father would have forewarned me. After the fall of Holland I asked for a word of his Dutch nephews. Weeks passed without a reply, despite the privileged news I had sent from a "part-time operative" describing the Zionists' desperate answer to Britain's latest reneging on Balfour's promises. "Jews," I said, "at last have taken up arms to rescue the helpless migrants at sea — they're spiriting them ashore under the cover of darkness." I received no answer.

A month's spell of mild but discomfiting illness explained the silence, in a letter meant for my birthday, which arrived late — June 22, 1940 — the morning that France surrendered. Most probably, his difficulties in writing by hand rose from his anxious haste to touch on all that had happened, from the brilliant retreat to England under an air umbrella of hundreds of thousands of stranded soldiers at Dunkerque, to cryptic news of his nephew Sigmund's flight from Paris, to questionings of the whereabouts of my old French poet, Spire. He had also taken the time while convalescing "to reconsider in depth the autobiography project." Someone "with more perspective" — meaning myself — should do the writing; he would furnish full accounts in seven installments. In fact, he was on the trail of a stenotypist who, he hoped, might come to his home after working hours.

Surprisingly, he had failed to mention the new Nazi technique of lightning war, the *Blitzkrieg,* that stupefied enemy armies. I supposed he saw no need to bemoan what everyone knew. That the spectacle of a Hitlerized Europe never left his mind suddenly struck me when I read the card that followed his letter:

> Rummaging through my ancient lecture notes on Heine, I found these words from the man who wrote *Die Lorelei,* which the Nazi textbooks attribute to Author Unknown. The passage was written a hundred years before Hitler: "The day will come when you will hear the storm of German lightning . . . German armies will plow through Europe mercilessly and tear up the roots of the past, reviving the forces of paganism." N.B. Vide your teacher Prescott's chapter on Poets as Prophets.

Lying awake in the dark for the midnight airwaves to bring in words from abroad, I realized how our dreads and hopes, griefs and joys, lowered and leaped with the changing fate of numberless faceless strangers miles from our shores. We were being lived by their lives — much of the time, not all, for everyone did his workaday tasks as before, drawn by needs of the moment. Nor did I bother to ask how my father spent his hours; what mattered most was its thought, which sprang to life from his words. They were few, rarely touching on happenings widely known. Typical was the way he dealt with my glee at the failure of Nazi daylight raids over London

I lost all feelings of warmth toward Britain after I learned through our underground what the head of her Foreign Office Refugee Section said last week when the steamboat bound for Turkey with 200 Jews from Bulgaria (a third of them children) sank in the Sea of Marmora: "There could be no more opportune disaster from the point of view of stopping this traffic." It could make one almost proud of Zionist terrorists. P.S. We had better gird ourselves for more of the same. When struggles worsen, people grow less humane. Dec. 10/1940.

Erica's letter in March, mailed from Nice, though it said nothing of Sigmund, offered, between the lines, reassurance concerning the lost Dutch nephews. I probably shouldn't have followed it up by telling my father that Spire — two or three years his senior — was coming by ship "with a brand-new middle-aged wife who had *espérances*," for he wholly ignored the news, even my added "Pseudocyesis?" All that he sent in reply was a postcard "Am mailing Installment One, which will raise some questions. How could I tell how much you recall of my early years?" His packet arrived May 10th, as it happened, a crucial date in the war. Hitler, faced with England's defeat of his airforce and with Churchill's refusal to listen to peace, aimed his killing machines in a changed direction: Greece, the Balkan countries, Yugoslavia. Six weeks later his troops invaded the U.S.S.R. Newsmen readied themselves for defeat on a scale too large to envisage: 3,000,000 well-trained Germans poised over 2,000 miles of front versus 2,000,000 Russians whose fighting skills had never been tested.

Perhaps it was simply the shock of the *Blitz* on Moscow or the suddenness of Japan's attack, or both that made my father take stock with a "Balance Sheet as of January 1942." In paired columns, he entered items he judged as Pro or Con, adding numbers to give the relative force of each. He had made this kind of picture before, at critical moments, "to clear the fogs from my eyes." Anxious to check his natively hopeful bent, he decided, before concluding, to undervalue the Pros — "and yet," he wrote, "the net prognosis is comforting, even omitting two facts: (1) that Japan's reputedly 'sneak attack' did more to unite Americans than 1,000 rallies at best could have done; (2) as for Hitler's *Drang nach Osten*, even Napoleon gave up the quest." Cautiously self-convinced, he resumed his usual tasks, keeping a watchful eye on his school, making notes for the new "Installments," answering two or three HSGS alumni who had sent him belated greetings.

Soon, he announced with unusual eagerness, he and Ethel were going to do "their bit" for the cause. Quite as suddenly, his joyous elation changed. He received a tersely worded letter from Erica. Nazi officers, aided by turncoat Frenchmen, finally ferreted Sigmund, his wife, and children out of their hiding place. Only eleven days ago did she finally learn they had all been herded in deportation trains bound for German "detention camps," the meaning of which nobody knew. Two or three hopeful words ended her letter: Maurice, a cousin, agreed to take her daughters (twins) "to Mexico first." It was well arranged. We might hear from him "soon." Also about the family from Alassio. Nothing had changed . . .

> You can use a distraction [I wrote]: I'm sending a book I'm proud to have published: writings by Negroes from Frederick Douglass to Richard Wright, edited by my old-time friend and professor-poet, Sterling Brown. Yesterday I offered it to your former HSGS club-leader Harry Scherman as a choice for his Book-of-the-Month Club. He answered: "A book of writings by *Negroes*? . . . for *our* membership? Out of the question." It did no good to quote the Sunday Times and others that call it "a great book."

It did no good to urge it upon my father. Although, as he put it, "no one can doubt its importance," his overriding concern right now was the plight of Jews. Somber reports of mass killings had rumbled through London late last year: they fell on deaf ears. A Vilna girl swore she had seen thousands of corpses of Jews in a ditch twenty miles from her ghetto. No one believed her — no one wished to believe her — except one man, the underground said, who sent out a call for Jewish "arms and is now a Partisan leader roaming the Polish woods."

A week later my father sent a note that surprised me:

> Your friend "the part-time operative," as you call him, is here, doing his best these days to make me a Zionist! Of course the Jews need a haven, but he calls for a full-fledged nation, which would drain unbelievable sums from Diaspora pockets. To which he replies with a searching argument: antisemitism in other places would lower or disappear if the Jews had a land of their own to go to . . . Of course England will have to honor the Balfour commitment, even though last September, Eden (reportedly) said that he "loves the Arabs and hates the Jews." . . . I pointed out to your friend that the Jews inhabited the Promised Land only 550 years out of 3200. Irrelevant, he insists: of no account right now even if all the rumor-reports turn out to be fantasies — which they well might be . . . I hope I shall live long enough after this war to see what comes of Herzl's dream. . . .

I had never heard him speak in this vein before. Nor had I viewed him as old. The possibility of his being "cut off before his time" — whatever his time might be — stopped me. On the other hand, so long as I could recall, he had been a model of health, confident strength, inexhaustible energy — patterned, as my mother once said, on his octogenarian father.

Installment Three arrived July the 3rd, one day after the British had halted Rommel's "invincible force" at El Alamein. Experts announced that "the tide of the war had turned for the world's future." It had also turned for my father's, at least in my eyes, for whatever fate or caprice might do, it was now too late to rob him of knowing that Light and another chance for Justice would triumph. A scribbled line on the typescript read "One of these days I'd like to look at your 'paradigm.'" When, I wondered? Safer of course to wait till after his last Installments, but what if he asked for it now? He had more than a right to know before going on. I had nothing on paper to send him. Clearing my desk, I pulled out a sheet and started

The story of this immigrant Jew of exceptional gifts and achievement — one of whose "realized dreams" had brought him the kind of renown reserved for the few — stands for vastly more than a New World success. His career is a paradigm of the modern idealist Jew who starts out life as a son of the Great Enlightenment, a believer in its One Universal Religion, in the power of Education, in the irreversible Progress of Man toward a shining future ruled by Reason and Brotherhood . . . only to witness in later life the advent of Nazi savagery and its frenzied battle to root out civilization and all that man had achieved . . . but then, at last, in the blackness, to see the glimmering rays of the dawn of a world self-rescued, of the triumph of Light, of a new future for Reason, Justice, even Compassion.

Offered the choice in his thirtieth year of a brilliant public school career versus the ever uncertain prospect of salvaging children victimized by misfortune and persecution, he cast his lot with the second, thus launching himself on a lifelong future in which his conception of education broadened into a species of Biblical social mission: to do for victims of "fate" — orphans, at first, then people of all ages who were disadvantaged in varying ways — what a just and merciful Deity "ought to have done." So at least in his private, agnostic hours he defined his role, and was able as well, in times of reversal, to find consolation, while at other moments upbraiding himself for the possible "sin" of teaching the Lord a lesson by preempting his role. The next decades he spent in putting to work for entire Jewish communities the innovative proposals that the world of welfare had come

to expect of one who still held fast to his faith in the endless human potential for reason and brotherhood . . . till Germany set all Europe on fire in
a conflagration of hate   . . . . . .

I read the page quickly. Too many nouns with capitals, yet the draft such
as it was would do as a start — though something was missing: the ever-
worsening rumor-reports from unknown sources, including the friend of a
friend of a friend. "Fantasies," people had called them — "morbid projec-
tions of fear." I wondered what the undergrounds sought to accomplish.
More than once, fragments that first appeared in their tales surfaced later
in news reports as facts — a phenomenon hard to ignore though scarcely
conclusive. And yet . . . there was Erica's note on Sigmund: why the quotation marks for "detention camps" unless she was trying to tell more than
she dared . . . ? As the high holidays neared, one of the undergrounds urged
all Jews to remember the slaughter at Kiev, of the year before, describing
again how thousands of men, women, and children were marched through
the streets by the Germans, into the desolate outskirts of Babi Yar to be
shot, their corpses dumped into ditches.

Some of my father's friends took their cues from the *Jewish Frontier,* a
monthly founded a decade ago, which was widely known for its "balanced
judgments." Thus when the Socialist Polish Bund's London report of May
reached its desk in August, one of their editors noted "After reading this
detailed account of the functioning of the Nazi extermination centers, we
rejected it as a macabre fantasy of a lunatic sadist," yet they printed a part
in smaller type at the back of the issue, so "the atrocity tale, surely untrue,
should not be emphatically publicized." I had never seen the journal; only
clippings my father had sent from time to time. Hence my enormous surprise when I found the "Special November" double-issue outside my door.
"Jews Under the Axis: 1939–1942," the editor's page 3 statement, more than
atoned for its errors:

> In the occupied countries of Europe a policy is now being put into effect
> whose avowed object is the extermination of a whole people . . . This
> issue attempts to give some picture of what is happening to the Jews of
> Europe. It is of necessity an incomplete picture because reports have to
> be smuggled out and evidence has to be pieced together. Consequently,
> we have hesitated to include any material whose authenticity was in any
> way doubtful. The information we print is vouched for by sources of un-
> impeachable authority. The best test of the credibility of these reports is
> furnished by the statements of the Nazis themselves, whose repeated pub-

lic utterances make no secret of their intentions in regard to the Jewish minority. We have paid the Nazi spokesmen the compliment of not believing their monstrous professions. The reports in this issue, however, substantiate the Nazi claims . . . The tempo of this planned slaughter is being speeded up. Unless it is checked, we are faced with the possibility of the murder of a whole people. . . .

The editors' six-page account of "The Plan of Destruction" preceded "German Police Testifies." The largest section, on Poland, published part of the London Bund report that the editors, two months earlier, had attributed to "a lunatic sadist." Articles dealing with Germany, Rumania, Lithuania, Czechoslovakia, France, and Holland completed the issue.

I tried, vainly, to telephone to my father — not that I had any message; I thought I might learn from his voice what the revelations had done. The next day's mail brought me his letter: "Now we know." He added a single sentence: "Half of Europe's Jewry have already met their doom in the German death camps — so Secretary Welles informs Stephen Wise."

The news flashed over the world, though not till December 17th did the House of Commons officially hear that Jews were being transported from Nazi-occupied lands to Eastern Europe "where they were either worked to death in labor camps or deliberately slain." Frantic appeals for Allied air-raids to stop the slaughter brought no response. John J. McCloy, Assistant Secretary of War, twice vetoed the pleas of Weizmann and Shertok to bomb the Auschwitz death-camps, which lay within five miles of his target, I. G. Farben. Nor did Roosevelt's officers alter their plans in response to the protests, meetings, memorial services, rallies, and demonstrations that swept the country from coast to coast. I explained my failure to reach my father by telephone by his presence at some such meeting. How wholly misled I was, his letter made evident

> You no longer need to send me your 'paradigm.' Mine has been looming in front of my eyes for the last three days — and even after I've dozed to sleep, it's there when I wake. — I must do something quickly to drive it away. How, I wonder? Not many options left at my age, as we're both aware. — Meanwhile a sentence dear to my father — not his words but a poet's — hums in my head . . . almost as though the corpses of Babi Yar were shouting up from their pits and commanding ruthlessly in the mute shrill voice of the dead *Du musst dein Leben ändern*! What I'm saying here seems mad, but this has been going on for days. No need to answer this letter.

I strove to absorb the phrases. Once or twice I thought of calling my sisters, but stopped when I raised the receiver. Friends dropped in; without explaining, they made their visits brief. When they left I felt relieved, though for no reason other than wanting quiet. As the afternoon wore on, I lay on my bed, stared into the ceiling, while chimes from the neighborhood numbered the hours.

I must have slipped away in a waking dream, for my father's screams were bursting my head. "Moses, what if the Goodness you brought is a lie? — if the Power that peopled this earth mocks at the agonized screams of people trying to force their pitiful will on the chaos? — even hurling their precious first-born into the flames as a final plea for the Mercies . . . ? What of your truth, Moses? Answer! What must we do? Murder ourselves or defy the fiend by creating out of our helpless hands what your Promised God should have done? Can you swear it, Moses? swear it is not a lie? Then swear it, Moses! Swear it, swear it! — "

Steady telephone ringing pulled me suddenly out of wherever I was. By the time I seized the instrument, it had stopped. Streetlamps flooded up from the pavements into my window, till the dark inside my room exploded in blackness, uttermost blackness — a hollow abyss blocking out every glimmer of possible light. I rushed to my desk, copied the paradigm notes I had scribbled off months before. Though Hitler's empire roared from the heights, I mobilized every positive sign, whatever its source: Allied landings in Africa — Algeria, Morocco — "that had turned the tide for good"; Russians fiercely counterattacking from Stalingrad, "the Germans' defeat now a certainty"; France's sudden turn-about, sinking its fleet at Toulon. . . . "Nothing," I shouted, "could hold us back now. It was time to summon up arms for saving the unblemished good from the hells of war — for guarding forever against man's future destruction!" — I was overstating, knowingly, yet utterly sure that my affirmations's claims would in time prove true . . . Even more certain that the paradigm's victory-light had erased the abyss.

At about this time, a friend of my sister Marie, who accompanied her to all HSGS alumni events, called on her — unannounced — to broach the idea of a gala party "as a tribute to your father. It will keep what he stands for alive for the new generation — they don't even know his name. But how go about it? We want it to be a great surprise, yet we also have to make sure he'll attend. There's time, of course, and we've picked the date: May 4th, his birthday. Two full years away — he'll be seventy-five. We'll have to prepare soon, and we'll need your help, if you like the idea. By *that*

May 4th the War will surely be over and we'll all be thrilled with the great new Victory world. Perfect time for making sure that all that he gave us won't be forgotten."

"Write to him now," Marie cried out. "He's had about all he can bear with the death-camp news, and his nephews seized by the Germans . . . If you write him now of your plans, he can start enjoying them now — he could live with them over and over again, long before the event. That's how he's been, living things over and over again in advance . . . But, of course, no matter how you decide, count on me! And please think of all that I've said . . . I can almost see him walking on clouds." A good many days would pass before the alumni group would act. Long before, I sent them my thanks, also offering to do whatever might help.

During these weeks I decided to ask my father's advice about a book we were trying to plan — one that might "make a difference — helping the so-called intelligent citizen to grasp the *political* difficulties that the Allied Powers would have to face when the fighting ended." We exchanged ideas — the challenge delighted him, even the working title I pulled from the air, and my fanciful roster of "ideal writers." Only a person of broad knowledge and high regard could serve the needs of this project. He would act as the General Editor and, as such, the responsible author, though the planning of every page and the writing itself would be done by other hands, under the guidance of one of my closest friends, whose grasp of world affairs was surpassed by no one.

In the midst of our live correspondence, newspapers startled the world with reports of an unbelievable armed attack by Warsaw's Jews on the Nazi soldiers surrounding their ghetto. April 19th, when the battle broke out, less than 40,000 were left of the once 600,000 men, women, and children herded behind brick walls into hideous streets under constant Nazi surveillance. Ranging themselves into 22 units, 600 fighters (men and women), armed with 60 pistols and paltry munitions, launched their attack by day, fleeing below at night to their bunkers and cellars to celebrate the Passover. Utterly stunned by the storm of home-made grenades and flaming benzine bottles that ruined their tanks, the Nazis counterattacked with unheard of fury. Every ghetto house was set on flame. Yet the rebels replied with bullets from smoking barricades, while others climbed through sewers and drains to attack from behind the enemy lines. Given three days to crush the rebellion, the Germans stopped the engagement, leaving their wounded and dead on the streets. The battle continued through six more weeks, some of the rebels carrying on for another month. As the end approached, all but four of the fighters chose to die — by their own hands, as Masada's zealots had done. The survivors made their way to Partisan units in Poland's forests.

The battle brought to the light other facts that were known only to those in continual touch with the underground. News now raged of rebellions in other ghettos, slave camps, death camps, even naming some of the places: Maidanek; Treblinka, Auschwitz, whose prisoners blew up a crematorium; Sobibor, where some SS guards were killed as they fled in escape. In addition to fighting their captors, ghetto survivors and others were forming Partisan groups of their own or joining Resistance units. Not since the Roman wars of Vespasian and Hadrian had Hebrews defied their conquerors; they had lost the will of defying death in the course of two bleak millenia of trusting the Lord's redemption, reason, and Torah. "A new chapter in history," said a note from my father, putting together reports of "Jewish Resistance" that shattered the age-old picture of helpless submission.

How should one face the irony? — that the triumph-defeats of Jewish rebellion lifted and quickened millions of hearts bleeding in grief for the Holocaust. But the "Never Again!" defiance of 600 Warsaw Jews who held off a Nazi army had become much more than a slogan, as Middle East Britishers and Arabs, as well as Nazi soldiers, already had come to learn. A New Jew had arisen, resolute, fearless, who would stop at nothing to safeguard his place in the world.

Good luck seemed to shadow my steps as I strove ahead with the book-idea I shared with my father. Sumner Welles, my choice for editor, not only gave his agreement to all I proposed but also offered not to "do anything else till this most important volume has seen the light." He even approved my title — *An Intelligent American's Guide to the Peace* — which I feared might ring in some ears like a play on Shaw's primer for women, though there the resemblance ended; for "the Welles book" would introduce any literate man and woman to the multiple opportunities — and complexities — awaiting the victor nations. The project seemed important enough for the *New York Times* to contribute the use of its maps, one for each of our chapters.

Two "great" pieces of news [my father replied in the same day's mail] — Yours about Sumner Welles and a wonderful invitation from the HSGS Alumni. They're planning a gala event for my birthday-after-next. I've already started to make some notes about what to say. . . . I hope I'll be able to recognize at least some of my former "boys and girls," though it's been so long — more than twenty-five years.

A third surprise would greet him soon. Pauline, Marie, and her daughter had been planning a California trip for the summer to come. When their letter arrived "it sounded too good to be true," he told them by 'phone that evening. Ethel and he would begin at once to look for accommodations. "I wish my oldest daughter and youngest son could join our reunion, and I know they will if they possibly can. Meanwhile nothing delights me more than the thought of being together. I'll be counting the days."

From all I was able to learn, the eight-week visit surpassed all hopes. Hasty letters and postcards gave me at least a notion of how they were spending the visit:

> Our days begin late in the morning — after we've had our swim — Pop and Ethel arrive by car at our Santa Monica place; then we start out driving — a little while — though by now we've been over hundreds of miles of this countryside. After lunch, back to our place "to relax" and prepare for the routine hiking excursion. He's still an incredible walker, but there's more. To get to the Palisades (our route high over the ocean) you must climb 110 steps. What a picture he makes, counting off ten at a time (in German) and rarely losing his breath . . .
>
> We have dinner together each night, often with some of his friends, and a musical evening weekly — German *Lieder* of course, the ones we were nursed on. Modern music: *verboten*.
>
> You asked if we talk of the war. Of course we know of the Landings in France and the German missiles in London; but the only ones who bring up such things are his cronies. Without having made a pact, we steer quite clear of whatever might stand in the way of our goal — to live these weeks as joyously as we can. He himself has set the tone, with his avid talk about traveling all through Mexico, after the big celebration next May with the HSGS alumni. . . . If I tried to describe his state, I'd say it was resignation overlaid by a firm desire to gather the most from whatever time he has left, though nobody mentions *that* subject. One topic of course is taboo — the fate of the hunted in Europe . . .

But in fact he tried each day to learn the whereabouts of his niece's two young daughters, who, Erica wrote, would be taken to Western Mexico. Nothing came through. Had their mother told them to sail back home, now that Paris was freed? Would he hear from Erica? . . .

After my sisters' departure he began again to send me handwritten notes by means of which, for seven whole years, we had kept close touch with each other. I showered him with journals and clippings after he wrote that he now had taken "to scanning scores of books in the local stacks" — and "for no good reason," he added. That his new habit reflected some striving need, I was certain. Yet I couldn't seize on the reason, which seemed to dart in and out of his letter that came in October:

> Yesterday, while visiting friends, I happened to cast my eye on the books, as I usually do. Don't ask me why it lighted on Tolstoy's *The Kingdom of God Is Within You,* except that the title (a paperback) seemed unfamiliar in English. I mention this now because of something I found in the introduction, written by one of your poet-friends. The passage struck me at once — I reread and reread it again. I copy it off for you now, for reasons you'll see when you read it. If you give me your friend's address, I'll send him my thanks. "The mature man lives quietly, does good privately, assumes personal responsibility for his actions, treats others with friendliness and courtesy, finds mischief boring and keeps out of it. Without this hidden conspiracy of good will, society would not endure an hour."

There was no gainsaying the words. Taking them one by one, then all together, I felt myself oddly relieved — yet also disbalanced, and quite at a loss to understand my response. All I was certain about was a sense of closure; but of what? for how long? — Answers, I once believed, might emerge in dreams, and then some "scientist proved" that dreams merely kept a sleeper from waking. As I lay in bed, sleeping, the message seemed to sail high over the earth: a glistening banner-of-words that clouded the aeons of "civilized knowledge" below. In the morning when I awoke my head still reeled with pictures of hurrying people racing through hundreds of ages, each of them wildly searching about for a voice's answer. I looked for the current address of the author of those lines, Kenneth Rexroth. He could never suspect he had written the coda words for my paradigm.

"Mirable dictu!" my father wrote in November. "Erica's girls are here, though 'here' is 70 miles from the border. Ethel must handle the whole affair since I'm much too busy — more than in years. I have to make sure my address to the HSGS Alumni will be worthy of such kind honor." Hurried postcard-notes that followed brimmed with ebullience "Living my early years again — part of my preparation. Makes me forget where I am: though my body's in California, my thought's in the East! Filling up pages of notes, more than I need. Can't seem to stop." And a day or two later "One thing's decided. Near my conclusion, I'll quote the 'Hidden conspiracy' adage. My thanks for the author's address." I urged him to hold onto all the notes. He answered at once that he'd take them along in the spring, adding "Happy news! Erica's girls may be here for New Year's — the one success of my family-rescue mission — with a saga past belief, which I'll save for the spring." Three days later another note "Just to tell you, before I forget, that I'm making special plans for our coming reunion. Secret plans. — We shall more than make up for your absence here when we're *all* together in May. Don't try to guess what I have in mind! It's a real surprise. — P.S. I'm thinking about a Pleasantville trip. The maples we planted when you were six should be glorious in the spring."

Ethel, who served in the United Service Organization recreation center, had volunteered to run the party on Christmas Eve, so her Gentile colleagues could have their holiday free. Returning long after midnight, she found my father tossing about, racked with pains he had struggled against for hours. His cure-all — walking — brought no relief, and by early morning a doctor was summoned, who took him at once for tests. After a day under oxygen, he started to act like his usual self, despite his nurse's insistence that he hold off questions about his heart and quietly rest instead. Smiling and shaking his head, he began to sing as she left the room. When she returned he was dead.

The body was flown for burial beside my mother's grave in the hills of Westview, and we ordered a granite boulder to set near the one I had sent from Maine thirteen winters before. What of the text for the plaque? The same that his daughters and son in their early years had heard him repeat, never failing to add that, despite the injustice around them, men for their sanity's sake must assert its truth. Although the source had been long forgotten, the will of the Psalm cried on *I have been young and now I am old but never have I seen the righteous forsaken or his offspring begging for bread.* In the war's last winter the words were too bitter to bear, but within a year the derisive overtones quieted as the salvaged nations, their triumph secured, buried the rest of their dead.

STEVENS' "MR. BURNSHAW

AND THE STATUE"

Originally published in *The Sewanee Review* 69 (Summer 1961): 355–66, as "Wallace Stevens and the Statue" by Stanley Burnshaw. Copyright 1961 by the University of the South. Reprinted by permission.

Like others interested in Wallace Stevens, I try to read what I can about his meanings, for despite the zeal of his commentators, I still find it hard to understand some of his most attractive poems, especially one directed to me that appeared a quarter-century ago. I first learned about "Mr. Burnshaw and the Statue" from an editor of *The New American Caravan,* who telephoned out of the blue to announce, with great glee, that I had just been immortalized: Stevens had sent him a wonderful poem written as a reply to a review of *Ideas of Order* which I had published in *The New Masses.* The poem was magnificent; I was sure to be delighted; and, best of all, it would appear between the same covers that had already made room for a slight lyric of my own. Not yet in my *an trentiesme,* and frankly overwhelmed that the author of *Harmonium* had even bothered to read what I had written, I awaited the heralded poem with a certain awe. But when I finally got hold of the text, its meaning eluded my efforts. And twenty-five years later, whenever I finish a discussion of the poem, I wonder if it will ever be adequately explicated.

It will not, so long as critics fail to interpret the originating circumstance *from within* its period context. Trigant Burrow once horrified his fellow social scientists by showing why they would never understand a system so long as they remained on the outside. His warning has equal point for literary critics, particularly those who write about books of the desperate, guilt-ridden thirties from the blasé and serener standpoint of our decades. Obviously both the review and Stevens' reply were of a piece with the period in which they appeared: they are nothing more nor less than actions of their time. Judge them out of their context and they become grotesques.[1] But it is never easy for a critic to shed his assumptions, and it is especially difficult for an American, in our anti-Marxist midcentury, to give up, even temporarily, the attitudes that compose his security. Yet unless he is able to do this, he will never understand the writings of the thirties for what they were.

Some reporters of the episode make out the onlie begetter to be a meaner relative of Belloc's anti-Chesterton Don; some are more charitable; and occasionally the controversy is discussed with unexceptionable clarity (as by Louis Martz, in the *Yale Review,* Summer 1958). But there is always a suggestion of oversimplicity. Frank Kermode, for example, introduces the affair by stating that the reviewer "criticized Stevens' apparent indifference to what was going on in the world,"[2] which is exactly what the review did not do. Mr. Kermode writes in England, where a 1935 issue of a foreign periodical may be a trouble to obtain; but can one write several pages of respectable first-hand criticism by referring only to what others have said? And will the next discussant carry on from this newest authority? Obviously there would be no point in arguing with Mr. Kermode or with anyone else who has had his say on the subject. What is needed, rather, is light and more light upon a literary decade that is becoming increasingly darkened by myth. If Martz is right in stating that the critique was "so largely true" and "left the mark," it may be worth knowing something of its genesis.

To begin with, then, a few facts about the reviewer, with due attention to the pranks of selective memory. He was young and little known. Such reputation as he had came not especially from poems he had been publishing in avant-garde journals (*Dial, Transition, Poetry,* etc.) but from a book of essays and translations (*André Spire and His Poetry,* 1933) which had been widely reviewed and vastly overpraised. What value it possessed lay in its technical study of syllabism and accent in French prosody and the origins of *vers libre.* Like Stevens, he had been deeply involved with the Symbolist poets by night and with a business job by day; but unlike Stevens, he quit a remunerative career for the hope of teaching. When his first book appeared, he was writing a thesis on the relationship between poetry and mysticism, at Cornell University, where he had gone in order to study with F. C. Prescott, author of *Poetry and Myth* and *The Poetic Mind.* Armed with a graduate degree but unable to find a teaching job, he returned to New York (1933) with the notion of living by his pen. Apathy greeted him everywhere except in the office of an impoverished journal, which accepted some of his "proletarian" verse and offered him books for review.

He had arrived at his peculiar political position through seemingly inevitable stages. Born into a comfortable middle-class family, he had never given a thought to social problems until he found his first job — in a mill-town outside Pittsburgh (1925). What he witnessed there of human misery and degradation was enough to convince him that something was terribly wrong with a social system whose "haves" could splurge *à la* Fitzgerald while others suffered without hope. He had no solution of his own other than to expunge the dark satanic mills, and even he recognized its absurdity. Hence his response, a few years later, to the one shining program of concrete action for ending want and suffering. Some fifty serious writers had already endorsed the Communist Party's 1932 presidential platform. Though Prescott had told him that a radical was a liberal in a hurry, he had also hastened to add that one doesn't play the violin when the house is on fire.

When in 1934–35 he found himself writing about books and plays, he knew he was practicing criticism of a very special sort, its attitudes and emphases determined by a particular moment in time. He was writing for a new *New Masses,* directed at the same audience to whom *The Nation* and *The New Republic* appealed, but from a wholly radical point of view.[3] How speak to such an audience? None of his associates was quite sure; there were no precedents to turn to in American journalism; and, as the managing editor never tired of reminding them, they were blind men leading the blind. But tentativeness and humility were unthinkable: the world was separating into two enemy camps and time was running out! One had to act in behalf of mankind, and for anyone with a brain there could be no choice. Like the rest of the intellectual Left, they moved in the serenity of certainty, naive examples of what Mann calls "the automatic tendency to believe that the intellect, by its very nature, takes its position . . . on the 'left,' that it is therefore essentially allied with the ideas of freedom, progress, humanity . . . a prejudice which has often been disproved." That "the intellect can just as well take a position on the 'right,' and, moreover, with the greatest brilliance" was inconceivable except to a few of these people — and their days of service were numbered.

As it turned out, the days of every seriously literary Marxist critic were numbered, for this was a criticism for the time-being-only. And the more perceptive practitioners recognized the temporal limitation, if not soon then before long. The overriding test — social amelioration — was quick to wear. After one applied it to a novel or poem or play, how much farther could one go in depth and range into the work of art itself? It was like any other extraliterary consideration — the psychoanalyst's, the historian's, the religionist's; once he had exhausted its possibilities, the critic would soon find himself carried into the literary structure; into a concentration upon form, which, as Stalin later made clear, was simply a bourgeois' basic desire for decadence. Inevitably, therefore, the critic dedicated to literature was foredoomed to give less and less attention to the very concern that accounted for his presence within the Left. Someone else would eventually have to take his place — until he too tired of the task (and a task it was, requiring deliberate effort) of looking at books in a certain way: the way of ultimate social welfare.

But for the time being — and until the unthought-about day of his departure — the critic could see some results of his contributions. More and more writers, some from the most unexpected places, were knocking at the door and asking to be let in. In 1934–1936 *The New Masses* printed work by Hemingway, MacLeish, Saroyan, Dos Passos, Elmer Rice, Erskine Caldwell, Richard Wright, Waldo Frank, Rolfe Humphries, Nelson Algren, Samuel Putnam, Edward Dahlberg, Horace Gregory, Kenneth Burke, to list some of the names that are especially familiar today. Controversies raged; the world of books had suddenly come alive with excitement. Audiences crowded into theatres and often argued out loud. Literature was reaching sectors of the population that one never regarded as part of the reading public. And better still, they seemed to care.

This startling experience, this sense of direct relationship with one's readers, was not only new in American letters; it could go far to sustain those writers within the Left who were wrestling with their private angels. The reviewer of Stevens, for example. In his darker moments, he would confront his own misgivings about the glory of the life-to-come in the stateless utopia. It would be ushered in, of course, by the Goddess of Industrialization whose handiwork he had already observed in a grim milltown. Little wonder he could not feel the thrill that others felt as they read a remarkable American poem about a new Soviet hydroelectric plant, with its climactic line: "billions and billions of kilowatt hours." If he was certain of anything about the future, it was that in the long run economic improvement could do little for human beings unless a comparable change took place in the spirit of man.[4] And what was he doing here anyway, in this world that worshipped the logic of dialectics, he who valued above all else the gifts of the intuitive mind? How far would he be able to go, in the days ahead, in applying to his criticism the multiple-meanings principle he had learned from Prescott, or the fact that often "the real poetry will be between the lines"? True enough, he had already been laughed at for his academic concern with the golden scales and absolute literary worth — but he had countered with an unMarxist line from Marx, on the "eternal" charm of Greek art. He had also been advised that formal analysis could lead to futile complexities, and that a too-temperate stance was simply a foolish timidity. And yet, nobody had tried to speed up his slow political "development" by flashing a party-membership card under his nose. And none of his words had ever been corrected by the red pencil of a commissar. He could do as he pleased — for he *would* do no wrong. Like the others around him, he deeply believed in the necessity for promoting the Ultimate Good, whatever the circumstances. But within a year after writing the Stevens review, his private angel had pinned his shoulders to the ground. Until his departure, however, he continued to do as he had done, without wavering from his public position, perhaps hoping unconsciously that the very act of repeating beliefs might make them unquestionable for him.

I have described one case because I know it best, but other cases could serve equally well to suggest the absurdity of the unhistorical view. For to think that the Marxist critics were an undifferentiated right-thinking Left-minded phalanx is to create a monster that simply did not exist. Not only were the wars within the compound frequent and fierce. Even more important: any number of these writers were troubled or torn, each for his private reasons; but the tendency was to keep one's reservations under control, for what mattered was the task at hand — ending the material miseries of the many, extinguishing the dangers of Fascism. The basic economic problems of our society had to be put to rights so that one could go back to the business of living. Was the "final conflict" a glorious prospect? It was a tragic, an unnecessary class war: if only the Opposition would see how fine things would be if . . . As for enforced comradely associations, it was often possible to wriggle away from the nonsense, the piety, the dreariness; and when Marxist togetherness became too cozy to bear, one could always get conveniently ill.

The discomforts, the discipline, even the inner conflicts could be borne so long as these writers felt that they were responding to something greater than an organizational alignment of time and place. Mann put it best when he called Communism "an idea which is badly distorted in its reality, but whose roots reach deeper than Marxism and Stalinism and whose pure realization will again and again confront mankind as a challenge and a task." One could accept official membership, or continue in voluntary association, or remove oneself completely, depending upon the value he attached to the current carrier of this "idea." That so many stayed for so brief a time suggests the judgment that they had to make: the traffic in and out of the literary Left was surely the heaviest in American cultural history. Some departed in quiet and others shouted, "I have been deceived." Still others crept into corners to lick their wounds.

The review that follows, reprinted only because of its documentary relevance to the Stevens poem that it evoked, is offered without the slightest pride of authorship — indeed, with much relief that it is less incomprehensible than other reviews from the same pen. Certain words and assumptions, however, may bewilder readers unfamiliar with reviews of the Left in the midthirties. For their benefit, then, the following minimal gloss:

1. The world, so pleasingly simple, is divided according to one groundplan only: We (Left), They (Right), and You (Left, Right, or Middle), with the Escapists in limbo. Reading the opening paragraph, one squirms at the trade-jargon current twenty-five years ago, as possibly others will squirm at the trade-jargon of our own decade twenty-five years hence.

2. Caveat with respect to irony: Marxist critics were often stupendously literal, earnest, humorless. To find "ambiguity" here is to do creative reading of the most misleading kind. To be taken straight.

3. Re final paragraph: these critics held the naive belief that a book could and would affect directly and even shape the minds of readers; hence, in a war between classes, each "nonconfused" book was an instrument for either the Left (*read* Good) or the Right (*read* Bad). Today we are much wiser; even sociologists have armed us with their construct of the "intervening variable" (prefigured by a few Marxist critics as a "seepage" of ideas, from the opinion-making illuminati to the benighted). Both sociology and life were simpler twenty-five years ago. One could take bearings and know where everyone stood pro tem. Authors of "Middle-ground" books were, of course, confused and in need of direction, which was often generously offered by the reviewer. It requires no expertness in Freud to perceive that the present reviewer's concern with Stevens' confusion was at least in part a projection of his own.

4. At times one might make broad statements which one would not normally make, simply because they were supposedly required by the Ultimate Good. To add qualifications was to please one's petty pride and, besides, such impedimenta would weaken the march of mankind toward excellence. The overriding concern — the greatest good for the greatest number — was also a principle whose morality was beyond question, regardless of what might be required in its name.

5. Tone: not to be viewed as a separable element or as something in-

jected to add power. If, as Martz says, the review was written "with a condescending tone," it was not for lack of visible provocation. *Ideas of Order* was offered to the reading public of the thirties by a man not in the least ignorant of the issues or, for that matter, of the controversies and the codes — after all, he had been reading *The New Masses*! Hence, when Stevens used a certain tone, he did so with full awareness. One example (not mentioned in the review): he could not help knowing that the word "nigger" was scrupulously avoided by white people who had now become acutely aware of its extreme offensiveness. Yet the longest poem in the book is called "Like Decorations in a Nigger Cemetery." Whether the title is actually essential to the poem, is beside the point. If Stevens had entitled another piece "Like Decorations in a Sheeny Cemetery," even his worshippers might have squirmed.

6. Comparative data: *The New Republic* (literary editor, Malcolm Cowley) devoted sixteen lines to *Ideas of Order* and twice as much to *Pittsburgh Memoranda*. Theodore Roethke, after remarking that "the times and a ripened maturity have begun to stiffen Mr. Stevens' rhetoric," concludes: "It is a pity that such a rich and special sensibility should be content with the order of words and music, and not project itself more vigorously upon the present-day world" (July 15, 1936).

TURMOIL IN THE MIDDLE GROUND

Among the handful of clichés which have crept into left-wing criticism is the notion that contemporary poets — except those on the left and extreme right — have all tramped off to some escapist limbo where they are joyously gathering moonshine. That such an idiot's paradise has existed no one can deny; but today the significant middle-ground poets are laboring elsewhere. And the significant trend is being marked by such writers as Wallace Stevens and Haniel Long: poets whose artistic statures have long been recognized, whose latest books (issued in middle age) form a considered record of agitated attitudes toward the present social order. Like all impressive phenomena of the middle ground, *Pittsburgh Memoranda* and *Ideas of Order* show troubled, searching minds.

As a matter of record Haniel Long has been struggling for a "solution" ever since his singular stories and poems appeared in the liberal magazines a dozen years ago. [*The next six paragraphs deal exclusively with Long.*]

Confused as it is, *Pittsburgh Memoranda* is a marvel of order alongside Wallace Stevens' volume; and yet to many readers it is something of a miracle that Stevens has at all bothered to give us his *Ideas of Order*. When

Harmonium appeared a dozen years ago Stevens was at once set down as an incomparable verbal musician. But nobody stopped to ask if he had any ideas. It was tacitly assumed that one read him for pure poetic sensation; if he had "a message" it was carefully buried and would take no end of labor to exhume. Yet he often comes out with flat judgments and certain ideas weave through the book consistently:

> The magnificent cause of being,
> The imagination, the one reality
> In this imagined world

underlies a number of poems. Realists have been bitter at the inanity of Pope's "Whatever is is right," but Stevens plunges ahead to the final insolence: "For realists, what is is what should be." And yet it is hard to know if such a line is not Stevens posing in self-mockery. One can rarely speak surely of Stevens' ideas.

But certain general convictions he admits in such a poem as "To One of Fictive Music." Bound up with the sovereignty of the imagination is his belief in an interfusion of music among the elements and man. And "music is feeling . . . not sound." This trinity of principles makes the business of living to him a matter of searching out the specific harmonies.

Harmonium, then, is mainly sense poetry, but not as Keats's is sense poetry, because this serener poet is not driven to suffuse sensuous imagery with powerful subjective emotions. This is "scientific," objectified sensuousness separated from its kernel of fire and allowed to settle, cool off, and harden in the poet's mind until it emerges a strange amazing crystal. Reading this poetry becomes a venture in crystallography. It is remembered for its curious humor, its brightness, its words and phrases that one rolls on the tongue. It is the kind of verse that people concerned with the murderous world collapse can hardly swallow today except in tiny doses.

And it is verse that Stevens can no longer write. His harmonious cosmos is suddenly screeching with confusion. *Ideas of Order* is the record of a man who, having lost his footing, now scrambles to stand up and keep his balance. The opening poem observes

> . . . This heavy historical sail
> Through the mustiest blue of the lake
> In a wholly vertiginous boat
> Is wholly the vapidest fake. . . .

And the rest follows with all the ironical logic of such a premise. The "sudden mobs of men" may have the answer;

> But what are radiant reason and radiant will
> To warblings early in the hilarious trees . . .

Sceptical of man's desire in general, there is still much to be said for the ordering power of the imagination. But there remains a yearning — and escape is itself an irony. "Marx has ruined Nature, for the moment," he observes in self-mockery; but he can speculate on the wisdom of turning inward, and a moment later look upon collective mankind as the guilty bungler of harmonious life, in "a peanut parody for a peanut people." What answer is there in the cosmic law — "everything falls back to coldness"? With apparent earnestness he goes a step beyond his former nature-man interfusing harmony:

> Only we two are one, not you and night,
> Nor night and I, but you and I, alone,
> So much alone, so deeply by ourselves,
> So far beyond the casual solitudes,
> That night is only the background of our selves . . .

And in a long poem he pours out in strange confusion his ideas of order, among them:

> If ever the search for a tranquil belief should end,
> The future might stop emerging out of the past,
> Out of what is full of us; yet the search
> And the future emerging out of us seem to be one.

Paraphrase, always a treacherous tool, is especially dangerous when used on so *raffiné* a poet as Stevens. Does he talk of himself when he explains that "the purple bird must have notes for his comfort that he may repeat through the gross tedium of being rare"? Does he make political reference in declaring "the union of the weakest develops strength, not wisdom"?

Asking questions may not be a reviewer's function, but uncertainties are unavoidable when reading such poets as the two under review; for the texture of their thought is made of speculations, questionings, contradictions. Acutely conscious members of a class menaced by the clashes between capital and labor, these writers are in the throes of struggle for philosophical adjustment. And their words have intense value and meaning to the sectors within the class whose confusions they articulate. Their books have deep importance for us as well.

Of course, objectively, neither poet is weakening the class in power — as yet they are potential allies as well as potential enemies — but one of them looks for a new set of values and the other earnestly propagates (however vaguely) some form of collectivism. Will Long emancipate himself from his paralyzing faith in inner perfection? Will Stevens sweep his contradictory notions into a valid Idea of Order? The answers depend not only on the personal predispositions of these poets but on their full realization of the alternatives facing them as artists.

(The New Masses, Oct. 1, 1935, p. 42)[5]

Notes

1. Note that Stevens cut the poem and changed its title to "The Statue at the World's End" for the Alcestis Press edition (1936); that he made other revisions for the version in *The Man with the Blue Guitar* (1937); that he omitted it altogether from *Collected Poems*. (The original version of "Mr. Burnshaw and the Statue" appears in *Opus Posthumous*.)

2. *Wallace Stevens* (New York, 1961), p. 63. See below: Gloss, Item 5, and penultimate paragraph of the review.

3. Differences in critical judgments were, however, frequently tenuous. See, for example, "Two Kinds of Against," a review by Kenneth Burke of *No Thanks* by E. E. Cummings and *Poems* by Kenneth Fearing, *The New Republic,* June 26, 1935. See also conclusion of Burke's review of *Pittsburgh Memoranda* by Haniel Long: ". . . it unquestionably suggests the magnitude and the quality of the philosophical issues arising from the confused ways in which capitalism both stimulates and frustrates ambition" (*The New Republic,* August 28, 1935).

4. *The Bridge* (New York, 1945), a play in verse drafted at this time but not completed for several years.

5. Mr. Burnshaw made, in a letter to the editor, some further comments that are added with his permission: "I have probably omitted a few things of possible relevance — I had never had any direct contact with Stevens, either in person or by letter; I have never been consulted by any writer on the episode; I am personally unacquainted with all of them. The sole intermediary, if he can be called that, was Alfred Kreymborg, to whom Stevens had given the long poem for publication in *The New American Caravan*. Kreymborg told me that at the time he received the MS, he had given Stevens a 'marvelous description of' me; but as to Stevens' response, I learned nothing. Once or twice, when Stevens was still alive, I had thought about paying him a visit. But his reputation for dealing with uninvited guests discouraged me. Needless to add, I often regret my lack of courage, and now that I've written on the subject of our 'exchange,' I find myself wishing that he could read it.

"My own questioning as to the importance of the whole affair subsides when I realize that despite what Stevens later did with the poem, the scholars concentrate upon the original (uncut) version and have made it part of the essential study of Stevens. Samuel French Morse includes the uncut poem in *Opus Posthumous*. More important, William Van O'Connor judges 'Owl's Clover' (of which 'Mr. Burnshaw and the Statue' is Part II) to be Stevens' 'finest long poem.' I disagree with O'Connor, but my opinion can hardly count for anything in this instance."

THE POEM ITSELF:

"DISCUSSING POEMS INTO ENGLISH"[1]

From the introduction to *The Poem Itself: Forty-five Modern Poets in a New Presentation,* edited by Stanley Burnshaw. First published by Holt, Rinehart and Winston in 1960; currently available in an edition published by the University of Arkansas Press. Copyright 1960, 1981, and 1995 by Stanley Burnshaw.

Thirty years ago in *This Quarter,* I published "A Note on Translation" which suggested that the only way one could experience the poetry of a language one did not command was by learning to hear and pronounce (if only approximately) the sounds of the originals and "simultaneously" reading literal renditions. Since the poetry inheres in the tonal language (the sounds of the poem in its original tongue), how could one possibly experience a Spanish poem in any language but Spanish, a French poem in any language but French? The "Note" appeared at a time when translators felt free to do anything: they were "re-creating originals"! Bilingual editions had not yet become familiar — nor had Frost's definition of poetry as "that which gets lost from verse and prose in translation." Before long a publisher expressed interest in my notion, and I embarked on a small anthology. But then he insisted that verse translations also be included, despite the danger of confusing and distracting the reader. And so for the time being I abandoned the project, certain as ever that mine was the only means by which a reader could begin to experience the poetry of other languages.

But my method had not gone far enough, as I discovered many years later when I found myself working on some poems by Mallarmé. My literal renditions were scrupulous, yet in certain key places a single French word could not be rendered by a single English word — pieces of two or even

---

1. ". . . [Y]ou don't try to translate poems — you *discuss them into English.*" — Robert Frost, see *Robert Frost Himself,* pp. 136 f.

of three might be required. Other words, with double denotations in the French, had to be halved in English or equated by impossible compounds. And certain phrases that looked easy in the dictionaries carried quite untranslatable connotations essential as meaning. As for syntax, the reader would have to untangle it for himself. And the allusions — though at times they might hold the key to the poem, they could not even be considered, since they stand outside the purview of all translation.

What sort of experience, then, did my confident method offer? Obviously a most inadequate one: a great deal more would have to be added before an English-speaking reader could begin to experience Mallarmé. And if this were true of so familiar a poet, then it must be true of other "difficult" moderns, such as Rilke, Vallejo, Montale; it must be true to some degree of every participant in the poetic revolution of the last hundred years. The method had to be expanded, the line-by-line rendition enriched, at least with alternate equivalents where necessary and with leads where ellipsis and syntax might frustrate a reader. Other clues had also to be given: to telescoped images, private allusions, specialized symbols, systems of belief, and similar problems. And what of the poem as a work of sonal art? For a reader who wishes to hear and pronounce the original, however approximately, any number of interesting points might be signalled; not only of rime, assonance, meter, and strophe, but of graces, stops, turns, and the sonal felicities of the whole. To be faithful to its intent, the method had to be enlarged into a literal rendering plus commentary — into a discussion aimed at enabling the reader both to *understand* the poem and to begin to *experience it as a poem.*

The result of these thoughts — which can be read on pp. 362–363 — fell short of its maker's ideal, yet it served to show others how a somewhat "difficult" poem in a foreign language could be made accessible to English-speaking readers through a new type of presentation. The first to examine "Don du poème" not only approved the theory and the practice but also made fruitful suggestions. When the specimen was next submitted, to other scholars and to poets, the response took the form of immediate offers to collaborate. One poet-critic thought that the discussion should be made twice as searching, but he soon saw the unwisdom of trying to analyze too much. For once the reader begins, he can plunge as deep as he wishes. The aim is to help him *into* the poem itself.

There are, of course, various ways of approaching foreign poetry; when a writer uses one, he does not thereby surrender his right to use others. Those of us who are drawn to particular poems in other languages will always be free to revivify them with English verses — and as one of this group, I applaud the practice and hail the occasional achievements. But these are personal preoccupations, and translation is of public concern. English versions of foreign writings abound, but the reader who wants to experience the poetry of other literatures must look elsewhere; the vast stock of verse translations provides no answer.

It provides no answer for several reasons. First, and overwhelming, a verse translation offers an experience in *English* poetry. It takes the reader away from the foreign literature and into his own, away from the original and into something different. The instant he departs from the words of the original, he departs from *its* poetry. For the words are the poem. Ideas can often be carried across, but poems are not made of ideas (as Degas was informed by Mallarmé): they are made of words. Regardless of its brilliance, an English translation is always a different thing: it is always an *English* poem.

In this fact about words lies the source of all the slanderous remarks that have been made about translators, from Frost's sentence quoted above to the notorious Italian pun *traduttore-traditore* ("translator-traitor"). Says Poggioli: "Both original and translation deal with a single substance, differentiated into two unique, and incommensurable, accidents"; and Nida: "There can never be a word-for-word type of correspondence which is fully meaningful or accurate."[2] When Coleridge proposed as "the infallible test of a blameless style" "its *untranslatableness* in words of the same language without injury to the meaning," he took care to "include in the *meaning* of a word not only its correspondent object, but likewise all the associations which it recalls." For every "meaningful" word is a unique totality — unique in sound, denotation, connotation, and doubtless much more.

But the order that words make is no less crucial to the translator than the words themselves. For when they appear in a sequence (as in a poem) they begin to mean in a special way — their uniquenesses act, as it were, selectively. The position that each word holds in relation to the others causes parts of its content to be magnified and other parts diminished. Yet even though some meanings recede as others come to the fore, all of them are to some degree also active — whence the multiform richness of feel-

2. *On Translation,* ed. Reuben A. Brower, Harvard University Press, 1959; Renato Poggioli, "The Added Artificer," p. 138; John Nida, "Principles of Translation as Exemplified by Bible Translating," p. 13.

ing and thought conveyed (the "suggestions, ambiguities, paradoxes, levels of meaning" of current terminology). These facts may be read into Coleridge's definition of poetry as "the best words in the best order," especially into his famous remark about "a more than usual state of emotion, with more than usual order." Today we talk of the "affective" phrase or sentence, whose word arrangement differs from that of prose; we say each poem is an organization of such phrases. But some critics go further: each affective phrase is a rhythmic metaphor — a poem is a series of rhythmic metaphors which evokes a physical response in the reader's body, in his internal and external muscles. Not only the mind, but the total organism moves with and "mirrors" the rhythmic pattern of the words. For a translator to evoke this response by different words and word order would of course be impossible. But, all corporeal concurrences aside, could a translator even think of trying to carry across into a different language the "more than usual order" of the original words?

And yet, with all its limitations, verse translation has given us almost all we know of the poets of the rest of the world. And from what we have been given we have formed our judgments. Can they be trusted? The only works we could read have been those that happened to appeal to translators who happened to succeed in turning them into English poems that happened to get published. This fortuitousness should be enough to make us suspect that the picture has been skewed; but there is more. We naturally judge the quality of a foreign poem by the quality of the English poem it inspired, even though we know such correspondence is rare. As a result, verse translation being the poorest subdivision of English verse, we must continually assure ourselves that the originals are much better — which is safe enough, but only a wishful assumption. And what of all the poetry that has never been carried across because it seemed too long or too compact or too difficult or too delicate to fashion into an English poem?

The method of *The Poem Itself* should overcome all three obstacles we have noted in verse translation. Because each word of a foreign poem is unique in itself and in its order, we ask the reader to read the original along with our English approximations (usually set in italics, with alternate meanings in parentheses and explanations in brackets). Our comments on allusion, symbol, meaning, sound, and the like will enable him to see *what* the poem is saying and *how,* though the poem itself is an unparaphrasable

"Don du Poème" as it is presented in *The Poem Itself* appears on the two pages that follow.

STÉPHANE MALLARMÉ

DON DU POÈME

Je t'apporte l'enfant d'une nuit d'Idumée!
Noire, à l'aile saignante et pâle, déplumée,
Par le verre brûlé d'aromates et d'or,
Par les carreaux glacés, hélas! mornes encor,   4
L'aurore se jeta sur la lampe angélique.
Palmes! et quand elle a montré cette relique
A ce père essayant un sourire ennemi,
La solitude bleue et stérile a frémi.   8
O la berceuse, avec ta fille et l'innocence
De vos pieds froids, accueille une horrible naissance:
Et ta voix rappelant viole et clavecin,
Avec le doigt fané presseras-tu le sein   12
Par qui coule en blancheur sibylline la femme
Pour les lèvres que l'air du vierge azur affame?

(Poésies. 1887)

"Gift of the Poem" this is entitled, and the specific poem is identified in the first line: "I bring you the child of an Idumean night." For a year Stéphane Mallarmé (1842-1898) had been working upon a verse drama for the stage, named for a princess of Edomite (Idumean) ancestry. "*Hérodiade*" was to embody a new poetic theory: "To paint, not the thing, but the effect it produces"; and though the undertaking filled him with terror, he could scarcely foresee that it would remain uncompleted at his death thirty-four years later.

The setting appears in the first eight lines. The writer has been laboring at his desk throughout the night, the lamplight glistening on the window, the images of Hérodiade's world all about him. Finally at dawn something has taken form, has been completed—a poem, such as it is, has been born. He takes this child of his thought into the adjoining room where the child of his body lies sleeping with its mother. He presents it to her and asks if she will give it nourishment.

Except for the indefiniteness created by the punctuation, the setting can be literally transcribed thus: (1) *I bring you the child (offspring) of an Idumean night!* (2) *Black (dark), with wing bleeding and pale, [its feathers] plucked,* (3) *Through the window burnt with spices and gold,* (4) *Through the icy panes, alas, still bleak (dreary),* (5) *Dawn hurled itself upon the angelic lamp.*

The word *Palmes!* suddenly appears, an exclamation whose import we are left to imagine; then the description continues: (6) *Palms! and when it [dawn] showed that relic* (7) *To this father [who was] attempting a hostile smile,* (8) *The blue and sterile solitude trembled (shuddered).*

(9) *O singer (of lullabies), you who rock the cradle, with your daughter and the innocence* (10) *Of your cold feet, welcome (greet) a [this] horrible birth:* (11) *And, your voice recalling viol and harpsichord,* (12) *With your faded finger, will you press the breast* (13) *Through which in sibylline whiteness woman flows* (14) *For the lips made hungry by the virgin azure?*

This poem, like a number of others by Mallarmé, dramatizes the birth-process of art. But why does the solitude tremble? why is it sterile? And why does the father look on his offspring with animosity? Both the actions and attitudes of this poem cannot be perceived apart from Mallarmé's lifelong obsession with his own creative impotence, with his fear and his struggle against it, and with his seeming horror of the birth-process itself. The child of this nightlong labor, a pale, bleeding bird born in the icy dawn, will die if it is not nourished. But the one who gave birth to it can do nothing more for it.

It has been a strange, almost sterile birth, such as might bring into the world the strange poem of the princess Hérodiade, who rejects all human contact and for whom barrenness is the burning ideal. "Yes, it is for myself, for myself that I flower alone. . . I love the horror of being virgin . . . I want nothing human / O final joy, yes, I feel it: I am alone. . . ." Denis Saurat points out that the kings of Edom were supposedly able to reproduce without women. The poet also—and in this instance it is a blood-soaked, horrible birth. But once born, the offspring of the mind must be nourished in order to live. Brought into the world, it must be welcomed and sustained by the world.

Certain English "equivalents" in our version of this quasi-sonnet are too bare.

"Plucked" (2) is too concise for the broad, slow sounds of *déplumée*, a word which carries the further implication that a pen has been removed. "Spices" (3) lacks the exoticism and aroma of *aromates*. *Ce père* (7) means much more than "this father": it implies pity for the poor, exhausted poet with his faint, ambiguous smile. Similarly *la berceuse* (9) carries overtones of intimacy and tenderness toward the wife and mother. It might also be the lullaby itself.

A number of other elements are curiously evocative. *Noire* paired with *pâle* (2), and *lampe angélique* with the other ecclesiastical touch *relique* (5-6). The "innocence of your cold feet" (9-10). The change from the intimate pronoun *ta* (*fille*) to the more distant *vos* (*pieds*). And the breast of the nourisher-and-sustainer —it will be pressed by a finger that is "faded," "withered."

A number of the images in this poem occur elsewhere in Mallarmé, almost as his signatures (*bleue et stérile, viole et clavecin, vierge azur*); but what shall we make of *Palmes!*? A French critic found a line in Virgil containing both *palmas* and *Idumaeas*, but does this help? To some American scholar-critics the exclamation symbolizes both martyrdom and victory. Other readers suggest that the dawn threw itself suddenly, like elongated, irradiating palms, or Homeric rosy fingers—and that the very sound suggests something broad, spread-out flat, like a bird wing, to which dawn has been related implicitly (2). But perhaps *Palmes* simply occurred to Mallarmé and he retained it because he felt that he had to—much as he introduced in another poem the word "ptyx" because this pure invention struck him as being both right and necessary for his purposes.

totality. As to how much the reader will hear of the sound of the poem, this depends on what knowledge he already has and on what effort he is willing to invest in learning to hear. This book, then, offers poems and the means toward experiencing them.

But the means vary, for each work is a unique problem: how can it best be presented in terms of this book? The extent to which each author has differed from my Mallarmé "model" may be judged in the varied approaches of the other 140 commentaries. Each author has, of course, been free to write in his characteristic way, and to emphasize certain things in a poem and pay little attention to others. Individuality of response is no less apparent in our way of presenting a poem than in a verse translation. Indeed, most of the poems in this book were chosen by the contributors themselves. But the editors have also been free to respond in their characteristic ways, and to do more than was ever intended, entirely (I like to think) out of necessity, in a collaborative undertaking dedicated to a new method.

THOMAS MANN TRANSLATES

"TONIO KRÖGER"

From the introduction to *Varieties of Literary Experience: Eighteen Essays in World Literature,* edited by Stanley Burnshaw, New York University Press, 1962. Copyright 1962 by Stanley Burnshaw.

The title of this volume [*Varieties of Literary Experience: Eighteen Essays in World Literature*] calls for explaining, especially the first part, with its echo of William James. By dropping the definite article from *The Varieties of Religious Experience* and changing the adjective, I intend neither depth nor mystery. A reader prone to pry may smile at my disclaimer, that I simply could not find more faithful words for describing this assemblage of eighteen essays — on writers, novels, plays, poems, movements, themes, ideologies, approaches — each of which embodies a set of assumptions, a style, and a method of its own. Such variety, deliberately sought for, seems worth adducing at a time when every critic is supposedly enrolled in one of a handful of "schools."

So much for the main title of the book. The five words that follow are another matter, and though they might lead to a variety of questions, they particularly suggest that we ask ourselves what we mean by the term "world literature." If it denotes a library of volumes, each section of which contains the complete published writings of a specific language, then "world literature" has only academic interest: it could be experienced by few if any living persons, for one can *experience* only as many literatures as the languages he commands. Most readers (including most scholars and critics) can never be truly at home in more than a very few foreign tongues. Hence "world literature" *as it is read* is by no means the totality of writings produced by the peoples of the world — not the alien originals at all but domestic imitations.

All this may be obvious enough until we remind ourselves that every piece of literature in translation is a very different thing from the work from which it was transported. The domestic imitation is made of different words. We "know" this, of course; we "know" that every translation is a new work; and yet we approach it not as we approach a new work originally written in our own language but with a special and pervasive awareness of difference. And we make charitable allowances, even to the extent of downgrading the translation by seeing the original enclosed in a halo of imagined superiority to whatever we find in the words before us. This curiously impeding awareness operates not only with dissatisfying translations. No matter how affecting the words before us, we "know" that the work they derived from must surely have been superior, for we properly assume that something precious has been lost. The moment we become aware that we are reading a translation, the normal relation between book and reader breaks down. The translated book is, of course, no longer entirely foreign — but neither is it "genuinely" English. What then can it be but a species of limbo literature?

Though such a question would always seem ungracious, it sounds particularly so today when translators are more productive than ever before and publishers promise them support. Dazzled by the first revelations of a goldening age, many readers may quickly reverse their ancient habits, and, in pursuit of the new, long-hidden joys, push aside everything including thoughts they long held to be true. Somewhere along this enchanted line, they may start telling themselves that all the essential differences between first-hand and second-hand literatures are merely a matter of theory, and then with a pragmatic wave of the hand, dismiss these differences as no longer worth considering. Merrily bound for the other extreme, they may even find themselves believing that the impossible has been accomplished: that the translation "problem" has at last been solved for all time.

Other readers, however, especially those with a weakness for books about literature, are likely to remain unchanged; for if recent criticism has contributed anything importantly new it has been to point up the implications of the ever obvious fact that a book is a matter of words. It is always and overwhelmingly a matter of words — as colors are the painter's materials, so are words the writer's; but whereas colors have no fatherland, words are stopped at each linguistic frontier. It is *Zapiski iz Podpolya* for readers of Russian and *Notes from the Underground* (or *Letters from the Underworld*) for readers of English: from title to conclusion, two structures of different words, which is also to say: two different structures. But in all such structures we find, in addition to the words, a variety of abstractable creations. How many, we may never be able to say; nor does the arithmetic count. What matters is that certain of these creations can be carried over from language to language without decisive loss — story, plot, fable, myth, allegory, generalized analogy. Ideas can also be translated to the extent that two languages possess terms that are reciprocally appropriate. Occasionally idioms may show something like a one-to-one correspondence, as will some elements of form in the gross. But such types of equivalence are as much as can be hoped for at best, for if literature is made of language, then it is changed when its language is changed — changed for better or worse, but in every case changed.

Nobody will deny that these statements hold true of poetry — besides, given certain aids, every reader can experience foreign poems in their original words[1] — but what of prose? That the English tongue possesses some fine works of fiction in translation is beside the point; their excellence has nothing to do with their difference from what they purport and are taken to be. And it is mainly because excellence here does away with full awareness of difference that readers need to realize what can happen even to prose in the process of change.

No handier example can be suggested, I think, than the following passage from *Tonio Kröger,* since Thomas Mann himself presided at the ceremony of analysis that took place at Colorado College in the spring of 1941.[2] Some thirty teachers and students of German had been asked to translate this paragraph from the middle of the story:

> Und Tonio Kröger fuhr gen Norden. Er fuhr mit Komfort (denn er pflegte zu sagen, dass jemand, der es innerlich so viel schwerer hat als andere Leute, gerechten Anspruch auf ein wenig äusseres Behagen habe), und er rastete nicht eher, als bis die Türme der engen Stadt, von der er ausgegangen war, sich vor ihm in die graue Luft erhoben. Dort nahm er einen kurzen, seltsamen Aufenthalt.

The discussion began with the fifth word: why had Mann used, instead of *gegen,* the archaic *gen?* Was there some connection with Siegfried's trip north to Iceland? Mann explained that he had striven for a balladesque atmosphere. As for the fourth word, *fuhr,* he had used it in the sense of *zog;* hence *traveled* would be too "pedestrian." *Norden* had been intended in what Mann called "a certain symbolical sense." *Er fuhr mit Komfort* had been written with technical comfort in mind. The word *innerlich* gave rise to much difficulty. *Schwer haben* turned out to be a deliberate understatement. *Anspruch haben* was finally translated as *entitled,* though Mann regretfully permitted the omission of *gerecht* (*rightfully*) for the greater good of simplicity in translation. *Creature comfort* was too explicit for *äusseres Behagen,* he said; and as for *rastete,* there was simply no exact English equivalent. The penultimate *seltsamen* had a dreamlike or fantastic connotation for the author; but *fantastic* was a bit exaggerated, *strange* would be unmelodious. The best solution was *a brief, enchanted stay.* After eighty minutes of deliberation, the following version was accepted by all present, including Thomas Mann, who considered it to be more faithful than any of the three published renderings of the same passage:[3]

> And Tonio Kröger went north. He went in comfort, for he always said that anyone who had so much more to bear inwardly than other people was surely entitled to a little outer ease. And he did not stop until there rose before him in the gray sky the spires of the cramped little city from which he had once set out. There he made a brief, enchanted stay.

Faced with such a demonstration in rendering so small a part of so long a story, a reader may throw up his hands. Frost was all too right! — "Poetry is that which gets lost from verse or prose in translation." — the quotation repeated again and again: it cannot be repeated too often. And yet, the "poetry" is by no means the main element contributing to the massed-up effectiveness of a foreign novel or play rendered into English. Its untranslatable charges of meaning may prove crucial only in isolated passages or they may inform every sentence from beginning to end; but even when this poetry is lost or weakly imitated, other important structures may remain in the domesticated version — the many "abstractable creations" noted earlier and the new constructions (character, situation) to which they give rise. All such things of course owe their existence to the original words from which they have now been cut off; but the life they lead and the power they exert no longer depend on those words.

They depend on the newfound words that compose their natures, which is to say that differences always arise. How many or how decisive depends on the "veil," if we think of translation as that which hangs between the original and our eyes. The veil distorts, as it must; it conceals; at times it darkens. But there is still much to be seen. The image behind it glows with curious light. And like every object viewed through a veil, it may sometimes seem to us finer than it really is. Not necessarily because we endow it with virtues we should like it to possess (as some Frenchmen have done with Poe), but rather because of the texture of the veil. Is there any reason why a prose translation cannot, as literature in a new language, be superior to the original? Is the King James Bible, for example, less great than the Hebrew? Even such exhilarating questions can only affirm the fact of difference. They should also make us alert to our limits, especially when we try to see all that a critic tells us he has seen in a work of world literature. How easy to forget that his sometimes seemingly excessive pronouncements or incredible findings, in a Dostoevski novel, for example, developed in the course of his involvement with *Zapiski iz Podpolya,* whereas we may have read only a book entitled *Notes from the Underground,* or *Letters from the Underworld.* Better to realize why such readers as ourselves must always stand outside: not only the original work but every critique it engenders will always remain not quite within reach, clad in obscuring veils.

Notes

1. As I have tried to show in *The Poem Itself.*
2. As reported by Hans Rosenhaupt, in *The History of Ideas News Letter,* Vol. 3, No. 3 (July 1957), pp. 60–63. Reprinted by permission of Dr. Rosenhaupt.
3. The three published renderings follow:

And Tonio Kröger journeyed northward. He traveled comfortably (for he was wont to say that any one who has so much more distress of soul than other people may justly claim a little external comfort), and he did not rest until the towers of the cramped city which had been his starting-point rose before him in the gray air. There he made a brief, strange sojourn.
　　　　　　　　　　　　　　　　　　— *Trans. by Bayard Q. Morgan*
　　　　　　　　　　　　　　　　　　　(*German Publication Society, 1914*)

And Tonio Kröger traveled north. He traveled with comfort (for he liked to say that anyone who was so much more disturbed internally than other people had a perfect right to a little external comfort), and he never stopped until the towers of the narrow city from which he had come rose up before him into the grey air. There he made a brief, strange stop-over.
　　　　　　　　　　　　　　　　　　— *Trans. by Kenneth Burke*
　　　　　　　　　　　　　　　　　　　(*Alfred A. Knopf, 1925*)

And Tonio Kröger travelled north. He travelled in comfort (for he was wont to say that anyone who had suffered inwardly more than other people had a right to a little outward ease); and he did not stay until the towers of the little town he had left rose up in the grey air. Among them he made a short and singular stay.　　— *Trans. by H. T. Lowe-Porter*
　　　　　　　　　　　　　　　　　　　(*Alfred A. Knopf, 1936*)

A FUTURE FOR POETRY:

PLANETARY MATURITY

For James Dickey

This chapter consists of notes for a lecture delivered at the universities of California, Minnesota, and Texas and first published in the "Stanley Burnshaw Special Issue" of *Agenda,* London, 1983/84. The author and publisher gratefully acknowledge the following publications in which poems quoted in this chapter previously appeared: From Eugenio Montale, *The Storm and Other Things,* translated by William Arrowsmith (New York: W. W. Norton and Co., 1985), reprinted by permission of the publisher. "Nudities" by André Spire and "Bread" from *In the Terrified Radiance* (New York: George Braziller, 1972), copyright 1972 by Stanley Burnshaw, reprinted by courtesy of the publisher. "Lovers in August" from *Selected Poems* by Miroslav Holúb, translated by Ian Milner and George Theiner (Penguin Books, 1967), copyright 1967 by Miroslav Holúb, translation copyright 1967 by Penguin Books. "The Fiend" is reprinted from *Buckdancer's Choice* by permission of James Dickey and Wesleyan University Press; copyright 1965 by James Dickey. "Ode to Hengist and Horsa," copyright 1963 by Donnan Jeffers and Garth Jeffers, reprinted from *The Beginning and the End and Other Poems,* by Robinson Jeffers, by permission of Random House, Inc. Excerpts from "To Robinson Jeffers," copyright 1988 by Czeslaw Milosz Royalties, Inc., from *The Collected Poems, 1921–1987,* first published by the Ecco Press in 1988; reprinted by permission. "Nature's Questioning" and "Dead 'Wessex' the Dog to the Household," reprinted from *The Complete Poems of Thomas Hardy,* edited by James Gibson (New York: Macmillan, 1978), by permission of the publisher; the latter poem copyright 1928 by Florence E. Hardy and Sydney E. Cockerell, copyright 1956 by Lloyds Bank Ltd. "Neither Out Far Nor In Deep" is reprinted from *The Poetry of Robert Frost,* edited by Edward Connery Lathem, by permission of Henry Holt and Co.; copyright 1936 by Robert Frost, copyright 1964 by Lesley Frost Ballantine. The quotation from Alberto Caeiro is reprinted from *Selected Poems* by Fernando Pessoa, copyright 1971, the fourth volume in the Edinburgh Bilingual Library. The quotations from the work of Umberto Saba are reprinted by the courtesy of New York University Press from *Modern Italian Poets* by Joseph Cary, copyright by the New York University Press. "The Far Field," copyright 1962 by Beatrice Roethke, administratrix of the Estate of Theodore Roethke, from *The Collected Poems*

"A future for poetry" — what do these words portend? I propose to single out a new attitude, a new point of view, a new state of being: it is all these things and more — which are with us already in some degree, and are sure to affect more and more people — and in time transform us, readers and poets alike.

How fine it would be to begin with a plain definition, then reel off examples, and end with a Q.E.D. But this new something I speak of only rarely is found in a "pure state." Usually it is intermixed with the old. The newness is missed — as often occurs when an art develops from one condition to another. But here the change is a radical one indeed: a movement away from what poems — with rare exceptions — have been in the past: *culture-bound* — hemmed in by the limits of purely human concerns and wishes, feelings, and laws, which, if viewed from a ship in space, would look so self-regarding as to seem myopic.

And yet most poetry, regardless of theme, has mirrored the culture of men and women, with the rest of creation a backdrop for their actions. The change that I aim to describe is *away* from poems that are culture-bound to something else . . . which will tend to define itself as we carry forward. But first, a warning. When I use the generic *Homo sapiens* or *man,* as I must for grace or brevity's sake, please take it as *shorthand only,* for male *and* female: both.

Let me start with a poem by a girl, Margie Twayaga. She wrote it in high school in Uganda. It's short and the title simple: "My Buttocks."

> How useful are my buttocks!
> And how helpful they are to me!
> How then am I proud of my buttocks!
> I am proud of their use to me.
> They give me shape.
> They help me when it is time for sitting.

I love my buttocks very much
Because they are so useful to me.
The trouble with me and my buttocks is
I love them very much
But they hate me more than I love them.
First, they hate me because I usually sit on them.
Then they hate me because
When I do bad things,
They are beaten!
I spend the day sitting on them and tonight
When I am thinking while sleeping,
I sleep *against* them.

Ha! my buttocks! my buttocks!
What can I do for you so that you will love me?
I love you more than any other part of mine.

The lines express something of the joy we feel to be stirring in a baby, kitten, or puppy as it suddenly discovers some new delight in its body. Yet this poem is *not* pure delight. More than half lists the "trouble[s] with me and my buttocks." Joy at the start, then uneasiness: where did it come from? Only one possible source: the culture that nurtured the speaker. It infused her — just as it infuses us all — with notions of right and wrong . . . and consequent feelings of "trouble": guilt. My buttocks "hate me because when I do bad things / They are beaten" — and she then proceeds to think of the other ways in which she offends them. Rights and wrongs, punishments, rewards. — Now, when I speak of "the culture" — and I shall be doing so often — I do *not* refer to manners or breeding or receptiveness to beauty and humane feelings. I refer to "all those historically created designs for living, explicit and implicit, rational, irrational, and nonrational, which exist at any given time as potential guides for human behavior." "Potential guides for human behavior" — the anthropological view.

"My Buttocks" of course is a poem of self-discovery within the purview of the culture. What happens when self-discovery cannot go further? We know nothing of its course with other creatures, but with people, self-contemplation deepens and darkens till it comes to a stop . . . resolving itself into any number of forms: ineffably joyous faith at the hopeful extreme to suicide. Most of us settle somewhere between on the spectrum, but long before, we do what Margie Twayaga does: we celebrate ourselves *while we also* condemn ourselves. There are wonderful poems, as you know, on our self-celebration but few that temper delight with pained awareness. When you think in these terms, it is not a great leap from our young girl's poem to the one John Davies wrote in the 1600s. It is called "Affliction." Anthologists frequently print just the last two stanzas. I give you three-and-a-half:

> Myself am centre of my circling thought,
>   Only myself I study, learn, and know.
>
> I know my body's of so frail a kind
>   As force without, fevers within, can kill;
> I know the heavenly nature of my mind,
>   But 'tis corrupted both in wit and will;
>
> I know my soul hath power to know all things,
>   Yet is she blind and ignorant in all;
> I know I am one of nature's little kings,
>   Yet to the least and vilest things am thrall.
>
> I know my life's a pain and but a span,
>   I know my sense is mocked with everything;
> And to conclude, I know myself a man,
>   Which is a proud, and yet a wretched thing.

Is there nothing more to be said about being human? Not if one's view is circumscribed by the culture, where man is the center of all. A good many people no longer can bear that view. Faced with our decade's menaces — nuclear war, pollution, famine, genocide — they are forced to approach the world from a vantage point *outside* the culture, which reveals *Homo sapiens* as being, above all else, a *creature;* and despite his spectacular gifts and works, as much "in thrall" to the laws of existence as every other creature. The awesome burden that fell on us when we made ourselves able to kill *all* life upon earth compels us now to look at all life with *responsible* eyes. It is forcing on us, even against our wishes, the humbling condition of "planetary maturity."

Planetary maturity: *accepting* ourselves as above all else creatures bound by the laws that control all other creatures. What have such things to do with a future for poetry? Everything! So it seems to me — so it may seem to you as we read some verse from our country and other countries. I call them "creature-poems," in part or in whole. What is a creature-poem? To paraphrase St. Clement and Samuel Johnson, it is easier to say what it is *not* than what it *is*. For one thing, most well-known poems about birds, fish, or animals are anthropomorphic expressions — Shelley's "Ode to a Skylark": not a creature-poem at all. As for Margie Twayaga's "My Buttocks," it begins in a creaturely way only to break its promise, and John Davies's "Affliction" is a wonderfully clear example of a culture-centered poem. Let us take off, then, in the other — the future — direction! . . . with complete short poems or relevant fragments, arranged into three main groups . . . arbitrary but useful.

I call them LOVING and DYING and SEARCHING. LOVING and DYING need no explaining; SEARCHING includes *all* things an inquiring mind might care to pursue or consider. We begin with LOVING — poems about any act that propels the life of a creature onward — loving in the broadest sense — *all* modes of sex as well as of reproduction. At once we run into conflict with the scientists, who declare that each has a different function: enhancing variability in one case, propagation in the other. My first example disagrees. It's a well-known lyric by the late Eugenio Montale. Like our other translations, this one will give you the sense, but not the sensation, of course, of the foreign poem. For our purpose, however, the sense will suffice. The poem is called "L'anguilla," "The Eel" — a celebration of the dauntless, tremendous drive of a creature that is, for Montale, the very symbol of *fertility* which he *also* calls "the arrow of *love* on earth." And so that we can't mistake his intent, he capitalizes *love* — or rather *Amore*. The poem is addressed to a woman — the translation is William Arrowsmith's:

> The eel, coldwater
> siren, who leaves the Baltic behind her
> to reach these shores of ours,
> our wetlands, marshes, our rivers,
> who struggles upstream hugging the bottom, under the flood
>   of the downward torrent,
> from branch to branch, thinning,
> narrowing in, stem by stem,
> snaking deeper and deeper into the rock-core
> of slab-ledge, squirming through
> stone interstices of slime until
> one day, light,
> exploding, blazes from the chestnut leaves,
> ignites a wriggle in deadwater sumps
> and run-off ditches of Apennine
> ravines spilling downhill toward the Romagna;

eel, torchlight, lash,
arrow of Love on earth,
whom only these dry gulches of our burned-out
Pyrenean gullies can draw back up
to Edens of generation;
the *green soul* seeking
life where there's nothing but stinging
thirst, drought, desolation;
spark that says
all things start when all seems
ashes and buried branches;
brief *rainbow,* twin
of that other iris shining between your lashes,
by which your virtue blazes out, unsullied, among the sons
of men floundering in your mud: can you
deny your sister?

If this poem is obscure, the cause is the poet's love of compression. Note the ending, where the light-streaked rainbow-colored body of the eel is called "brief *rainbow,*" twin-sister to the one that you set in-between your lashes — the iris of the woman's eye. The Italian word *iride* means both rainbow and eel. Montale's poem exalts the sisterhood of two species of earthly creatures: womankind and eel in a celebration of the driving power of *Amore* — arrow of love on earth. Shall I reread it? A show of hands will guide me.

My next poem comes from France, where I heard it in 1927 — years ago at a Sorbonne lecture. The poet is André Spire and the title "Nudities." The work has two parts. In the first a woman reasons with a man; in the second, he shouts his reply. The epigraph, from the Talmud, reads, "Hair is a nakedness." But first some background to point out a strange irony. The poem appeared in a France still shaking with antisemitic furies stirred by the Dreyfus Affair. The woman says: she has come to the man as a comrade; they're both comrades working to find a haven for victims of persecution. She's firm about this comradeship, insisting, "I am your equal, not a prey." — Hear, then, the poem, whose only recondite word is *chignon,* a round bun or coil of hair worn at the top or the back of a woman's head:

> *You said to me:*
> I want to become your comrade,

I want to visit you without fear of troubling you;
We shall spend long evenings in talk together,
Thinking together of our murdered brothers;
Together we'll travel the world to find
A country where they can lay their heads.
But don't let me see your eyeballs glitter
Or the burning veins of your forehead bulge!
I am your equal, not a prey.
Look! — my clothes are chaste, almost poor,
And you can't even see the curve of my throat.

I answered:
Woman, you are naked.
Your downy neck is a goblet of well-water;
Your locks are wanton as a flock of mountain goats;
Your soft round chignon quivers like a breast . . .
Woman, cut off your hair!

Woman, you are naked.
Your hands unfurl upon our open book;
Your hands, the subtle tips of your body,
Ringless fingers that will touch mine any moment . . .
Woman, cut off your hands!

You are naked.
Your voice flows up from your bosom,
Your song, your breath, the very heat of your flesh —
It is spreading round my body to enter my flesh —
Woman, tear out your voice!

Spire has written other lyrics, one of which questions the scientists' view that I cited before. In a poem about young men and women skating on a lake, he describes their interweavings, partings and meetings, only to note at the end how male and female seem to be driven toward each other by a force outside their willing — magnetized toward each other in a civilized mating dance. The longer he watches, the more deeply he sees *past* the persons themselves till the dancers-skaters — faceless, clothesless, fleshless — appear to be merely "bearers, conveyors, of" "germs that yearn to merge."

Spire was not a scientist, but Miroslav Holúb, a Czech immunologist, has written an even more "clinical" creature-poem about loving. Unfortunately it's a difficult work to follow, with its references to entropy and to Maxwell's demons. But its singsong refrain both before and after the lovemaking act mark it with affirmation: "All this has happened before / All this will happen again" — once more I quote — "In the random and senseless universe."

> Your hand travelled
> the Aztec trail
> down my breast.
> The sun popped out like the egg
> of a platypus
> and aspens pattered
> their leafy Ur-language.
> All this has happened before.
>
> The jellied landscape
> was furrowed with happiness.
> You worshipped me
> like the goddess of warm rain.
>
> But in each corner of our eyes
> stood one of Maxwell's demons
> loosening the molecules
> of rise and fall
> back and forth.
>
> And in and out, round and about,
> in and out,
> through the cracked lens of the eye
> unendingly,
> surface behind glass
> entropy mounted
> in the random and senseless universe.
>
> All this has happened before.
> All this will happen again.

The first half is very simple description — the man speaking to the woman about their act of lovemaking. Your hand traveled, in ritual fashion, "the Aztec trail down my breast." The sun popped out like a duck-bill's egg, while trees pattered in their primeval language. The shimmering landscape was marked with joy as you worshipped me like an ancient goddess —

and "all this has happened before." But — and now the scientist explains what happened next, as he alludes to the Laws of Thermodynamics. According to the Second Law, heat always moves from the hotter body to the colder one — and we presume this has happened here also. But it is the Third Law — about entropy — that he dwells upon till the end. According to this law, as energy decreases, entropy increases: as he says, "entropy mounts in the random and senseless universe." That is, entropy — or "heat-death" — leads to a universal state of inert uniformity. The speaker introduces entropy by an ironical reference to a theory of James Clerk Maxwell, the nineteenth-century physicist, who posited an imaginary agent — called "Maxwell's demon" — that could somehow stamp out entropy. But in the poem, the very opposite happens: "entropy mounts," it increases the general trend of the universe toward death and disorder . . . in which the love of these lovers must wane . . . And all this takes place in a "random and senseless universe." "All this has happened before. / All this will happen again." And no such scientific "Law" has ever stopped any lovers from loving. Nor will it do so ever.

I find this — despite the seemingly hopeless observation, perhaps even because of it — an essentially affirmative poem. For Holúb words speak out in a creature-acceptance of the way things are. By implication, it scorns any howling against fate and so on, in its calm, matter-of-fact, yet witty self-acceptance.

How far can acceptance go in such matters? I think as far as you wish. For it proffers freedom from culture's proscriptions, from all its "noes." Think of the difference in terms of seeing the world either with your naked eyes or through spectacles contrived by the culture. When you look through the lens of the culture, certain behaviors look right, certain others look wrong. But once you remove the spectacles, the distinctions vanish. And then such a work as James Dickey's "The Fiend" is a creature-poem about loving. And yet, if again you put on the culture's spectacles, what can the speaker seem — the "worried accountant . . . moodily passing window after window of her building" — what can he seem but a pervert, an obsessed *voyeur*? Please cast aside the spectacles while I read two specimen passages. The first comes after the worried accountant sits on a limb of an oak-tree, gazing:

> This night the apartments are sinking
> To ground level   burying their sleepers in the soil   burying all floors
> But the one where a sullen shopgirl gets ready to take a shower,
> Her hair in rigid curlers, and the rest. When she gives up

Her aqua terry-cloth robe the wind quits in mid-tree   the birds
Freeze to their perches round his head   a purely human light
Comes out of a one-man oak   around her an energy field   she stands
Rooted   not turning to anything else   then begins to move like a saint
Her stressed nipples rising like things about to crawl off her   as he gets
A hold on himself. With that clasp she changes   senses   something
Some breath through the fragile walls   some all-seeing eye
Of God   some touch that enfolds her body   some hand come up
        out of roots
That carries her as she moves   swaying   at this rare height.

And then — ten lines later:

By this time   he holds in his awkward, subtle limbs the limbs
Of a hundred understanding trees. He has learned what a plant is like
When it moves near a human habitation   moving closer the later it is
Unfurling its leaves near bedrooms   still keeping its wilderness life
Twigs covering his body with only one way out   for his eyes into
        inner light
Of a chosen window   living with them night after night . . .

And so on for many more lines. To the consternation of some, I read "The
Fiend" as a love-poem, much as Lionel Trilling read *Lolita* as a love-story.
If this seems perverse, I urge that you now recall that serious thinkers in
the Middle Ages conceived of love as a virtually physical force that held
the universe together. What *sort* of love? The question is crucial. And I
find the most sensible answer in Plato, in Lacordaire, in Freud, each of
whom thought in the encompassing terms, attributing its multiform manifestations to a *single generative power.* For the Greek philosopher Plato, love
"ascended" from sexual lust to desire for all objects of physical beauty to
a longing for union with beauty of mind and soul. For the French theologian Jean Lacordaire, it was love of God. For the Viennese psychoanalyst
Freud, instinctual impulse. Since our present concern is poetry, I may add a
fourth manifestation, taking the words from a poem of my own addressed
to Whitman called "Poetry: The Art." The relevant lines are "The poetries
of speech / Are acts of thinking love." That is, a poem is an act of thinking
love. For any poem worthy of the name is a bodily act that bears the life of
a creature onward, *lifeward,* as I said when discussing the use of the term
LOVING.

    And now let us turn to the opposite theme: DYING. We're familiar with all the varied ways in which our *culture-bound* poets have talked of death. To put it grossly, death has been either defied or welcomed; and each of these polar attitudes exhibits variety — though mainly the second. Some of them speak out of faith in the bliss that God will give to the worthy (Dante et al.). Some have welcomed more secular joys (Browning in "Prospice"). In Alfred de Vigny's monologue, the speaker Moses, exhausted by his achievements and the pain they have brought, asks but for respite: "Let me sleep the sleep of the earth." And Miguel de Unamuno, in our own day, cries, "For human life is sickness / And in living sick, I die." One can cite related attitudes, from Whitman's "Come lovely and soothing death" to the Emily Dickinson poem that domesticates death and dying. "A wife at daybreak I shall be" concludes

> Softly my Future climbs the stair,
> I fumble at my childhood prayer —
> So soon to be a child no more!
> Eternity, I'm coming, Sir —
> Master, I've seen that face before.

No earlier poems about dying had been so intimate, so confessedly autobiographical. And yet, in the last decade, we have all been exposed to death-poems which go even further — those on suicide and death made popular by Sylvia Plath and Anne Sexton. I, for one, recoil from what seems to verge on a tragic flirtatiousness, but I hold a minority view.

Moreover, one ought to avoid the autobiographical fallacy in any discussion of verse, for a poem, as we know, is a dramatized experience in which a speaker speaks for himself or herself and not for the author. When we say that Dickinson thinks thus-and-thus about dying, we mean the speaker in the poem. And yet in poems about dying, autobiographical attribution seems difficult to avoid. Yet avoid it, we must. Shakespeare's sonnets immediately come to mind with their proud assertion of art's power to frustrate death. The procedure varies but the end of Sonnet 18 is typical —

> But thy eternal summer shall not fade . . .
> Nor shall death brag thou wander'st in his shade
> When in eternal lines to time thou grow'st . . .
> So long lives this and this gives life to thee.

This mode of defiance was, of course, a Renaissance convention — one of the accepted kinds of rationalization, which takes many forms: Herrick's

"Gather ye rosebuds" is one, Donne's "Death, be not proud" is another . . . and one so familiar that even a candidate for President quoted the opening in a campaign speech. It's also a culture-bound poem *par excellence,* and I know of no keener reaction than John Crowe Ransom's. Donne begins, as you know:

> Death, be not proud, though some have called thee
> Mighty and dreadful, for thou art not so:
> For those whom thou thinkst thou dost overthrow
> Die not, poor Death; nor yet canst thou kill me.

As Ransom says, "Donne sets up a figure, a metaphor, proceeds to go through an argument and as a result of the argument — which in reality applies only to the figure — calmly informs death that it's dead." Ransom calls it absurd and indeed the logic is shaky. But shaky or sound, such an attitude is at farthest remove from Thomas' cry to his father, "Do not go gentle into that good night," with its "Rage, rage against the dying of the light" repeated again and again. No rationalization here. A creature's cry but — and this is essential to remember — *not* a self-accepting creature's. A creature who rejects his fate.

Are there actually any creature-poems about death? Let me read from Robinson Jeffers' posthumous volume his "Ode to Hengist and Horsa." They were brothers — Jutes — who invaded England about 450, and they aided the British king in his war on the Picts. Hengist is said to have ruled Kent, Horsa was killed in battle —

> Recently in the south of England
> A Saxon warrior was found in the rich earth there, old hero bones
> Of a man seven feet tall, buried with honor
> Under his shield, his spear beside him, and at his hand
> The Saxon knife: but every bone of his body was broken
> Lest he come forth and walk. It was their custom.
> They did not fear the living but they feared the dead,
> The stopped-off battle-fury, the stinking flesh.
> They honored and perhaps had loved him, but they broke his bones
> Lest he come back.
>   For life, the natural animal thinks,
>   life is the treasure.
> No wonder the dead envy it, gnashing their jaws
> In the black earth. He was our loyal captain and friend,

But now he is changed, he belongs to another nation,
The grim tribes underground. We break their bones
To hold them down. We must not be destroyed
By the dead or the living. We have all history ahead of us.

A poem by one writer rarely evokes a counter-reply, but this one did —
from Czeslaw Milosz. He contrasts two "opposing" human societies. Part 1
depicts his Lithuanian background in affectionate terms; Part 2, the world
of Jeffers; Part 3, his charge and conclusion. The title, "To Robinson
Jeffers."

If you have not read the Slavic poets
so much the better. There's nothing there
for a Scotch-Irish wanderer to seek. They lived in a childhood
prolonged from age to age. For them, the sun
was a farmer's ruddy face, the moon peeped through a cloud
and the Milky Way gladdened them like a birch-lined road.
They longed for the Kingdom which is always near,
. . . .
And you are from surf-rattled skerries. From the heaths
where burying a warrior they broke his bones
so he could not haunt the living.
. . . .
Above your head no face, neither the sun's nor the moon's
only the throbbing of galaxies, the immutable
violence of new beginnings, of new destruction.

and so for ten more lines, then:

What have I to do with you? From footpaths in the orchards,
from an untaught choir and shimmers of a monstrance,
from flowerbeds of rue, hills by the rivers, books
in which a zealous Lithuanian announced brotherhood, I come.
Oh, consolations of mortals, futile creeds.
And yet you did not know what I know. The earth teaches
More than does the nakedness of elements. No one with impunity
gives to himself the eyes of a god. So brave, in a void,
you offered sacrifices to demons: there were Wotan and Thor,
the screech of Erinyes in the air,

. . . .

Better to carve suns and moons on the joints of crosses
as was done in my district. To birches and firs
give feminine names. To implore protection
against the mute and treacherous might
than to proclaim, as you did, an inhuman thing.

No attitudes could be more dissimilar, yet both are culture-bound, each reflecting a specific human society. Milosz "implores protection against the mute and treacherous might." The preliterate world of Hengist proposes to break the warriors' bones . . . so they cannot come back. But neither work, gentle or violent, is a creature-poem.

There is, however, a lyric by Thomas Hardy which accomplishes the impossible on this subject. It consists of words that a dead dog, Wessex, supposedly speaks to the people he used to live with:

> Do you think of me at all,
>> Wistful ones?
> Do you think of me at all
>> As if nigh?
> Do you think of me at all
> At the creep of evenfall,
> Or when the sky-birds call
>> As they fly?
>
> Do you look for me at times,
>> Wistful ones?
> Do you look for me at times,
>> Strained and still?
> Do you look for me at times,
> When the hour for walking chimes,
> On that grassy path that climbs
>> Up the hill?
>
> You may hear a jump or trot,
>> Wistful ones,
> You may hear a jump or trot,
>> Mine, as 'twere —
> You may hear a jump or trot,
> On the stair or path or plot;

> But I shall cause it not,
> > Be not there.
>
> Should you call as when I knew you,
> > Wistful ones,
> Should you call as when I knew you,
> > Shared your home;
> Should you call as when I knew you,
> I shall not turn to view you,
> I shall not listen to you,
> > Shall not come.

The poem imagines what a nonhuman creature might say to his mourners. "Wistful ones," he calls them: those who feel or evince yearning but with little hope. Do you think of me, the dead dog asks? Look for me? Hope that I haven't died? So, at times, you may almost believe, but I shan't be there, even if you should call as you used to call when I shared *your* home — *your* home, not *ours*. The distinctions are unmistakable, and what follows makes them deeper. If you should call as "when I knew you, / I shall not turn to view you, / I shall not listen to you, / Shall not come." Not a touch of wistfulness in the final speech. He has grown away from them. That's how it is. Creature-acceptance.

I've touched on LOVING and DYING; what of SEARCHING? It includes almost anything an inquiring mind might pursue or consider — a huge territory. But I've only two creature-poems to offer, each taking a different view of searching. The first is Frost's "Neither Out Far Nor In Deep":

> The people along the sand
> All turn and look one way.
> They turn their back on the land.
> They look at the sea all day.
>
> As long as it takes to pass,
> A ship keeps raising its hull;
> The wetter ground like glass
> Reflects a standing gull.
>
> The land may vary more;
> But wherever the truth may be —
> The water comes ashore,
> And the people look at the sea.

They cannot look out far.
They cannot look in deep.
But when was that ever a bar
To any watch they keep?

What are they doing? In expectation of something? Is it some faith that holds them there, looking out as into infinity itself, out of which occasionally something emerges — something finite, familiar, a ship . . . or are they waiting for something else to rise up suddenly — an *unknown* something? How account for this waiting, this patience, foreknowledge, though they can neither look out far nor in deep? Theirs is not the only reported case of unexplained human behavior. As J. Z. Young, the biologist, has said, from very earliest times, *Homo sapiens* developed the habit of gathering in great assemblies — "he tends to come together at intervals in huge swarms," tends to form great gatherings on hills. We can't explain such behaviors without resorting to words like rite and ritual, which do not explain at all. Yet a purpose, we feel, must be present. So we have no choice: we accept this creature-strangeness, which ultimately means accepting ourselves as we are. This is what Frost's short poem impels us to do, and, to borrow Keats's phrase, "without any irritable reaching after fact and reason." The people standing there seem most strange till we recognize them as ourselves.

Frost pictures a human action, but Hardy, in our next poem, enlarges the roles. I'll read the seven stanzas slowly; careful listening is needed. The title is "Nature's Questioning."

When I look forth at dawning, pool,
  Field, flock, and lonely tree,
  All seem to gaze at me
Like chastened children sitting silent in a school;

Their faces dulled, constrained, and worn,
  As though the master's ways
  Through the long teaching days
Had cowed them till their early zest was overborne.

Upon them stirs in lippings mere
  (As if once clear in call,
  But now scarce breathed at all) —
'We wonder, ever wonder, why we find us here!

The poem imagines that field, flock, pool, tree once asked aloud the questions that follow:

> 'Has some Vast Imbecility,
>   Mighty to build and blend,
>   But impotent to tend,
> Framed us in jest, and left us now to hazardry?
>
> 'Or come we of an Automaton
>   Unconscious of our pains? . . .
>   Or are we live remains
> Of Godhead dying downwards, brain and eye now gone?
>
> 'Or is it that some high Plan betides,
>   As yet not understood,
>   Of Evil stormed by Good,
> We the Forlorn Hope over which Achievement strides?'
>
> Thus things around. No answerer I . . .
>   Meanwhile the winds, and rains,
>   And Earth's old glooms and pains
> Are still the same, and Death and Life are neighbours nigh.

By hearing nonhuman speakers ask the same unanswerable questions that confound people, the poem unites all members of creation into one mystified family. Not only men and animals, but pool, field, and tree are bound together in our helplessness to explain why we are here. Is life the work of some Vast Imbecility which abandoned it to caprice? Was it fashioned by an Automaton oblivious to our pains? Or are we living vestiges of a failed divinity — "live remains / Of Godhead dying downwards, brain and eye now gone"? Or is there some lofty but imperceptible plan in which the Good may destroy Evil? The poet-speaker doesn't presume to reply. "No answerer I," he says. Meanwhile — "Earth's old glooms and pains / Are still the same, and Death and Life are neighbours nigh."

The poem calls to mind the quite different view of Fernando Pessoa, the Portuguese poet who died not long ago. He wrote under four different names. I quote from the one he christened Albert Caeiro:

> What does a river know of this, what does a tree know,
> And what do I know, who am no more than they?

Whenever I look at things and think of men's thoughts about them
I laugh like a brook coolly babbling over stones.

For the only hidden meaning of things
Is that they have no hidden meaning at all.
It's stranger than strangeness itself,
Stranger than the dreams of all poets
And the thoughts of all philosophers,
That things really are what they seem,
So that there's nothing to understand.

There! That's what my senses learned unaided: —
Things have no meaning: they have being.
Things are the only hidden meaning of things.

This predates the philosopher Whitehead, who asks "whether nature does not in its very being show itself as self-explanatory."

Nonetheless we keep looking for answers, marked as we are by traits peculiar to our species, as others are marked by their own. Some of the latter are more like ours than we formerly thought. The exploratory drive displayed by various creatures is a striking example. Another is play, common to numerous animals, at times resembling elaborate, organized games. Ethologists go so far as to name "nonspecific arousal" as "conscious effort." As for culture itself, once thought our unique possession, its presence in certain species is well confirmed. And for all we know, other creatures may carry on acts *comparable* to ours when we muse or question. *Comparable* must be stressed. Only lately have we learned that communication in parts of the nonhuman world is effected by odor, vibration, or sight. Again I stress the word comparable as I think of the ultraviolet hue that a bee can see in a flower which we cannot see, but also of colors *we* see that are missed by others. Facts of this kind foster man's self-acceptance. They neither diminish nor exalt him but clarify our knowledge of what we are with our own capacities and limits while compelling us to grant the same in all other creatures. Once we look from this vantage point, the world opens up to reveal realities, affinities, that could never be seen through the narrow, distorting lens of the human culture.

These thoughts call to mind the Italian, Umberto Saba, and the closing lines of a sonnet he wrote as a soldier in World War I. "Today my eyes see the earth / In a way I think no artist has known it. So beasts see it maybe." At the end of his life, he wrote of nonhuman creatures who — I quote —

"by the simplicity and nakedness of their lives . . . are close to the truth . . . that can be read in the open book of creation." Joseph Cary, the critic, remarks that Saba found among animals "*his* quintessential creatureliness, a consciousness of a common ground of elemental life shared with the whole of creation. Men, like the beasts, are creatures, therefore *fratelli* [brothers]."

Could Saba have heard of Christopher Smart's poem on his cat, written two hundred years earlier? . . .

> For I will consider my Cat Jeoffry.
> For he is the servant of the Living God, duly and daily serving him.
> For at the first glance of the glory of God in the East he worships in
> his way.
> For this is done by wreathing his body seven times round with
> elegant quickness.
> For then he leaps up to catch the musk, which is the blessing of God
> upon his prayer.
> For he rolls upon prank to work it in.
> For having done duty and received blessing he begins to consider
> himself.

and so on for seventy-four lines. Surely Saba never read "Of Jeoffry" nor of Theodore Roethke's poems. Where Saba observes from a distance, Roethke sees from as close as his eyes allow: "I study the lives on a leaf: the little / Sleepers, numb nudgers in cold dimensions, / Beetles in caves, newts, stone-deaf fishes, / Lice tethered to long limp subterranean weeds" and so on in a poem called "The Minimal." When he studies his own kind, the perspective changes. Roethke's last book contains these self-reflecting words:

> — Or to lie naked in sand,
> In the silted shallows of a slow river,
> Fingering a shell,
> Thinking:
> Once I was something like this, mindless,
> Or perhaps with another mind, less peculiar . . .

And these lines

> Near this rose, in this grove of sun-parched, wind-warped madronas,
> Among the half-dead trees, I came upon the true ease of myself . . .

As if another man appeared out of the depths of my being. . . .
And I rejoiced in being what I was:
In the lilac change, the white reptilian calm . . .

Though neither Smart nor Roethke was known to Saba, Walt Whitman probably was. Yet I cannot learn if he'd read these words from the 1885 edition of *Leaves of Grass:*

> The sharphoofed moose of the north, the cat on the house-sill, the
>   chickadee, the prairie-dog,
> The litter of the grunting sow as they tug at her teats,
> The brood of the turkeyhen, and she with her halfspread wings,
> I see in them and myself the same old law.

Saba would have warmed to these lines as to many more famous others by Whitman, who believed that "a leaf of grass is no less than the journeywork of the stars" — that "the cow crunching with depressed head surpasses any statue, / And a mouse is miracle enough to stagger sextillions of infidels." The same Whitman who avowed "that every thing has an eternal soul! The trees have, rooted in the ground . . . the weeds of the sea . . . the animals . . ."

Trees rooted in the ground. Thus far our creatures have been animals. "To the Pomegranate," by T. Carmi, an Israeli, goes a step further:

> Get away from here! Get away!
> Go to other eyes!
> I wrote about you yesterday.
> "Green," I said
> To your branches bowing in the wind
> And red red red
>
> > [Echo: Holy, holy, holy is
> > the Lord]
>
> To the drops of your fruit,
> And I brought your root to light
> Your moist, dark, stubborn root.
>
> > [Literally: "I released into the
> > light your root" — poet has
> > creator-power]
>
> Now you no longer exist!
> Now you block off the day from my view
> And the moon that hasn't yet risen!

[But this troublesome tree,
though commanded to
disappear, persists!]

Come, my love
(I wrote about you the day before yesterday
And your young memory
Inflames my hands like nettle).
Come and see this odd pomegranate tree:
His blood is in my soul, on my head, in my hands
And he still stands where he stood.

All creatures — poet, tree, girl — are taken for granted as equal. And despite the poet's power to create things *into* existence and as readily make them vanish, this tree that he orders to leave *refuses*. It will not go. It's there in the eye of the speaker as much as himself and the girl.

A creature-poem involving the world of plants can go further. Kenneth Rexroth heads his poem "Lyell's Hypothesis Again" with a sentence from Sir Lyell's text on geology: "An attempt to explain the former changes of the earth's surfaces by causes now in operation." Rexroth's words compose a love-poem in which man, woman, and the lignite rock of a cliff are joined in an earthy kinship. The first lines give the setting. Scarlet larkspur flowers glitter in the April morning sun where the couple lie in the lee of a cliff of lignite, the brownish mineral, half-coal, half-peat, beside a waterfall. Here — I'm quoting — "insuperable life" is "flushed with the equinox" and the selves of the lovers seem "As passionate, as apathetic, / As the lava flow that burned here once: / And stopped here; and said, 'This far / And no further.' And spoke thereafter / In the simple diction of stone." Let me now read on as the man speaks to the woman:

Naked in the warm April air,
We lie under the redwoods,
In the sunny lee of a cliff.
As you kneel above me I see
Tiny red marks on your flanks
Like bites, where the redwood cones
Have pressed into your flesh

You can find just the same marks
In the lignite in the cliff
Over our heads. *Sequoi*

Langdorfi before the ice,
And *sempervirens* afterwards,
There is little difference,
Except for all those years.

Here in the sweet, moribund
Fetor of spring flowers, washed,
Flotsam and jetsam together,
Cool and naked together,
Under this tree for a moment,
We have escaped the bitterness
Of love, and love lost, and love
Betrayed. And what might have been,
And what might be, fall equally
Away with what is, and leave
Only these ideograms
Printed on the immortal
Hydrocarbons of flesh and stone.

The woman and man are beyond the petty contentions, the human self-centered concerns. "What might have been / And what might be, fall equally / Away with what is, and leave / Only these ideograms / Printed on the immortal / Hydrocarbons of flesh and stone." The marks of the redwood cones on *both* the woman's flesh and the lignite rock join two presences of earth: animate woman, "inanimate" rock.

I began with a poem by a high-school girl of Uganda, a poem of discovery. I close with another poem of a girl and discovery, but here the girl, a woman, sits at a dinner table with others. Quite casually she asks for a piece of bread. As the man offers it, something happens. Bread and woman appear as part of the cycle of earthly sustenance. But let the man speak for himself in this poem called "Bread" [The complete text of this poem appears on p. 5]:

This that I give you now,
This bread that your mouth receives,
Never knows that its essence
Slept in the hanging leaves

Of a waving wheatfield thriving
With the sun's light, soil, and the rain,

A season ago, before knives
And wheels took life from the grain

That leaf might be flour — and the flour
Bread for the breathers' need . . .
Nor cared that some night one breather
Might watch how each remnant seed

Invades the blood, to become
Your tissue of flesh, and molests
Your body's secrets, swift-changing
To arms and the mounds of your breasts,

To thigh, hand, hair, to voices,
Your heart and your woman's mind . . .

Possibly some of you wonder at my intent. Do I propose that most or the best of poems to come will be creature-poems? Hardly. Poets belong to the human culture: *what* they write cannot help but reflect the concerns of that culture. Hence it is not a question of theme or subject but point of view, change in the point of view.

As I hope my examples have shown, writers of creature-poems do not see the world in an anthropocentric vision. They do not look at life through the lens of the culture: rather they look at culture and life through the lens of earthly existence.

As he gazes from a kind of planetary vantage-point, *Homo sapiens* no longer appears as Nature's king, its master, the center of all. He sees himself as one of a host of beings . . . Inevitably relationships change, values change, meanings change. Having accepted their quintessential creature-liness, men know that they share with the whole of creation a common ground of elemental being.

Does the world become a more comforting place to live in? The pained realities on which we could shut our eyes, ignore, or condemn as aberrant evils now must receive acceptance as components of earthly existence. Planetary maturity, the inevitable next stage in man's evolution, is in no respect a more soothing state that reconciles kindness and cruelty. But maturity never is.

Notes for Expanding Lecture into an Essay

1. "Planetary maturity" — needs expansion with regard to the difficulties of accepting the griefs that call to mind Hardy's "Vast Imbecility," e.g., random horrors: infants born without spines, autism, etc. Discuss anthropocentrism as example of human infantilism. Relate planetary maturity to danger of destruction of earth by global warming ("greenhouse effect"), nuclear explosions, ruining the rain forests, etc.

2. Meaning of "inanimate" according to current scientific position.

3. Counter-reaction to creature-acceptance as shown by kinds of self-condemnation of man as a species. Examples from Robinson Jeffers and others. To be followed by examples of remarkable human accomplishments in the form of matters not very well known — best example, Fibonacci series of numbers as related to opposing spirals in daisies, pine cones, etc., and to the Golden Section in art (architecture, painting, etc.). These to be followed by examples of remarkable "capacities" of nonhuman creatures, such as migratory patterns of birds, fish; animal architecture (see Frisch volume); crow's capacity for abstraction; etc. (See *The Seamless Web*, 198ff.)

4. Discuss religious beliefs as a human phenomenon, so far as we know, and their existence in poems that exemplify creature-acceptance as well.

5. Discuss the unexplained way in which *Mimosa pudica* responds — "process not well enough understood," say botanists. The fact that plants lack nervous systems offers no final answer, since other systems, to date undiscovered, may possibly exist and account for the *Mimosa pudica* response.

6. Added examples of self-condemnation by human beings, based on the many unspeakable ways by which animals are made to suffer for the greater glory of science — Draize tests on rabbits' eyes for cosmetic research; breaking dogs' feet to determine threshold of pain; strapped-down primates in NASA programs, etc. Growing movements against such victimization of nonhuman creatures.

7. Discuss Ralph Hodgson's "The Bull" and Galway Kinnell's "The Bear"?

THE SEAMLESS WEB

Chapter 6 of *The Seamless Web: Language-Thinking, Creature-Knowledge, Art-Experience,* copyright 1970 by Stanley Burnshaw and reprinted by courtesy of George Braziller, Inc.; reissued in 1991 with a foreword by James Dickey. Some words and phrases have been altered for clarification and numbered cross-references to earlier pages in the book have been removed. The opening paragraph is drawn from the closing section of Chapter 5.

At a certain time, says Loren Eiseley, ancestral man entered his own head. All that our kind has become goes back to this crucial moment, for to see oneself, to feel, to know oneself as an other is to do as much with the world. To break through the seamless web — no longer to be part of all that one senses and knows — is to enter a strangeness from which there is no return. Paradigms of the fate can be found in ancient myths which compress to a single moment long ages during which men slowly came to realize what they had "done." The tales of the race's childhood are songs of paradise lost, of homelessness, helplessness: the lament of a creature aware of his alienation from the whole of living creation.

Although everyone knows that humanity is only one strand in the web of creation, one can rarely speak about man's condition as a creature without eliciting defensiveness and confusion. Part of the problem grows out of language. "At-oneness," for all its plainness of statement, carries a portentous ring. "Seamlessness" is a wholly negative abstraction. Still more difficult to envisage is the "mixedness" of man's condition. Though physical reality recedes from him as his symbolic activities advance, man obviously does not live in indirectness all or even most of the time. Moreover, the innermost tendencies of his organism regularly insist on obtaining satisfaction: he is still very much a creature of earth despite all he knows of control. Indeed one of the largest mysteries in his behavior is the source of the balance he is able to maintain between his learned restraint and the needs that propel his organism.

Those needs, drives, instincts cause endless problems for the expert who would classify and define them and chart their courses. But whether they be presented as the "dominant" few (nourishment, reproduction, aggression, flight) or as more numerous "inborn behavior patterns" does not matter at all. For the experts totally ignore the organic tradition of man's biological evolution — of his drive to regain, to recover, his primary organic unity with the rest of creation: his "seamlessness," which endured through his millions of years, whose heritage is inscribed in his myths, his religions, his arts, his rituals. One is strongly tempted to explain the omission, but the reader can readily do this for himself, aware of the mind's self-protective way of "forgetting" things which might threaten its balance. Besides, at this point a more productive paradox beckons. The very capacities of the mind that were and are involved with man's divisiveness act toward fulfilling his drive toward unification. A part of the sickness itself must work toward the cure.

Drive, Desire, and Public Object

Readers of Malinowski's *Coral Gardens and Their Magic* may remember one of the incantations of the Trobriand Islanders as translated into commonplace English:

> It passes, it passes,
> The breaking pain in the thighbone passes,
> The ulceration of the skin passes,
> The big black evil of the abdomen passes,
> It passes, it passes.

The Trobriand Islanders did not need to be lectured on the evocative power of their words. Like the rest of humanity, they were acting as it were "on the knowledge" that something deeply desired can be imagined into believable existence. Their incantations imagine with words, words marked by rich phonetic, rhythmical, metaphorical, and alliterative effects, (according to Malinowski), by weird cadences and repetitions. But such language is only one variety of the several materials that the mind can use in attempting to fulfil the pressing demand for a much desired reality.

At this point a reader anxious to define imagination may try to choose from among the offerings of philosophers, critics, psychologists, writers, scientists. He may separate imagination from the fancy (as Hume, Dryden, Hunt, Wordsworth, Emerson, Croce, and many others have done in respectively different ways). Or he may break imagination itself into two or more modes, such as "productive and reproductive" (Kant), "primary and secondary" (Coleridge), "formal and material" (Bachelard), "penetrative, associative, contemplative" (Ruskin), and so on. This arbitrary list gives no idea of the modes of speculation, which often encoil metaphysics, philosophy, semantics. And on the whole the verbal arrangements tell more about the originators than the subject, since imagination can be made to include as little or as much as one chooses, issuing, as it does, from the mental power of forming images: "ideal" or "actual," spontaneously or with deliberateness. To be sure, in everyday affairs we draw on the publicly held store, whereas in visionary thought they arise on their own to lead a life of their own. Yet even this self-evident distinction does not hold; for whatever else it may be said to be — memory, invention, association, imitation, and so on — an image is always a symbolic representation responding to some need of a particular human organism.

This emphasis may seem too obvious until one realizes, with Suzanne Langer, that the image "which presents with something like the objectivity of a percept, still bears the stamp of the thing it really is — part of the cerebral process itself, a quintessence of the very act that produces it, *with its deeper reaches into the rest of the life in which it occurs*" (my italics).[1] Each person's images (whether they appear when he is awake, entranced, or asleep) are passages from the life of his own and particular brain. The quaternions came to Hamilton, a mathematician; the vision of dry bones to Ezekiel, a prophet. "Kubla Khan" was dreamed by Coleridge, a poet; the "Devil's Sonata" by Tartini, a composer.

One head of a state, "finding" an image to picture his social program, speaks of a "New Deal"; another, of a "New Frontier." A business-man, reaching out for words which others will be able to envisage, coins a phrase about "a product mix." By contrast, a mystic falters when he attempts to describe what he beheld. "The deliciousness of some of these states is too subtle and piercing a delight for ordinary words to connote," says St. Teresa of Avila, for whom union was not a vision but "rather some overmastering idea." And when the mystics proceed to represent it with any language, the imagery fails — as, moreover, they insist that it must. Wherefore Dr. Johnson reasoned, concerning Boehme, that "If Jacob had seen unutterable things, Jacob should not have attempted to utter them." Yet Jacob's fellows crowd line after line with imagery which evokes deep meaning only for themselves.[2] As do numberless non-mystics also. The inspiring sights and feelings fail to come alive on the page for others; they remain private possessions. Whereas the imagining that we call "creative" gives rise to public objects. Its touchstone is the power of the recorded enactment to be meaningfully "known" by others, to be a source of affecting, enlarging experience for others.

This power is of course the hallmark of the productions of creative artists and scientists, none of whom is primarily concerned with discovering what philosophers refer to as "knowledge": statements which are absolutely certain, irrevocably true. What Karl Popper observed of science — that it is cosmology, the problem of understanding the world, ourselves, and our knowledge as part of it — holds equally for all the arts. And the imagination is the only instrument available to a mind with this primary concern. In the arts obviously, but also in "the purest and driest parts of science, imagination is as necessary as in lyric poetry" (Russell). There is indeed no logical path leading to the universal laws which give a picture of the world, as Einstein stated decades ago: "They can be reached only by intuition, and this intuition is based on an intellectual love of the objects of experience." One thinks of Rilke's earlier declaration about works of art: that "only love can grasp and hold them." By now, to be sure, the essential identity among all approaches to "cosmology, the problem of understanding the world and ourselves," is no longer questioned. "The pioneer scientist," says Planck, "must have a vivid intuitive imagination for new ideas, ideas not generated by deduction, but by *artistically* creative imagination." The dedication of a recent book on *Scientific Uncertainty and Information* affirms that "An artist's inspiration or a scientist's theory, reveal the unpredictable power of human imagination."

The statement might as easily have been made a half-century ago, even earlier, for the involuntary nature of creative enactment had already been witnessed widely. In music and poetry the "unpredictable power of human imagination" had become an established tradition, pointed up with a number of cases of entire works composed at a single stroke, some of them during dreams.[3] But quite as spectacular were some of the reports from science. Poincaré's theory of Fuchsian groups arrived one night when, contrary to his custom, he had drunk black coffee and could not sleep: "Ideas rose in crowds; I felt them collide until pairs interlocked, so to speak, making a stable combination." Kekulé von Stradonitz literally beheld one of his most important discoveries — of the benzine ring — one evening when he was trying to prepare some pages of a chemistry textbook. The writing did not go well:

> . . . my spirit was with other things. I turned my chair to the fireplace and sank into a half-sleep. Again the atoms flitted before my eyes [taking the pattern of rings]. Long rows, variously, more closely united; all in move-

ment, wriggling and turning like snakes. And see, what was that? One of the snakes seized its own tail and the image whirled scornfully before my eyes. As though from a flash of lightning I awoke; this time again I occupied the rest of the night in working out the consequences of the hypothesis.

("Let us learn to dream!" Kekulé urged his fellow-scientists.) Sir William Rowan Hamilton while walking with his wife to Dublin came up Brougham Bridge and "then and there felt the galvanic circuit of thought close; and the sparks which fell from it were the fundamental equations between i, j, k [quarternions]; exactly as I have used them ever since." Karl F. Gauss, having tried unsuccessfully for years to prove a certain arithmetical theorem, finally succeeded, but "not on account of my painful efforts. . . . Like a sudden flash of lightning, the riddle happened to be solved."

Suddenness, spontaneity — von Helmholtz had already discussed them in a pioneering speech to scientists in 1896. Today we take them for granted, together with the fact that creativity does not end with illumination in the arts or in the sciences. The flash, the dazzling intuition, the dawning recognition must be exposed to the common light and verified, "perfected": moved toward "completion" — submitted to the inscrutably collaborative processes that in poetry are called, misleadingly, "conscious artistry." Poets consider words in the full range of their meanings; scientists, symbols of quantity and logical sequences. Each specific procedure takes a different direction, whereas the over-all processes take the same. Today it is usual to hear it remarked that in the testing of hypotheses as well as in their discovery, imagination is the indispensable factor.

Though we have come to learn something about the course of creative activity, we still remain mystified by its genesis. Whence — not to ask Wherefore — this imaginative projection? Bacon held the use of poetry to consist in giving "some shadow of satisfaction to the mind of man in those points wherein the nature of things doth deny it." Centuries later, in the era of Freud, Théodore Ribot (who exalted scientific creativity far above art) maintained that "all invention presupposes a want, a craving, a tendency, an unsatisfied desire." When on a later page in the same *Essai sur l'imagination créatrice* he declares the origin of all imaginative creation to be "a need, a desire," the effect is mainly to give scientific caste to proverbial notions — necessity has been the mother of invention for two thousand years just as the wish has been the father to the thought. Desire if impeded may begin a visionary action of thought; but the origin, says Ribot, can also be a need. The word "desire," which is understood to be the attraction toward something we want to possess or to do or feel or know, is broad enough to include almost anything, and the same may be remarked of "need." But the two are not the same unless we choose to make them the same. And if we do, we shall have to take account of the *modes* of desire-need that are associated with creativity and its productions.

One mode will be seen to consist of what it is that the creator of the poem desires-needs to possess or do or feel or know as embodied in the references of his lines to experiences (feelings, ideas, objects, events) within the culture. A wholly different order of desire-need arises from his human condition as a creature inhabiting the earth: a specific type of creature (as noted earlier) in whom the desire-need expresses itself as a burden upon his organism — malaise, irritation, tension, even torment, which finds relief in the act of composition.

Creativity cannot emerge without an unburdening of the organism whether the disturbance be remarked or not and regardless of degree. Alongside Byron's bravura passage on "the lava of imagination whose eruption prevents an earthquake," Donne's couplet is comparatively calm:

> Griefe brought to numbers cannot be so fierce,
> For, he tames it, that fetters it in verse.

And Wordsworth's lines are plain:

> To me alone there came a thought of grief;
> A timely utterance gave that thought relief,
> And I again am strong.

In fact, Newman's prose remark that "poetry is a means of relieving the overburdened mind" might be mistaken for a paraphrase. Odd as it may seem, few people have gone so far as Newman's contemporary, the High Anglican cleric and professor John Keble, who argued in his *Oxford Lectures* and reviews that to innumerable persons poetry "acts like a safety-valve to a full mind," at times "preserving men from actual madness."[4] Whether or not one accepts the last phrase, there can be no ignoring of the fact that the pressure exerted by these desires-needs upon the organism may at intervals be sufficient to direct much of its behavior. Or that they may continue to do so over long periods of time despite the counter-pressure of its livelihood desires-needs. All too many careers of musicians, painters, writers, and scientists show the sign of obsessive dedication, often at the cost of deprivation and suffering and with little or no likelihood of worldly reward.

To wring one's hands at the adulation some of them receive only post-humously is irrelevant if their kind of creating involved little choice. In a sense, volition plays the same part here as in composing. At least, most typically creative persons do not seem to be able to help themselves from doing what they "have to" do, susceptible as they are to those accumulating burdens whose arrivals cannot be predicted or controlled. Much like other events which upset the balance of the organism, these particular desires-needs demand to be disposed of . . . by the classic means for regaining stability. We are back to "The Body Makes the Minde," to the cycle of creative accumulation and release, to the inspiration that sets it in motion.

We are also back to the third paragraph of the present chapter: to the paradox and to the need omitted from the lists. Whatever may be their total number, each basic drive must show its own disturbances, periods of crisis, directions, effects, and so on, but no one could pretend to have perceived more than a miniscule amount of the manifestations of all that must drive the organism, or to expect the enormous complexity of these phenomena to exhibit parallel behaviors. On the other hand, no one doubts that the drive to perpetuate the species manifests itself in the desire for sexual union with another human body. And if there are any discernible manifestations of the drive to recover primary organic unity with the rest of creation, one of them surely is adducible in the public objects produced by creative imaginers: in the act by which they are created as well as in the supposed recapitulation of this act as re-lived in the re-experiencing of the object.

The foregoing pages of this book have focused on the creator; the remainder of the present chapter is concerned both with ourselves as participants in what the creator has made and with the creature-drive for unity instinct within us. Analogies here may be difficult to find, yet it would seem that if the reproductive drive can fulfil itself when it finds release through union with another human body, this other human-creature necessity, when it finds its release through imagination's symbols, can unite us with the "body" of the world.

How is such a statement to be justified? What is there about the creative symbol that makes possible any union with the world? In all that has preceded I have referred to various forms of creative productivity, but in facing this question I limit myself to the form I know best, which is poetry, while continuing to assume the essential nature of all creative imagining to be the same.

Fusions of Resemblance

A poem is made of words as a musical composition is made of tones: words are the public materials composing the private, irreducible entities — the metaphors, similes, other figurative structures; the questions, exclamations, propositions, other statements — and the terms denoting their relationships. No single one of these expressive units is itself a *sine qua non*. If Western readers show surprise at discovering that a poem can be effective without any figures of speech, it is because they have grown used to regarding metaphors and similes as indispensable. And, of course, the metaphor is not only the commonest figure in verse; as the naming of an imaginative fusion of resemblance which has already occurred in the poet's mind, it is emblematic of the poem itself. Personifications and imaginative similes (basically varieties of metaphor) are also functions of resemblance. As for the so-called "tropes of connection" — the synecdoche ("blind mouths"), the metonymy ("When I consider how my light is spent") — though technically fusions of contiguity, they are obviously also expressions of resemblance, and of a highly compressed kind.

One might expect that figure-less verse must, by contrast, be weak in impact. So narrow a notion of poetic condensation can be tested by trying to bluepencil Goethe's "Wanderers Nachtlied, II," H. D.'s "Lethe," Eliot's "Rhapsody on a Windy Night," or longer works such as Cavafy's "Waiting for the Barbarians," the best of the Scottish ballads, some of the *Cantos* of Pound. Structure proves as various in figure-less verse as elsewhere — as poetic logic itself. And if each picture in a figure-less poem acts as a term of a multiple fusion, much the same can be said of figure-less poems in general: each expressive unit holds together with the force of resemblance to the totality they form, as a part of the work or as the whole. That is, each poem is a total unification composed of smaller unifications; through its fusions of resemblance, it identifies a relational unity. To say that a poem which fails to do so fails as a poem, is a circular way of reaffirming the demand we make that a work be a whole. So we speak of the organic unity of a successful poem, attributing to it the power of a life of its own within the reader. Can such life fail to stir in him empathetic feelings of unification, since (whatever the fusions employed) its action proceeds by bodying forth similitude?

British writers of the nineteenth century, fascinated by imagination's gift for identifying resemblances, discovered in it the essential of poetic thought. "This intuitive perception of the hidden analogies of things," wrote Hazlitt, "or, as it may be called, this instinct of the imagination, is, perhaps, what stamps the character of genius on the productions of art more than any other circumstance; for it works unconsciously like nature, and receives its impressions from a kind of inspiration." Moreover, the making of "strange combinations out of common things" (Shelley) is an act of emotion. "Imagination, purely so-called, is all feeling; the feeling of the subtlest and most affecting analogies" (Leigh Hunt). And so on. Some of these writers remarked on an accompanying disturbance, as noted earlier in citations from Byron, Wordsworth, and especially Keble; yet nowhere is it viewed as bringing on a type of assault to which the brain responds with its characteristic drive to "make sense" of it. In assimilating the new to what it already knows, it may seize on things that turn out later to make bad sense, if sense at all. The organism's resumption of balance in itself cannot assure validity. There is no telling what its headlong action to contain the assault may lead to. Indeed no pathways conceal so many pitfalls as the ones that the mind may take in its "intuitive perception of hidden analogies." The French *philosophe* J. B. Robinet declared that life's principal effort is to make shells, and his *Philosophical views on the natural gradation of forms of existence, or the attempts made by nature while learning to create humanity* was for a time regarded as a scientific contribution. The world's recorded verse must be populated with images of every range which are as valid as this large one of Robinet's, and since the same doubtless holds true in other provinces of creative imagining, it makes all viable intuitive perceptions the more astonishing and precious. Moreover, the drive toward similitude reflects itself not only in linguistic fusions of resemblance but in countless other actions within the poem — obviously, for example, in parallelism, refrain, antithesis. Poems in fact are steadily engaged in the work of con-fusing, for the paradigm of poetry — metaphor — pervades its every act.

If, as Oliver Goldsmith remarked, metaphor is a kind of magical means "by which the same idea assumes a thousand different appearances," it is also the means by which the same appearance stands for a thousand different ideas. The two actions are simultaneous and indivisible. We "understand" by perceiving-feeling likenesses and unlikenesses, by bringing some things together and, in so doing, setting other things apart — assimilating/distinguishing. This amounts to regarding likeness and difference as reflexive parts of the process of relational thinking, the one implying the other. They are aspects, not antitheses. That likeness is not identity nor difference always contrariety, is generally — and curiously — ignored despite the glaring fact that much less than we suspect in experience can be fitted into neat little packets of black-and-white. The engulfing universe exemplifies variety in uniformity, as Plato had discovered long before British poets and critics rediscovered its significance for art. Coleridge said "poetry produces two kinds of pleasure . . . the gratification of the love of variety, and the gratification of the love of uniformity," which correspond to the "two master-movements or impulses of man." Wordsworth, in pointing to the second ("which the mind derives from the perception of similitude in dissimilitude") as the drive at the center of poetry, anticipated the view of the contemporary scientist. "A man becomes creative, whether he is an artist or a scientist," says Bronowski, for example, "when he finds a new unity in the variety of nature . . . finding a likeness between things which were not thought alike before. . . . An innovation in either field occurs only when a single mind perceives in disorder a deep new unity." For Wordsworth the necessity for such perceiving flows out of the depths of the organism. It is "the great spring of the activity of our minds, and their chief feeder. From this principle the direction of the sexual appetite, and all the passions connected with it, take their origin. . . ."

What of anterior causes, what of the great spring's sources? Man's actions and thoughts could hardly be impelled by and drawn toward the interrelatedness of all that surrounds him unless at the depth of his organism he believed in its unity and felt and knew it to exist, as ancestral man had felt and known it in his capacity as a participant.[5] At these innermost creature levels of feeling and knowledge, the arbitrary cannot find room. Nature's buzzing and blooming confusion that engulfs our senses is not suddenly ordered and unified and interinvolved in all its parts merely because post-Eden creatures would wish it to be. Such statements as Anaxagoras' (that everything is latently involved in everything else) or Emerson's (that everything is convertible into every other thing) are but feeble and partial intuitions in latter-day symbols of the primary organic unity of a creature who himself had been part of the seamless unity of the "All."

If the sciences, like the arts, are busy with new unifications, in their encompassing physical laws as in minor equations, every such enactment of the imagination is a mirror-image of the all-involving unity whose existence it affirms and toward which it reaches out with the only means we possess: the microcosm of a symbol. The passion impelling such creations underlies not only transcendent dramas and murals of paradisal grandeur; even in casual-seeming sculptures assembled from industrial debris its forces are at work, manifesting the same uniquely human need for perceiving kinship among the disparate, wholeness beneath the chaos. And if every such created object is a unification, it is so not only in its totality but equally in the smaller fusions that make it one. So it happens that when, in experiencing a poem, we respond within us to such large and small embodiments of language, we participate in a re-enactment of unification, whether we know it or not — and by the means (the symbols of language) provided by the very capacities of mind that were and are involved with divisiveness.[6]

That only certain types of imaginative creation can impart a sense of cosmic identification has sometimes been insisted on by philosophers and poets in particular. The greatest of all of poetry's attempts "to say one thing in terms of another," writes Frost, "is the philosophical attempt to set matter in terms of spirit, or spirit in terms of matter, to make the final unity." The duality is quite as plain in Karl Jaspers' remark that "We call great art the metaphysical art which reveals, through its visuality, Being itself." The differences in the terms employed by Frost and by Jaspers count less than the common belief both statements avow:

> Poetry begins in trivial metaphors, pretty metaphors, "grace" metaphors, and goes on to the profoundest thinking that we have.
>
> — *Frost*

> Fundamentally, just art and therefore skill bare of philosophic significance is the non-transcendental manner of representing, of decorating, of producing the sensuously attractive, in as much as it exists in isolation and has no metaphysical bearing.
>
> — *Jaspers*

In a conversation with Wilhelm Furtwängler, the philosopher was still more insistent. "In art there are two layers: one is metaphysically sincere, the other, while showing vital creativeness can at best please but it cannot impress itself in an essential manner. This sharp division cannot be made with objective certainty, but I consider it of fundamental importance."[7]

Division of art into a hierarchy may also grow from quite different thinking — from a "new ontology of the imagination," for example, as described by Gaston Bachelard in *The Poetics of Space*. Renouncing both his earlier "objective" method and his "interpretation through depth," the

French philosopher-historian of science distinguishes formal from material imagination, the second of which bodies forth poetic "purity." In an attempt to help others recognize in the image *being is round* "the primitivity of certain images of being," he pursues "the phenomenology of roundness" with the addition of statements on roundness collected from LaFontaine, Michelet, Van Gogh, Rilke, and others. Bachelard's "pure imagination" — which he names "metapsychological" — is neither the "profoundest thinking" of Frost nor the "revelation of Being" of Jaspers but the experiencing of being itself ("we find ourselves entirely in the roundness of this being").

For each of these thinkers there are two different species of poetry, variously defined. Yet how would one go about separating poems which fuse spirit with matter, matter with spirit, from those which do not? Or poems which are metaphysically sincere from those in the underlayer which show vital creativeness only? Or poems which are metapsychological from the lowlier others? In all such cases, two different species presuppose two different births or sources. Are there, then, two different creative processes? Or, at the level of sources, two different sets of impelling needs, drives, compulsions? Furtwängler rejected Jaspers' dichotomy as a misconstruction of the genesis of art. Even the most insignificant tune, he assured him, originates in the same indivisible source of creativity. Both musician and philosopher clung to their convictions, neither succeeding in proving that the other was wrong.

Proof in matters of this kind seems all but unreachable. (How validate Auden's assertion that "every poem is rooted in imaginative awe"? As Mark Van Doren "answered," in a similar discussion, "If you have to prove it, then it can't be very important.") Furtwängler, however, might have added that any attempt such as Jaspers' to rank imaginative works into a higher and a lower species rests on a misconception of subject matter in art. To look, with Jaspers, for the metaphysical — or with Matthew Arnold, for the solemn-serious — is to ignore what a poem *does* in favor of what it seems to be "about." As remarked before, the experiencing of a work of art is indivisible; hence any thinking about, any focusing upon, a partial aspect of the whole can take place only within our analytic heads. Nevertheless we have no instruments for dealing with matters of rank except for our analytic heads; and when we use them to cope with this question a number of conclusions confront us.

First, every successful poem, regardless of whatever else it is and does, embodies similitude. It embodies it, as we have noted, through the action of its language, through its fusings of resemblance, in the whole and in the parts, irrespective of how each happens to be formed grammatically and irrespective of the experiences, objects, events, and/or ideas in the culture to which it happens to refer. This is to say that regardless of what any poem may happen to be "about," all the resemblance-making actions begin and end with unification. Furthermore, we may even conceive of these unifications of poetry as comprising a generic mode of love. This would be doing the kind of thing that Plato, Jean Baptiste Lacordaire, and Freud, for example, have done in attributing its multiform manifestations (love of woman, of parents, of a cause, etc., etc.) to a single generative force. For the Greek philosopher, it was mind; for the French theologian, love of God; for the Viennese psychoanalyst, instinctual impulse. To conceive of each poem as "an act of thinking love" implies an even vaster emotion, one which takes these three great forces as themselves but partial expressions of man's organic desire for reunion with creation itself.[8]

Resonance and Reverberation

Whether all human feelings flow out of a single source, whether, as Otto Rank believes, "every emotion which is admitted in its totality manifests itself as love,"[9] poetic thought, no matter which aspects of reality it embodies, proceeds by enacting union. Viewed thus in terms of what it does, every successful poem is a binding-together. And since binding-together is fundamentally what every poem is "about," we meet a seeming paradox. The substance or referents of a poem appear to serve as the vehicle for the making of unifications; or, in more familiar terms, it is a poem's "form" (structuring) that constitutes its ultimate "subject" (unification) — the act of unifying forms the poem, its referents subserve this action. But it is in this sense only that every poem must embody the identical theme, for "form" is always a structuring of particular referents. And *what* a poem binds together are elements drawn from the writer's private experiences, elements possessing public meaning and interest, which are therefore able to resound in the experience of the reader.

These *resonances* depend on and evoke the world of their culture, its events, ideas, objects, and so on. Unlike the "ultimate subject," which transcends human time and place, the resonance-world is walled in always by the specific culture it arises from and speaks to. A less apparent limitation inheres in the speech it is borne on. "In a symbol," says Carlyle in *Sartor Resartus*, "there is concealment yet revelation" — and for this reason it is a "wondrous agency." One of the sources of the conflict was noted earlier, in the disparity between the terms of a metaphor and the counterpull away from resemblance. A second relates to one of the modes of desires-and-needs discussed earlier in this chapter. That an impulse to reveal encounters an impulse to conceal is an axiom of behavior within the culture. And that the poet may be unaware of their effect upon his thinking also may be taken for granted, as well as their conflict, for the characteristic ways by which poetry speaks make its presence plain. We have already noted the tendency of poetic language to obscure the directness of reality, to throw over it a sort of half-consciousness of unsubstantial existence — to reveal the fervent emotions of the mind under certain veils and disguises. Revelation yet concealment — and, as a consequence, a tension which marks the very nature of poetic resonance, adding to the other forces it exerts upon the reader a further power: that of a message which "still seems to be trying to express something beyond itself."[10]

What can be found of the reader's response to the poem's *act* of uniting? Hopeless though it may seem to ask where or how, some light yet glows from the crucial fact that this action does not address itself to bits and pieces of nameable cultural experience. It speaks purely as a force of feeling. And when this force "sounds" upon the feeling-capacities within the reader, his organism vibrates with responsive aliveness; it fills with *reverberations*. F. W. H. Myers, like a good many others, acknowledges the apparently "mysterious power by which mere arrangements of sound can convey an emotion which no one could have predicted beforehand, and which no known laws can explain."[11] And despite the great attention given by scholars to the linguistic structures of poetry, one essential effect — if not the profoundest effect — has been ignored. That a poem embodies rhythm together with other patterns of recurrence (rime, assonance, parallelism, antithesis, and so on, as the case may be) has been taken for granted. But taking for granted totally misses the emotional symbolism — and consequent import — of recurrence, associated as it is with other cycles of recurrence, with diurnity, the seasons, and the deep creature reassurance that they bring. Similarly, taking for granted fails to appreciate what the presence of these expectation-patterns implies for the reader as structural reflections and embodiments of uniting in the over-all action of uniting that is every poem.[12]

None of the foregoing observations so much as implies any possible notion of separating the meanings of any word in a poem from its sounds.[13] So far as I can see, every attempt to do so has greatly confused by suggesting, when not asserting, that a word actually leads two separate lives. At times the sequence of sounds in a poem of an unknown tongue can be so "musical" as to delight a listener who has no idea of their meanings; and if the word "musical" can ever be applied to verse, it is here: to a sonal pattern with no denotation at all. A special kind of meaning, however, is held by some writers to exist in certain words. F. E. Halliday, for example, speaks of an "aural symbolism lying deep in the unconscious and fully operative and evocatory only when experienced in the semi-hypnotic condition induced by verse, and to a lesser degree by rhythmical prose such as that of the Bible and Sir Thomas Browne." This "elemental significance" would be possessed by only certain sounds and sound-combinations "which are echoed and partially reproduced in words like *lie, light, foam, sea, beat, grave, stone, day, glory.*"[14] But even agreement with this writer that "Far more words are onomatopoeic in origin than is generally realised" could not affect the fact that every word is a complex of sounds and of meanings which acts upon the reader as an indivisible totality — just as his response to a poem is an indivisible experience of what I have called resonances and reverberations. In the same passage (on the "poetic state"), Valéry gives his own characterization of the first:

> Under these conditions familiar objects and persons somehow undergo a change in values. New affinities are felt to exist between them, new relationships never observed in ordinary circumstances.

and of the second:

> There is a tendency to discover a complete new system of relationships in which men, things, and events . . . also seem to have some indefinable though marvelously exact relation to the modes and laws of our general being.[15]

The most telling and neglected aspect of the reverberative process must now be considered, one which was foreshadowed in the opening words of this book: "Poetry begins with the body and ends with the body." As Collingwood in his *Principles of Art* says of "psychical expression," it consists in the doing of involuntary and perhaps wholly unconscious bodily acts, related in a peculiar way to the emotions they are said to express. Not only are the two "elements in one indivisible experience" but "every kind and shade of emotion which occurs at the purely psychical level of experience has its counterpart in some change of the muscular or circulatory or glandular system . . . which expresses it." Thus, "the mere sight of some one in pain, or the sound of his groans, produces in us an echo of his pain, whose expression in our own body we can feel in the tingling or shrinking of skin areas, certain visceral sensa, and so forth."[16]

This involuntary expression of "sympathy" by the organism is central to Spire's massive study of the biological foundations of poetry, *Plaisir Poétique et plaisir musculaire*. By its organization of rhythm, says Spire, which is so different from that of the verbal structure in a typically logical sentence, and by its more or less strong accents, the affective word-order of verse "echoes" the internal physiological motions of the poet during composition as well as those of the reader during his experiencing of the poem. "Indeed, it models itself on these internal motions; it is their external and communicative aspect. The movements and attitudes of our muscles — those hidden in our organs and in the rest of the body as well as those of the face (especially the mobile and sensitive muscles associated with responses of sight and taste) — *translate* the ideas and feelings experienced in the poem." ("I read sentences of Goethe as though my whole body were running down the stresses" — Kafka.)

Since the poem produces patterns of motion in the body which parallel those set forth by the words, one might almost be tempted to say that in its own way the organism "reads" these motions. In any case, it clearly participates in them. As counterpart, as psychical expression, they are represented — and therefore "known" — by the organism in ways that antedate by millennia the life of the culture. For reaction-with-the-body is an archaic type of identification; hence to be expected in the expressions of a type of person who is (as Eliot calls him) "more primitive, as well as more civilised, than his contemporaries," one whose imagination can draw him toward the very depths of his creature nature — and his reader with him.

Knowledge

To respond to a poem is to know its resonances-reverberations — but do they equal knowledge? The question touches on categories, leading away from all knowledges which complete themselves in abstractions whose validity must be verified, regardless of the thinking processes out of which they had been born. Science, of course, is the exalted example. Every truth it proposes must survive testing by "value-free, objective" analytic procedures before it can gain acceptance. By contrast, certain types of knowledge become true or untrue according to criteria which are "subjective." And here the exalted example is religion — toward which our question of knowledge is inevitably magnetized.

So often and so surely has the closeness between religion and poetry been stressed that most people who think of the relationship probably suspect that the two must ultimately be one. Or agree with Arnold that most of what passes for the first will in time be replaced by the second.[17] If all poems are rooted in imaginative awe, so are all religious experiences, the most voluble witnesses to which are the mystics. But as they never fail to avow, the feeling-knowledge that they behold in their ecstatic visions simply cannot be conveyed. Though poetic inspiration may already be on the decline when composition begins (as Shelley maintained), great poetry nevertheless succeeds in affecting readers profoundly, even if it is (as Shelley added) only a feeble shadow of the poets' original conceptions. This basic difference in capacity to impart does not in itself clear up the question of knowledge. To do so, one has first to define religion — if one can.

Sir James G. Frazer's definition, which was generally shared — that it is "a propitiation or conciliation of powers superior to man which are believed to direct and control the course of nature and of human life" — has been despatched for filing in the dustbin of history by replacements both legion and ingenious. Yet while the new verbal arrangements may rule out the supernatural, even the type that proposes "an expanded new religion based on the new materialism" makes room for a kind of divinity — for example, one that is "not truly supernatural but transnatural," growing out of ordinary nature but transcending it (Julian Huxley). Thus the poetic knowledge conveyed in Wordsworth's Immortality Ode and numberless other intimations in verse of cosmic-identifications-cum-beneficence must be nothing else or more than religious knowledge. Although this reasoning does not lead us quite back to archaic cultures, where poetry was at one with prophecy and other rituals, it dismisses all the distinctions that emerged when (as noted before) the single personage who was a poet-possessed, God-smitten, and a seer gradually split into the specialized figures of the prophet, the soothsayer, the mystagogue, and the poet as we know him.[18] We should have to shut our eyes to the outcome: to the fact and all its compelling implications that the primordial composite type, the *vates,* evolved into different persons who must use different means for achieving their ends. For a person who believes that means and end are ultimately inseparable, that the one cannot help but condition the other, the relation between poetry's knowledge and religion's knowledge is decisively settled. The road available to poetry is not a road available to religion. Nor is it necessary to belabor differences in interest and temperament. "I cannot answer for the experience of others," wrote Ruskin, "but I have never yet met with a Christian whose heart was thoroughly set upon the world to come, and so far as human judgement could pronounce, perfect and right before God, who cared about art at all."

Though poetry's knowledge (no matter how viewed) is neither trans- nor super-natural, some of its advocates, constrained to make it respect- able, try to prove it able to compete with or even exceed the knowledge of science. A critic sets out to establish "the empirical status of the work of art" (Read), a poet argues the basis for teaching poetry (MacLeish), a philosopher analyzes the "truth-value" of art (Feibleman) or art as knowl- edge (Ross). . . . With their dependence on analytic reasoning, some of the demonstrations make a curious spectacle since science itself is unable to justify its existence by analytic reasoning. While value-free, science is based on values, freedom from value-judgements being one of the first, as Eric Weil points out. And since "science and consistency are unable to justify fundamental values, and particularly themselves, as necessary," "logically, scientific thought seems to have undermined its own basis."[19] Moreover, unless the theorems of Kurt Gödel and of Alfred Tarski do not hold, the very ideal that science pursues will continue to be hopeless. As for complete objectivity, one of its most precious principles, it is now acknowledged to be unattainable even in the segment of existence to which science applies. The apologists for poetry's knowledge may lay down their arms.

The understanding that poetry brings I call by the name of "creature- knowledge" in the hope of suggesting the entirety and profundity of the reader's involvement with the All. The poem's resonances-reverberations submerge the aspects of divisiveness that qualify his ordinary thoughts and feelings. Nor can future or past, of time or of place, exist in this here-and- now. "All possible objects of the ordinary world, exterior or interior, beings, events, feelings, and actions, remaining normal as far as appearances are concerned, suddenly fall into a relationship that is indefinable but won- derfully in harmony with the modes of our general being" (Valéry).[20] For the poem as a whole and in its units is, above all, an act of uniting. And to respond by experiencing its act of uniting is to relive, for the duration and with the whole of one's being, an indefinable sense of organic creature unity such as pervaded our creature-existence when it "knew" itself part of the seamless web of creation. That a man is an alien, that divisiveness bur- dens his nights and days, that his organism is instinct with the drive toward primary unity, make his need for re-living acts of this kind more crucial than he can know. For isolate man, as he lives ever more in himself, from others, and apart from the world that contains him, creature-knowledge has become no less than a necessity for his survival.

Notes and Comments

1. This, Langer says (*Mind,* pp. 98 f.), is the second thesis of Jean Philippe's *L'image mentale (évolution et dissolution),* Paris, Alcan, 1903, p. 5. Malinowski, *Carol Gardens and Their Magic,* Indiana, 1967, vol. 2, pp. 236–237, *cf.* p. 213.

2. "They continuously and bitterly complain of the utter inadequacy of words to express their true feelings but, for all that, they glory in them; they indulge in rhetoric and never weary of trying to express the inexpressible in words. All writers on mysticism have laid stress on this point." — Gershom G. Scholem, *Major Trends in Jewish Mysticism,* Schocken, 1961, p. 15; see also pp. 58, 135. • Not every mystical experience must remain unaffecting for others: the "visions" re-presented by the creative imagination in certain poems of St. John of the Cross, Traherne, Dickinson, for example.

3. Karl Popper, *The Logic of Scientific Discovery,* London, Hutchinson & Co., Ltd., 1958, preface, cited in A. M. Taylor, *Imagination and the Growth of Science,* Schocken, 1967, p. 1. • To the examples given earlier (Chap. 2) may be added the account of composition presented by Mozart: "[M]y thoughts come in swarms and with marvelous ease. Whence and how do they come? I do not know; I have no share in it. Those that please me I hold in mind and I hum them, at least so others have told me . . . and all these morsels combine to form the whole. Then my mind kindles, if nothing interrupts me. The work grows, — I keep hearing it, and bring it out more and more clearly. . . . I then comprehend the whole at one glance; and my imagination makes me hear it, not in its parts successively as I shall come to hear it later, but, as it were, all at once (*gleich alles zusammen*)." — Paul Chabaniex, *Le Subconscient,* Paris, Alcan, p. 94, quoting *Mozart* by Jahn, vol. III, pp. 424 f. • After "Kubla Khan," the most celebrated work assigned to composition during dream may be "Il Trillo del Diavolo" by Giuseppe Tartini ("I heard [the Devil] play with consummate skill a sonata of such exquisite beauty as surpassed the boldest flights of my imagination . . ." • Jacques Hadamard, *The Psychology of Invention in the Mathematical Field,* p. 7, gives an authenticated report of the mother and sister of a prominent American mathematician, who had spent a long, futile evening over a certain problem in geometry: "During the night, [the] mother dreamed of it and began developing the solution in a loud clear voice; the sister hearing that, arose and took notes. On the following morning, she happened to have the right solution which the mother failed to know."

4. Keble's *Lectures on Poetry* were delivered in Latin in 1832–1841, published in 1844, and translated into English by E. K. Francis in 1912.

5. Bronowski in *Scientific American,* Sept. 1958, p. 63. See Conrad Aiken's "the miracle of interconnectedness" in his poem "The Crystal," *Selected Poems,* Oxford, 1961.

6. Symbols of language, in literature; and by extension, in the other arts, by their respectively different symbols.

7. Robert Frost in "Education by Poetry," *Amherst Graduates' Quarterly,* Feb. 1931. Karl Jaspers in *Von der Wahrheit,* Munich, 1947, as translated by J. P. Hodin, *Prism,* No. 1, 1962.

8. ". . . Wherefore the syllables / Reach outward from the self in an embrace / Of multi-

tudes. The poetries of speech/Are acts of thinking love. . . ." — Burnshaw, *Caged in an Animal's Mind,* p. 109.

9. Rank's sentence continues: "yes, one might also identify love with totality, just as fear, and all its negative emotions, are one with partiality." — *Will Therapy,* Knopf, 1936, p. 197.

10. The last two sentences of this paragraph are a mosaic of quotations cited earlier in *The Seamless Web* from Wordsworth, Keble, and A. C. Bradley.

11. F. W. H. Myers, "Essay on Virgil," precedes the words that I quote: "[Poetry] as a system of rhythmical and melodious effects — not indebted for their potency to their associated ideas alone — it appeals also to that mysterious, [etc.]."

12. "The rhythmic oscillation becomes the distinguishing mark of the functions of life-structures. The pulsations, the rhythmic flow of the functions of cells form the law of life. . . ." — J. C. Smuts, *Holism and Evolution,* Macmillan, 1926, p. 175.

13. Gerard Manley Hopkins, in a student paper of 1865, says the following: "The structure of poetry is that of continuous parallelism [which I should call recurrence here as he does later], ranging from the technical so-called Parallelisms of Hebrew poetry and the antiphons of Church music up to the intricacy of Greek or Italian or English verse. But parallelism is of two kinds necessarily — where the opposition is clearly marked, and where it is transitional rather or chromatic. Only the first kind, that of marked parallelism, is concerned with the structure of verse — in rhythm, the recurrence of a certain sequence of syllables, in metre, the recurrence of a certain sequence of rhythm, in alliteration, in assonance and in rhyme. Now the force of this recurrence is to beget a recurrence or parallelism answering to it in the words or thought and, speaking roughly and rather for the tendency than the invariable result, the more marked parallelism in structure whether of elaboration or of emphasis begets more marked parallelism in the words and sense. . . ." — *The Journals and Papers,* London, 1959.

14. F. E. Halliday, *Shakespeare and His Critics,* London, Gerald Duckworth & Co., 1949.

15. Valéry, "Poetry," in *The Forum,* April 1929, p. 251.

16. Collingwood, *op. cit.,* pp. 229–231 *passim.* Remy de Gourmont: "Le véritable problème du style est une question de physiologie." Kafka quotation from his *Diaries, 1910–1913.* • "Echoes" is a poor word here because of its denotation of a time interval, which would raise a question which does not affect these psychical expressions (do we blush because we are ashamed? vice versa? "The common-sense view is right, and the James-Lange theory wrong," says Collingwood). • See discussion of the unity of perception and movement in Ernest G. Schachtel, *Metamorphosis,* Basic, 1959, Chap. 9, esp. p. 213. • The quoted passages from Spire are slightly revised from the highly telescoped translation I made for Cleanth Brooks and Robert Penn Warren, *Understanding Poetry,* 3rd edition, Holt, 1960, p. 124. • "In laughter the whole body becomes, to a varying degree, an 'apparatus for expression'; archaic pleasure in movement is reactivated and is socially permissible." — Kris, *op. cit.,* p. 225. Eliot's phrase ("more primitive . . .") recalls the suggestion of F. W. H. Myers that men of poetic genius may be progenerates — may not "their perturbation mask an evolution which we or our children must traverse when they have shown the way?" — *Human Personality and Its Survival of Bodily Death,* London, Longmans, Green, 1903, vol. I, p. 56.

17. J. G. Frazer's definition is from Chapter 4, *The Golden Bough,* Macmillan, 1949.

18. Here I follow the phrasing of Huizinga in his *Homo Ludens.* I am indebted to Sir Kenneth Clark for the Ruskin quotation from *Stones of Venice,* vol. 2, Chap. 4, par. 58. Poems on religious subjects tend to be handicapped to the measure in which they evoke objects and events connected with a specific creed, in having appeal only to readers who are able to accept and believe in the referents.

19. Eric Weil, in *Daedalus,* Winter 1965, pp. 183–186 *passim.* According to Gödel's theorem, the consistency of any system cannot be proved within the system itself, yet unless it has consistency it cannot be a system. Tarski's theorem shows why there cannot be a universal description of nature in a single, closed, consistent language. • "The power of modern man is based on 'objectivity.' But look closer and you'll see that this power is possessed by objectivity in itself — and not by man himself. He is becoming the tool — or slave — of what he has discovered or evolved . . . a way of looking." — Valéry, *Idée Fixe,* Pantheon, 1965, p. 79. See also "Passion in Clear Reason," by David Krech, *The Nation,* March 28, 1966. The outcome for "complete objectivity" of the work of Werner Heisenberg and Niels Bohr requires no restating. For the hopelessness of the scientific ideal, see "The Logic of the Mind," American Association for the Advancement of Science Lecture, by J. Bronowski, *American Scientist,* Jan. 1966, p. 4.

20. Valéry, *Poésie et pensée abstraite,* Oxford 1939, p. 8. (Cf. translation in *The Art of Poetry,* Pantheon, 1958, p. 59.) Creature-knowledge, regardless of the source from which it is drawn, is not supernatural, transnatural, or divine. It is a reliving of the indefinable sense of organic creature unity at the *creature level,* not "above" or "beyond," though the rules by which human thinking organizes the brain tend to endow any such indefinable and timeless sense with the transcendental, with divinity of some sort. There is, of course, no correlation between the significance of the creature-knowledge that a person may draw in experiencing works of creative imagination and the quality of these works as art.

TOWARD THE "KNOWABLE" FROST

From *Robert Frost Himself,* copyright 1986 by Stanley Burnshaw and re-printed courtesy of George Braziller, Inc. Identifications: Alfred C. Edwards ("ACE"), senior vice-president of Henry Holt, Inc.; Kay, Mrs. Theodore Morrison; Edgar T. Rigg, president of Henry Holt, Inc.; Lawrance Thomp-son, Frost's official biographer; Wade Van Dore, author of *Wade Van Dore and Robert Frost,* Wright State University Press, 1986; Elinor, Mrs. Robert Frost.

After a busy twelve-day stay with his biographer Newdick, Frost (for the first time calling him "Dear Robert") sent him a warning word:

> I'll never forget my visit with you — what I read to you and what you said to me. The point I tried to make was that I was a very hard person to make out if I am any judge of human nature. I might easily be deceiving when most bent on telling the truth.
>
> *(December 2, 1938)*

The words differ in tone and context from those that he typically made to Thompson: "I grow curious about my soul out of sympathy for you in your quest for it" (1948); "I trust my philosophy still bothers you a little. It bothers me." (1959). Frost was aware of the problems he presented to biographers, and his private professions of badness helped no more than his words to the press — "I contain opposites" or "I'm not confused. I'm only well mixed." To dismiss such words as meaningless play would make no sense with a man deeply aware of his "moods" and their cost to himself and others. When his friend Rabbi Reichert quoted a well-known play on words from the Talmud, he quickly accepted the sting: "I'd have no trouble with the first two. It's the last, 'temper,' I have to watch":

> By these three things is a man recognized as worthy (is a person's char-acter determined): by his cup, his purse, his anger — *Koso,* Kiso, Ka-a-so. B'koso — if his wisdom is in equilibrium; *B'kiso* — if he acts with his fellow-men with integrity; *B'ka-a-so* — if he is not more hot-tempered (quick to anger) than needed.

Urging Frost to reform was far from the rabbi's intent; his friend was no normal mortal. Sidney Cox hadn't even approached the truth when he called him the "original 'ordinary' man."

It was John Ciardi who saw Frost plain:

> Robert Frost was a primal energy. There were serenities in the man as time brought them to him, but there was in him a volcano of passion that burned to his last day. . . . To be greatly of the earth earthy demands the bitter sweat and scald of first passions. That heat could erupt into cantankerousness at times, and even into the occasional meanness of which violent temper is capable. But the splutters of cantankerousness and the violences of temper were only surface bubbles on the magmatic passions of the man, part of the last traits that accompany intensity. . . .
>
> It is just that passionate intensity that must be realized before the man can be loved, mourned — and read — in his own nature. . . . His genius, wild and ardent, remains to us in his poems. It is the man we lose, a man salty and rough with the earth trace, and though towering above it, never removed from it, a man above all who could tower precisely because he was rooted in real earth.

There seemed nothing to add, yet the picture led many people to think of examples that glossed the passage above, attesting to the "more than usual" will and desires, powers and needs, of this surely "excessive man" — to his conversations that might have gone on forever: part of his hunger for people, which was balanced at the other extreme by a need to be wholly alone ("Desert me, desert me!"). His "contradictions" — mocked by hostile critics, mis-taken by others — dealt with so many received ideas as to brand him perversely rebellious despite his desire to hold close to a commonsensical center. But not to moderation — "I should hate to get stuck in the golden mean," he forewarned Thompson. Yet he knew as well as anyone else from Emerson's "Experience" that "The line he must walk is a hair's breadth," that "The wise through excess of wisdom is made a fool." Few could do better than Frost in walking the hair's-breadth line through the beckoning maze of ideas, seeking out and treasuring "the least display of mind," while never losing sight of the limited reach of human thought.

When the Unitarian Church of Martha's Vineyard asked me to speak on the poet, I named my talk "The Unknowable Frost" — not out of false modesty: the better I'd come to know him, the more I found him immense-in-complexity. The date was August 1962, long before I had read one word of *The Letters of Robert Frost to Louis Untermeyer*, of Thompson's

Selected Letters; even longer before I would go through the *Family Letters of Robert and Elinor Frost,* the *Selected Prose,* the *Interviews,* the lectures in Cook's *Robert Frost: A Living Voice.* The *Vineyard Gazette's* report — "Burnshaw Sees Robert Frost as the Most Elusive and Subtlest Poet" — was faithful to what I believed at the time — and still believe. But today I should qualify "unknowable." Would Frost approve? The reply would be no more predictable than the poet himself, who defied at times all efforts to enter his privacy but at others confessed with astounding candor "facts" he had kept from the world. The bluntest observers spoke of the man as a "bundle of contradictions"; others, using the gentler "paradoxical," threw up their hands, though the contradictory aspects might have been born out of wholly acceptable premises. For me, Frost's "baffling" behavior asks to be seen in terms of Carlyle's discussion of symbols, that "wondrous agency," because, as he said, it contains not only concealment but revelation as well.

"I have written," wrote Frost in an early note to Cox, "to keep the over curious out of the secret places of my mind both in my verse and in my letters." Thus could he chide a friend and would-be-biographer. A poem might bear the same warning: "any eye is an evil eye / That looks in onto a mood apart." On the other hand, writes Theodore Morrison, "When the mood was on him, he could spill out confidences with a recklessness the very opposite of the man who made himself a place apart and hid his tracks." Mere contradiction or a twofold need? No one was more aware of this question than Frost, in spite of his letter to Cox, for as Jarrell safely observed, "anyone who has read his *Collected Poems* and *Selected Letters* has entered some of the secret places of his mind." And as Frost himself confessed of his poems to a Dartmouth audience, on a subject he liked to avoid, "So many of them have literary criticism in them — *in* them. And yet I wouldn't admit it. I try to hide it." This was late in his last November. But the same need to be known-and-unknown had been part of his earliest book. In "Revelation" the speaker is drawn toward opposed positions, both of which he must take:

> We make ourselves a place apart
> 　Behind light words that tease and flout,
> But oh, the agitated heart
> 　Till someone really find us out.
>
> 'Tis pity if the case require
> 　(Or so we say) that in the end

> We speak the literal to inspire
> The understanding of a friend.
>
> But so with all, from babes that play
> At hide-and-seek to God afar,
> So all who hide too well away
> Must speak and tell us where they are.

The poem asks to be rightly read, with full concern for every word (lines 3, 4, 5, 6, 11, 12 in particular), and the final phrase — not "who" nor "what," but "where." Paradox or a constitutional urge toward divergent "goods" — desiderata, each ministering to a need of the total self. So in his wish for protection from being "found out" in matters too private for most people, he could say that he sometimes hoped to be misunderstood. Yet, with a very limited few, he might show a glimpse of part of himself which he yearned to conceal, as occurred in a letter to Untermeyer. Within twenty-four hours he wrote: "Please burn it. Be easy on me for what I did too emotionally and personally" — an appeal we might have expected from one for whom excessive response was the norm. A man who feared he had bared too much could also enlarge small insults into causes for rage or remark at the close of his last public performance: "It's a wonderful world . . . To hell with it."

Such incidents — except for those who, with Eliot, separate the person who suffers from the mind that creates — stand in the way of comprehending Frost's total achievement. Like others who understood its range, he viewed the prose and the verse as parts of a whole. "Most of my ideas occur in verse. But I have always had some turning up in talk that I feared I might never use because I was too lazy to write prose." Some, however, that turned up in talk were used — and not in prose. Peter Davison, who had listened to him for years, tells about one:

> He tried on the sounds of words to see if they would fit his ideas, his jokes, his turns of wit. Often you could watch him working out a poem in conversation, testing an idea in different suits of clothes. I heard him, over many months of playing with the contrast between tools and weapons, finally come up with a couplet which had been solicited by the United Nations for their Meditation Room . . . : "Nature within her inmost self divides / To trouble men with having to take sides."

Lazy though he called himself about writing prose, he "produced" four books of letters; a number of prefaces, introductions, and other works besides the *Selected Prose.* And vastly more of his "talk" than he might have suspected found its way into print: public lectures, interviews with the press, personal conversations with various friends. One of the most assiduous, Reginald Cook, found that: "The difference between Frost as poet and Frost as talker is more a matter of method than of style. In the run of his talk, I heard passages in cadences as moving as any of those in his poetry," some of which can be heard in the first of Cook's two Frost volumes. As for the lectures, many of which he recorded, they invariably "*sound* better than they read." For "the voice on the sound track, with its pauses, hesitancies, repetitions, and stresses, enlivens the talk and evokes a remarkable presence."

He had moved far from the poet of 1909 who, after painful trials, learned to lessen his fear of facing an audience — filling his shoes with pebbles, dousing the back of his neck with ice-cold water. Biographers need not say why a man driven to writing poems can also be husband, father, teacher, farmer; but how explain the "remarkable Frostian presence," described by Cook, who, when asked to recite a poem to a group in Derry in 1906, had to implore a friend to read in his place? The bare facts of a life cannot give the answer as they follow from birth the body's genetic uniqueness — a uniqueness making for differences in development, since no organism long responds with the full capacities with which it was born. From its earliest moment, some are inhibited, some diminished, others lost in the course of its meeting events — the accidents and effects of its encounters. The organism responds with the functional remnant of all it at first possessed; and as it learns and grows and changes, makes its unforeseeable ways of responding-behaving, drawing on powers and weaknesses that outer events may lead, at best, into seeming self-transcendence.

As early as his eighteenth year Frost confessed that he found even in his failures all the promise he needed "to justify the astonishing magnitude of [his] ambitions." "Into My Own," the first poem of *A Boy's Will,* offered a hidden answer — "They would not find me changed from him they knew — / Only more sure of all I thought was true." A manifesto of fixity? — if wrongly taken. "One of the greatest changes my nature has undergone is of record in To Earthward," he professed to DeVoto, "and indeed elsewhere for the discerning." Of the last words of "Into My Own" he explained in 1959, "The new thing with me has always included the old. Those lines are really about loyalty." Loyalty? — to what he knew that he was, which the world would never learn? Biographers who searched or pried would be thrown off track, but he might have guessed, in spite of his willed concealments, that all his "talk, mythologizing, or lies" would fail IF one could finally know how to read his writings: to "discern" the poems and the prose. A crucial, decisive IF. Yet a twentieth-century John Keble whose skill as perceiver matched his insight as critic might be able to "see" the work for what it must be: "unconscious autobiography."[1] Not, of course, of the total person: part of the life, parts of the self which lie "too deep for tears" never might find their words. Yet a man whose work seemed to ask to be read biographically promised more than enough: the "subtlest and most elusive poet" might, with lucky discerning, prove to be, to some degree, knowable.

Frost had been writing poems for twenty-three years before he gained recognition. Sudden fame awaited and, despite the vicissitudes of taste, it seemed to grow wider. Much as the public's praise helped his faith in himself, no one's approval meant so much to him as Elinor's. Yet this was only one of her contributions which, when added together, formed so great a part of his life that to *know* Frost is impossible unless one knows something of Elinor. Comments by certain biographers offers us glimpses: striking, candid, for the most part brief, limited by times and places of meeting — a "vital part of his picture . . . inscrutable in many ways, shy" and "untamed, and fiercely watchful" (John Holmes).

All who saw her speak of her physical presence — her fine head, with its coiled braids and classic Puritan features, an "arresting New England beauty purified . . . into an almost desperate calm" (Sergeant's words, much like my own impression), to which she adds: "a hint of melancholy and somber pessimism." Part of the time. Not always — even after the grief over Marjorie's death. Sitting with both Frosts in The Gulley kitchen, Reginald Cook and his wife chatted at ease, the poet in the corner, his chair tilted back, his wife close by. "Mrs. Frost, an animated talker, had as pleasant a voice as I have ever listened to, and her warm, friendly smile quickly overcame any constraint we might have felt." Henry Dierkes' account of a luncheon visit adds another dimension: "Mrs. Frost had probably become accustomed to sitting in the shade of her illustrious husband, but when the conversation turned to poetry she entered into it and spoke with a confident authority." — phrases that would have seemed quite just to Van Dore, who, after years as part of her household, offered a two-word summary: "sweet-severe."

---

1. M. H. Abrams, *The Mirror and the Lamp,* Oxford, 1953, pp. 259 ff., quoting George Lyman Kittredge as well: "Unquestionably the man is there, the real Shakespeare is somehow latent in his plays. . . ."

I had a good number of hours alone with her, because Rob almost never got up before 10, while she usually was about by 7 or half-past. Many times just the two of us had breakfast together. Often she was the first in the kitchen. I would find her quietly sitting smoking a cigarette — a habit she had picked up from the wives of their friends in England. I doubt she smoked over two a day through 1925–35 when I was with her the most. Very seldom would she be reading a newspaper or book. From what she called her "sitting room" she didn't need to look out a window. She just sat there — one-third dreaming and two-thirds thinking of or planning for her family. That seemed to be her role. When it looked as if he might succeed as a poet, I'm sure she wanted that to happen — without having faith that it would. Constitutionally she had become a pessimist, but she didn't enjoy suffering or sadness. . . . Elinor felt that she truly owned her Rob and she wasn't keen about sharing him with anybody. When I describe her as "sweet-severe" I mean her overall kind, mild manner. . . . She had piercing black eyes. One liked just to look at her.

Through their first six months at Derry she could get along without curtains, even an indoor pump; but Frost at times had to be "forced" into working. "Rob!" — he was deep in talk with Sidney Cox — "It's after nine o'clock, and you *must* go milk. It's not good for her to wait so long." Frost preferred to delay the chores; Elinor hated housework. Most of the time they could take each other's ways without apology.

Not until 1964, in *Selected Letters,* could we gain a sense of another Elinor Frost. And eight additional years would pass before the *Family Letters of Robert and Elinor Frost* provided the nearest thing we have to a full-length portrait of a thoughtful, sensitive woman who lived for the present, her family, her home. To the poet's large correspondence her fifty letters added acute variations, counterpointing his judgments. Their views often collided; she was scarcely less opinionated than Frost. As Arnold Grade remarks, the "influence of this firm, intuitive, highly intelligent woman who brought order and discipline to the farmhouse of art was enormous" — not only in family matters and in shaping the work of the writer but, most important of all, in their man-woman relationship. "F is as considerate of Mrs. F," reads one of Newdick's research entries of 1935, "as a lover in his teens. And her eyes shine from their depths as they rest on him." Some forty years later, Poirier would declare that Frost was not only "a great poet of marriage, but maybe the greatest since Milton, and of the sexuality that goes with it." And in several important poems, he explores the subject — which others approach with unwarranted confidence, usually through "The Subverted Flower," with its "clear" biographical basis, its long-delayed publication, the purported tension between the maiden's reserve and the male's animal wildness. More to the point is the implication of Poirier's earlier statements, remarking upon: "The magnificent clarity of his love for his wife which is full of a critical respect for her individual separateness." I do not know of any body of English verse that brings to its treatment of women the perceptiveness, the compassion, the respect, the attributive wisdom that we find in Frost's.

Nor do I know of a poet so eager to give the woman who shared his life all he considered her due: "She has been the unspoken half of everything I ever wrote, and both halves of many a thing from My November Guest down to the last stanzas of Two Tramps in Mud Time." The words hold true of more than his writings. It was Elinor who went alone to speak to Grandfather Frost when her household lay in crisis, winning his promise to help them start their life anew at the farm in Derry. It was she who wrote to every absent child (two or three times weekly); who tried to protect Frost before, during, and after his frequent attacks of illness. Months after Marjorie's death, though hardly able to "go on living from day to day," she saw no choice: "Robert depends on me, and the other children do to some extent," she confessed to a friend. "I *must* keep up." Not only was she able to "keep up"; she displayed surprising resilience. She took delight in Marjorie's "bright, forward, exceptionally merry" daughter. She relished the prospect of choosing a permanent house for their Florida winters. She was still the woman who lived for her home, for her family, for the present.

And not, to be sure, for any posthumous glory. The gifted high-school girl whose poems and essays praised "the ideal . . . as surely the best of life" had long since disappeared. It might have been years before the death of their first-born in July 1900 with its shattering grief that kept her speechless for days. Frost, unable to bear the torment, burst into self-accusations. It was God — God's wrath come down on his head for failing to summon a doctor in time to save the young life. Elinor, when she finally spoke, lashed at his wild self-punishing talk and his "senseless belief" in a God concerned with human affairs. Living was hateful; the world too evil to bear — yet bear it she must, with a second child in her arms. There were four more offspring to come — three would survive.

In his letter to Untermeyer of March 21, 1920, Frost doesn't explain the cause of his sudden announcement: "Elinor has just come out flat-footed against God." To his playful countering arguments — "How about a Shelleyan principal or spirit coeternal with the rock of creation" — she replied bluntly, "Nonsense and you know it's nonsense, Rob Frost, only you're afraid you'll have bad luck or lose your standing in the community if you speak your mind." But in fact his "mind" was not what her words assumed, nor what he wished it might be. Their thoughts on faith would keep moving farther apart till the rift would become unbridgeable. And yet, if as Frost told Lesley after Elinor's death, she had "colored" his thought "from the first," through the rest of his days her atheistic certainty never quite left his mind despite his determined self-dedication to faith and belief.

In the same letter (March 1, 1939), he goes on to remark: "She dominated my art with the power and character of her nature" — a phrase implying very much more than it states. That she stopped him from publishing "The Subverted Flower," has long been known (were there others also?). That he counted on her to judge his poems, we learn from a letter he sent with her list of titles to Untermeyer, who was making a new anthology. "Domination" of a different sort comes to light in another intimate letter: "Pretty nearly every one of my poems will be found to be about her if rightly read . . . they were as much about her as she liked and permitted them to be." With a number of friends he gladly spoke of her gifts as a critical reader and how they affected his work. She "could hurt him" by saying what she wouldn't let pass in a poem, he had told John Holmes. He explained to Mertins: "an imperfect line, or flash of beauty spoiled, hurt her worse, both physically and spiritually, than I ever knew. This was the only goad I needed. . . ."

"Domination" welcomed and prized — but not always: the "Roosevelt" poems, for example ("To a Thinker," "Build Soil"), that she pleaded with him to withhold. * * To which must be added other species of fear. Frost tried hard to make light of the fact that as early as 1917 she had grown "especially wary of honors that derogate from" what he mockingly called "the poetic life she fancies us living." She was no less wary of "reputation, that bubble" — what if Newdick, his early biographer, were left one day with the sudden eclipse of "his" poet? There was also the deep, half-hidden fear of the plight of Frost as triumphant public performer for the harm it might do to the poet-artist.

In the letter that said she was "wary of honors" Frost added: "She wouldn't lift a hand or have me lift a hand to increase my reputation or even save it." Had she changed? Were the words untrue? After *A Boy's Will* appeared, she was "somewhat disappointed": The reviewers should have done better, for how could "they help seeing how exquisitely beautiful" were some of the poems. Moreover, Yeats had said that the book was "the best poetry written in America for a long time. If only he would say so publicly," she added. Some twenty years later she made no attempt to hide her elation at Frost's success: "It is certainly *grand* about the Book-of-the-Month Club" choice of *A Further Range,* she wrote to the publisher's wife. She probably felt the same of "The Critics and Robert Frost," a paean by DeVoto in the *Saturday Review,* based on Holt's recently issued *Recognition of Robert Frost.* She read it aloud — "I sat and let Elinor pour it over me," he said in a letter of thanks to the author on December 29, 1937. Within three months the one about whom "pretty nearly every one of [his] poems had been written" died. For more than forty-five years the finest gift he could make was a poem that fulfilled her hope. There were more than a few. When, after *Mountain Interval* appeared, the widow of an Amherst colleague, assisting her in preparing sandwiches, asked, "Don't you think it's beautiful yourself?" Elinor dropped her knife and clasped her hands. "Beautiful," she said in a voice close to tears. The place and time was Franconia, 1917, twenty-five years since the poems that each had been writing brought them together.

Not long after, their quietsome world of two had become a house of childhood bustling with four young lives. By now, however, the special delights of the early years — that readers can live in *New Hampshire's Child: The Derry Journals of Lesley Frost* and the book of *Family Letters* — had long since passed. Gone, the Christmas parties or made-up stories or tales about elves and fairies; no more morning winters piled with snow too high for walking which they watched their father shovel clear from the house to the barn to the mailbox, from the pump to the maple they christened the woodpecker tree. As Frost recalled, rather wistfully in his aged years, "I played with them more than most fathers," showing them how to read the tracks of foxes, rabbits, and squirrels, of chickadees and partridges, asking their help each spring with the garden beds and the plants they discovered together, tramping the woods. Elinor spoke to an Amherst friend of a Christmas Eve when Rob was carving small wooden animals for the children. One was a pig for Carol, but at 2:00 A.M. he decided it needed a pen. He sat there, whittling till daylight, and "I sat there with him. I went to sleep as I rocked and woke at dawn. . . . Rob had just finished the pen!"

The cherishing hope of the early years gave way to worry and fear for three of the children. Carol, now in his sixteenth year, "has absolutely no one to play with," his mother wrote to Lesley. "He just does nothing a good deal of the time and that drives me almost distracted." Irma's actions at times foreshadowed her problems, alienating Frost from a former student for a fancied sexual advance. "Take the way with her that will keep the peace," Frost urged Lesley a few years later. "Her strictness is part of her nature. Don't try to make her over. Some of it she will outgrow, but not all." Marjorie, the youngest, frailest, lonely now and discouraged, was intermittently plagued by illness, overwork, and "nervous prostration." Her parents did all they could, but they strained to do more, whatever the cost. Elinor's death saved her the grief over Carol's suicide and Irma's fate. Frost had striven to help his son by reinforcing his self-assurance in writing, going so far as to call his "Stratton" poem "powerful and splendid," "written with a man's vigor," "richly attractive," "with so much solid truth, such condensation and intense feeling." Two months later: "That was another good poem. . . . Your way is certainly your own." And in 1935, the highest praise he could give: Your "apple-crating poem . . . has a great deal more of the feeling of real work and country business than anything of mine could ever pretend or hope to have." Nothing availed. As he wrote to Untermeyer after the suicide, "I tried many ways and every single one of them was wrong. Some thing in me is still asking for the chance to try one more."

What would become of Irma? He had shielded her from Marjorie's death: "Irma is in no condition to face the terribleness" of the news, he had warned her brother. Twelve years later, John Cone, her husband, wrote to her father to explain why, after close to two decades, he felt forced to end the marriage. Frost wasn't greatly surprised to learn of his daughter's jealousy, prudery, of her frequent hysterical outbursts, of her fears of being persecuted. Once the divorce was final, she was quite unable to try to fare for herself. Frost sought to find a suitable place where she could live. After a number of failed attempts, he knew she would have to be placed in an institution. On the day of her formal commitment in Concord, New Hampshire, he strove to make her see that her stay would help her recover. "Get out of here," she replied. On the day after Christmas, 1947, he wrote to his friend Margaret Bartlett of "the sad ending to Irma's story. She is at once too insane to be out of an institution and too sane to be in one. So she suffers the sense of imprisonment where she is."

He was used to tragedy; by now he had gained a composure and strength that none of his intimates would have dreamed possible after Elinor's death. No one could talk again, as Hervey Allen had done in 1938, of a powerful engine "wracking itself to pieces from running wild after the loss of its flywheel." Frost had resolved to survive. Four months after Elinor's loss he "refused," he wrote to a friend, "to be bowed down as much as she was by other deaths," though the forms this refusal was taking appalled both friends and foes. Then the hoped-for change began: Unter-meyer and others could see: "By December the worst of his long period of blackness was over." His friends the Morrisons helped in essential ways, with Kay's agreeing to serve as his secretary-manager. Installed in a Boston apartment, the man who throughout his marriage had lived in thirty-five houses or more was about to be settled down and "watched" for the rest of his days. In 1939 he bought the Homer Noble Farm in Ripton, Vermont, for the summers; in 1940, Pencil Pines in Florida, for the winters; in early 1941, the house at 35 Brewster Street for the other months of the year. A "diastolic-systolic motion," Sergeant had termed the decades ahead, taking him forth to read, teach, talk, take part in the world at large, then return to one of his homes. More and more friends were replacing his family losses. There were also more and more writings, lectures, interviews; good-will missions (Brazil, Britain, Israel, Greece); honors, medals, degrees, awards, birthday dinners; calls from posts of political power, topped by the invita-tion to read the Inaugural poem and President Kennedy's bid for a special mission to Russia. The older he grew, the more commitments he welcomed and kept, till the morning after his final public speech and the doctor's hospital orders he couldn't refuse.

His final public speech betokened a basic change. "The poem," he now made clear, was "the song itself," and poetry stood above the world of "con-tentions" — politics, education, and even above religion. In 1956, in three consecutive talks in New York, he had made some specifications:

> I reached a point lately where I could finally divide life into three parts, the three greatest things in human thought: Religion, Science, Gossip. At the top, the exaltation part, they are close together. . . .

> Science . . . first for glory, not for use. The top is discovery for discovery's sake.

> Gossip. I venture to say that the greatest of the three is Gossip. It may be defined as our guessing at each other in journalism, novels, poetry in that order. Gossip exalts in poetry. Poetry is the top of our guessing at each other. . . . The beauty of gossip is that it is the whole of our daily life. It has flashes of insight. The height of imagination is there.

On a much more telling note in a talk two decades before, he spoke of his years of writing after "My Butterfly" (1894), "the first poem that I got any personal satisfaction from. Twenty years of it when I was out and in and didn't know what I was and didn't know what I wanted, nor what the feeling was that I wanted to satisfy. Not having anything in mind, no formula, just seeking, questing."

The last two words can serve for the years that followed, for the poet *knew* that "seeking, questing" goaded him on till the end. Do these words offer the clue to the knowable Frost? All his days and nights were marked by the quest. It reflected itself as he strove with the great "three things in human life," clearly in the words he wrote and uttered, but vividly also at times in his acts — public or privately known — in the things he feared, dared, risked, played with, loved, hated, believed, and hoped he would finally know.

"Writing, teaching a little, and farming. The three strands of my life," he told a reporter in 1960. Teaching "a little"? If his interviewer had scanned his career, he would have smiled: "Educating" for Frost had been second only to writing. "I taught every grade" — kindergarten, at home, school, college, he said to me once, smiling, with bittersweet pride, "And I like the academic in my way . . . and I know, up to a certain point, that the academic likes me." He didn't care to stop to say why, nor did I ask, though the academic seemed less than half of what he had been as a teacher. "It takes all sorts of in- and outdoor schooling," from a couplet of *In the Clearing,* rose to my mind. I was now in the midst of the second ("To get adapted to my kind of fooling."); the first, I hoped, would some-day come to light through those of his colleagues who might be helped by indoor students who had seen him perform.

Meanwhile we have data enough to follow his teaching career after he gave up study at Dartmouth (in 1892, before completing his first semester) to help in his mother's private school in Methuen, Massachusetts. From there he taught in a district school in Salem, New Hampshire; then, after marriage, joined his mother again. He became a special student at Harvard in September 1897; he left in March 1899. Not until nine years later did he finally give up poultry-raising and farming to earn his living by teaching:[2]

2. 1906–1911: Pinkerton Academy, Derry, New Hampshire.
    1911–1912: New Hampshire State Normal School, Plymouth.
    1917–1920: Amherst College.
    1921–1923: University of Michigan (Poet-in-Residence, then Fellow in Creative Arts).
    1923–1925: Amherst College (Professor of English).
    1925–1926: University of Michigan (Fellow in Letters).
    1926–1938: Amherst College (under various arrangements, including his Charles Eliot Norton Lectures at Harvard 1936).

He planned, he said, to write a book about teaching and schools. He never did. But words by Frost (and by others on Frost) abound on the subject. It would be no large undertaking to gather enough for an essay or at least a full report of his sayings. For example:

> [T]he only education worth anything is self-education. All the rest consists of schoolwork, textbooks, training, aids to help distinguish one fact from another without helping us to tell true values from false. But that doesn't mean I don't believe in people learning as well as learned people. I'm for educated humanity all the time — except in an undiscriminating way. All men are born free and equal — free at least in their right to be different. Some people want to mix the weak and the strong of mankind; they want to homogenize society everywhere. . . . I want the cream to rise.

> I ought to have been poet enough to stay away [instead of returning to Amherst in 1923]. But I was too much of a philosopher to resist the temptation to go back and help show the world the difference between the right kind of liberal college and the wrong kind.

> I never taught long enough to carry anything out. I was a symbolical teacher. After giving a class a chance to say if there was anything in the bunch of themes on my desk they wanted to keep and satisfied myself there wasnt I threw them unread into the waste basket while the class looked on. If they didn't care enough for the themes to keep them I didnt care enough for the themes to read them. I wasnt going to be a perfunctory corrector of perfunctory writing.

> I have long thought that our high schools should be improved. Nobody should [enter them] without examinations — no aptitude tests, but on reading, 'riting, and 'rithmetic. . . . A lot of people [want] to harden up our education or speed it up. I am interested in toning it up, at the high school level. . . . establishing named chairs . . . to create tenure and prestige for teachers.

"I'm going to leave you with the motto: 'Don't work, worry!'" he said to his Harvard class before a fortnight's absence. He had hoped they would understand the point of his thought: "worry about ideas." But as often happened, he expected too much.

Pronouncing himself, with a twinkle, "the greatest living expert" on

---

1939–1940: Harvard University (Ralph Waldo Emerson Fellow in Poetry).
1943–1949: Dartmouth College (Ticknor Fellow in Humanities).
1949– :　Amherst College (Simpson Lecturer in Literature).

education, he could also speak with gratitude of the institutions that have been "so patient with my educational heresies." As to how extreme these heresies were, we have various comments from first-hand observers: scattered in books most of which can be found in libraries only. Many are well worth reading — for example, a Normal Training School student's remarks as of 1911; Dorothy Tyler's "Robert Frost in Michigan"; Gardner Jackson's "Reminiscences"; recollections by several Dartmouth colleagues in the *Southern Review*, October 1966; Frost's own "Education by Poetry" in *Selected Prose*. * *

Many ideas important to Frost came out in his conversations. Did he hit his stride at midnight? Some of his listeners thought so, but not all — witness his endless hours of daylight talk at the Phillips Academy and "The Master Conversationalist at Work" in Ciardi's report of his 1959 visit to Pencil Pines.

"In twenty years I have walked many miles with Frost — always in conversation, entertaining ideas" — I quote Hyde Cox from *You Come Too*. "We all speak of having ideas but entertaining them is an art. . . . It is almost the heart of education." For hearers, of course; but also for Frost himself — "self-education" as noted by numerous listeners, trying out sounds of words, turns of wit, notions, testing, viewing-reviewing long-past moments for possible hidden meanings.

How many people alive today were lucky enough to have heard "the very best talker I've ever known" — the usual phrase one meets in accounts of his listeners. To help re-create the experience for those to whom it smacks of the mythical, more is required than a list of topics combined with attempts at describing bodily gestures, tones of voice, glances, twinkles, and so on. Frost had spoken of in- and outdoor schooling as "education by presence." The presence is gone, yet a sense of what it could mean for a listener can in part be recaptured with the help of people with whom he had often conversed. Reginald Cook, for example, who had talked with Frost intimately over a period of forty years:

> His talk-spiels were legendary; marathon nocturnal sessions, continuing from two to four or five hours. He could talk anywhere, anytime, and with the greatest of ease. Yet the length of the talks was hardly more remarkable than the range. Once he launched into a diatribe on doctoral dissertations, shifted key to the reading of poetry, alluded to prize fighting, and reacted vigorously to the current popularity of the anti-Keynesian Adam Smith. Another time — October 4, 1952 — he covered the spectrum, talking about baseball, the presidential campaign, educa-

tion, poetry, language, the Greeks (notably Herodotus), Shakespeare's songs, Russia, slavery, loyalty, and writers (Jesse Stuart, Robert Penn Warren, Ernest Hemingway, William Faulkner, and Erle Stanley Gardner). After a formal lecture, he unwound in the house of a stranger, talking about witches, politics, great Americans, and words with three n's in them, like *noumenon*. Following another formal lecture and reception, he talked from eleven o'clock until three in the morning, discussing en route Morgan horses, psychiatry, Catullus, politics, Tung oil, spun-glass fishing rods, philosophy (categorizing philosophers into two groups — the annalists and the analysts), education, Generals Lee and Grant, the Imagists F. S. Flint, T. E. Hulme, and Ezra Pound. He wrapped up the nocturnal session, expressing a preference for Immanual Swedenborg's "Heaven" to Dante's "Hell."

Frost's talk is not pyrotechnic or febrile. On the contrary, it is social, genial, and expansive. There are few unintended pauses in it. One thought starts another, and he rambles on while the deep-set blue eyes, the blunt nose, the expressive lips, the formidable chin and the shock of white hair all help to pin a point down. . . . He always seems at random like a blue-bottle fly on a hot midsummer day. . . . His voice is medium in pitch, rather low than high, but not gutteral; and it registers sensitively shades of feeling. . . . Just as the charm of the man comes to focus in his talk, so the total force of the poet comes to focus in the resonant voice . . . readily able to reproduce the brogue of Irish speech tones, or nuances in colloquial idiom and the accent of a countryman, or blank-verse paragraphs of Miltonic eloquence. . . . In Frost's poetry the meaning is partly in the tone. Similarly, in his conversation one has to hear the voice intonate the thought to catch the total meaning.

The aim of all education, for Frost, was self-cultivation, as everyone knew who read "Build Soil," his Phi Beta Kappa poem that created a storm in the thirties. Twenty years later his solicitude for "the individual" above "the group" was, if anything, firmer: "The best things and the best people rise out of their separateness." He took pleasure in telling the tale of the chunk of iron from Sweden and the poem the United Nations asked him to write for it — and then rejected. He also spoke of his welfare-minded granddaughter Robin's challenge: "Don't you believe it's important to do good?" "It was more important," he said, "to do well." Yet he didn't quote her reply, nor say how he answered her, if he had — a clash of wills that the advocate of "the individual" ought to have relished and doubtless did, at least in part, knowing the risks involved: "the individual," the core problem of all societies, old and new.

Whitman, democracy's dauntless advocate, saw and stated it plain: "the big problem, the only problem, the sum of them all — adjusting the individual to the mass." But the dangerousness implicit in Whitman's fear, for Frost was a challenging virtue. "Democracy means all the risks taken — conflict of opinion, conflict of personality, eccentricity. The tone is freedom to the point of destruction." These words announced in his eighty-sixth year almost repeat a notebook jotting of unknown date: "A nation should be just as full of conflict as it can contain, physically, mentally, financially. But of course *it must contain*. The strain must be short of the bursting point — *just short*" (italics added). And indeed, as he told a reporter: "I like all this uncertainty that we live in, between being members and individuals." Although he was deeply opposed to "everything and everybody that want people to rely on somebody else," he declared that for reasons of "the public health, / So that the poor won't steal by stealth / We now and then should take an equalizer." The seeming contrariety is one of a number encountered before, at the time when Frost was attacked as a rockbound New England conservative. He was fully aware of having been "too much one way and then too much another through fifty years of politics," as he told a Bread Loaf audience in 1961. The poem that he read — "Take Something Like a Star" — was one in which he "hated" himself for his shifting about. "Maybe I'm one who never makes up his mind," he had said to a friend a decade before.

"Maybe?" It was one of his needs and necessary strengths in his life-long seeking, questing: Keep open to change. "It's well to have all kinds of feelings; for this is all kinds of a world," he'd told Sidney Cox. It is even better, he came to believe, to be able to welcome growth and change and to let it be known to friends and to "the discerning." His statements about poetry and the "great issues were continually growing and changing," to quote from the introduction to *Selected Prose*. "Great issues were among the things he loved most and lived with most intimately." They were one of his long addictions — trying out new ideas, playing with them, hoping to learn by stating what he believed at the time and might find to be less than the waiting truth it seemed. If seeking, questing led him to self-contradiction, it was part of the costly process of self-education.

No more striking example is known than the letter he wrote to the Socialist leader, Norman Thomas, but did not survive to complete. "I yield to no one in my admiration for the kind of liberal you have been, you and Henry Wallace." The letter explains what he hoped to tell Khrushchev in person:

. . . we shouldn't come to blows till we were sure there was a big issue remaining between us, of his kind of democracy versus our kind of democracy, approximating each other as they are, his by easing downward toward socialism from the severity of its original ideals, ours by straining upward toward socialism through various phases of welfare state-ism. I said the arena is set between us for a rivalry of perhaps a hundred years. Let's hope we can take it out in sports, science, art, business and politics before ever we have to take it out in the bloody politics of war. It was all magnanimity — Aristotle's great word.

(September 28, 1962)

Magnanimity? An odd word for Frost to use, his critics would say. Jealousy, rather; competitiveness, campaigning — noisome parts of the poet's career which even his admirers conceded. Few had attempted to look at the under-surface. They could turn the other way, pretend that they hadn't heard him say that "jealousy is a passion I approve of and attribute to angels." Or when he explained to an Oberlin audience in 1937: "What is jealousy? It's the claim of the object on the lover. The claim of God that you should be true to Him, and so true to yourself. The word still lives for me." Twenty-two years before he had hoped to avoid "the odium of seeming jealous of anybody," but by then he had entered the fray. As the author of *A Boy's Will* and *North of Boston,* he was part of the writers' world. Could he close his eyes to the rivalries, the politics, the thirst for success all about him? "I wonder," he asked his friend the poet Alfred Kreymborg after his third book appeared, "do you feel as badly as I do when some other fellow does a good piece of work?" Kreymborg peered at me sadly as I listened many years later: "Frost had hopes for *Mountain Interval* but it failed badly, badly. The reviews simply missed the wonderful poems. He was hurt and of course he was jealous — but worse: *worried* — worried about the future." He shrugged. "Even now, with all his successes, he's secretly worried. I could tell from something he said and the way he said it — afraid the bubble might burst."

In his 1960 interview for the *Paris Review* a seemingly different Frost let himself go on the theme of performance. "The whole thing is performance and prowess and feats of association." But for Poirier, the most revealing statement of all was "Scoring. You've got to score. They say not, but you've got to score — in all the realms." Few people possessed the gift to hear what Poirier heard in those seventeen words:

Frost even in his mid-eighties still had to remind himself that he was tough enough to live. Of course no man really tough would be so sententious about it, or so lovably anxious to dispel the guilt of having had to be so fiercely competitive in order to live at all.

The words appeared in a double review of *Robert Frost: The Early Years* and *The Letters of Robert Frost to Louis Untermeyer* (206). In discussing the second, Poirier points to some of the ways in which Frost resorted to playfulness "to keep his image from solidifying" even for himself:

> He mocks his own foxiness . . . and describes nearly all his meetings and relationships with rival poets as if he were a kind of shrewd buffoon. . . . Being at once fiercely ambitious and genuinely contemptuous of literary politics, Frost was at times close to nervous collapse "from the strain of competition." His efforts at creating a benign public image were motivated less by cynicism than by the emotional necessity of escaping the wear and tear of such competition by seeming to be above it.

Escape was not always possible; the wear and tear could be wounding enough to force him to break a commitment. But most of the time he could gather strength for a challenge. "The object in life is to win — win a game, win the play of a poem," one of his notebooks reads. "Obviously," he might have added, for how could competing be wrong? It was Nature itself. "I divide my talks," he explained to Cook, "into two parts, both in this world. First, there is the basic animal faith which leads me to believe in playing to win. And, secondly, at a higher level, there is a lift or crest where . . . you hope you don't make too much of a fool of yourself in the eyes of *It*."

In the eyes of the less exalted, the hope sometimes failed, sometimes succeeded. Four years after Eliot's speech in praise of Frost at the Books Across the Sea dinner in London and Frost's graciously thankful reply, he could still cry out in resentment: "Did any government ever send Eliot anywhere?" And yet he wholly approved the inclusion of "rival poets" in the Untermeyer anthologies; and he fostered the series of Michigan poetry readings in 1922 by Padraic Colum, Amy Lowell, Vachel Lindsay, and that "most artificial and studied ruffian" Carl Sandburg. He publicly lauded the work of Robinson, Ransom, and Moore. Although he "hated" Masters, he couldn't "say for certain" that he didn't "like Spoon River. I believe I do like it in a way." In 1951, when Sandburg won the Pulitzer Prize, Frost quickly agreed he deserved it. The "fiercely competitive" Frost who maintained: "There's only room for one at the top of the steeple" bowed to Yeats as "undoubtedly the man of the last twenty years in English poetry." And so on and so on. . . .

There would be no point in trying to reconcile the Elinor Frost of her husband's letter of 1917 ("She wouldn't lift a hand or have me lift a hand to increase my reputation") with the woman who "only" hoped that Yeats, having praised the poems of Frost as "the best written in America for a long time," "would say so publicly." Frost's concern with gaining readers is vividly clear in the published letters, which also reveal an Elinor Frost striving for and taking delight in the poet's success. No less anxious than Whitman to be read by a very large audience, he had made a start even while living in England, *vide* his letters to Sidney Cox and to John Bartlett. Pound, the master promoter, and Pound's behavior, good and bad, had "told" him what could be done, but Pound never advised him how or where to begin.

On February 22, 1915, all six Frosts and Edward Thomas' son Mervyn landed at Ellis Island. An unfamiliar magazine, *The New Republic,* caught his eye on a newsstand as he sauntered about 42nd Street near Grand Central Station. To his great surprise, the contents page listed a review of *North of Boston* by Amy Lowell, one of the movers and shakers of the famed Imagist movement. He hastened to read her response. Some of her reservations struck him as wrong; others as almost absurd; yet her review was impressively long and her verdict highly favorable — "certainly one of the most American volumes of poetry which has appeared for some time." A happy sendoff for Elinor and the children, who were going by train to New Hampshire as paying guests at the home of friends in Bethlehem! Frost would remain in New York. He had Mervyn's immigration problems to solve. And how could he possibly leave without paying a call to his new-found publisher, Henry Holt?

The call was the first of numberless visits Frost would make in the course of his long career. Greeting him with surprising warmth, his editor Alfred Harcourt, chief of the Trade division, told him at once how *North of Boston* came to be published: it was Mrs. Holt's discovery. He also gave him a check from *The New Republic:* $40 for "The Death of the Hired Man," published some weeks before. It would be worthwhile, Harcourt went on, for Frost to make the acquaintance of various people who might prove of help in the future. Frost agreed to follow his mentor's counsel — to attend an open meeting of the Poetry Society, to lunch with the staff of *The New Republic:* Walter Lippmann, Herbert Croly, Francis Hackett, Philip Littell. Neither Harcourt nor Frost, however, had been aware that the poet's work had been sharply attacked at a Poetry Society meeting two months before, or that Frost's conservative views would be quite at odds with those of his luncheon hosts.

What mattered most was the tie he had made with Harcourt and the latter's concern with arranging "helpful relationships." With this in mind, he decided to try the *Atlantic Monthly,* though every *North of Boston* poem he had sent them always came back with: "We are sorry we have no place in the *Atlantic Monthly* for your vigorous verse." Why, Frost started to reason as he fidgeted in the reception room, would the editor, Ellery Sedgwick, one of Boston's cultural greats, put aside his tasks to talk with a man whose work he rejected? But before he could think of leaving, Sedgwick suddenly stood in front of him, holding out both hands in an effusive greeting. Amy Lowell, he said, had told him of *North of Boston,* but would the poet himself consent to tell him the story now? . . . Before the visit was over, Frost agreed to join the dinner party that night at the editor's home and to stay as his overnight guest. A round of literary meetings followed — at the Boston Authors' Club, with Nathan Haskell Dole, Sylvester Baxter, and William Stanley Braithwaite of the Boston *Transcript.* "If you want to see what happened in Boston," Frost wrote from Bethlehem to Sidney Cox, "look me up in the Boston Herald for Tuesday March 9 under the heading Talk of the Town." Baxter had written: "The homecoming of Robert Frost has been the sensation of the day. . . ."

Alfred Harcourt's advice had led not only to "helpful results" but also to troubles. Amy Lowell and Frost — in spite of their effort to bear with each other's difference in taste, theory, and manner of person — never arrived at a sympathetic relationship. In William Stanley Braithwaite, the magazine-verse anthologist, Frost hoped to find a poetry critic unreserved in support and in admiration. Pritchard's summary words on Frost's behavior are a model of kind restraint: ". . . in the case of Braithwaite and Lowell there was a large disparity between the way he dealt with them publicly and what he said about them in the privacy of letters to people he trusted." The lines one reads in the letters, although they form a dismaying picture, call for the reader's awareness that Frost knew that his earning abilities depended on his reputation as poet, reciter, and "presence." And not with "the critical few" alone. On the contrary: "to arrive where I can stand on my legs as a poet and nothing else I must get outside that circle to the general reader who buys books in their thousands." This was his goal, he explained to Bartlett from Beaconsfield in November 1913. He might not succeed but he wanted his friend to realize how much he "believed in doing it — dont you doubt me there. I want to be a poet for all sorts and kinds. . . . I want to reach out."

Frost, of course, succeeded, helped by readers, editors, teachers, believers, reporters, by reviewers and critics, none more zealous than Untermeyer, from the time he discovered "The Fear" and "A Hundred Collars" (December 1913). Frost welcomed and sometimes asked support in the face of attacks, but alongside Whitman and Melville, he makes a most unimpressive sight as a self-promoter.[3]

However amateurish Frost as a self-promoter may appear today, as a "poet-speaker-performer" he was unsurpassed. From years of barding around, he learned that not only "everything written is as good as it is dramatic" but also everything said in a hall of listeners. "I have myself all in a strong box where I can unfold as a personality at discretion," he wrote about publishing poems; but the words apply to his platform presence as well. In the early days of success (1916), he had grown aware of his problem: how to prepare a "face" to present to an audience. The solution probably called for introducing some acting, some pretending, some masking of what he considered his frailties. The poet of 1909, who learned to lessen his fear of facing an audience — filling his shoes with pebbles, dousing his back with ice-cold water — sought to meet the need of his listeners or what he thought it to be. And, inevitably, at certain times before some groups, "something" differed in Frost. I quote the negative view of Randall Jarrell:

> I want to appreciate more than his best poems, I want to exclaim over some of the unimportantly delightful and marvelously characteristic ones. . . . But first let me get rid, in a few sentences, . . . of what might be called the Peter Pan of the National Association of Manufacturers, or any such thing . . .

Jarrell's words on the "public self" that "gets in the way of the real Frost, of the real poems" can neither be dismissed nor accepted. For the "plat-

3. Thompson termed Frost "a campaigner" (*The Years of Triumph*, p. 718). Whitman planted anonymous reviews written by himself. Melville "followed the fortunes of *Typee* with zest, and even wanted to manipulate the controversy through a planted newspaper review of his own." *Publishers Weekly*'s recent charge against Frost for publicity-seeking makes ludicrous reading in the 1980's, when the serious writer V. S. Naipaul blandly refers to visiting Oslo to promote his current book: the scholarly Italian professor Umberto Eco does the same, speaking of his "autumn promotion tour of the U.S.A."; and so on.

form self" of any writer, teacher, or other performer varies with time, place, mood, and numberless other conditions. The public Frost of his famous Norton lectures obviously bears no relationship to Jarrell's Peter Pan of the N.A.M. "Frost had us all in the palm of his hand," wrote one of his critic-poet-listeners at Harvard, "simply by being himself . . . But what a self!" Or to make the phrase precise, *which* public self?

He had the audience in the palm of his hand, but at what personal cost? Questions keep crowding in about winning, scoring. "They say not, but you've got to score — in all the realms." What if it took too great a toll at times? Were his efforts at building a public image — to return to Poirier's words — motivated mainly by his need to escape the wear and tear of competing by seeming to stand above it, being both fiercely ambitious and truly contemptuous of having to show some part of his private self to strangers who had come to be pleased, carried away, entertained, held in the palm of his hand? And what — beneath their laughter and applause — did they think and feel him to be? He had long ago "found" the answer in "fourths" — those he worried about were the "25% who hated him for the right reasons." How did he feel about *them*? "The best audience the world ever had" could be found in the little college towns all over the land. There he could talk in earnest — they would weigh the words. He could tease — they would take it as play. He might test their reading by "saying" poems they had missed, and they would thank him for it. As for those who came "for the wrong reasons," he would have to judge, guess, ready himself to act the parts that would hold them till the end. Once when Cook approached as he left the stage to say how well he had spoken, he glowered: "That's what *you* would say, anyway." — hurrying off without giving a clue as to why he "knew" he had failed. What had he done or said to have caused five or six people to leave before he'd finished? The thought might pain him for days or fade, only to reappear at a worried moment. Every time he stepped to the podium, he knew that, however sure he might feel at the start, the outcome would be uncertain.

Once a performance was over, he could give himself to the person-to-person relationships that became his life. "I have come to value my poetry almost less than the friendships it has brought me," he volunteered eight months after Elinor's death. Among such friends were many whose work-a-day lives were not involved with the writing of poems — a physician (Jack Hagstrom), a teacher (Howard Mumford Jones), a printer (Joseph Blumenthal), a painter (Andrew Wyeth), a rabbi (Victor Reichert), a cultural leader (Hyde Cox). There were also farmers, librarians, men in business, scientists, journalists, government people — the list runs on and on. Two of his deepest friendships — the short-lived one with Edward Thomas, the tie that lasted till death with Louis Untermeyer — are now quite widely known. But something needs to be said of other relationships, largely unknown, which widen our knowledge of Frost as poet and friend.

Thompson's thirteen pages on "Encouraging Younger Poets" offer little beyond six summarized sketches and long quotations from Frost's lectures on writing and his introduction to a student anthology. Two of the writers "encouraged" by Frost wrote prose: Lawrence Conrad and B. F. Skinner. For one of the four poets, Joseph Moncure March, author of *The Wild Party* and *The Set-up,* Frost entertained high hopes, till he turned from verse to creating Hollywood scripts. Two others — Kimball Flaccus, Clifford Bragdon — seemed to gain from Frost's guidance, but also gave up poetry. All but Wade Van Dore ceased to be writers; four became teachers and scholars. Hence, according to Thompson, Frost had but one success and — in Thompson's account, which Van Dore derides as false — success of a very odd kind. I refer to the two poems that led to the making of "The Most of It."[4]

In a 1928 interview, Frost, though known to be frankly jealous of rivals, willingly named four younger poets as likely to win importance: among them, Robinson Jeffers, Archibald MacLeish, Stephen Benét, and Raymond Holden. Twenty-six years later he told another reporter that among the "individuals of great worth in the younger generation" were Elizabeth Bishop, Karl Shapiro, Robert Lowell, Richard Wilbur, and Leonard Bacon. He also expected to see "good things of others," including Delmore Schwartz. But who the "others" had been turns into guesswork, except where records exist. From my own conversations with Frost, from private letters and books, I can list as some of the poets encouraged or helped or praised by Frost: John Holmes, Donald Hall, Charles Foster, Robert Francis, William Meredith, I. H. Salomon, Peter Davison, Theodore Roethke, E. Merrill Root, Wade Van Dore, Henry Dierkes, Robert Lowell, Richard Wilbur, Thomas Hornsby Ferril, James Hearst, Charles Malam, Peter J. Stanlis, John Ciardi, Melville Cane, David Schubert. These are merely the names I happen to know; others can doubtless be added.

Frost on occasion contributed introductions to new anthologies, some by students, some by young published poets. The unexpected excitement

4. See my *Robert Frost Himself,* p. 22.

he felt in reading *Poetry*'s special issue of verse by living Israelis moved him to send the editor the gift of a warm response. One even more surprising was made by Frost when he learned that a former student, Reuben Brower, was starting a little poetry journal and also planning to marry. He wired at once: 1934 SEP 4/ STOP PRESS YOU'VE GOT ONE COMING TO YOU TOMORROW. The "one coming" was the manuscript of "Provide, Provide" accompanied by a letter: "Accept the enclosed for the New Frontier as a wedding present. I owe it to you anyway for a day in class made memorable by your reading of the falling out of faithful friends./ Ever yours/ R.F."

Frost's encouragements varied from spoken praise to counting on friends to repeat his comments. They could also take other forms: a testing challenge, a sharp demand to revise "defective" passages, a reasoning "plea" to remove the kind of self-indulgent imbalances he abhorred. Rarely were his words allowed to appear on a book jacket. Rarely would he speak as he did to Wilbur — "The Puritans" was "the best little poem" he had seen in a year or so. A useful book could be made to present Frost in his varying roles as helper. There are surely records to draw on. One of them, by Hugo Saglio, on file at Amherst, quotes the considerate excuse of Frost to save a blind student the problem of making his way to his house: "Why don't I come to *your* room? People keep coming here and the telephone keeps ringing. We can talk better there. . . ."

Meanwhile we can turn to three books that provide a beginning of sorts. I have already drawn on *Robert Frost and Wade Van Dore: The Life of the Hired Man,* a first-hand account of unique value for everyone concerned with the poet-as-person. Unlike Van Dore, Henry Dierkes was close to Frost for three years only (1934–1936), but they bore unusual fruit; witness his *Robert Frost: A Friend to a Younger Poet:*

> We swapped poems for a while [I quote from his letter] before he suggested that I should have a book and from that point on he was most helpful in the decisions about which poems should be included or left out. What is really remarkable is that Frost had very little use for free verse because he said he wouldn't know how to break off the lines without doing it "hocus-pocusly." What Frost didn't know was that when I lacked half a dozen poems to fill out the book manuscript I sneaked in some of what I considered my best sonnets by typing them as if they were free verse. I didn't tell him and he never discovered it.

The title poem of Dierkes' book, *The Man from Vermont,* points not only to peace and the end of wars but to poets as the agent of the change. Milton

Hindus believes that Frost may have attempted "a dialectic refutation" of Dierkes' optimistic view of the future — "What roused the everlasting 'oppositionist' in Frost . . . may be surmised" from his 1957 Christmas poem, "The Objection to Being Stepped On." Whether Hindus is right or wrong in his introduction to Dierkes' book matters much less than the comments by Frost on specific poems. For the first time (I believe) we can read about some of the ways in which the teaching-poet guided writers in whom he believed: glimpses of Frost at work as critic-and-helper.

In the midst of a New York reading at the New School in the winter of 1930, Frost spotted the face of an Amherst student, David Schubert. Expelled in his sophomore year for missing chapel, cutting classes, and similar failings, he was now living from hand-to-mouth and trying to write. After the lecture, Frost walked with him to his boarding-house cell and listened to his poem on Faustus. They talked together for hours. Before leaving, Frost promised to urge Amherst to take the young man back; he also gave him some money and offered to send the same amount each week (in the thirties, $3.00 could help one survive). Schubert was readmitted, then dropped for good in December 1932.

Frost sent him to meet with another former Amherst student, Peak Crawford, who was selling books at Brentano's. Within five minutes they were friends. Frost heard nothing more from Schubert himself, but he came upon some of his poems in the *Saturday Review,* the *Yale Review,* and *Poetry,* which in 1936 gave him a prize. Five years later Frost read him again in the New Directions' volume *Five Young American Poets.* That was the last till the evening after his lecture at Bard College in the forties. He and his host, Theodore Weiss, talked about universities and writing and Frost started to reminisce about young poets he had known. Suddenly he quoted: "Atta boy Jesus Christ Professor." To his great amazement, Weiss replied: "O, yes, David Schubert." The two proceeded to talk of publishing a book of Schubert's poems. Frost applauded the project and offered to help in spite of his age. Time passed. In the summer of 1946 the Weisses' *Quarterly Review of Literature* featured a large group of Schubert's poems. Frost quite probably learned from friends who had read the issue that the author he had striven to help had died in April.

"Generosity" does not appear in Thompson's topical indexes. Frost, to be sure, never regarded himself as "a nice person." No one was more aware than he of the "terrible things" he might possibly do or had already done (as his letters reveal). He could even hide in a closet the morning after some act that he gravely regretted ("I was too ashamed to face you . . ."). As in other respects — one is tempted to say, in almost all — he would over-react, over-blame. But sometimes even extreme self-punishment failed to assuage the pain — "I'm the kind that can't get over things[.] I have to say they have never been. Annul[,] not divorce." And yet he knew he was not alone in self-entrapment: "You want to believe that great writers are good men," he said to Van Wyck Brooks. "It's an illusion that dies hard." To which Maxwell Perkins added, "They are all sons of bitches."

Can "badness" stand as the norm, or — to be more specific — did Frost in dealing with people, for the most part act in reprehensible ways? The question sounds absurd to ask of a person known for his numerous friend-ships — and yet, on certain occasions, Frost behaved in ways deplored by even his admirers. I offer three examples of the supposedly "worst," based — so far as possible — on data given by those who were either on the scene or part of it.

The "search" for a fit biographer brought on problems years before the poet selected Thompson. In 1926 there were three possibilities: Edward Davison, an English poet who called at Bread Loaf during the Writers' Conference; Wilfred Davison, Dean of the School of English; Gorham B. Munson. Edward Davison's opening chapter troubled Frost by its sharply negative treatment of Louis Untermeyer. At once the writer agreed to prepare a revision, assuming, since nothing else had been said, that all was well. Frost, however, had other ideas, stirred by an essay he read in a March issue of the *Saturday Review* which named him "the purest clas-sical poet of America." In the fall he took a train to New York, reached the author, Munson, by telephone, and proposed that he write a mono-graph for the series edited by John Farrar. The project, discussed over din-ner that evening, moved so fast that the writing was done by June and sent to the printer. The poet's many suggested corrections arrived too late to be made. *Robert Frost: A Study in Sensibility and Good Sense* appeared November 1, 1927.

Its closing chapter led reviewers to mistake Frost for a follower of Irving Babbitt, chief of the "New Humanists," whose harsh attacks on William James and Henri Bergson were more than the poet could stomach. His re-lationship with Munson came to an end, but not the relationships with the two Davisons. The Dean's "disappointment was great," Farrar informed Frost, who, so far as I know, did nothing. With the English poet, how-ever, he tried to make reparations, and in minor ways succeeded, helping to promote his lectures and enabling him to receive a Guggenheim grant. Davison, in turn, was more than generous. "Let's not have the biography between us always as our reason for meeting or avoiding each other," Frost proposed. "Let's consider it dropped." Davison agreed, and the two remained friends.

Another case of Frost's unseemly behavior also involved an English poet, but one of a special brand. The scene: St. Botolph's Club, November 1932; the occasion: a dinner in honor of Eliot, currently Harvard's Norton Professor of Poetry. Sergeant's "possibly mythical composite" derived from witness accounts from Frost, Ferris Greenslet (who chose the date so that Frost could attend), and David McCord. * * Frost "began the evening a bit antipathetic — with a touch of the old jealousy," he remarked years later with some contrition. But as things moved on, he had all he could do to control his disgust with the way that Eliot, then at the height of his fashion, patronized his questioners, who approved with pious solemnity every last word he said. At a certain point, "Eliot announced that Burns could not be considered a poet at all — in fact no poetry had been written north of the River Tweed except for Dunbar's gloomy 'Lament for the Makers.'"

"Eliot sounds like a Border name," said Frost, his Scotch blood rising. "We were Somerset Eliots."

"Might we consider Burns a *song writer?*" Frost countered ironically. Eliot finally conceded "One might grant that modest claim." By then, Frost had had enough, but one of the guests, holding the text of "The Hippopotamus," proposed that each of them read a poem of his own.

> He offered [wrote Frost to Untermeyer] to read a poem if I would read one. I made him a counter-offer to *write* one while he was reading his. Then I fussed around with place-cards and a borrowed pencil, pretending an inspiration. When my time came I said I hadn't finished on paper but would try to fake the tail part in talk when I got to it. I did nine four-line stanzas on the subject "My Olympic Record Stride." Several said "Quite a feat." All were so solemn I hadn't the courage to tell them that I of course was lying! I had composed the piece for my family when torn between Montauk, Long Island, and Long Beach, California, the summer before. So be cautioned. They must never know the truth. I'm much to blame, but I just couldn't be serious when Eliot was taking himself so seriously. . . .

Another "poetry competition" occurred at the Bread Loaf Writers' Conference on August 27, 1938, an evening lecture and reading by Archibald MacLeish, whose growing importance and warm reception proved too much for Frost to accept with civility:

Early in the proceedings [I quote from Wallace Stegner's account] Frost found some mimeographed notices on a nearby chair and sat rolling and folding them. . . . Now and again he raised the roll of paper, or an eyebrow, calling the attention of his seat mates to some phrase or image. He seemed to listen with an impartial, if skeptical, judiciousness. About halfway through the reading he leaned over and said in a carrying whisper, "Archie's poems all have the same *tune*." As the reading went on, to the obvious pleasure of the audience, he grew restive. The fumbling and rustling of the papers in his hands became disturbing. Finally MacLeish announced "You, Andrew Marvell," . . . a favorite. Murmurs of approval, intent receptive faces. The poet began. Then an exclamation, a flurry in the rear of the hall. The reading paused, heads turned. Robert Frost, playing around like an idle, inattentive schoolboy in a classroom, had somehow contrived to strike a match and set fire to his handful of papers and was busy beating them out and waving away the smoke.

There was more to come. Charles H. Foster, a former Amherst student then living at Bread Loaf on a scholarship in memory of Elinor Frost, wrote an account in his *Journal:*

Frost did not take kindly to Archie's talk, I found out, when I met him in the kitchen. He was mixing himself a drink of a tumbler of whiskey. . . . Ted Morrison asked him to be good and he said he'd be all right when he put what he had in his hand where it should go. When we went into the living room everyone felt the tension and Benny DeVoto was pacing around. . . . "God-damn it to hell, Charlie. Robert's acting like a fool. Archie wasn't talking against him." . . . [MacLeish now read *Air Raid* which provoked a heated discussion between Morrison and DeVoto]. I went over to see how Frost was stirring the waters. I sat next to Frost on a davenport and after a time Archie came over and sat on the arm of it. Frost had one arm around me and as more drinks were drunk and the discussion arose, Archie balanced himself with an arm around my shoulder. . . . Frost said that it made him mad when "a young squirt" like Spender gave what he had worked on all his life a phrase, and tried to take the credit for it. . . . "Jesus H. Christ, Robert," said Archie. . . . "You're the foundation and we all know it." "I'm an old man. I want you to say it, to say it often. I want to be flattered." . . . Archie then tried to make the conversation less personal and Frost said "God-damn everything to hell so long as we're friends, Archie." "We are friends, Robert." . . .

One week before, according to Foster's *Journal,* Frost called himself "a God-damn-son-of-a-bitch, a selfish person who had dragged people roughshod over life. People didn't understand who wanted to make him good." Elinor had been dead since March; his long "period of blackness" had not yet ended. "I've been crazy for the last six months," he wrote in September to Untermeyer. "I haven't known what I was doing. . . . Do you think I'm still living in this world? Tell me the truth. Dont spare me."

What of the decades after the poet's recovery? Having never witnessed a burst of his bad behavior, I approached various friends who had long been close to the poet — only three were able to give examples. The first — from Professor Robert N. Ganz, who in 1956 or 1957 drove Frost across Vermont to a party near Dartmouth:

> I showed up at the Homer Noble Farm about 20 minutes late. He hated people to be late, a sign to him of disrespect. He showed this feeling by speaking with disdain of my Volkswagen. Perhaps he may also have been disappointed that his chariot was not to be more comfortable. In any case, he said, as he descended into the seat — anything but a throne — "I wouldn't trust *you* in a war with the Germans." (I might have replied, "When we have wars with the Germans, I go and you don't." But I didn't.) In addition to being a rebuke, Frost's comment, of course, was funny. Still, I'm sure, he regretted his show of temper. Near the end of our trip — we got a bit lost — he complimented my car's maneuverability. This was, obviously, a kind of apology. Then, because the car didn't have a fuel gauge, we ran out of gas — at the foot of a large hill or small mountain. He was *very big* about this as we started to trudge up the road. We were soon picked up by other guests and Frost continued to comfort me, to be gentle with my ego. I recall his saying, as we approached the house, there were better men outside than in — another effort to minimize my embarrassment. He did the same at another time when a driver rudely honked. Leaning out of the window, he yelled in a burst of loyal belligerency, "What's the matter with *you*?"

My second reply came from Alfred Edwards — he had been at Holt since 1945 — who had seen "very few examples of Frost's 'bad behavior' ":

> For the most part he was considerate with almost everyone though occasionally very short with Thompson when Larry's probing questions made him feel the "official" biographer might slant RF's image to fit *Thompson's predetermined image* of the poet.

> Only once was I victim of a tantrum. RF was one of very few American authors of his time to be paid a 20% royalty on all copies sold. When I negotiated a contract with him in 1958 for *You Come Too*, I lowered the

royalty to 15% as children's books carry lower royalty scales and are priced accordingly.

RF's pride was hurt, he was furious. Over the telephone he gave me a tongue lashing including some colorful language. He would not listen for my answer so I dropped the receiver terminating his call.

Several hours later he called back to apologize, later signing the offending contract. Neither ever mentioned the incident thereafter. Years later Kay told me Frost admired my guts and was glad he named me sole executor and trustee in his will, a fact I did not know until after his death.

My third reply was made by Joseph Blumenthal, who states that the incident he reports "should be stressed as being the only time in our 30-year association when Frost ever blew his top with me":

> The setting was early January, 1962, when I was visiting the Howard Mumford Jones' in Cambridge for the weekend. At the end of the evening I told Robert that I had an extra set of proofs of *In the Clearing*, that his OK was imperative if the book were to be completed in time for the dinner in Washington for his birthday in March. Robert asked me to call at Brewster Street "tomorrow at two."

> Promptly I rang the bell. He opened the door, his eyes angry, shook his finger in my face, said "Damn you!" and barred the way, indicating that something was wrong. It was the first time in a thirty-year friendship that I had encountered him in such a state of agitation. I knew no reason for his anger with me unless he felt that I was putting undue pressure on him to release the proofs I had under my arm. I offered to leave for New York at once and take the proofs back with me. But he said no, to "come on in." Mrs. Morrison was already there. We three sat around his dining table, each with a set of proofs, and the agitation quickly subsided. Frost read the proofs aloud and made a number of corrections as he went along. After three or four relaxed and harmonious hours, he handed me his set with "OK as corrected" and invited me back for breakfast next morning.

Something more must be said about Frost: first, as a "racist," and second, as a "mythologist." From all I have learned, the racist charge hangs on his use of *nigger.* "The world hates Jews and despises Blacks. I'd rather be hated than despised," he remarked, typically, to Reichert, for whom the poem "The Black Cottage" demonstrates Frost's "puzzlement" on the whole subject of race (lines 61, 75–83, 105–110). Frost was "acceptance personified" when compared with such other poets as Stevens ("Who's the lady coon [Gwendolyn Brooks]?" "I don't like this place. Too many Jews come in here.") and MacLeish ("I find race feeling runs pretty hot in my veins.") To say nothing of words by Pound, Eliot, Auden, Tate, Williams, Lowell. None of which erases the fact that Frost on occasion muttered or shouted "nigger" in anger over some petty event, imagined slight, discourteous act, or similar provocation. But Frost didn't say "nigger" only in anger. At my house, at our breakfast table, he used it to test my wife's and my daughter's reaction, knowing I saw through his game, since he'd spoken warmly to me of Sterling Brown and knew of our intimate friendship — the Browns had been guests at our daughter's wedding and Sterling would attend the party for Sergeant's biography. * * But whether spoken in anger or play, "nigger" remains a racist word. Hyde Cox holds a different view on the whole subject:

> I don't think the word should be applied to Frost at all. I could go on at length to prove that he was not basically anti any race. *He relished diversity.* There were — we both know — occasions when he seemed to be using race difference to vent his frustration with an individual (he was highly competitive) but such behavior in him had no root. "We love the things we love for what they are."

The line quoted by Cox applies in a curious way to Frost's recollections. "Mythologizing" his past not only served when needed to confuse biographers; it could also cause him concern, as with Pound's review of *A Boy's Will* in *Poetry* (18). The line between deliberate reshaping of one's past and simple forgetting often cannot be marked. "Trust me on the poetry, but don't trust me on my life" may be a "way of admitting that he couldn't always trust himself to tell — or even to see — the entire truth about himself" — so Thompson believed. How can anyone find "the entire truth"? That Frost tried to recall events as they had happened hardly needs to be stressed: nor that he sometimes failed; nor that he felt compelled to insist about "certain things" that "they never have been": to "Annul[,] not divorce."

This phrase from his *Prose Jottings,* more than all others involving the past, points to his need for maintaining a view of his life he could bear. Seen in this light, his contradictory statements — on time, place, people; on what he had or hadn't done, loved, or hated — bespeak his concern that the place he had earned might be lost to him, not of his doing but out of the workings of chance, fashion, taste — forces beyond control or foreseeing. Or to use the vast, encompassing word: fear. One might make an anthology of instances of varying sorts and intensities, from mild insecurity to darkest dread, from the early days with his reckless idolized father to the final words uttered in public that — whatever else they intended — voiced a defiant life-without-hope misgiving.

James Dickey "felt sure" that "the motivating emotion in Frost was fear." Randall Jarrell remembered that the poet "could never seem to forgive people" who scared him "within an inch of his life." In his comments about Robinson's *King Jasper,* Frost stressed two fears: the fear of God; the fear "that men won't understand us and we shall be cut off from them." Years before, he had taken especial care with Sidney Cox to explain that he "didn't believe it did [him] the least good to be told of the enemies he had had to defend [him] from." Out of hearing, out of mind, and, if possible, out of sight: he stayed away from Pound on his Washington visits to avoid confronting those who were out of their senses. "We all have our souls — and minds — to save, and it seems a miracle that we do it, not once, but several times. He could look back and see his hanging by a thread," John Bartlett noted after a talk with Frost. Page after page could be filled with acts observed, friends' quotations, lines of prose and verse, whole poems — on fear. In counter-response, Frost celebrates daring, courage, taking risks. * * ("I'd rather be taken for brave than anything else," he told Lesley.) Or hides, shielded by humor. "Be careful how you offer to take care of me in my last days," he teased Van Dore. "You never can tell about a poet's future." And yet, though "any form of humor shows fear, . . . [b]elief is better than anything else." And of all beliefs, even the most exalted, belief in one's self must come before all others, whatever one is stirred to do or say or imagine to assure its safety.

If fear is this poet's motivating emotion, and if humor in *any* form shows fear, what is one to think of the "serious" Frost? Ironically, as Sidney Cox has written, Frost frequently said: "It's a funny world."

> If he said it once, he has said it a thousand times. He said it sadly, he said it mockingly, he said it calmly as he slowly shook his head at the solemn explanations of the great minds, and he said it smiling as he made an opening for more truth. . . . Seriously, it's funny. It's seriously funny. And it's funny because it's serious. You often have to wait a while before you are amused. And even then most good smiles have a disappearing trace at least of ruefulness.

Untermeyer was quick to stress Frost's "extraordinarily playful spirit," but his book of *Letters,* though rich with examples, merely implies its range. At the "lowest" extreme: puns, good, bad, brilliant, sometimes "impossible" (Schenectady-synedoche). At the "highest": looking hard at the meanings of "you bet your sweet life" or, in the closing quatrain of "Two Tramps in Mud Time," joining "love and need" with "work [as] play for mortal stakes." Better than high and low would be breadth of kinds, which offers a world in itself — reveling in baseball talk; challenging the Poetry Society of America audience with a famous Sir John Davies poem (he had bet they would miss); insisting "I'm never serious except when fooling"; testing a reader's "rightness" by saying "My truth will bind you slave to me"; quoting his fee for a sonnet to an ex-world heavyweight champion ("because the last two lines . . . don't mean anything anyway"); taking "oppositionist" stands in an argument without concern for where they might leave him stranded; testing an audience after receiving a medal with "Oh, if my mother could only see me now" without acknowledging Kipling as its author; trying the patience of friends with comments he hoped would lead to a battle of wits; starting a punning contest he knew he might lose . . . To which one could add dozens of better examples. More to the point is Frost himself on the subject:

> I own any form of humor shows fear and inferiority. Irony is simply a kind of guardedness. So is a twinkle. It keeps the reader from criticism. . . . Belief is better than anything else, and it is best when rapt, above paying its respect to anybody's doubt whatsoever. At bottom the world isn't a joke. We only joke about it to avoid an issue with someone to let someone know that we know he's there with his questions: to disarm him by seeming to have heard and done justice to his side of the standing argument. Humor is the most engaging cowardice. With it myself I have been able to hold some of my enemy in play far out of gunshot.

> When the question comes up . . . what in the world are we to do next, the answer is easily either laugh or cry. We have no other choice. It takes wit to supply the laugh, yes and the tears too I guess.

> [S]tyle is the way the man takes himself; and to be at all charming or even bearable, the way is almost rigidly prescribed. If it is with outer seriousness, it must be with inner humor. If it is with outer humor, it must be with inner seriousness. Neither one alone without the other under it will do.

> Play no matter how deep has got to be so playful that the audience are left in doubt whether it is deep or shallow.

Pritchard considers this last sentence "perhaps his deepest word on the subject." He never professed to be giving the whole of the truth in any assertion; how could he possibly do so, convinced as he was of the limiting power of thought, all human thought? Everything he says about play, for all its sureness of tone, is a grain of truth — large, probing, provocative, beyond any sensible doubt at times but only at times; or, to make him witness against himself: earnest acts of playing with truth, playing for truth, which can take the mind as far as mind can go in its "seeking, questing." So he is able to write that "The way of understanding" with its outer or inner seriousness is always "partly mirth."

The *Centennial Essays II* devotes six of twenty-two chapters to "play." "Acceptance in Frost's Poetry: Conflict as Play," by Professor Marjorie Cook, argues "that Frost finds balance through his ability to see conflict as play. Serious play," in fact, "is the crux of Frost's poetics," which calls to mind Pritchard's belief that "everything he did or wrote could be thought about in the light of the [fact that one] of Frost's favorite words for poetry was 'Play,'" and poetry means "not just the poems but also the prose reflections: essays, interviews, notebooks — above all, the letters," to which I should add the talks and conversations.

With a poet of Frost's complexity, readers do well to look from a number of vantage points, to consider other assumptions. For example, Poirier's words "To the Reader":

> Frost is a poet of genius because he could so often make his subtleties inextricable from an apparent availability. The assumption that he is more easily read than are his contemporaries, like Yeats and Eliot, persists only in ignorance of the unique but equally strenuous kinds of difficulty which inform his best work. He is likely to be most evasive when his idioms are so ordinary as to relax rather than to stimulate attention; he is an allusive poet, but in a hedging and off-hand way, the allusions being often perceptible only to the ear, and then just barely — in echoings of earlier poets like Herbert or Rossetti, or in metrical patternings traceable to Milton; he will wrap central implications, especially of a sexual kind, within phraseologies that seem innocent of what they carry. The conclusion of "The Need of Being Versed in Country Things" — "One had to be versed in country things / Not to believe the phoebes wept" — sounds like a formula ready made for the delectation of critics who can then talk, as indeed I do, about poetry in nature, nature in poetry. But the proffered interpretation is compelling enough to mask other possibilities which would greatly enrich it. . . .

His poetry is especially exciting when it makes of the "obvious" something problematic, or when it lets us discover, by casual inflections or hesitations of movement, that the "obvious" by nature *is* problematic. . . .

He leads us toward a kind of knowing that belongs to dream and reverie. . . .

His practices derive from his passionate convictions about poetry as a form of life. . . .

"Most folks are poets. If they were not," Frost told a reporter, "most of us would have no one to read what we write." Nothing was said about critics and how they might help, for the date was 1921, years before the land was flooded with New Critics who could hardly wait to proffer the *real meanings* of any poem they happened to have at hand. Classrooms echoed with interpretations — brilliant, wild, clear, obtuse — but rarely without some technically provable basis. In 1958 Professor M. H. Abrams put "Five Ways of Reading *Lycidas*" into an essay which also included his own critique so that readers could know what was going on all around them and judge for themselves. By now the anything-goes approach has been driven away by others equally doomed — while the poems remain unchanged, to be used by newcoming readers and critics to minister to their wishes; that is, to respond to the temper of each. One reads according to one's ability *and* one's needs. For example, Professor Helen H. Bacon delivers a lecture on "In- and Outdoor Schooling: Robert Frost and the Classics." And others do the same: They view the poems in the light of their own inclinations and knowledge. Thus, in limiting ways, does Frost, "the subtlest and most elusive of poets," come to be "known" *at the start,* and so remains unless readers seek the help of a "world" that is waiting to open their ears and eyes. And a world it is. By now the poems have been studied, discussed, brooded upon by so many writers that specialists find it difficult to encompass them all. Such riches are not without hazards, but a reader can guard himself by reviewing essentials, many of which Frost provided in comments, letters, talks.

"Everything written is as good as it is dramatic." The test holds true of many, possibly most, of Frost's poems — notably in "Mending Wall" and "The Death of the Hired Man," household items for years. Two "contradictory" speakers, both of them "right" up to a point, and only when they are joined is the poem resolved — and then in an "open-endedness." As much holds true of "Provide, Provide": though "sung" by a single speaker, the contradictory voice is heard through implications that cannot be missed;

and again the poem says all that is needed without an overt "conclusion." "Life sways perilously at the confluence of opposing forces. Poetry in general plays perilously in the same wild place. In particular . . . between truth and make-believe." A duality, as one might suppose, commonly forms the base of the poet's dramatics, but not always: witness poems marked by more than two forces, attitudes, "voices" living in conflict ("Directive," "Two Tramps in Mud Time," "The Draft Horse"); or in which the opposing "something(s)" are hypothesized ("I Could Give All to Time," "Acquainted with the Night," "The Most of It").

Though open-ended "conclusions," like works which ask the reader to add what the writer omitted, are considered typicaly modern, often other critical touchstones are used. For example, if the twentieth-century vision is characteristically bleak, pessimistic, Frost as "a poet who terrifies" must be rated "modern." And so he is for more than a few critics. Not, however for Rexford Stamper, who holds that "the juxtaposed interpretations of facts reveal Frost's modernity." Nor for Lloyd N. Dendinger: Yeats, Eliot, Stevens, "the poets most often held up as the most modern," all follow the nineteenth-century pattern of " 'replacing' what has been lost to the poet as a result of the scientific, industrial, and political revolutions," the loss "lamented as early as Wordsworth's cry" in "The world is too much with us," in Arnold's "Dover Beach" and "Stanzas from the Grande Chartreuse," in Eliot's "Prufrock." Frost's "modernity rests primarily in the fact that . . . he turns neither to Eliot's 'chambers of the sea' nor to Yeats's prophetic vision of some 'rough beast' . . . but rather to the 'real' world [that Howells described] as the 'poor real life' of the largely impoverished countryside of New England." James Dickey, however, notes that "through this stealthy rusticity" Frost is able "to say the most amazing things without seeming to raise his voice . . . that the modern poet is trying to express — bewilderment and horror, wonder and compassion, a tragic sense of life, which he . . . suggests without bitterness or whining." Frost's innovations in verbal texture are too apparent to need attention ("let what will be, be"; "stay us and be staid"; "Back out of all this now too much for us"), or his openness to revolutions in syntax. What he valued in Christopher Smart's "Where ask is have, where seek is find" was the "cavalierliness with words." Indeed, "The height of poetry is a kind of mischief."

In letters, speeches, and conversations — everywhere — Frost talked about his art:

> The sound is the gold in the ore. . . . We need the help of context — meaning — subject matter. That is the greatest help toward variety. All

that can be done with words is soon told. So also with meters — particularly in our language where there are virtually but two, strict iambic and loose iambic. . . . The possibilities for tune from the dramatic tones of meaning struck across the rigidity of a limited meter are endless. . . .

Then there is this wildness. . . . it has an equal claim with sound to being a poem's better half. If it is a wild tune, it is a poem. Our problem then is, as modern abstractionists, to have the wildness pure; to be wild with nothing to be wild about. . . . so the second mystery is how a poem can have wildness and at the same time a subject that shall be fulfilled.

It should be of the pleasure of a poem itself to tell how it can. The figure a poem makes. It begins in delight and ends in wisdom. . . . It begins in delight, it inclines to the impulse, it assumes direction with the first line laid down, it runs a course of lucky events, and ends in a clarification of life — not necessarily a great clarification, such as sects and cults are founded on, but in a momentary stay against confusion.

No tears in the writer, no tears in the reader. No surprise for the writer, no surprise for the reader. . . . [L]ike giants we are always hurling experience ahead of us to pave the future with against the day when we may want to strike a line of purpose across it for somewhere. . . . Like a piece of ice on a hot stove the poem must ride on its own melting.

— "The Figure a Poem Makes," *1939*

Everything written is as good as it is dramatic. . . . Sentences are not different enough to hold the attention unless they are dramatic. . . . All that can save them is the speaking tone of voice somehow entangled in the words and fastened to the page for the ear of the imagination.

— Preface to "A Way Out," *1929*

[Metaphor]: saying one thing and meaning another, saying one thing in terms of another, the pleasure of ulteriority. Poetry is simply made of metaphor. So also is philosophy — and science, too. . . .

Every single poem written regular is a symbol small or great of the way the will has to pitch into commitments deeper and deeper to a rounded conclusion and then be judged for whether any original intention it had has been strongly spent or weakly lost. . . . Strongly spent is synonymous with kept.

— "The Constant Symbol," *1946*

Poetry begins in trivial metaphors, pretty metaphors, "grace" metaphors, and goes on to the profoundest thinking that we have. Poetry provides the one permissible way of saying one thing and meaning another.

— "Education by Poetry," *1931*

A poem . . . begins as a lump in the throat, a sense of wrong, a homesickness, a lovesickness. It is never a thought to begin with. It is at its best when it is a tantalizing vagueness. It finds its thought and succeeds, or doesn't find it and comes to nothing. It finds its thought or makes its thought. . . . It finds the thought and the thought finds the words.

— Letter to Louis Untermeyer, January 1, 1916

Poetry — it's the ultimate. The nearest thing to it is penultimate, even religion. It's a thought-felt thing.

— Oxford Lecture, June 4, 1957

Earlier than any of these statements is the one Frost made to Bartlett (July 4, 1913) on the audile imagination. Convinced that Swinburne, Tennyson, and others whose effects arose largely from assonance were on "the wrong track or at any rate on a short track," he felt confident enough to write:

I alone of English writers have consciously set myself to make music out of what I may call the sound of sense. Now it is possible to have sense without the sound of sense . . . and the sound of sense without sense. . . . The best place to get the abstract sound of sense is from voices behind a door that cuts off the words. . . . The sound of sense . . . is the abstract vitality of our speech . . . pure sound — pure form. . . . [but] merely the raw material of poetry. . . . [I]f one is to be a poet he must learn to get cadences by skillfully breaking the sounds of sense with all their irregularity of accent across the regular beat of the metre. [Eight months later he added:] A sentence is a sound in itself on which other sounds called words may be strung. . . . The sentence-sounds . . . are as definite as words. . . . They are gathered by the ear from the vernacular and brought into books. . . . *The ear does it.* The ear is the only true writer and the only true reader. . . . [T]he sentence sound often says more than the words.

So much, then, for theories. What of his practice? "Perfection is a great thing," he said at his 1954 birthday dinner. He "determined to have it" for Elinor's sake as much as his own, but long before (six months after her death), he not only "ceased to expect it [but] actually crave[d] the flaws of human handwork." Such craving isn't evident in his writing. As late as 1959 his "utmost ambition" was still "to write two or three poems hard to get rid of." That he strove for perfection, I knew from watching him try out last-minute changes with the proofs of his final book. None, however, approached the depth of difference in the two versions of "A Minor Bird"

(129) or "Design" (entitled in 1912 "In White," published in 1922 with all lines changed but four).

A full account of Frost's revisions is as useless to hope for as the composition dates of the poems. But his borrowings are sometimes easily traced. J. Donald Crowley cites a few ("A Drumlin Woodchuck," "Neither Out Far Nor In Deep," "Desert Places") in his essay "Hawthorne and Frost" that stresses the source of "The Wood-Pile," together with Frost's "confession that it was his habit to make deliberate borrowings." Speaking in 1955 of the reader's need to give himself over completely to his book, he declared that "every single one of my poems is probably one of these adaptations . . . taken" from what he was "given." Things dropped into his mind to come back on their own or were consciously drawn from Emerson, James, Santayana, and who can say how many more, knowing the "smokeless powder" source of "The Wood-Pile."

Many of Frost's beliefs about critics and theory I have cited before — poetry as "correspondence" (172), the role of the New Critics (182), what is truly lost in translation (123), to name but three. One "idea" which he seldom mentioned but to which he had given much thought was the "inappropriateness" of being termed a "Symbolist" poet. "If my poetry has to have a name, I'd prefer to call it Emblemism," not "Symbolism, [which] is all too likely to clog up and kill a poem." I know of only one writer to cope with this difference, Samuel Coale, who considers the early "Stars" the clearest example:

> The stars "congregate" above "our tumultuous snow" as if they were symbols of some more permanent meaning, as if they symbolized a "keenness for our fate." Frost, however, rejects such personification of natural objects, rejects the "symbolism" he describes, and prefers to take the stars *as they are* "with neither love nor hate." They are significant by virtue of their permanence as natural objects, by their very existence and distance from us . . . ; they remain not allegoric or symbolic but in Frost's terms emblematic of man's encounter with the very presence of existence itself. . . .

No attempt is made to force the stars to reflect a mood of the poet, to humanize and incorporate it into some allegorical mirror of the human soul. Nature remains a permanent "other" beyond our comprehension, yet significant since people and nature both are part of some great cosmic encounter. Thus each natural fact is emblematic of "something" whose existence we can know only in the thing itself. Not every poem by Frost conforms to this principle. "Stopping by Woods . . ." (he named it his "best bid for remembrance") succumbs to the very poetic Symbolic reverie that the emblematic encounter purports to deny. Yet Emblemism is what he hoped his work as a whole would embody and be understood as portraying.

"My poems —" he said in his early fifties, "I should suppose everybody's poems — are all set to trip the reader head foremost into the boundless." Thirty years later, when questioned about some proffered meanings of "Stopping by Woods . . . ," he replied, "Now, that's all right; it's out of my hands once it's published," which didn't stop him from saying of its being a death-poem, "I never intended that but I did have the feeling it was loaded with ulteriority." He often talked of specific poems, occasionally of how they were written, most often of when or where. Did the comments help? To speak for myself only: A poem is a virtual object added to the landscape — virtual because it cannot be touched or seen; the experience it offers is never actual as the warmth of the sun is actual. The poem speaks to readers indirectly in a mode of dramatized speaking addressed to their own experiences, their own desires. Response depends on what they bring to the poem and what they are able to "hear." At best they may think that they hear it all. If they hear little, they may search for help.

For me, at times, merely a passing word or part of a friend's tale of a talk with the poet has opened my ears to meanings. But many comments (including some of Frost's) have hindered or seemed irrelevant. I gained nothing at all from being told that "The Road Not Taken" involved Edward Thomas; that "Into My Own" was "really" about loyalty; that England was the birthplace of "The Sound of the Trees"; that the heroine of "The Lovely Shall Be Choosers" was the poet's mother. In any event, how is one helped to "know" "The Subverted Flower" by being informed that Elinor White was part of the scene? Whether "The Silken Tent" was "about" Mrs. Frost (as Lesley recalled) or Mrs. Morrison (as Thompson insisted) may matter to Frost's biographers, but not to a reader involved with the poem itself. Yet with certain writings, background help is essential. Few readers can fail to benefit from Pritchard's discussions of *North of Boston* and *A Witness Tree*.

Frost's poems, as everyone knows, are sometimes difficult, always subtle, and in some degree elusive. By saying that "The poet is entitled to all the meanings the reader can find in his poem," he not only stressed the likelihood of clashing interpretations but also proposed its rightness and, by implication, fostered repeated encounters with the very same poem. He could sometimes play a game by keeping readers off balance. Of "The Most of It" he might say dryly, "It's another one people have bothered around about — the meaning of — and I'm glad to have them get more out of it than I put in. . . . I do that myself as the years go on." Throwing dust in the eye was almost a pastime, Cook implies, quoting some of his comments — "Neither Out Far Nor In Deep" was a "rhymy little thing," "a joke on microscope and telescope." And although with "Kitty Hawk" he took great care to state what it meant, most of the time he chose to insist that his poems were clear if "rightly taken" — if he had wanted to make them clearer, he would have used different words. And, in any case, a poem should not "be pressed too hard for meaning." True, certain ones had to be "taken doubly," others singly (as he wrote in *A Further Range*); but most of his poems could and would be taken in multiple ways. At times the most perceptive of critics and readers emerge from identical poems with thoughtfully differing judgments — with apparently irreconcilable recognitions. * *

Which amounts to saying in a somewhat oblique paradoxical way that much of Frost is "obscure." That "His subject was the world that is so familiar and that no one understands" — true though it be — doesn't lead to an answer. Nor that his poetry fails to be helped by the kinds of explication that help readers of Eliot, Yeats, or Stevens. There are no adducible fixed-and-findable treasures at the end of the analytic rainbow: no Eliotic neo-Christian myths, no "systematic" Yeatsian *Vision,* no ascending steps on Stevens' stairway of imagination. Frost's poetry calls for more than the tracking down of allusions, ambiguities of language, echoes from other writings, and the other "strategies" which, once exhausted, presumably end the need to explore. Eliot, Yeats, Stevens (as others also have found) are "easier" writers than Frost. There would be no imperative point in saying of them that "The poet is entitled to *all* the meanings that the reader can find in his poem"; whereas with Frost this seemingly evasive remark showed the way toward "the answer." Read, for example, "I Could Give All to Time," then see what such thoughtful critics as Poirier, Jarrell, Brower, Pritchard, and Cook have to say. Does any one of these comments satisfy a reader avid to know the meaning of *every line*? Hyde Cox, with whom Frost often discussed his work, waives the question: "The poem suggests more than one can specifically nail down, and that is as it should be." Which leads back to Frost's assertion that poetry was "the one permissible way of saying one thing and meaning another" *and its hazards;* for it presupposes being "rightly taken," which cannot be counted on when a crucial part — or parts — of the rest of the meaning is missing. (As noted above, "Don't work, worry!" he told his Harvard students, only to be forced to add later: "I meant worry about ideas.")

"Rightly taken" — Frost "explains" — holds the key to his meaning. "They say the truth will make you free. / My truth will bind you slave to me." What does the couplet say? "You can talk by opposites and contraries with certain people because they know how to take you," he told a college audience. What if they do not know? What happens to the meaning? And what led Frost, within a month, to hint at the couplet's missing part by urging a different audience: "Having thoughts of your own is the only freedom" — *telling* them how to take his poems? One might hope that everyone knew by now. But more must be taken into account than his talking by opposites or omitting parts of implicit meanings. To understand a Frost poem calls for putting together "*all* the meanings that the reader can find" — those that are clearly stated, others plainly or even vaguely implied, still others only suggested — then drawing out of all that is found, intimations of the *poem's* intention. For the meaning itself rises out of the mixed totality which most surely includes the seeming contrarieties that themselves form much of the "message," as they well might do in the work of a poet for whom "everything written is as good as it is dramatic." To take rightly a poem by Frost is to open one's ears, eyes, and all other senses to the indefinably subtle ways with which he played his language in the hope that the "thought-felt thing"[5] he created would find continuing life in the life of his reader.

A thought-felt thing: "Poetry is the thought of the heart. I'm sure that's what Catullus meant by *mens animi.*" Though "feeling is always ahead of thinking," "poetry must include the mind as well . . . The mind is dangerous . . . but the poet must use it." Use it with "fear and trembling"; use it with full concern for the limits of knowledge: "there is nothing anybody knows, however absolutely, that isn't more or less vitiated as a fact by what he doesn't know." Granted — yet thinking is a gift to treasure. "No one can know how glad I am to find / On any sheet the least display of mind." No one can know how he felt by "gradually [coming] to see" that in his poem "Give All to Love," Emerson meant "Give all to meaning. The freedom is ours to insist on meaning." On meaning and more. On the freedom to "stay" as Emerson stayed throughout his life: like the hero of " 'Uriel,' the greatest Western poem yet," to look with "cherubic scorn," with "contempt for a person that had aged to the point where he

5. One may take a Frost poem rightly and still not learn its meaning. Pritchard may be correct: Some of the poems may be "ultimately not quite understandable." Frost "likes at times to be misunderstood — in preference to being understood wrongly," Sidney Cox assured Newdick.**

had given up newness, betterness." One could — and should — remain immune from cherubic scorn without forgetting that few blessings, if any, come unmixed.

Those of science — to take the clearest case of Frost's concern with thought and its ceaseless searching — "It's the plunge of the mind, the spirit, into the material universe. It can't go too far or too deep for me." Lost in admiring science, he let nothing stop him, given his lay limitations, from learning enough to be able to follow some of its great explorers. Niels Bohr went out of his way to tell the host of a dinner discussion that the poet's questions were more incisive than those of any professor-scientist present. Frost not only was overjoyed by all that science had learned; he also mocked the fear of its possibly robbing existence of mystery or romance — at the same time, loathing the smallness of mind, the arrogance, the "cocksureness," of many professional scientists he encountered. "It is not given to man to be omniscient." After so many years of remarkable searchings, they're still unable to do much more than ponder three great questions: where we came from, where we are going, what the steering principle of human living has been. And Darwinism, great as its founder was, seemed in its fixed determinist form to be marked by an all-explaining pretentiousness ruling out everything else — "passionate preference," Bergson's *élan vital,* Jamesian free will — that made of our lives far more than mechanical applications of ordained behavior. Evolution itself, moreover, confirmed the basic belief in progress, about which Frost held strong reservations: "The most exciting movement in nature is not progress, advance, but the expansion and contraction, the opening and shutting of the eyes, the hand, the heart, the mind."

If science, with its ceaseless testing of all it learns of the world outside, brings no light to the three great questions, what of philosophy, which is based on nothing beyond our mind's self-knowledge? "Logical systems [are] nonsense," Frost maintained, for "even the most impersonal processes [are] determined largely by influences controlling the logician but altogether excluded from the system and ignored." Thus in 1915; twelve years later: "I'm less and less for systems and system-building. . . . I'm afraid of too much structure. Some violence is always done to wisdom you build a philosophy out of." For example, the systematization of science which proceeds by assuming it possible to find all the answers when the most it can find are "pieces of wisdom," grains of truth. Much the same for politics, for here also the answers, if any exist, lie past the reach of the human mind — which didn't keep him from weighing the proffered solutions. "Communism, democracy, socialism . . . all complex problems of our time . . . have to be examined seriously." "A deeper understanding of socialism" was what he was wishing to "get" in Russia, he informed *Izvestia* in September 1962. Eight years before, after attending the World Congress of Writers in Brazil, he declared: "I'm a nationalist and I expect other people to be." Yet during World War II, he had called himself "a Lucretian abstainer from politics."

Frost's beliefs on politics, many of which I have quoted, appear to some as a model of contradictions. But to others his contrarieties result from observing the same phenomena from differing points of vantage, each of which leads to a different perception possessed of its own validity. Various pages set forth the poet's response to the Great Depression and the government's efforts to save the system by methods that some considered a threat to their freedom. Where did Frost "really" stand at the time of ferment, and why? * * More important: What was his stand on social justice after the thirties had passed into World-War conflict and emerged to confront the peace? His effort to set forth answers would have to appear in works such as the *Masques,* for the problems basic to politics were basic as well to religion.

Frost, with what seemed like a quip, refuted the charge that he contradicted himself: "I'm not confused; I'm only well-mixed." "I *am* the conflicts, I *contain* them." He was deep in his eighty-fifth year, having often in letters and talk and some of his best-known poems given the source of his contrarieties. For example, on the meaning of "Mending Wall," he denied that he had any allegory in mind other than

> . . . the impossibility of drawing sharp lines and making exact distinctions between good and bad or between almost any two abstractions. There is no rigid separation between right and wrong.

> The Emersonian idea of being pleased with your own inconsistency I never had. I always hoped that the thing would tie together some way. If I couldn't make it, that was up to God.

> All truth is a dialogue.

> All a man's art is a bursting unity of opposites.

> Hegel taught a doctrine of opposites, but said nothing about everything's having more than one opposite.

> But even where . . . opposing interests kill, / They are to be thought of as opposing goods / Oftener than as conflicting good and ill.

Everything in life contains a varying blend of order and riot, from the individual to nations.

We look for the line between good and evil and see it only imperfectly[,] for the reason that we are the line ourselves.

You'll have plenty to do just keeping honest — that is to say[,] reporting your position truthfully from phase to phase.

If "Frost appears to contradict himself, the explanation," says Tharpe, "is simple: he tried to tell the truth. In the everyday world, a thing appears at times to be true, and at times its opposite appears to be true." Though such contrariety was an ever-beckoning mystery and necessity, it was not beyond transcending. In 1926 he wrote to Sidney Cox:

> Having ideas that are neither pro nor con is the happy thing. Get up there high enough and the differences that make controversy become only the two legs of a body, the weight of which is on one in one period, on the other in the next. Democracy monarchy; puritanism paganism; form content; conservatism radicalism; systole diastole; rustic urbane; literary colloquial; work play. . . . I've wanted to find ways to transcend the strife-method. I have found some. . . . It is not so much anti-conflict as it is something beyond conflict — such as poetry and religion that is not just theological dialectic.

We are into a subject that needs a book in itself. What did he *really* believe? How far did his faith take him? We have bits and pieces from others, as well as his works to guide us. Do they offer enough? To avoid being wrongly taken, he took unusual care, at times, in his public use of "spirit" and "soul," equating the first with "mind" and the second with "decency" or "integrity." But "God" he used unglossed, in spite of or maybe because "The thought it suggests to the human mind," as Shelley had warned, "is susceptible of as many varieties as the human minds themselves."

> I despise religiosity. But I have no religious doubts. Not about God's existence, anyway.

> [God] is that which a man is sure cares, and will save him, no matter how many times or how completely he has failed.

> I never prayed except formally and politely with the Lord's prayer in public. I used to try to get up plausible theories about prayer like Emerson. My latest is that it might be an expression of the hope I have that my

offering of verse on the altar may be acceptable in His sight Whoever He is.

[T]he self-belief, the love-belief, and the art-belief, are all closely related to the God-belief . . . the relationship we enter into with God to believe the future in — to believe the hereafter in.

My fear of God has settled down into a deep inward fear that my best offering may not prove acceptable in his sight. I'll tell you most about it in another world.

My approach to the New Testament is rather through Jerewsalem than through Rome and Canterbury.

Is that agnosticism [he asked after reading from Sir John Davies' "Man"]? [T]he rest of the poem would show you that it's very religious. What fills up the knowing is believing.[6]

The God Question. Religion is superstition or it is nothing. It is still there after philosophy has done its best. . . . [P]hilosophy is nothing but an attempt to rationalize religion.

[Religion] is a straining of the spirit forward to a wisdom beyond wisdom. . . . And the fear of God always has meant the fear that one's wisdom, one's own human wisdom is not quite acceptable in His sight.

Greatest of all attempts to say one thing in terms of another is the philosophical attempt to say matter in terms of spirit, or spirit in terms of matter, to make the final unity. That is the greatest attempt that ever failed. . . . But it is the height of poetry, the height of all thinking.

Why will the quidnuncs always be hoping for a salvation man will never have from anyone but God? . . . How can we be just in a world that needs mercy and merciful in a world that needs justice. . . . If only I get well, I'll go deeper into my life with you than I ever have before.

To these citations more could be added without implying the sort of coherence that several scholars and friends have sought to provide. I find

6.   I know my soul hath power to know all things,
           Yet she is blind and ignorant in all;
           I know I'm one of Nature's little kings,
           Yet to the least and vilest things am thrall.

           I know my life's a pain and but a span;
           I know my sense is mock'd in everything;
           And to conclude, I know myself a Man —
           Which is a proud and yet a wretched thing.

the most rewarding pages in Cook's *The Dimensions of Robert Frost* (188–194) and the three *Centennial Essays,* especially Reichert's (415–426, I) and Hall's (325–339, III). Of the other works that may yet appear, one of especial import would result if the poet's friend Hyde Cox were to put in writing some of their talks on God. It might offer more of revelation than concealment, though the two in Frost seldom are found apart.

Take, for example, "something," the most significant single word in the poems. Forty years ago McGiffert, in three close pages filled with examples, speculated about its use and suggested answers. Two more books were still to come, also a verse concordance that lists 135 lines for "something," sixty-eight for the closely related "someone," and eight for "somehow." Of all these uses, sixty-five exemplify what McGiffert calls Frost's "refusal to define the indefinite [by] creating his special blend of fact and implication." It refers to the tangible or, as he notes, the intangible; more often to both. In "The Grindstone," the speaker is "all for leaving something to the whetter." Leaving what? In "Maple," the search for the secret of the girl's odd name was in vain, but "it proved there was something" rewarding in the search itself. This is not the "something" of line twenty-one in "The Code," which is followed by clear defining; nor the wife's partial attempt (in "The Death of the Hired Man") at explaining "home" as "Something you somehow haven't to deserve." Nor even the menacing implications in the "something" the waters "thought of doing . . . to the shore" in "Once by the Pacific." It is rather the ineffable-elusive at the close of "For Once, Then, Something," the intimation of knowledge beyond human grasp in "A Passing Glimpse," the unaccountable "someone" whom the killer had to obey in "The Draft Horse." It is present also behind the words of the "altogether remarkable poem" of Poirier's altogether remarkable study of "A Star in a Stone Boat," in which the speaker explains that he goes about "as though / Commanded in a dream" by something or someone that somehow "promises the prize / Of the one world complete in any size / That I am like to compass, fool or wise."

In a speech to the American Academy of Arts and Sciences on receiving its Emerson-Thoreau medal, Frost ascribed his religious beginnings to his Scotch Presbyterian mother. Reading Emerson made her a Unitarian, until, reading on into *Representative Men,* she became a Swedenborgian. "I was brought up in all three of these religions . . . [b]ut pretty much under the auspices of Emerson." What happened to Frost's beliefs from this point on has been studied by too many writers to call for more than a few remarks on his meeting with three other thinkers: William James,

Henri Bergson, Henry Thoreau. From all he learned of their thoughts, he proceeded to draw what became his unique composite of principles, beliefs, predilections, meanings, and convictions. James and Thoreau reinforced his inherent drive to confront "the essential facts of life" unveiled and without any turning away from its hard realities. But James went on to provide him with vastly more — all he could need — from his first encounter in 1897 at Harvard with the *Principles of Psychology* on to *The Will to Believe,* to *Pragmatism,* and then to whatever else he may have decided to study.[7] That James was his greatest teacher, Frost was proud to proclaim, and critics and scholars have zealously shown the indebtedness. Readers have only to turn to Poirier, Brower, Squires, Cook, Pritchard, and the three *Centennial Essays* for extensive examples, some of which also discuss the relation of Frost to Emerson, Hawthorne, and others, including Bergson, whose crowning work, *L'Evolution créatrice,* he found in 1911 when it first appeared in English. There is more to life than intellect can explain. By *intuiting* experience from within, we learn that its essence is an *"élan vital":* a life-force that thrusts, pushes, flings itself on, and expands outward in a ceaseless struggle against the decline of nature in a reaching back

---

7. James expanded Charles Peirce's pragmatic idea of meaning into an instrumental theory of the mind as serving our lives: — The basis is sense experience: a continuous flowing consciousness, varied and multiple, which likes some feelings and dislikes others, rejecting, neglecting the rest. Hence the world of things is largely made of our *choosing.* And the same selectiveness operates with our ideas. We attend to and promote whatever gives our total nature the most satisfaction, which is to say that the nature of truth is pragmatic — for something to be true, it must "work." Reality is nothing but experience borne on the stream of consciousness which expands and contracts and interacts with other human streams. But man has always felt around and about him the presence of a different experience, sympathetic, akin to his own striving for good over evil. The true way of interpreting this psychological experience, which is also metaphysical, calls for believing that it comes from another consciousness: one like our own, with which we commune, which loves and wishes to help us. We may conceive of God as limited (the world being visibly imperfect and full of real evils) and ourselves as striving by His side together to counteract these evils. There are obstacles: man's unwillingness to work with God, also the factor of chance (Peirce's "tychistic" view: the unpredictable element that may work against efforts of God-and-man). Existence is therefore a gamble, with enormous stakes and tremendous risks, but well worth taking. When no evidence is at hand or obtainable, it is permissible to believe; and a positive belief is more consonant with the health of mind and soul than a distrustful one. "God," James concluded in *The Varieties of Religious Experience,* "is the natural appellation . . . for the supreme reality, so I will call this higher part of the universe by the name of God. We and God have business with each other; and in opening ourselves to his influence our deepest destiny is fulfilled."

toward the Source. Like James, Bergson interpreted human experience in both down-to-earth and metaphysical terms based on neither science nor Christianity but the individual's knowledge.

By the time that Frost was arranging poems for his first book, *A Boy's Will,* he had come to a view of faith and God that prepared the pattern of all that he later learned through seeking, questing. He defined himself as "an Old Testament believer." He confessed having had revelations: "Call them 'nature's favors.' An owl that banked as it turned in its flight made me feel as if I'd been spoken to . . ." Although he publicly called it "a curse to be an agnostic," he feared that certain remarks he had made might be misconstrued as a skeptic's; hence, he "commissioned" an intimate friend to convince Thompson that he truly believed in God. The couplet-prayer "Forgive, O Lord, my little jokes on Thee . . ." would probably only seldom be wrongly taken, but what of his shrugging off sectarian theology, churchly trappings, even some venerated Christian tenets as "froth"? How many people would know that his kind of belief drove him to draw the line "between trivialities and profundities"? Yet there can be no doubt that at times he felt less than sure. Seven months after Elinor's death he suddenly turned on Newdick: "Where is this God I hear so much about? Where *is* he?" Thompson refers, ten years later, to Frost's having said "he [had] moved from skepticism to almost complete mystical faith and back again," but he does not quote a word to support his interpretation. Nor are we given a clue to the last of a trio of letters to Untermeyer, each with a verse beginning "To prayer." The first and second (July 7, September 26, 1921) seem easy to grasp, but the third (January 15, 1942)? "As your editor, Louis," I said to Untermeyer, "may I read your editorial explanation?" He shook his head. I quoted the closing: " 'Oh, if religion's not to be my fate / I must be spoken to and told / Before too late!' — he says that he *had* been spoken to but adds 'I believe I am safely secular till the last go down.' No comment at all, Louis, not even on 'till'?" He smiled, handing me the next manuscript page. "This one's about my sixth revised — transgression."

Frost defined a religious person as one who "can say he aspires to a full consent" — "All I do in [*A Masque of Mercy*] is reach for something." Aspiration: strong desire. "To believe is to wish to believe," wrote Unamuno, "to believe in God is, before and above all, a wish that there may be a God." More than once in intimate moments, Frost dwelt upon *Mark,* Chapter 9:23–24: "Lord, I believe; help thou mine unbelief." One thinks of his credo: Belief is "best when rapt, above paying its respects to anybody's doubts whatsoever." Doubts were as much a part of his trial by existence as his faith, aspiration, and all-too-human moods. "Play me some great music, something you think is great," he asked Hyde Cox in the course of a visit. His host played part of a Handel *Messiah* recording. As it closed with the aria, "I know that my redeemer liveth," Frost listened intently. "Hyde, do you know your redeemer liveth?" he asked half-teasing. "Sometimes I think so," came the reply, "do you?" "Oh, I don't know," Frost answered, "but I do know there's such a thing as redemption." In the autumn after his trip to Russia, at a party in Reichert's Ripton home, he asked out of nowhere, "Victor, what do you think are the chances of life after death?" "I teased Frost by reminding him that when you ask a Jew a question, you don't get an answer; just another question: 'What do you think?' I asked. He became deeply silent. Then he said to me, 'With so many ladders going up everywhere, there must be something for them to lean against.'" His words, echoing James ("The mutable in experience must be founded on immutability"), cannot be heard apart from all he had sought in his life of seeking. So Marice Brown — like others close to the poetry — sees Frost as "a spiritual explorer . . . not only driven to understand the *how* of God's ways but . . . also deeply concerned with the *why*. . . . The thread that runs through it all is the quest itself."

In his *Letter* of 1935 to *The Amherst Student* the ostensible subject was the special badness of the present age, but the heart of his message was "form." The "evident design" in the situation facing people "may vary a little" from age to age. Its background has always been "in hugeness and confusion shading away from where we stand into black and utter chaos." But . . .

> There is at least so much of good in the world that it admits of form and the making of form. And not only admits of it, but calls for it. We people are thrust forward out of the suggestions of form in the rolling clouds of nature. . . . When in doubt there is always form for us to go on with. Anyone who has achieved the least form to be sure of it, is lost to the larger excruciations. I think it must stroke faith the right way. The artist, the poet, might be expected to be the most aware of such assurance. But it is really everybody's sanity to feel it and live by it.

For the maker he was, ever "seeking, questing," much that he learned became the stuff of poems and of other writings and talks that are virtual poems-in-prose. "Any little form [he was able to] assert upon the hugeness and confusion [had] to be considered for how much more it [was] than nothing, [also] for how much less it [was] than everything."

The thoughts foretoken "The Figure a Poem Makes," the preface to his 1939 *Collected Poems*. No words by Frost on "the poem" are so widely quoted: "It begins in delight, it inclines to the impulse, it assumes direction with the first line laid down, it runs a course of lucky events, and ends in a clarification of life — not necessarily a great clarification of life, such as sects and cults are founded on, but in a momentary stay against confusion." The last five words lead us to James (". . . if a reader can lapse back into his immediate sensible life at this very moment, he will find it to be a big blooming buzzing confusion") and to Frost's paraphrase ("The present/ Is too much for the senses, / Too crowding, too confusing — / Too present to imagine"). Besides this assault on the senses, "There is always tragedy. That is what life is. . . . [N]othing," however, "is so composing to the spirit as composition. We make a little order where we are. . . . We make a little form and we gain composure." "Each poem clarifies something. But then you've got to do it again" "because confusions keep coming fresh." Will there be no end? Can "what seems to us confusion" be "but the form of forms," as Job supposes in *A Masque of Reason*? "Directive" offers a promise: "Drink and be whole again beyond confusion." Moreover, "the good of the world" not only admits the making of form but demands it — "it is really everybody's sanity to feel and live by it." This is the human lot: to be called to achieve some form, some order out of the hugeness, buoyed upon faith in assurances that may bring acceptance.

No one can say what acceptance meant to the poet without bearing in mind certain "givens" of existence as he saw them:

(1) The human mind is limited; we do no more than we can, drawing on every type of thought we are able to summon, from pure intuition and "passionate preference" to the fine complexities of reason. *All* are fallible: At one extreme, "The White-Tailed Hornet's" thought-by-instinct (aimed at a fly, "he swooped, he pounced, he struck; / But what he . . . had was just a nailhead. / He struck a second time. Another nailhead"); at the other extreme, science, which by virtue of testing itself, "goes self-superseding on."

(2) Living entails freedom of choice with responsibility. We can choose to will to believe, to believe things into existence; we can even consider ourselves to be working with God to perfect the universe. At the end, we shall have to account for our lives, hoping that all we have done and all we have been will be deemed acceptable.

(3) Much that we do must be done solely by faith in the outcome: We must willingly dare, take risks, gamble our lives. ("You're always believing ahead of your evidence" — Frost; "It is only by risking our persons from

one hour to another that we live at all" — James.) Fear, the obbligato of courage and daring, "is the great thing to exorcise; but it isn't reason that will do it" (James). Frost experienced fears too many and varied to name, from imagined slights to crucial doubt that his offering would prove "acceptable in the sight of God."

(4) "You are not safe anywhere unless you are at home with metaphor," hence the need to be educated by poetry; for "all there is of thinking is the metaphor whose management we are best taught in poetry." "All metaphor," however, "breaks down somewhere." Even the greatest "of all attempts . . . to say matter in terms of spirit, or spirit in terms of matter [has] failed." And yet we must keep on striving to perceive in disorder new and profound unities. For Wordsworth, the necessity for such perceiving flows out of the depths of the organism. It is, as he wrote, "the great spring of the activity of our minds, and their chief feeder. From this principle the direction of the sexual appetite, and all the passions connected with it, take their origin; it is the life of our ordinary conversation. . . ." Wordsworth and Frost, as Poirier notes in a recent essay, "are nearly identical in their theories of poetic 'strain' and of the pleasures it affords."

(5) We learn not only through poetry: The study of nature at times yields knowledge too precious to miss. For Emerson, the "moral law lies at the center and radiates to the circumference." No such belief is found in Frost, although, as he wrote: "We throw our arms wide with a gesture of religion to the universe." In his attitude toward nature, Frost resembled Thoreau,[8] who wished "to front the essential facts . . . [to] learn what [they] had to teach," for with all its moments of bleakness, a "true account of the actual is the rarest poetry." Frost never worshiped nature, yet some of his finest poems are prayers, petitions, "instructions to the season." One need only leaf through his books — from the early "Rose Pogonias," "A Prayer in Spring," "October," and on. The worlds of nature, which he never ceased to explore from both afar and up close, stirred him into reachings beyond the "reports" of the senses. "I'm always saying something that's just the edge of something more," he answered a man who called his work "a vast symbolic structure." More than that he avoided saying, aware that his brightest and darkest pages and those of neither extreme had been born in response to "somethings" seen or heard or imagined in the natural world.

(6) When questioned on some of his work in which sensitivity to nature's beauty is allied with poignant awareness of the suffering within the

---

8. Frost: "A poet must lean hard on facts, so hard, sometimes, that they hurt."

natural order, he replied, "Where is there any benevolence of purpose?" His words apply no less to certain poems on the human condition — "A Servant to Servants," "Out, Out — ," "The Housekeeper," "Home Burial," and similar works that led Trilling to refer to Frost as "a poet who terrifies." None that were known to Trilling had gone so far as "The Draft Horse." Written in 1920, it remained unpublished until 1962:

> With a lantern that wouldn't burn
> In too frail a buggy we drove
> Behind too heavy a horse
> Through a pitch-dark limitless grove.
>
> And a man came out of the trees
> And took our horse by the head
> And reaching back to his ribs
> Deliberately stabbed him dead.
>
> The ponderous beast went down
> With a crack of a broken shaft.
> And the night drew through the trees
> In one long invidious draft.
>
> The most unquestioning pair
> That ever accepted fate
> And the least disposed to ascribe
> Any more than we had to to hate.
>
> We assumed that the man himself
> Or someone he had to obey
> Wanted us to get down
> And walk the rest of the way.

No gloss can suffice. The poem reflects the "tychistic" belief that James shared with Peirce: the objective reality of pure chance as a central factor in all earthly existence. The words speak to each other; they speak to the poem as a whole. Not a syllable about purpose — "a lantern that wouldn't burn," a grove "pitch-dark" and "limitless," and yet one word ("invidious") moves the poem out of the world of pure chance.

(7) One is tempted to read the poem as more than "A true account of the actual": as justice-mercy on a cosmic scale, unlike the equivalent in human affairs where at least in theory "solutions" at times are con-

ceivable. Frost's most extensive effort at "explaining" justice-mercy was made in the *Masques* — with no greater success in resolving than explaining usually achieves. Could the conflict be traced to the nature of people, to the stuff we are made of, as the conflict of a different sort inheres in the metal chunk of "From Iron" — "Nature within her in-most self divides / To trouble men with having to take sides"? Justice-versus-mercy troubled him till the end. Did he still believe it to be "a natural conflict built into the moral universe"?

(8) As natural, perhaps, as his need to be with people? — a need common to most mortals, but with Frost — like almost everything else — found in a heightened state. From infancy till Elinor's death, he had never lived by himself and then, with the help of the Morrisons, he was much of the time surrounded by people, and alone only by choice. In 1943 he invited Van Dore to "come up and help with the haying . . . and at least we can talk." Not long after his visit, Wade was asked to "stay permanently" as his helper and companion. Van Dore had become deeply aware of the poet's "need never to be alone." He had often escaped from solitude into Wade's presence, and when not talking together — as they did each night, often till morning — he was always companioned by his dog. His loneliness expressed itself in various ways. Obviously: when he wrote of "the fear that men won't understand us and we shall be cut off from them." Indirectly: in his poetry's most common situation — a man, or a man and wife, alone in a small isolated house — or in one of his "favorite" figures — a house abandoned, with ruin as an image of heroism "against hopeless odds."

(9) Hopeless odds — humanity's impotence within the world that engulfs him. In his Norton lecture ("Does Wisdom Signify?"), referring to problems of the universe, he declared, wagging a lively finger, "The surest thing you know is that we'll never understand. And we'll never lack resources to stay here, to hang onto the globe." "At Woodward's Gardens," a poem that was soon to appear, bore the subtitle "Resourcefulness Is More Than Understanding." Twenty-three years later the line disappeared. Why? So far as I know, he was never asked nor ever explained. It would seem, however — whatever "resourcefulness" signified — that his passion to understand had regained control. Not that any admitted change had driven him closer to "knowing." Nothing he said after dropping the line implied any notably new understanding. In that very year (1959) he said that his forthcoming book would be named *The Great Misgiving*. The final title, *In the Clearing*, failed to reflect the book as a whole. Moreover, the poems defined

by Joseph Kau as "creational" showed that Frost "metaphysically was never 'in the clearing.'" Frost continues to wrestle with faith and fear; he wills to believe. He places "The Draft Horse" after his "Cluster of Faith" section and ends the book with the group that he calls "Quandary." It was three months after *In the Clearing* appeared that he said he had always hoped that all the contradictions and inconsistencies of life on earth would "tie together some way. If [he] couldn't make it," the problem "was up to God."

In 1953 Jarrell opened the eyes of a good many critics and readers to the greatness and profundities of Frost, "exclaiming" not only over "some unimportantly delightful and marvellously characteristic poems" but also selecting others that reveal him "for what he really is." Jarrell focused on poems that the modernist elite had missed, works "unique in the poetry of our century and perhaps in any poetry." The essay led to Trilling's birthday speech that likened Frost to Sophocles, the poet "his people loved most . . . chiefly because . . . they felt, perhaps, that only a poet who could make plain the terrible things of human life could possibly give them comfort." In spite of a controversial response, the ascription changed the course of critical views, the dark overshadowed the light, but not entirely and not for long. Within a year G. W. Nitchie published his "case against" Frost, which was followed by numerously varied studies, notably in the three *Centennial Essays.*

In the first volume, while Robert Rechnitz stressed "The Tragic Vision of Frost," Marjorie Cook, in Volume Two, maintained that the poet's view of existence is "ultimately affirmative and therefore comic." Neither term is adequate as a characterization of Frost, for the sense of "no harm being done" (epitomized by Miranda's speech in *The Tempest*) is the surely decisive sense of the comic that sets it apart from the tragic: that problems cannot always be solved; that even if evil is somehow destroyed, much good may be wasted also. The "ultimately affirmative" Frostian view may best be defined as "acceptance." But what kind of acceptance — gleeful, willing, reluctant, resigned? Could a gathering of some relevant lines point toward an answer? * *

> Heaven gives its glimpses to those
> Not in position to look too close.

> The fact is the sweetest dream that labor knows.

> It had to seem unmeaning to have meaning.

The only certain freedom's in departure.

Earth's the right place for love:
I don't know where it's likely to go better.

Anything more than the truth would have seemed too weak . . .

Keep off each other and keep each other off.

And of course there must be something wrong
In wanting to silence any song.

And tell me truly, men of earth,
If all the soul-and-body scars
Were not too much to pay for birth.

The trial by market everything must come to.

But even where . . . opposing interests kill,
They are to be thought of as opposing goods
Oftener than as conflicting good and ill . . .

Let the night be too dark for me to see
Into the future. Let what will be, be.

The way of understanding is partly mirth.

. . . the utmost reward
Of daring should be still to dare.

Nothing gold can stay.

But power of blood itself releases blood. . . .
Oh, blood will out. It cannot be contained.

We dance round in a ring and suppose,
But the Secret sits in the middle and knows.

[W]hat seems to us confusion
Is not confusion, but the form of forms. . . .

I have it in me so much nearer home
To scare myself with my own desert places.

And forthwith found salvation in surrender.

We may take something like a star
To stay our minds on and be staid.

Standing alone, some of the lines seem to be pointing less toward affirmant light than to darkness. But within their poems they attest to knowledge-sought in probing the actual; and whether or not answers were found, naming itself asserts a truce that implies acceptance. Only two of the passages come from the *Masques,* though their stage-characters, as in all such works, are partly the writer. All the poems, however, large and small, mirror the poet's seeking-questing for momentary stays in a world confused with beauty and bleakness. It is ours to choose to live with; the decision to stay bespeaks acceptance of all that awaits in a huge and ruthless place we shall never quite understand any more than what we are. To explore these unintelligibles is also to learn "There are roughly zones whose laws must be obeyed" despite our thirst for the limitless.

What Frost valued, of course, were the ever-recurrent occasions to discover something or make "a new start." Nor would it matter when searching brought back only pieces, glimmerings: "If you see the little truths with sharp delight or pain, you will not be anxiously straining to do final justice to the whole of reality." And if wisdom consists of enduring the world and our limits just as they are, our ability to know the whole of reality demands our trust in ultimates out of our reach. It also insists on less-than-final statements, partial insights which can seem to deny others. Frost so often spoke in terms of "as if" that its bearing on contrarieties in some of his poems may be lost on readers. Radcliffe Squires remarks in this regard on Melville's complaint: It was unfair to hold a poet answerable forever for what was true for him only in the moment. In every case, the less-than-final statements cannot be said to arise from Frost's refusal to take a stand, as his 1937 letter to Sidney Cox makes clear. * * Moreover, *A Masque of Mercy* (he called it his "Whole Bible") bewilders — by intention? — as forthright words and parody weave in and out, not to mention the contradictory words on courage. The effect of the lines approaching the end seems more than anything else to encourage uncertainty — which should not surprise us in Frost, an exemplar of the Negative Capability that Keats said Shakespeare "so enormously" possessed: "when a man is capable of being in uncertainties, mysteries, doubts, without any irritable reaching after fact and reason."

The *Masque* fails to reach a settled conclusion, yet changes occur, among them Jonah's conversion, which leads back thirty-four years to "the myth of 'The Trial by Existence.' In both poems," says Nitchie (who elsewhere censures Frost for the virtue lauded by Keats), "what really matters is . . . the joyfully, arduously willed acceptance of a world we never made." "A

Lesson for Today," printed a year before the *Masque,* would have served him better. In 160 rambling lines on the world and its ages, Frost acknowledges much that might cause despair — "Earth's a hard place in which to save the soul"; "The groundwork of all faith is human woe"; the "belittled human race [is] either nothing or a God's regret"; ourselves, "the total race, / The earth itself is liable to the fate / Of meaninglessly being broken off." In view of which "No choice is left the poet . . . / But how to take the curse, tragic or comic." Acceptance demands both: He replies with words for his gravestone — "I had a lover's quarrel with the world." But acceptance asks for more than a private epitaph. And of all his writings, one lyric alone dares hold up a mirror to the reader's eyes. "Neither Out Far Nor In Deep" moves calmly in simple words. But who are these people? Where is this shore, this sea? What are the watchers doing? Why? And the poem — what can it be but the emblem of the human condition: mystified, seeking-questing:

> The people along the sand
> All turn and look one way.
> They turn their back on the land.
> They look at the sea all day.
>
> As long as it takes to pass
> A ship keeps raising its hull;
> The wetter ground like glass
> Reflects a standing gull.
>
> The land may vary more;
> But wherever the truth may be —
> The water comes ashore,
> And the people look at the sea.
>
> They cannot look out far.
> They cannot look in deep.
> But when was that ever a bar
> To any watch they keep?

In the year after the poet's death, Jarrell reviewed the *Selected Letters.* These are his words toward the close:

In the end he talked as naturally as he breathed: for as long as you got to listen you were sharing Frost's life. What came to you in that deep grainy voice — a voice that made other voices sound thin or abstract — was half a natural physiological process and half a work of art; it was as if Frost dreamed aloud and the dream were a poem. Was what he said right or wrong? It seemed irrelevant. In the same way, whether Frost himself was good or bad seemed irrelevant — he was there and you accepted him.

The world was also there, and whether Frost thought his trial by existence worth the grief and scars, he had made the choice, had accepted the risks. In the end did it matter that the Secret could not be found, the Truth that would burn the eyes out? * * "All I would keep for myself," he had said, "is the freedom of my material — the condition of body and mind now and then to summons aptly from the vast chaos of all I have lived through." What of the words others were taking as Truth — the Incarnation, "half guessed, half understood" (Eliot) or "that the final belief / Must be in a fiction" (Stevens)? Earth's conditions and human nature scorned any more-than-human answer, pointing at best to intimations, hidden glimpses, to the momentary fulfillments of the will to know in a quest that itself was reward enough for one who had long accepted himself and the world.

Reference Notes

The numbers at the far left refer to pages in this book and the abbreviations in italics to the books from which citations have been made. These citations appear in the text either within quotation marks or in passages marked with a double asterisk (* *).

Ordin.	Sidney Cox, *Robert Frost: Original "Ordinary" Man,* Holt, 1929
Swinger	Sidney Cox, *A Swinger of Birches: A Portrait of Robert Frost,* New York University Press, 1957
Dimens.	Reginald L. Cook, *The Dimensions of Robert Frost,* Rinehart, 1958
Sergeant	Elizabeth Shepley Sergeant, *Robert Frost: The Trial by Existence,* Holt, Rinehart and Winston, 1960
Unterm.	*The Letters of Robert Frost to Louis Untermeyer,* Holt, Rinehart and Winston, 1963
Brower	Reuben A. Brower, *The Poetry of Robert Frost: Constellations of Intention,* Oxford, 1963
Bartl.	Margaret Bartlett Anderson, *Robert Frost and John Bartlett: The Record of a Friendship,* Holt, Rinehart and Winston, 1963
Sel. Lett.	*Selected Letters of Robert Frost,* Lawrance Thompson, ed., Holt, Rinehart and Winston, 1964
Early Y.	Lawrance Thompson, *Robert Frost: The Early Years, 1874–1915,* Holt, Rinehart and Winston, 1966

Interv.	*Interviews with Robert Frost,* Edward Connery Lathem, ed., Holt, Rinehart and Winston, 1966
Prose	*Selected Prose of Robert Frost,* Hyde Cox and Edward Connery Lathem, eds., Holt, Rinehart and Winston, 1966
Poetry	*The Poetry of Robert Frost,* Edward Connery Lathem, ed., Holt, Rinehart and Winston, 1969
Triumph	Lawrance Thompson, *Robert Frost: The Years of Triumph, 1915–1938,* Holt, Rinehart and Winston, 1970
Fam. Lett.	*Family Letters of Robert and Elinor Frost,* Arnold Grade, ed., State University of New York Press, 1972
P&P	*Robert Frost/Poetry and Prose,* Edward Connery Lathem and Lawrance Thompson, eds., Holt, Rinehart and Winston, 1972
Living	Reginald [L.] Cook, *Robert Frost: A Living Voice,* University of Massachusetts Press, 1974
Pictor.	Kathleen Morrison, *Robert Frost: A Pictorial Chronicle,* Holt, Rinehart and Winston, 1974
Centen.	*Frost: Centennial Essays — Centen.-I,* 1974; Committee on the Frost Centennial of the University of Southern Mississippi; *Centen.-II,* Jac Tharpe, ed., 1976; *Centen.-III,* Jac Tharpe, ed., 1978; all published by the University of Southern Mississippi
Newdick	*Newdick's Season of Frost: An Interrupted Biography of Robert Frost,* William A. Sutton, ed., State University of New York Press, 1976
Later Y.	Lawrance Thompson and R. H. Winnick, *Robert Frost: The Later Years, 1938–1963,* Holt, Rinehart and Winston, 1976
Poirier	Richard Poirier, *Robert Frost: The Work of Knowing,* Oxford, 1977
Jott.	*Prose Jottings of Robert Frost,* Edward Connery Lathem and Hyde Cox, eds., Northeast-Kingdom, Vermont, 1982
Pritch.	William H. Pritchard, *Frost: A Literary Life Reconsidered,* Oxford, 1984
Notes	Lawrance R. Thompson, "Notes on Robert Frost: 1939–1967," Manuscript Department, University of Virginia Library, Charlottesville

page
415 "I'll never forget my visit with you": *Newdick,* 218

"I grow curious about my soul": *Sel. Lett.,* 530

"I trust my philosophy still bothers you": *Sel. Lett.,* 584

"I contain opposites": *Interv.,* 271, 185

"I'd have no trouble with the first two. It's the last, 'temper,' ": Reichert, *Out for the Stars,* Cincinnati, 1969, p. 6

416 "Robert Frost was a primal energy": *Saturday Review,* Feb. 23, 1963

417 "wondrous agency": *Sartor Resartus,* Book 3, chap. 3

"I have written to keep the over curious": *Sel. Lett.,* 385

"any eye is an evil eye / That looks in onto": *Poetry,* 385

"When the mood was on him, he could spill": *Atlantic,* July 1967

"anyone who has read his *Collected Poems*": *Book Week,* Aug. 30, 1964

"So many of them have literary criticism": *P&P,* 458

"We make ourselves a place apart": *Poetry,* 19

418 "Please burn it. Be easy on me": *Unterm.,* 296

"Most of my ideas occur": Frost to Sidney Cox, *Sergeant,* 311

"He tried on the sounds of words to see if": Peter Davison, *Half-Remembered,* Harper, 1973, p. 207

419 "the difference between Frost as poet and": *Living,* 5–6

"*sound* better than they read": *Living,* 30

"to justify the astonishing": *Sel. Lett.,* 20, to Susan Hayes Ward

"one of the greatest changes my nature": *Sel. Lett.,* 482

"The new thing with me": Ciardi, *Saturday Review,* Mar. 21, 1959

"talk, mythologizing, or lies": see letter to Sidney Cox, "Look out I don't spoof you." *Sel. Lett.,* 435

420 "vital part of his picture": *Newdick,* 194

"arresting New England beauty purified": *Sergeant,* xviii

"Mrs. Frost, an animated talker": *Living,* 9

"Mrs. Frost had probably become": Dierkes, *op. cit.,* 68–69

421 "I had a good number of hours alone with her": letter to me

"It's after nine o'clock, and you *must* go milk": *Swinger,* 9

"influence of this firm, intuitive": *Fam. Lett.,* 275

"F is as considerate of Mrs. F": *Newdick,* 282

"a great poet of marriage": *Poirier,* 22

422 "The magnificent clarity of his love for his wife": *New York Times Book Review,* Nov. 6, 1966

"She has been the unspoken half of everything": *Unterm.,* 295–96

"Robert depends on me": *Sel. Lett.,* 410, to Edith H. Fobes

"Elinor has just come out flat-footed against": *Unterm.,* 101

423 "colored [his thought] from the first": see *Fam. Lett.,* 210

"Pretty nearly every one of my poems": *Sel. Lett.,* 471, to G. R. and A. Elliott

"could hurt him": See *Sergeant,* 293

"an imperfect line, or flash of beauty": Mertins, *op. cit.,* 229

**: *Sergeant,* 320

"especially wary of honors that derogate": *Unterm.,* 63

"reputation, that bubble": *Sergeant,* xix

"somewhat disappointed": *Sel. Lett.,* 78, to Margaret Bartlett

424 "It is certainly *grand* about the": *Sel. Lett.,* 429, to Nina Thornton

"I sat and let Elinor pour it over me": *Sel. Lett.,* 452

"Don't you think it's beautiful yourself?": *Sergeant,* 188

"I played with them more than most fathers": *Sergeant,* 77. See Frost's stories for his children, *P&P,* 216–24.

"I sat there with him. I went to sleep as": *Sergeant,* 78

"He just does nothing a good deal of": *Fam. Lett.,* 15 (Nov. 1917)

425 "Take the way with her that will keep the peace": *Fam. Lett.,* 102

"Stratton . . . powerful and splendid": *Sel. Lett.,* 390 (Mar. 1933)

"That was another good poem": *Fam. Lett.,* 153 (May 1933)

"apple-crating poem . . . has a great deal more of": *Fam. Lett.,* 183

"I tried many ways and every single one of them": *Unterm.,* 322–23 "the sad ending to Irma's story": *Sel. Lett.,* 528. Lesley removed Irma to a nursing home in Vermont, the expenses paid out of the income from Frost's will. See *Unterm.,* 345.

"wracking itself to pieces from running wild": *Unterm.,* 315

"to be bowed down": *Triumph,* 511, to J. J. Lankes, Aug. 3, 1938. See *Unterm.,* 103, end of letter, Apr. 12, 1920.

426   "I reached a point lately where I could": *Sergeant,* 408–9

"the first poem that I got any personal": *Swinger,* 85

427   "Writing, teaching a little, and farming": *Interv.,* 242

428   "[T]he only education worth anything": *Unterm.,* 376

"I ought to have been poet enough": *Sel. Lett.,* 293, to W. L. Cross

"I never taught long enough to carry anything out": *Unterm.,* 289

"I have long thought that our high schools": *Interv.,* 193, 181

"I'm going to leave you with the motto": see *Centen.-III,* 151

"the greatest living expert [on education]": *Interv.,* 193

429   "so patient with my educational heresies": *Interv.,* 101

**: *Newdick,* 317–19; Tyler, *Centen-III;* Jackson, *Triumph,* 100

"In twenty years I have walked": *You Come Too,* Foreword

"His talk-spiels were legendary; marathon": *Centen.-III,* 134

430   "Frost's talk is not pyrotechnic or febrile": *Dimens.,* 12–15

"Don't you believe it's important to do good?": *Unterm.,* 372–73

431   "Democracy means all the risks taken": *Interv.,* 194

"A nation should be just as full of conflict": *Jott.,* 109

"I like all this uncertainty that we live in": *Interv.,* 213

"everything and everybody that want people to": *Interv.,* 213

"the public health, / So that the poor won't": *Poetry,* 363

"too much one way and then too much another": *Living,* 183

"Maybe I'm one who never makes up his mind": *Living,* 200

"It's well to have all kinds of feelings": *Ordin.,* 16

"I yield to no one in my admiration for": *Pictor.,* 115

432   "we shouldn't come to blows till we": *Pictor.,* 115–16

"jealousy is a passion I approve of": Oberlin *Alumni Magazine,* May 1938

"the odium of seeming jealous of anybody": *Unterm.,* 18

"I wonder . . . do you feel as badly as I do": Alfred Kreymborg, *Troubadour, An Autobiography,* Boni, 1925, p. 336

"The whole thing is performance": *Poirier,* 294

433   "The object in life is to win": *Jott.,* 53

"I divide my talks into two parts": *Centen-III,* 165

"Did any government ever send Eliot anywhere?": letter to me from Robert Fitzgerald, see p. 155 above.

"say for certain [that he didn't] like Spoon River": *Unterm.,* 75

434   "There's only room for one at the top of the steeple": *Interv.,* 197

"undoubtedly the man": *Sel. Lett.,* 93, to Sidney Cox

435   "If you want to see what happened in Boston": *Sel. Lett.,* 156

"in the case of Braithwaite": *Pritch.,* 113. See *Triumph,* 535, note 53. When I edited

Unterm., the manuscript contained no hint of any such substitution, nor did Untermeyer mention a change.

"to arrive where I can stand on my legs as a poet": *Sel. Lett.,* 98

436   "I have myself all in a strong box": *Unterm.,* 29

"I want to appreciate more": *Poetry and the Age., op. cit.,* p. 37

437   "Frost had us all in the palm of his hand": Selden Rodman, *Tongues of Fallen Angels,* New Directions, 1974, p. 43

"The best audience the world ever had": *Interv.,* 161

"That's what *you* would say, anyway": *Centen.-III,* 170; see also 107

"I have come to value my poetry": *Unterm.,* 314

438   "individuals of great worth in the younger generation": *Interv.,* 140

439   "1934 SEP 4/STOP PRESS": letter to me from Helen Brower

"The Puritans [was] the best": letter to me from Richard Wilbur

"Why don't I come to *your* room?": *A Reminiscence of Robert Frost,* 1980, Special Collection and Archives, Amherst College

"We swapped poems for a while": letter to me

440   "Atta boy Jesus Christ Professor": letter to me from Theodore Weiss; see Schubert, *Work and Days,* the QRL 40th anniversary, 1983.

441   "I'm the kind that can't get over things": *Jott.,* 137

"You want to believe that great writers are good men": Brooks, *From the Shadow of the Mountain,* Dutton, 1961, pp. 180–81

"Let's not have": letter from Frost, Dartmouth College Library

442   ** *Sergeant,* 313–16

"He offered to read a poem if I would read one": *Unterm.,* 231 (*Poetry,* 294)

443   "Early in the proceedings Frost found": Stegner, *The Uneasy Chair: A Biography of Bernard DeVoto,* Doubleday, 1974, p. 206

"Frost did not take kindly to Archie's talk": quoted in *Later Y.,* 371

444   "I've been crazy for the last six months": *Unterm.,* 311

"I showed up at the Homer": letter to me from Robert N. Ganz

"For the most part he was": letter to me from Alfred C. Edwards

445   "The setting was early": letter to me from Joseph Blumenthal

"The world hates Jews and despises": letter to me from Victor Reichert

"Who's the lady coon?": Peter Brazeau, *Parts of a World: Wallace Stevens Remembered,* Random House, 1983, pp. 195–96 and 249

446   "I find race feeling runs pretty hot in my veins": *The Letters of Archibald MacLeish, op. cit.,* p. 57

**: Frost also knew that my wife worked in a children's clinic in New York City's Harlem; that I had published *The Negro Caravan;* etc.

"I don't think the word should": letter to me from Hyde Cox

"way of admitting that he couldn't": *Early Y.,* xiv. See also note to p. 220 ("Trust me . . .").

447   "[James Dickey] felt sure": in conversation with me, 1972

"could never seem to forgive people": *Book Week,* Aug. 30, 1964

"that men won't understand us and we shall be": *Prose,* 60

"didn't believe it did [him] the least good": *Swinger,* vii

"We all have our souls — and minds — to save": *Sel. Lett.,* 212

**: "the utmost reward / Of daring . . .": *Poetry,* 19; 497, line 106

"I'd rather be taken for brave than anything else": *Sel. Lett.,* 595

"Be careful how you offer to": letter to me from Van Dore

"any form of humor shows fear": *Unterm.,* 166

"It's a funny world": *Swinger,* 40–41

448 "I own any form of humor shows . . . inferiority": *Unterm.,* 166

"When the question comes up": *Unterm.,* 366

"[S]tyle is the way the man takes himself": *Prose,* 65

"Play no matter how deep has got to be": Dartmouth College Library

449 "perhaps his deepest word on the subject": *Pritch.,* xvi

"The way of understanding is [always] partly mirth": *Poetry,* 306

"that Frost finds balance . . . Serious play": *Centen-II,* 223, 230

"everything he did or wrote": *Pritch.,* xvi

"Frost is a poet of genius because": *Poirier,* x–xii

450 "Most folks are poets. If they were not": *Interv.,* 32

"Five ways of reading *Lycidas*": *Varieties of Literary Experience,* Stanley Burnshaw, ed., New York University Press, 1962

"In- and Outdoor Schooling": *Robert Frost,* Lectures on the Centennial of His Birth, Library of Congress, 1975

451 "Life sways perilously at the": *Sel. Lett.,* 467, to R. P. T. Coffin

"the juxtaposed interpretation of facts": *Centen.-I,* 82

"the poets most often held up as": *Centen.-I.,* 273–74

"through this stealthy rusticity": *Centen.-I.,* 55

"cavalierliness with words": *Dimens.,* 50; *cf.* E. E. Cummings, *Poems: 1923–1954,* No. 34, p. 373, Harcourt, 1954

"The sound is": first four quotations from *Prose,* 17, 13, 23, 33

453 "A poem . . . begins as a lump in the throat": *Unterm.,* 22

"I alone of English writers": *Sel. Lett.,* 79–80, 110–11, 113

"ceased to expect it [perfection]": *Sel. Lett.,* 482, to DeVoto

"utmost ambition": Ciardi, *Saturday Review,* Mar. 21, 1959

"A Minor Bird," see *Robert Frost Himself,* p. 129

454 "Hawthorne and Frost": *Centen.-I,* 288–309

"every single one of my poems is probably": *P&P,* 420–21

"The Wood-Pile": see *Robert Frost Himself,* p. 164

"correspondence": see *Robert Frost Himself* for the pages cited

"If my poetry has to have a name": Untermeyer, *Robert Frost: A Backward Look,* Library of Congress, 1964, p. 3

"The stars 'congregate' ": *Centen.-I,* 98. See also 89–107 passim.

455 "My poems": *Sel. Lett.,* 344, to Leonidas W. Payne, Jr.

"Now, that's all right; it's out of my hands once": *Interv.,* 188

"It's another one people have bothered around": *Living,* 248

456 "Rhymy little thing": *Living,* 303

"be pressed too hard for meaning": *Living,* 240

**: for example, comments on "Directive" (*Poetry,* 377) in Poirier, Brower, Pritch.

"His subject was the world": *Centen.-III,* 101

"I Could Give All": compare *Poirier,* 174–77, Jarrell, *Poetry and the Age, op. cit.,* p. 51; *Brower,* 232; *Pritch.,* 234; *Living,* 257

"The poem suggests more than one can": letter to me from Hyde Cox

"the one permissible way of saying one thing and": *Prose,* 36

457 "Having thoughts of your own is the only freedom": *Centen.-III,* 150

"feeling is always ahead of thinking": *Living,* 207

"poetry must include the mind as well . . . The mind is dangerous": *Interv.,* 124. See also *Pictor.,* 47, interview in *The Scotsman,* May 1957.

"there is nothing anybody knows, however absolutely": *Unterm.,* 175

"No one can know how glad I am to find": *Poetry,* 358

"Give all to meaning.": *Prose,* 116

"cherubic scorn": *Living,* 130

"ultimately not quite understandable": *Hudson Review,* Summer 1976

**: Newdick, 219, to Sidney Cox. Frost or his editors could have supplied the English meanings of the Greek (*Poetry,* 427) or the Latin (*Poetry,* 394) that form parts of his poems. "Stopping by Woods . . ." was "the kind of poem he'd like to print on one page to be followed with forty pages of footnotes," he told Reichert, *op. cit.,* p. 13. Havighurst observed that certain poems were "so personal that [Frost] declined to read them on the platform": *Cent.-III,* 101

458 "It's the plunge of the mind, the spirit, into": *Living,* 212

"It is not given to man to be omniscient": *Interv.,* 64

"The most exciting movement in nature is not progress": *Ordin.,* 21

"Logical systems [are] nonsense": *Swinger,* 12–13

"I'm less and less for systems and system-building": *Sel. Lett.,* 343

459 "A deeper understanding of socialism": *Interv.,* 286

"I'm a nationalist and I expect other people to be": *Interv.,* 121

"a Lucretian abstainer from politics": *Unterm.,* 335

** See *Robert Frost Himself,* pp. 79–83

"I'm not confused; I'm only well-mixed": *Interv.,* 185

"I *am* the conflicts, I *contain* them": *Sergeant,* 406

Nine quotations in order: (I) *Interv.,* 112; (2) *Living,* 190; (3) *Dimens.,* 177; (4) Frost's notebook quoted in *Early Y.,* 427 and often repeated in conversation; (5) *Jott.,* 65; (6) *Poetry,* 350; (7) reported in the Amherst *Journal,* May 2, 1947; (8–9) *Jott.,* 144, 91

460 "Frost appears to contradict himself": *Centen.-I,* 603

"Having ideas that are neither pro nor con": *Swinger,* 28–29

"I despise religiosity" and the ten quotations that follow: (I) Rodman, *op. cit.,* 41; (2) *Ordin.,* 36; (3) *Sel. Lett.,* 530; (4) *Prose,* 45–46; (5–6) *Sel. Lett.,* 525; (7) *Living,* 181; (8) Notebook, Dartmouth College Library; (9) Sermon, Rockdale Avenue Temple, Cincinnati, Oct. 10, 1946; (10) *Prose,* 41; (11) *Sel. Lett.,* 596 (Jan. 12, 1963)

462 "something": John McGiffert, *English Journal,* November 1945

"altogether remarkable poem": *Poirier,* 305–313

"I was brought up in all three of these religions": *Prose,* 112

464 "an Old Testament believer": *Dimens.,* 190

"Call them 'nature's favors' ": *Centen.-I,* 424

"a curse to be an agnostic": *Interv.,* 194

"froth": *Dimens.,* 191

"between trivialities and profundities": *Notes,* 555

"Where is this God I hear so much about?": *Newdick,* 366

"he [had] moved from skepticism to almost complete": *Notes,* 426

"To prayer": *Unterm.,* 130, 136, 331

"This one's about my sixth revised — transgression": Untermeyer's characterization of his forthcoming poetry anthology

"All I do . . . is reach for something": *Dimens.,* 191

"To believe is to wish to believe": *The Tragic Sense of Life,* Dover, 1954, p. 114

"Lord, I believe": letter to me from Hyde Cox, Dec. 18, 1983

"best when rapt": *Unterm.,* 166

465   "Play me some great music": Hyde Cox quoted in *Later Y.,* 439

"Victor, what do you think": recounted to me in conversation

"a spiritual explorer": Marice Brown, *Centen.-I,* 4

"There is at least so much of good": *Prose,* 106

466   "It begins in delight, it inclines to the impulse": *Prose,* 18

"if a reader can lapse back into his immediate sensible life": *Some Problems in Philosophy,* Longmans, 1911, p. 50. See *The Seamless Web.,* op. cit., p. 42, n8.

"The present / Is too much for the senses": *Poetry,* 336

"There is always tragedy. That is what life is": *Swinger,* 174

"because confusions keep coming": *Times of London,* May 22, 1957

"Drink and be whole again beyond confusion": *Poetry,* 379

"he swooped, he pounced, he struck": *Poetry,* 278

"[science] goes self-superseding on": *Poetry,* 480

"You're always believing ahead of your evidence": *Interv.,* 271

"It is only by risking our persons from one hour to": *Philosophy of William James,* H. M. Kallen, ed., Modern Library, 1925, p. 25

467   "You are not safe anywhere unless": *Prose,* 39–43 (phrases reordered)

"The great spring": *The Seamless Web,* op. cit., p. 183

"are nearly identical in their theories of poetic 'strain' and": *New York Review of Books,* Apr. 25, 1985, p. 34

"moral law lies at the center and radiates to": *Nature*

"We throw our arms wide with a gesture of religion": *Prose,* 71–72

"to front the essential facts . . . [to] learn what": *Walden*

"a true account of the actual is the rarest poetry": Thoreau, *A Week on the Concord and Merrimack Rivers*

"instructions to the season": *Poirier,* 200

"I'm always saying something that's just the edge": *Interv.,* 268

"A poet must lean": *Swinger,* 10

468   "Where is there any benevolence of purpose?": *Interv.,* 165

"With a lantern that wouldn't burn": *Poetry,* 443

469   "a natural conflict": Stanlis paraphrasing Frost, *Centen.-III,* 280

"the fear that men won't understand us": *Prose,* 60

"against hopeless odds": see W. H. Auden, *The Dyer's Hand,* Random House, 1962, pp. 345–47. Compare: "I never tire of being shown how the limited can make snug in the limitless": *Living,* 65n, with regard to *Walden* and *Robinson Crusoe.*

"The surest thing you know is": *Boston Herald,* Mar. 19, 1936

470 "creational": *Centen.-II,* 100 (phrases reordered)

"tie together some way": *Living,* 190

"case against [Frost]": *Human Values in the Poetry of Robert Frost,* Duke University Press, 1960

**: Quotations from *Poetry:* pp. 248, 17, 475, 460, 122, 17, 324, 251, 362, 106, 350, 249, 306, 19, 222, 254–55, 362, 485, 296, 348, and 403, respectively.

472 "There are roughly zones whose laws must be": *Poetry,* 305

"a new start": See Auden, *op. cit.,* p. 349

"If you see the little truths": *Swinger,* 80, paraphrasing Frost

"as if": Radcliffe Squires, *The Major Themes of Robert Frost,* Univ. of Michigan Press, 1963, p. 51

**: *Sel. Lett.,* p. 436 ("I refuse to explain my position on a lot of things we . . . left unsettled . . . Why should I press home my conclusions everywhere.")

"the myth of 'The Trial by Existence'": Nitchie, *op. cit.,* p. 223

473 "Earth's a hard place . . ." and the other quotations here: "The Lesson for Today," *Poetry,* 350–55

"The people along the sand": *Poetry,* 301

"In the end he talked as naturally": *Book Week,* Aug. 30, 1964

474 **: *Poetry,* 517, lines 629–30

"All I would keep for myself": *Prose,* 20

INDEX OF POEM TITLES

AND FIRST LINES